ECONOMIC POLICY IN IRAQ
1932–1950

ECONOMIC POLICY IN IRAQ

1932–1950

JOSEPH SASSOON

FRANK CASS

First published 1987 in Great Britain by
FRANK CASS & CO. LTD.
2 Park Square, Milton Park,
Abingdon, Oxon, OX14 4RN

and in the United States of America by
FRANK CASS & CO. LTD.
270 Madison Ave,
New York NY 10016

Transferred to Digital Printing 2006

British Library Cataloguing in Publication Data

Sassoon, Joseph
Economic policy in Iraq 1932–1950.
1. Iraq — Economic policy
I. Title
330.9567'042 HC415.4

ISBN 0–7146–3305–4

Library of Congress Cataloging-in-Publication Data

Sassoon, Joseph.
Economic policy in Iraq, 1932–1950.
1. Iraq—Economic policy. 2. Iraq—Foreign relations—Great Britain. 3. Great Britain—Foreign relations—Iraq. 4. Iraq—History—1921–
I. Title.
HC415.4.S27 1987 338.9567 87–6577
ISBN 0–7146–3305–4

Publisher's Note

The publisher has gone to great lengths to ensure the quality of this reprint but points out that some imperfections in the original may be apparent

To Taffy, Rachel and Dena

CONTENTS

LIST OF TABLES

Notes on Transliteration, Currency and References

TRANSLITERATION

Arabic names and words have been transliterated according to the system adopted by the *International Journal of Middle East Studies.*

CURRENCY

Up to April 1932 the monetary unit in Iraq was the rupee. The Iraqi dinar (ID) was then introduced, each ID comprising 1,000 fils. The ID was valued at par with the pound sterling, being equal to $4.03. In 1949, with the devaluation of the pound sterling, it became equal to $2.80.

FOOTNOTES

The first reference to any source is given in full; subsequent references are abbreviated; British archival material is notated according to the List of Abbreviations; unless otherwise indicated, the files are at the Public Record Office. American archives are notated according to the number of the microfilm reel on which they appear at the Middle East Centre, Oxford.

LIST OF ABBREVIATIONS

ACR	American Consular Reports
Air	Air Ministry Files, PRO
ANA	American National Archives
BMEO	British Middle East Office
BOD	British Oil Development Company
BPC	Basra Petroleum Company
BT	Board of Trade Files, PRO
CAB	Cabinet Papers, PRO
CO	Colonial Office Files, PRO
DGFP	Documents of German Foreign Policy
DOT	Department of Overseas Trade
ECGD	Export Credits Guarantee Department
FEA	Foreign Economic Administration
FO	Foreign Office (files at PRO)
FRUS	Foreign Relations of the United States
FY	Financial Year
G	Top Secret Papers at PRO
IBRD	International Bank for Reconstruction and Development
IPC	Iraq Petroleum Company
KOC	Khanaquin Oil Company
LAB	Labour Ministry Files, PRO
MESC	Middle East Supply Centre
MEW	Ministry of Economic Warfare
MPC	Mosul Petroleum Company
PRO	Public Record Office
T	Treasury Files, PRO
UKCC	United Kingdom Commercial Corporation

MAP OF IRAQ

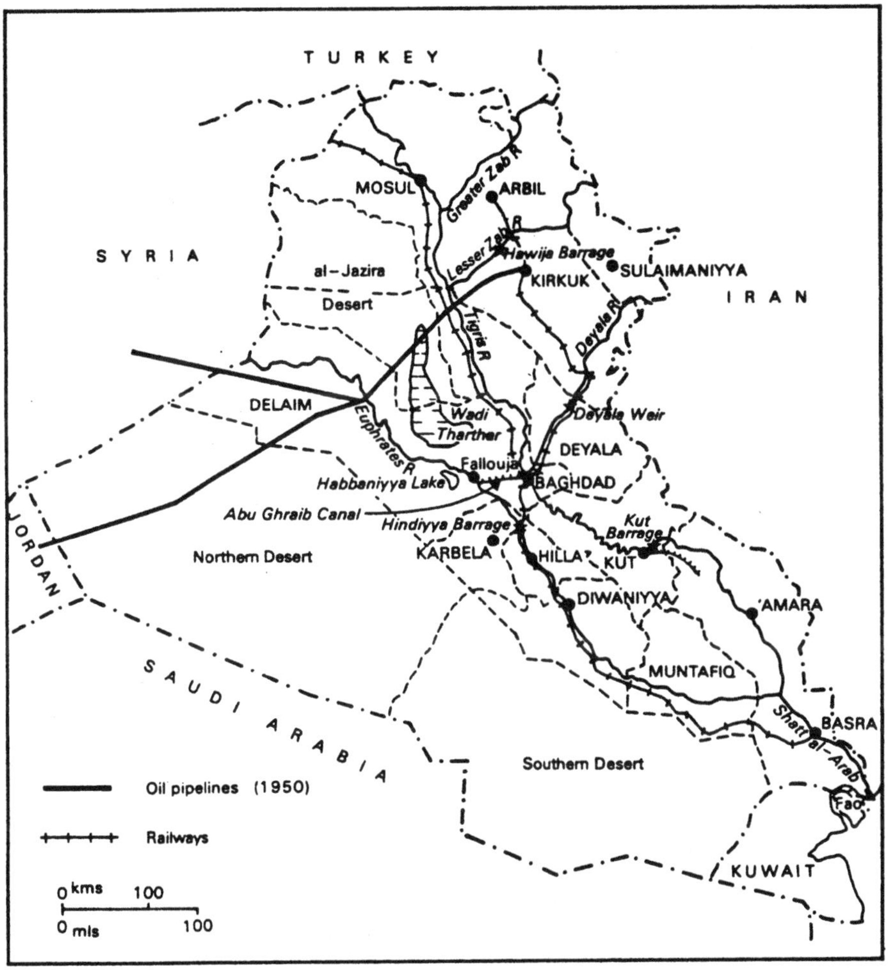
TURKEY
SYRIA
IRAN
JORDAN
SAUDI ARABIA
KUWAIT
MOSUL
ARBIL
Greater Zab R
Lesser Zab R
Hawija Barrage
SULAIMANIYYA
KIRKUK
al-Jazira
Desert
Tigris R
Deyala R
DELAIM
Euphrates R
Wadi
Tharthar
Deyala Weir
DEYALA
Fallouja
BAGHDAD
Habbaniyya Lake
Abu Ghraib Canal
Hindiyya Barrage
Kut
Barrage
KARBELA
HILLA
KUT
Northern Desert
DIWANIYYA
'AMARA
MUNTAFIQ
BASRA
Shatt al-Arab
Fao
Southern Desert
Oil pipelines (1950)
Railways
0 kms 100
0 mls 100

PREFACE

This book is an economic history of Iraq from October 1932, when it was admitted to the League of Nations as an independent country, until 1950, when comprehensive economic planning and the windfall of oil revenues began.

In researching this study, considerable use was made of the British documents in the Public Record Office and, to a lesser extent, the American Consular Reports from Iraq. Both these sources have been neglected in most of the work done to date on Iraq's economic history. In addition, the research also drew heavily on official Iraqi publications of the 1930s and 1940s (economic laws, statistical abstracts, and annual reports of various economic and financial institutions). Lastly, a very wide range of secondary sources (in English, Arabic, Hebrew and French) was consulted.

Although the writer did not have access to Iraqi archives, it should be emphasized that very few of the primary documents such archives contain deal with the subject of economic policy; most are files of the police or the Ministry of the Interior, and deal primarily (as such files do) with internal politics. But even copies of some of these appear in the Public Record Office.

A further relevant point regarding the sources consulted concerns the quality of their statistics, which in many instances suffer serious inaccuracies and discrepancies. Moreover, many statistics do not exist at all. (For example, calculations of national income were not made until the 1950s.) Despite this obstacle, however, repeated checking and comparing of such statistics as do exist convinced the writer that they adequately indicate the general trend of development in each sector. No figures of the late 1950s or the 1960s were used unless it was thought they accurately reflected the situation in the period under study.

This book is based on a D.Phil. thesis submitted to Oxford University in 1980. Special thanks are due to my thesis supervisor, Dr. Roger Owen, and to Mr. Albert Hourani, for their advice, comments and encouragement. I would also like to thank Connie Wilsack for her help in editing the book, Louise van Heyningen for her technical assistance, and my wife, Taffy, for her tremendous support throughout this work.

J.S.

INTRODUCTION

This study cannot properly be entitled 'Iraq's Economic Policy' because, due to the strong British influence on its governments, Iraq did not have the power to decide its own policy in a free and unrestricted manner. At the same time, it would be equally incorrect to say that economic policy in Iraq was purely British-determined since Iraq was, at least formally, an independent state in the period under study. The neutral term 'Economic Policy in Iraq' has therefore been chosen as the title least likely to distort the subject.

The period 1932–50 was chosen for a number of reasons. In 1932 the British mandate over Iraq was terminated and Iraq officially became independent, while 1950 marks a turning point in Iraq's economic history because after that year the oil boom began, and, with it, a form of comprehensive economic planning. The eighteen-year period between those two dates therefore constitutes a special stage in Iraq's economic history, encompassing the early years of statehood up to the stage of oil prosperity and comprehensive economic planning. It thus represents an interesting subject for the disciplines of economic history and political economy.

Politics and economics were closely related in Iraq during the period under study, and each reacted on the other. One cannot speak of a particular monetary policy, fiscal policy or even development policy. Economic decisions were taken for political reasons or because of economic need, or a combination thereof. In each chapter the study will try to pinpoint the factors which led to the formulation and implementation or abandonment of a certain policy. For example, in the agricultural sector the position of the sheikhs *vis à vis* the government and the British was an important consideration co-existing with the desire to improve Iraq's agricultural conditions; and in the foreign trade sector, British interests were a dominant factor in adopting policies which were sometimes even to Iraq's detriment.

In studying the economy of Iraq, one must remember that in this period Iraq was a quasi-independent or semi-colonial state, and shared many of the characteristics of other states having similar status at that time. Thus, it had many of the features of an 'under-developed' economy – a predominantly agricultural population, dependence on a few primary commodities, and so forth. Furthermore, the structure of its finances, the relationship between its landlords and politicians, the British–Japanese competition for its markets in the 1930s, its connection with the sterling area, its industrialization process and the nature of its oil concessions – all make Iraq resemble many other non-European countries during this period. (For example, the problems of concentration of land holdings, British–Japanese competition, and the link with the sterling area were all part of Egypt's economic history as well during the same period.) Anglo-American competition, another feature of that period, was to be found throughout the Middle East in the second half of the 1940s, as well as in other parts of the world.

The economy of Iraq also had certain distinctive features, of course. The potential of its oil reserves was becoming increasingly evident and its agriculture, unlike Egypt's, had tremendous possibilities in that there were virtually no obvious constraints on the expansion of the cultivable area. These advantages, together with the abundance of water and dearth of population, made Iraq very different from many other developing countries.

Iraq of the 1930s and 1940s is also an interesting case study in neo-colonialism. Having secured its own position and interests there during the mandate period, Britain proceeded to a policy aimed at maintaining and enhancing its gains without the need for either military occupation or a mandate. This policy was lucidly described by Sir John Glubb as 'control by influence': 'this is an art in itself, quite different from Colonial administration.'[1] Once again, Iraq was but one of many countries within the British sphere of influence where this form of indirect control prevailed.[2] In Iraq's case, this new 'art' largely depended on the presence of British officials serving as 'advisers' to the Iraqi government and on the continuation of political alliances between the British and certain groups of Iraqis (e.g. politicians like Nuri as-Said on the one hand and tribal leaders on the other). By such means, and as long as British interests were not infringed upon, Britain did not have to resort to direct intervention in Iraqi affairs. (The events of 1941, as will be shown later, were exceptional in this respect.)

The Iraqi political élite – as in most other ex-colonial countries, a group of a hundred or so eminent personages – were for their part well aware that their being in power depended greatly on their alliance with and support for the British. Most of this élite came from the same social background, and had once been Sharifian[3] officers. They shared many experiences and knew each other well, and some were even closely related – although this of course did not prevent strong and continuous competition among them.[4]

While it can accurately be said that the government controlled Parliament and there was no real democracy in Iraq, the government was nevertheless not without constraints upon its activities. Because of the strong competition among politicians, it was highly sensitive to criticism in Parliament or the press. Any failure on the political or economic front rendered it vulnerable, and this point should be borne in mind throughout the study.

Before proceeding to the main body of the study, a brief review of some of Iraq's basic demographic features will provide useful general background information to the more detailed reviews of the various sectors of the economy given in the relevant chapters.

During the period under study, Iraq was administratively subdivided into fourteen *liwas*, covering an area of 235,733 square kilometres (equivalent to 94 million *mesharas*), in addition to its three desert areas (known as the North Desert, the South Desert and the al-Jazirah Desert) which together comprised an area of 208,709 square kilometres – the total area of the country therefore being 444,442 square kilometres.[5]

Prior to 1947, when the first official census of Iraq's population was taken, a number of estimates were published by the Census Department (established in early 1926) and in various economic and agricultural surveys. In both 1930 and 1932 the population was put at about 2.83 million;[6] in 1935, 3.35 million;[7] in 1944, 4.25 million;[8] and in 1947, 4.82 million.[9] A study by the Food and Agriculture Organization (FAO) in 1959 concluded that the 1947 census underestimated the population, and a more correct figure would be 5.28 million.[10]

The annual rate of population increase was estimated at 1.7% between 1905 and 1919, 1.5% between 1919 and 1935, and 2.4% between 1935 and 1947. As one commentator has written, 'It is therefore clear that it was only during the period since 1935 that Iraq's population began to grow at a rate markedly higher than at any other time from the middle of the nineteenth century onwards ...'[11]

Most of Iraq's population was rural. In 1930 only 25% was urban, while 68% was rural and 7% nomadic. By 1947, 37% were classified as urban, as against 59% rural and 5% nomadic.[12] The increase in urbanization during the period 1930–47, which was in no small measure due to a mass exodus from distressed rural areas to the cities, had an important impact on the economy, as will be discussed in the chapter on agriculture.

According to the 1947 census, the economically active population (49.5% of the total) consisted of 22.5% male-active and 27% female-active. The data on the occupations of this economically active population are, however, inaccurate and ambiguous. Because the term 'occupation' was confused with 'industrial employment', what the 1947 census shows is in fact the number of workers employed in various industries. Moreover, the figures underestimate the proportion of working women (mainly in agriculture). However, based on the census and Hasan's article, one can say that in 1947 some 57–60% of the total active population were working in the agricultural sector.[13] A further 30–35% were engaged in commerce, public and domestic services, transport, and other administrative and professional services. The smallest sector was industry: only some 5–7% of the active population were employed in manufacturing industries, oil and handicrafts.[14]

Illiteracy was very widespread, only 8.5% being literate in 1947. Similarly, health conditions were very poor; even by as late as 1950 there were only 5,000 hospital beds, and an average of two doctors for every 10,000 people.[15]

The social and economic structure briefly reviewed above exhibits many of the characteristics of a developing country. This impression is further sustained by the fact that Iraq had a very young population (about half being under the age of twenty) and a very low average annual per capita income ($48 in 1939 and $85 in 1949, as against $100 for Syria and $125 for Lebanon in the latter year).[16]

When Iraq became independent on 3 October 1932, the managers of its economy inherited an undeveloped country with extremely low living standards. Though there had been important achievements during the mandate period preceding independence, mainly in the spheres of infrastructure and health, many of the shortcomings of the 1930s and 1940s also had their roots in those years of British occupation: a legacy of financial burdens, an inequitable land policy, and unfavourable trade agreements and oil concessions.

This study seeks to understand Iraq's economic history during the first eighteen years of its independence by examining policy in each sector of the economy and analysing the factors which caused Iraq, with its glorious past and impressive potential, to end the first half of the twentieth century with the majority of its people still living in poverty.

The first chapter examines British interests in Iraq, which played so crucial a role in shaping economic policy there. The second chapter concentrates on the Iraqi side of the equation, examining government attitudes towards economic policy and the mechanisms for its implementation. The third chapter looks at Iraq's finances: its budgets, its tax system and aspects of its financial policy. The fourth chapter discusses various facets of agricultural policy by exploring the triangular relationship among the Iraqi government, the British government and the landlords. The fifth chapter analyses foreign trade policy by examining the trade structure and various factors affecting commercial policy. The sixth and last chapter reviews the most important developments in Iraq's industry, oil and labour policies.

NOTES

1. Memorandum by J.B. Glubb, Officer Commander of the Arab Legion 1943. FO 371/34975, E 5925/2551/65.
2. For a general discussion of colonial development policy see: Stephen Constantine, *The Making of British Colonial Development Policy 1914–1940* (London, 1984).
3. 'Sharifian' refers to those who were associated with the Sharif of Mecca's revolt in the Hejaz against Ottoman rule.
4. See David Pool, 'From Elite to Class: The Transformation of Iraqi Political Leadership' in Abbas Kelidar, *The Integration of Modern Iraq* (London, 1979), pp.64–75. See also Hanna Batatu, *The Old Social Classes and the Revolutionary Movements of Iraq* (Princeton, 1978), pp.319–61.
5. Government of Iraq, Principal Bureau of Statistics, *Report on the Agricultural and Livestock Census of Iraq 1952–1953* (Baghdad, 1954), vol. i, p.15.
6. Ernest Dowson, *An Inquiry into Land Tenure and Related Questions* (Letchworth, 1931), p.12; *The Stateman's Year-Book 1935* (London, 1935), p.1033.
7. *The Iraq Directory 1936* (Baghdad, 1936), pp.481–506.
8. Statement of Director General of Census, FO 371/45338, E 2084/2084/93.
9. Government of Iraq, Directorate General of Census, *Census of Iraq 1947*, 3 parts (Baghdad, 1954), p.*h*.
10. Food and Agriculture Organization, Mediterranean Development Project, *Iraq*, Country Report (Rome, 1959), appendix ii, pp.1–2.
11. Mohammad Salman Hasan, 'Growth and Structure of Iraq's Population', *Bulletin of the Oxford University Institute of Statistics* xx (1958), p.340.
12. FAO, *Iraq*, p.7.
13. A similar percentage was suggested by Hashim Jawad, *The Social Structure of Iraq* (Baghdad, 1945), p.18.
14. *1947 Census*, Hasan, op. cit., p.348.
15. FAO, *Iraq*, p.9.
16. United Nations, *Final Report of the United Nations Economic Survey Mission for the Middle East* (UN 1949), part i, p.43.

1

BRITISH INTERESTS IN IRAQ

The importance of British interests as a factor influencing economic policy, and indeed all aspects of life in Iraq during the 1930s and 1940s, will become clearly evident in subsequent chapters. It is the purpose of this first chapter, however, to define just what those interests were and to examine the factors impinging upon them and the agents by which they were served.

We will trace the development of Anglo-Iraqi relations from 1930 to 1950, concentrating on the period preceding independence and other important turning points, such as the events of 1940–1 and the negotiations for, and cancellation of, the Portsmouth Treaty. We will also discuss the organizations responsible for shaping and implementing British economic policy in Iraq, such as the Middle East Supply Centre (MESC) and the British Middle East Office (BMEO).

Besides these organizations, which were established during and because of World War II, the main body responsible for protecting and advancing British interests in Iraq after it became independent comprised those British subjects employed by the Iraqi government as 'advisers'. Their role in Iraq's economic life and their relationship with the British and Iraqi governments will be examined at length.

The final part of this chapter deals with Anglo-American relations and American economic policy in the Middle East, showing how America's appearance in the region posed an implicit threat to Britain's position and led to a change in British economic policy towards Iraq during the 1940s.

ANGLO-IRAQI RELATIONS

Britain's interest in Mesopotamia before the twentieth century was strategic: to protect its route to India and Indian trade. With the beginning of this century, however, this interest was augmented by an additional factor: oil.

As the probability of Turkey's entering World War I increased, British policy-makers decided to safeguard British interests.[1] The campaign was launched in October 1914, and by 1919, after four centuries of Ottoman rule, the British occupation of Iraq was complete. For the next two years, Iraq was administered from Baghdad by a civil commissioner.

In April 1920 the San Remo conference assigned the mandates of Iraq and Palestine to Britain, and those of Syria and Lebanon to France. On 3 May it was officially announced in Baghdad that Britain had accepted the mandate for Iraq, stress being laid in the announcement on the fact that the object of the mandate was the development of independent institutions; and in October 1920 British military rule came to an end with the arrival of the first High Commissioner, Sir Percy Cox.[2]

During the period 1921–30, Iraq under the mandate was economically and politically little different from other countries under colonial rule. As regards government expenditure, for example, Iraq was similar to India, Cyprus, Trans-Jordan, Palestine and Syria in the sense that, as in these countries, 'there was no extensive colonization from the ruling European country, so that public services were oriented primarily towards the local population'.[3] In all these countries the government spent an average of 28.5% on general administration (in Iraq, during the period 1921–30, 34.6%). The combined share of administration and public security was about 60% (in Iraq 69%), while only 13.2% was devoted to development (in Iraq 7.7%).[4]

From a political point of view, the period 1921–30 witnessed the building of government organizations in Iraq, based mainly on the Indian model; and the creation of partnerships between the British and certain local groups, such as landlords, which were intended to protect British interests.[5]

By such measures Britain consolidated its own position to such an extent that by the end of the 1920s Britain concluded that it could secure its interests in Iraq even without the mandatory government. 'Control by influence', it was decided, was more advantageous than direct control, as it reduced local antagonism to British interests and saved expense. Thus, in the summer of 1929, Iraq was notified that the British government was prepared to support its candidature for admission to the League of Nations as an independent state.

Negotiations between the two countries began in April 1930 and concluded with the signing of a treaty in June of the same year. The resulting Anglo-Iraqi Treaty of Alliance formed the basis of their bilateral relations for more than two decades. It was to enter into force after Iraq's admission to the League of Nations and last for twenty-five years (Article 11), replacing all previous agreements between the two countries (Article 7).

The treaty and its annex granted Britain certain non-reciprocal rights and powers in Iraq. The British were entitled to maintain military forces in Iraq, as well as naval and air bases. The British diplomatic representative was to have the rank of ambassador and be the permanent senior diplomatic representative in the country. Iraq was obliged to give preference to British subjects in choosing military and civilian advisers, and to give preference to Britain as the country in which members of Iraq's armed forces received their military education. Finally, Iraq undertook, should Britain become involved in a war, to furnish it full facilities and assistance on Iraqi territory, including the use of railways, rivers, ports, airfields and so forth.[6] An American official reviewing Anglo-Iraqi relations commented thus on the treaty: 'It cannot be considered as a type of agreement which one sovereign nation is accustomed to enter with another.'[7]

From 1930 onwards the British did everything possible to secure Iraq's entry into the League of Nations, because of the importance of this step to Anglo-Iraqi relations.[8] The optimistic report, *Progress of Iraq 1920–1931*, presented to the League was one example of how the British tried to convince the League that their mandate had achieved great success in Iraq.[9]

The year 1931 witnessed a significant consolidation of Britain's position in Iraq: an important oil concession was granted to the Iraq Petroleum Company (IPC), a British-dominated firm; a currency law was promulgated stipulating that the Currency Board should sit in London; and agricultural laws were enacted which strengthened the landlords, Britain's local allies.

On 3 October 1932 Iraq was admitted to membership in the League of Nations as an independent state. There was, however, little excitement among Iraqis at the termination of the mandate because, in Sluglett's words:

> those in Iraq who understood the realities of the situation, and who were not members of the very small circle to whom power was actually entrusted, realised that there was little to be jubilant about. The real extent of British influence had not been perceptibly limited: while Britain could no longer overtly interfere in internal affairs, the 1930 Treaty had left her a considerable latitude in matters of defence and of administration, through the retention of senior British officials at key posts in important Ministries.[10]

These 'senior British officials' were also the British government's main source of information about events in Iraq, and access to information was a high Foreign Office priority during 1932. At first the secretary of state for India suggested that the British ambassador officially call upon the British advisers for information, but London realized that such an arrangement would be most awkward for the advisers, and would expose Britain to strong Iraqi and international criticism.[11] An informal arrangement was therefore reached with King Faisal and Iraq's prime minister, according to which the British ambassador would from time to time receive information from the adviser to the Ministry of the Interior (then Sir Kinahan Cornwallis), in his capacity as the most senior adviser.[12]

This arrangement worked to the British government's satisfaction; and after Iraq's independence the British ambassador obtained King Faisal's blessing for the continuation of close contacts between the British Embassy and the advisers: the king undertook that 'orders should be given privately to advisers that there should be no change in this respect'.[13]

The death of King Faisal in 1933 and the accession of King Ghazi to the throne did not significantly affect Britain's predominance in Iraq, nor did the various *coups d'état* between 1936 and 1938 or the death of King Ghazi in a motor accident in April 1939.[14] Secure in their position, the British continued their policy of giving the Iraqis more power in administering their own affairs, while continuing to influence them through the advisers. A good illustration of this policy was the 1936 agreement transferring ownership of the Iraqi State Railways to the Iraqi government, while leaving all the key positions in British hands.[15] Indeed, virtually no decline in British influence in Iraq was discernible until 1939. At the same time, it should be emphasized that even after independence most Iraqis (outside government circles) continued to resent British influence in their country, and the local press, whenever it had the chance, attacked British predominance in Iraq's political and economic life. This resentment, however, was not exclusively anti-British, for no foreign influence was viewed kindly during this period.[16]

On 5 September 1939, two days after Britain's declaration of war on Germany, Iraq broke off diplomatic relations with Germany and assured Britain of its co-operation. These two acts aroused criticism in nationalist Iraqi circles 'who had hoped that a German victory would free Palestine and Syria from British and French control'.[17] A week later a state of emergency was declared, and a decree was issued with regard to the organization of the country's economic life.

With the formation of the Rashid 'Ali government on 31 March 1940 and the fall of France in June 1940, anti-British feelings were strengthened. Iraqi politicians began to capitalize on anti-British feelings to gain political prestige.[18] Meanwhile, Iraqi politicians and officers were holding talks with Nazi Germany through Italy's representative in Baghdad. German documents from this period show that by the end of 1940 the Rashid 'Ali government had begun asking the Italians and the Germans for both military and propaganda support.[19]

British officials pressed Iraq to break off relations with Italy, take a more active pro-British stand and suppress German propaganda, but to no avail.[20] When the US informed Iraq of its full endorsement of British policy and urged it to take a more co-operative attitude in its relations with the British, this too proved fruitless.[21] At the same time, the Iraqis informally communicated to the British ambassador their readiness to alter their policy if three conditions were fulfilled: that Syria be granted complete independence; that there be immediate implementation of the White Paper on Palestine; and that Britain promptly furnish Iraq with sufficient quantities of arms.[22]

The gap between the two countries continued to widen, and the resignation of Rashid 'Ali's government on 30 January 1941 was therefore met with great relief in London. Britain's foreign minister, Anthony Eden, sent his congratulations to Ambassador Basil Newton: 'Resignation of Prime Minister [Rashid 'Ali] is highly satisfactory and I much appreciate the part Your Excellency has played in matter.'[23]

The new government set up by Taha al-Hashimi was no more responsive to British demands, however, and in any event Rashid 'Ali returned to power in April. At this point the new British ambassador in Baghdad, Sir Kinahan Cornwallis, favoured military measures to restore Iraq to a pro-British policy, though he was aware that the necessary forces could not be spared.[24] Relations continued to deteriorate: the Iraqis forbade Cornwallis to communicate in cypher, searched the British embassy, and forced the staff to haul down its Union Jack.[25]

Meanwhile Iraq pressed Germany for military aid;[26] and while the Germans held exhaustive discussions to decide what military aid to give, how to deliver it and what its impact would be,[27] the climax in anti-British feelings was reached: Iraq refused disembarkation rights to British forces at Basra, and hostilities erupted between the two countries with the landing of British forces at Basra on 29 April 1941.[28] The Germans did not provide significant military aid, and the British were able to recapture Iraq thirty days later – twenty-one years after their first occupation had terminated.

The reasons for Iraq's support of the Axis and the question of whether British military intervention was necessary are outside the scope of this study.[29] What is, however, important for us to consider is the impact of these events on British influence in Iraq. Basically, anti-British feelings did not subside after the reoccupation. (Certain Iraqi circles undoubtedly supported the Axis not out of sympathy to Germany and its ideas but rather as a result of antipathy to Britain.) Jamil al-Midfa'i, Iraq's prime minister between June and October 1941, followed a policy of compromise between British demands (e.g. severing relations with Italy) and nationalistic trends (e.g. not prosecuting members of Rashid 'Ali's government). By then, however, the British had enough power to demand more drastic changes in their favour. Nuri as-Said, their main ally, formed a new government in October 1941, and for the next two and a half years Iraq was, more or less, under British control.

British policy in Iraq (and throughout the Middle East) changed considerably during the war period, and the British mechanism in Iraq gained significantly in power. Moreover, Britain was quite satisfied with Nuri as-Said's government, which not only complied with its demands (e.g. declared war on Germany in January 1943), but even went to the extent of confining anti-British officials and other Iraqis to a detention camp established at Fao.[30]

With the relaxation of emergency restrictions at the end of the war, British influence was reduced but by no means lost entirely. New issues, such as Iraq's membership in the sterling area and the situation in Palestine, now came to dominate Anglo-Iraqi relations. The major issue in the political relationship, however, was the revision of the 1930 Treaty of Alliance. Towards the end of the war, the Iraqi press began calling on Britain 'to remove the last vestige of imperfection in Iraq's independence'.[31] The government formed by Tawfiq as-Suwaydi in February 1946 set up a committee to study the treaty's revision,[32] and the subsequent fall of Suwaydi's government three months later did not alter this trend of thought among Iraqi politicians.[33] British officials began reporting 'slight signs of increased anti-British feeling', expressed in sharp press attacks on British advisers.[34] Between March and July 1946, Baghdad witnessed many anti-British demonstrations, and the events in Palestine did nothing to help pacify the mood in the country. Probably as a result of this pressure, the British government decided, as a gesture of goodwill, to raise the status of the Iraqi mission in London to that of an Embassy; at the same time it informed the Iraqi government that it would no longer claim special precedence for the British ambassador in Baghdad.[35] Iraqi pressure continued, however, and throughout 1947, Iraqi governments and political parties still put revision of the treaty first in their programmes – if only because, apart from Palestine, it was the only issue for which they could count 'on the whole-hearted support of all politically minded elements in the country'.[36]

The British began to perceive the significant changes taking place in the Middle East. The Middle East (Official) Committee, in its examination of the situation, noted the gradual realization by the Arabs of the relative decline of Britain's military and financial power; the withdrawal of British forces from the area;[37] the continued rise of nationalist feelings; the increase in America's interest in the area; and the USSR's intention to increase its influence in the region.[38] Faced with these trends, Britain agreed to begin negotiations on the revision of the 1930 treaty. Foreign Secretary Ernest Bevin, writing to Sir Stafford Cripps, minister for economic affairs, in an effort to lobby for the new decision, said:

> The significance of Iraq for Great Britain is clearly growing, particularly in the light of the situation in Egypt. Egypt is a broken reed ... Iraq on the other hand is a country capable of enormous development and increase of population ... I am in fact convinced that we must now seek to make Iraq the keystone of our Middle East policy.[39]

Secret and informal talks began with the Iraqi government and the regent of Iraq (during his visit to London in August 1947).[40] Meetings continued in Baghdad, and in December 1947 an Iraqi mission headed by Prime Minister Salih Jabr proceeded to Portsmouth where Bevin was spending his holiday.[41] On 10 January 1948 a new treaty was initialled,[42] with the formal signing taking place five days later.

The Portsmouth Treaty thus replaced the 1930 Treaty of Alliance. It provided that 'Iraq and Britain would have a relationship of strong allies based on equality and complete independence'. Whilst its annex recognized the importance of British air bases in Iraq as 'an essential element in the defence of Iraq itself and of international security', Britain's use of them, in the event of war or threat of war, would be dependent on Iraq's invitation. A Joint Defence Board was established to discuss matters of defence, and Iraq pledged that it would continue to employ British subjects as military instructors and send Iraqis to Britain for military training.[43] In addition to the published treaty and its annex, a series of secret letters between Bevin and Jabr emphasized Iraq's willingness to put the air bases and all other military facilities at Britain's disposal whenever needed, and to pay compensation to British employees of the Iraqi State Railways (the 1936 agreement had stipulated that the important administrative and technical positions be filled by British subjects) and to Iraqi employees of the Royal Air Force.[44]

Although from the Iraqi point of view the 1948 treaty was certainly an improvement on the 1930 treaty, it was nevertheless met by fierce popular opposition. The mass insurrection against the Portsmouth Treaty became known as *Al-Wathbah* ('The leap'). It is clear now that the regent, Abd al-Ilah, and the small circle of Iraqis who ruled Iraq (such as Nuri as-Said) underestimated national sentiments, and the continual demonstrations led Prime Minister Salih Jabr (the first Shi'ite to occupy this high office) to resign.[45] The new government, led by Mohammad as-Sadr, informed Britain on 4 February that the Portsmouth Treaty was rejected by Iraq's Council of Ministers since it was 'far from realising the wishes of the Iraqi Nation'.[46] Anglo-Iraqi relations thus continued to be based on the original 1930 treaty until April 1955, when it was replaced by a special agreement in accordance with the Baghdad Pact.

It should be noted that the Portsmouth Treaty was abrogated not because of its contents but rather due to the circumstances surrounding its signature: the atmosphere of secrecy, and the fact that no Arabic translation of the text was prepared, aroused suspicions in nationalist circles in Iraq about the government's intentions.[47] The atmosphere of distrust was undoubtedly exacerbated by the financial crisis developing in Iraq in 1948, and by the events in Palestine (with the outbreak of war there, Iraq was put under martial law).[48]

British influence in Iraq reached a new nadir with Britain's embargo on arms supplies to all participants in the Palestine war. Even so, although 'it was practically impossible for H.M.'s Government to obtain a favourable decision on the smallest point',[49] Britain's position in Iraq did not deteriorate to the 1941 level. As after the 1941 events, Nuri as-Said was again called upon (in January 1949) to form a government with a very pro-British policy. Revision of the 1930 treaty now became a secondary issue to most Iraqi politicians, as their interest turned to lifting the arms embargo and negotiating a new agreement with the oil companies, and by 1950 Anglo-Iraqi relations were beginning to regain their former strength. In 1955 they reached a new peak with the creation of the Baghdad Pact.

BRITISH ECONOMIC POLICY IN IRAQ

The 1930 Treaty of Alliance, as shown above, concentrated on military and political issues. Though this emphasis might seem surprising in view of Britain's important commercial interests in Iraq, it was not accidental:

The omission from the Treaty of Alliance of all mention of commercial relations was intentional. It was considered that such mention would be likely to excite in foreign circles suspicion that His Majesty's Government were using their position as mandatory to secure a privileged position for British trade in Iraq after the termination of the mandatory regime. It was hoped to conclude a separate commercial treaty on the usual lines ...[50]

However, the idea of a separate commercial treaty lapsed after the League of Nations required Iraq, as a condition for termination of the mandate, to guarantee most-favoured-nation treatment to all members.[51]

Most British officials in Baghdad and London considered the economic benefits accruing to Britain as a result of the 1930 treaty to be substantial indeed. When in 1934 some British circles suggested a reassessment of Britain's position in Iraq, the British ambassador in Baghdad, Sir Francis Humphrys, argued that any revision of the 1930 treaty or reduction in Britain's involvement in Iraq would be a grave mistake. He sent a detailed report describing the ways in which Britain was benefiting from Iraq, concluding:

We have sunk millions in this country in less propitious times and are just beginning to obtain a return on our expenditure. It is not a question of throwing good money after bad, but of consolidating, at a relatively trifling cost, a hard-won position of pre-eminence on one of the world's important highways.[52]

The minority of officials in London who objected to the 1930 treaty argued that it would lead to a loss of British popularity in Iraq, which in turn would harm British interests there. This minority, however, as represented by G. W. Rendel of the Eastern Department at the Foreign Office, did not want to change the treaty in order to strengthen Iraqi independence but rather, on the contrary, to stem the rising tide of nationalism, which they viewed as a plague. In Rendel's words:

Personally, I have long felt increasingly doubtful as to the wisdom of the policy embodied in the 1930 Treaty – though it has always been strongly defended by Sir F. Humphrys, the Colonial Office and the Air Ministry, and (to a diminishing extent) by the War Office and Admiralty. Our determination to retain what one may perhaps call a military finger in the Iraqi pie seems to me to have acted as a kind of irritant and stimulus to the more extreme form of oriental nationalism (a disease which is strongly prevalent in Iraq ...)[53]

Thus, the 1930 treaty constituted not only the basis for serving

Britain's political and military interests in Iraq; it also provided the means for protecting and widening British economic interests there.

It is difficult to discern any clearly defined British economic policy in Iraq (or elsewhere in the Middle East) during the 1930s. Only the broadest terms were used to describe Britain's aims in Iraq:

a. The permanent maintenance and protection in all circumstances of the essential communications of His Majesty's Government.
b. The general object of maintaining predominant British influence in Iraq, or at least of guarding against any penetration of Iraq by other foreign countries.
c. The protection of other smaller British financial and commercial interests in Iraq, and of the predominant position won by the United Kingdom in the import trade into Iraq during the Mandatory period.[54]

Nor were many discussions held during this period on particular aspects of British economic policy in Iraq, for the promotion of which no organization was established. All this was in great contrast to what was to happen in the 1940s, particularly in the post-war period.

It was World War II which changed Britain's perception of the Middle East. The creation in April 1941 of the Middle East Supply Centre (MESC), intended to serve the specific purpose of overcoming supply shortages, constituted a turning point in the history of British economic policy in the Middle East.[55] The war and its impact on the various countries of the region had convinced the British of the necessity for planning a long-term policy towards the area. American participation in MESC and growing US interest in the area in general further strengthened the British in their belief that the formulation of a comprehensive economic policy in the Middle East was vital to British interests. Nevertheless, the main effort during the war was naturally devoted to tackling day-to-day problems. Parallel to MESC, a Middle East Supplies Committee was established in Washington to co-ordinate supply questions (mainly those related to Land–Lease),[56] while various other local committees were created throughout the region for the same purpose. But even before the war ended, committees began discussing economic policy in the Middle East in the post-war period.[57] In June 1943 the war cabinet discussed the situation in the area and emphasized that 'the economic stability – and consequent social and political contentment – of the Middle East is a major strategic interest of His Majesty's Government, and thus of the United Nations'.[58]

At first, influenced by the work of MESC, Britain was of the opinion that the Middle East should be considered a single regional unit: 'Our ultimate objective should be to create a Middle East Economic Council, as a consultative body representative of the Middle East Governments and of the Governments of external Powers (principally Great Britain and the United States) with major interests in this region'.[59]

It was only after the war, however, that Britain began to formulate its Middle East economic policy, still regional rather than specific to each country of the area, in concrete and detailed form. Meeting in London during 5–17 September 1945, British representatives serving throughout the Middle East adopted a number of guidelines for Britain's economic policy in the region, which may be summarized as follows:

1. Efforts should be made to further the economic development and amelioration of the social conditions of the people of the Middle East, to insure internal stability and increase the area's importance as a market for imported goods.
2. British representatives should guide Middle East governments in mobilizing and spending their ample sterling balances.
3. The recommendations made by the Board of Trade for the stimulation of British commerce in the area should be implemented: strengthening commercial diplomatic posts, exchanging trade missions, increasing travel facilities, encouraging preliminary survey work by British firms of consulting engineers, improving existing air-mail service, concluding commercial treaties with the countries of the region, and providing British technical experts.[60]

The adoption of these guidelines had an immense impact on the economic development of Middle East countries. In Iraq's case, we will see how the concept of economic development changed, what problems confronted the Iraqis when they tried to draw from their sterling balances to finance imports, and how the British attempted to impose their advisers on the Iraqi government.

In line with Britain's new policy, MESC was dissolved on 1 November 1945 (mainly because the Americans did not want to remain in an organization which they saw as a tool serving British interests), and the British Middle East Office (BMEO), based in Cairo, was created to carry on some of its functions, as well as some of those performed by the British minister-resident in the Middle East (a position abolished at the end of the war). Officially it was announced that: 'The experience of the war and the findings of recent scientific surveys of the economic problems of the Middle East have indicated that in certain directions such schemes must be formulated on a regional basis if they are to be effective.'[61] BMEO's function was defined as 'a channel through which British technical and specialist assistance is placed at the disposal of the Governments of the Arab countries, Persia, Ethiopia, the Arab League, and of any other regional organisation which may be established to co-ordinate economic policy in the Middle East.'[62]

BMEO's contribution to the economic development of the Middle East is beyond dispute. Its technical and specialist staff included men of high reputation in their professions, such as Dr John Murray (statistics), Sir Herbert Stewart (agriculture), Mr Audsley (labour) and others.[63] Many important surveys were conducted on the various economic sectors of each Middle Eastern country, and the resulting reports constituted bases for development plans.

But BMEO had political functions too. It was to prepare analyses of political events and make recommendations to London, give political guidance to the British commanders-in-chief in the area, and keep British missions and the British government informed of 'service matters likely to be of interest to them'.[64]

BMEO's political functions aroused bitterness and led to conflict with British embassies in the Middle East, particularly Egypt. These embassies felt that BMEO reduced their power and decreased their influence with the Middle East governments, and by 1948 British representatives were explicitly demanding that 'the B.M.E.O. should be reduced to a development agency'.[65] This pressure continued until BMEO was finally dissolved in 1949.

During the four years of BMEO's existence, British economic policy underwent a number of changes. Some of the guidelines adopted at the 1945 conference were found to be unrealistic because of the drastic transformations that occurred in the world in general and the Middle East in particular in 1946 and 1947.[66] The most important of these, which it seems was underestimated at the 1945 conference, was the extent of Britain's weakness – both economic and military – on the one hand, and of America's growing interest and ability to take Britain's place in the Middle East on the other. As a Foreign Office official put it:

> The deterioration in our economic and financial position renders impossible the maintenance of a British economic and financial predominance in the M.E. … .
> In view of this situation it seems essential, politically, that we should associate the United States with us in the M.E. … .
> Anglo-American co-operation … would provide the best opportunity for effective control of the M.E. in the interests of the maintenance of Anglo-

Saxon predominance, of the material progress of the M.E. and of the prevention of Russian penetration.[67]

Apart from the American factor, the continued rise of nationalism, particularly in Egypt and Iraq, and fear of communism also contributed to the need for redirecting British economic policy in the Middle East.[68] Nevertheless, the principal objectives of Britain's policy remained generally the same as in 1945:

(i) to retain our predominance in the area.
(ii) to raise the standard of living in order to increase the demand for our manufactured products, to give political stability and to resist communist encroachment.[69]

Resisting 'communist encroachment' was the only real difference in objectives in comparison with 1945. However, it was the means for attaining these objectives which changed. It was realized, for instance, that Britain could no longer afford to grant loans and thus it was decided to support an extension of operations by the International Bank for Reconstruction and Development (IBRD). With regard to the sterling balances held in London by Middle East countries, it was recognized that it would be impossible to continue opposing their withdrawal and therefore the main emphasis was to be placed on encouraging those countries to import goods from Britain, rather than to reduce imports in general, as had been recommended in 1945. Besides this general Middle East economic policy, in 1947 Britain also formulated a specific policy for each country. With regard to Iraq, it was decided that more attention should be paid to nationalistic demands in the economic sphere and that 'nationalistic schemes', like the creation of a central bank or a national shipping company, should not be opposed. Furthermore, the 1947 meeting of the Middle East (Official) Committee put forward a new idea that was to become one of the basic elements of Britain's economic policy in Iraq for the next three years: the establishment of a central development board, with foreign assistance (both British and American), to co-ordinate and approve development projects. It was felt in London that this would safeguard British interests and enable British firms to continue to receive Iraqi contracts. With regard to American competition, it was decided that although it was impossible to prevent Americans from exporting to Iraq, efforts should be made to limit Iraqi government imports from the United States to only those products which Britain could not then supply, like agricultural machinery. The committee also decided to have the British

Embassy continue to press Iraq to adopt measures designed to improve living standards in order to thwart communist trends.[70]

The policy adopted in 1947 did not change significantly despite important events, both regional (the war in Palestine) and local (Iraq's severe financial crisis). By 1949 British officials were well aware of the immense problems facing development in the area, but neither their policy nor their attitude of superiority changed – as the Foreign Office put it: 'The difficulties of promoting development are very great. The countries concerned are not only foreign countries, but Eastern countries.'[71]

In July 1949, a meeting in London of British ambassadors in the Middle East again took up the issue of economic policy in the region, but without significantly altering the 1947 guidelines. They did feel, however, that the time had come for Britain to push ahead vigorously in the field of development, since the survey and enquiry phase was largely completed.[72] Nevertheless, British development priorities for Middle East countries remained the same. In Iraq, the British encouraged agricultural produce (which Britain needed), while attaching but limited importance to industrialization (which might lead to competition with British goods). These priorities were re-emphasized at the 1949 conference:

> The great majority of the population in the Middle East were rural and therefore we were rightly concentrating primarily on food production projects. This might also have the effect of keeping the population on the land and stopping the drift to the towns – an important consideration in the anti-Communist campaign. The development of industry was of secondary importance, but we should avoid giving the impression of discouraging their industrial development in order to extend our markets.[73]

Iraq's decision to create a Central Development Board, as recommended by the 1947 conference, was met with relief by conference delegates.[74] (In the event, however, the decision was not implemented until 1959.)

As we have seen, the 1940s ended with a growing awareness on Britain's part of the strategic and economic importance of the Middle East. Two cabinet memoranda by Foreign Secretary Ernest Bevin clearly reflect the sources of this awareness. Oil reserves in the Middle East, particularly in Saudi Arabia and Iraq, were now known and recognized as vital to Britain's economy, while the cold war between East and West further increased the region's importance. These perceptions led the British to be both more responsive to the demands of Middle East governments (withdrawal of sterling balances was such an example, as will be seen below) and more prepared to co-operate with the United States.[75]

THE ROLE OF BRITISH ADVISERS IN IRAQ

In implementing British economic and political policy in Iraq British advisers constituted a most important means. Their impact on policy in each sector of Iraq's economy will be apparent throughout this study. In this section, however, we will concentrate on general issues affecting almost all the advisers in Iraq.

Subsidiary agreements to the Anglo-Iraqi Treaty of 1922 specified that British officials should be attached to Iraq's important government offices as advisers, directors, inspectors, and so on. The 1930 Treaty of Alliance, while acknowledging Iraq's sovereignty, contained two significant commitments by the Iraqi government: 'the Iraq Government will normally engage British subjects when in need of the services of foreign officials', and 'such officials will be selected after consultation between our two Governments'.[76] Though the treaty left the Iraqi government free 'to engage non-British officials for posts for which suitable British subjects are not available',[77] this was rarely done.

During the 1920s, the number of British officials was drastically, if gradually, reduced owing to the expiry and non-renewal of contracts: from 2,906 in 1920, to 1,829 in 1923, to 474 in 1926, and by September 1929 their number had fallen to 234.[78] Even so, this did not result in any significant decrease in British influence, as all senior government posts were still held by British subjects.

After Iraq's independence, the British advisers officially became employees of the Iraqi government, and the British government emphasized time and again throughout the period under study that they were in no way affiliated to the British Embassy. These denials, as we shall see, were clearly disingenuous.

Immediately following independence, the advisers were asked by the British government to continue reporting to the British Embassy, but in a slightly different manner: instead of writing directly to the Embassy they were to channel their information via the adviser to the Ministry of the Interior (usually the most senior British adviser).[79] British documents of the 1930s and 1940s leave absolutely no doubt that the advisers passed information to the British Embassy and the Foreign Office on a regular basis, mostly without the knowledge or consent of the Iraqis. While it is true that King Faisal had expressed his willingness for British advisers to continue keeping Humphrys privately informed of any important developments, the continual and regular flow of information almost certainly exceeded Faisal's intentions. In fact, even British officials were somewhat uneasy with the situation. For instance, when the 1933 Assyrian massacre occurred, Humphrys wrote privately to Rendel of the Foreign Office:

> Since the outbreak of the present Assyrian crisis, a considerable number of letters and reports by Stafford [then an official at the Ministry of the Interior] and Edmonds [then Adviser to the Ministry for Foreign Affairs] have been copied textually in the Embassy and sent home to the Foreign Office. The bulk of these were prepared by Stafford and Edmonds in their capacity as officials of the Iraq Government, whose permission was not obtained before they were passed to us.[80]

Humphrys went on to ask Rendel to treat information thus obtained as most confidential:

> The whole question of the liaison between the Embassy and the British officials in the Iraqi service is very delicate and it would clearly make the position of Stafford and Edmonds (and probably of other British officials employed in the administration) quite impossible if it became known to the Iraqis that the writings of their own officials were, so to speak, being used against them. It is therefore essential that no reference to British officials of the Iraqi Government as a source of information shall appear in any statement or document published by His Majesty's Government.[81]

Another example of the strong connection between the advisers and the Embassy is their reaction to the Iraqi decision, in 1933, to stop sending intelligence abstracts to the Royal Air Force stationed in Iraq. A British adviser working with Iraq's Criminal Investigation Department wrote to the RAF:

> If the Iraqis do stop sending their abstracts and publish only in Arabic, I anticipate no difficulty in obtaining an Arabic copy from their office regularly and making you translated extracts ... This being so it doesn't seem to matter much to us, what they [the Iraqis] do.[82]

Edmonds's private papers also give ample evidence of the dual role of the advisers. As adviser to the Ministry of the Interior in the 1940s, his influence was such that Iraqi prime ministers used to discuss with him such sensitive matters as the formation of new cabinets and the allocation of ministries, and he regularly forwarded the information to Ambassador Cornwallis.[83] An American diplomat serving in Baghdad summed up the relationship between the British advisers and the Embassy very lucidly thus:

> The British officials of the Iraqi Government maintain very close relations with the British Embassy, to which they report and from which, at times, they receive instructions and suggestions. Rarely do these officials feel their positions as employees of the Iraqi Government to be more of a moral responsibility than their allegiance to the British King; and they are to

think first as loyal Britishers and then as Iraqi officials. Their appointments are made (usually they are nominated) by the British Government.[84]

The British advisers were an important asset to the British government not only as a source of information but also, and more significantly, as a means of implementing British policy in Iraq. When the Iraqi government, for example, asked the British government to nominate an adviser to the Ministry of Economics and Communications, the British ambassador commented:

The post is one of great importance on account of the present disorganised condition of Irrigation and Public Works, while from the British point of view, the influence ... the incumbent can have over (a) railway affairs; (b) relations with oil companies; and (c) placing of works contracts, should be borne in mind.[85]

The importance of the advisers to the British government is clearly reflected in the latter's immense efforts, on the one hand, to impose such advisers on the Iraqi government, and, on the other, to prevent the appointment of non-British advisers even for purely technical positions. A few examples will illustrate this. For instance, the British frequently exploited Iraq's crises to have advisers appointed, and during the negotiations for the 1939 loan (see Ch. 3), the British continually pressed the Iraqis to employ an adviser to the Ministry of Finance. Houston-Boswall, of the British Embassy in Baghdad, wrote to the Foreign Office: 'Although the Iraqis have not yet asked for a new financial Adviser, I think they ought to have one and if they continue to show reluctance, means might be found to link this matter up in some tactful way with credits.'[86] Another example was Iraq's 1948 financial crisis when again the British linked the appointment of an adviser to financial aid. As the Foreign Office informed its Baghdad Embassy: 'We find it significant that the Iraqis have been without a Financial Adviser for a year and ... you should tell the Regent that the sooner they appoint a new one the sooner they are likely to establish financial stability without which they have no hope of securing foreign loans.'[87]

During the various conferences held in London to discuss British economic policy, the provision of experts to Iraq (and other Middle East countries) was always high on the agenda. It was believed that having British advisers in these countries would be 'one of the most vital elements in the success of any development policy in the Middle East'.[88] This belief remained paramount in 1947: when Britain and Iraq began negotiating a revision of their 1930 treaty, it was decided in London: 'We should do nothing to encourage the Iraqis to raise the Treaty position about advisers.'[89] And although it was known that the Iraqis were 'touchy about the implication of inferiority in the Treaty' evoked by the reference to the provision of experts, it was felt that Britain could not compromise with Iraq on this subject.[90] Indeed, Article 9 of the annex of the Portsmouth Treaty explicitly provided that Iraq would undertake to use British subjects as military instructors and experts.[91] As this treaty was immediately abrogated, the 1930 treaty continued to be the basis for providing British advisers to Iraq.

With regard to the nationality of advisers, the British followed a very consistent policy: whatever the adviser's function – military, financial, educational or medical – they made every effort to recruit a British subject. If none were forthcoming, they usually tried to defer the appointment until an appropriate British subject could be found. Only in rare cases did they agree to the appointment of non-British advisers.[92]

The result was that in April 1949 there were about a dozen non-British advisers (3 American pilots of agricultural planes, 2 Rumanian musicians, 1 Russian refugee who was a fish expert, 2 French teachers and about 6 Eyptian and Syrian teachers), compared with the 247 British advisers serving with Iraqi ministries and directorates, as shown in Table 1.1. Thirty-seven of these British officials were teachers, and 108 were junior technicians and fore-

TABLE 1.1 Number of British Officials with Iraqi Ministries and Directorates, April 1949

Ministry or directorate	British officials
Finance	1
Interior	8
Defence	8
Economics	9
Social Affairs	28
Education	37
Justice	1
Survey Directorate	2
Post, Telegraphs and Telephones	15
Public Works Department	4
Iraqi State Railways	40
Basra Port Directorate	33
Fao Dredging Scheme	61
Total	247

Source: FO 371/75068, E 2381/1053/65.

men. The rest held senior posts (apart from advisers to ministers, the directors-general of both the Railways and the Port of Basra, the president of the Court of Cessation, the controller of foreign exchange, the chief biologist, etc.).[93]

The numbers of advisers fluctuated between 1932 and 1950, but not drastically. According to one estimate there were 106 in 1932, 99 in 1933, and 87 in 1934,[94] compared with 113 in 1949 if we exclude those working at the Iraqi Railways, Basra Port and the Fao Dredging Scheme. Between 1939 and 1941, because of world events, there was a decrease in the number of officials, but with the reoccupation of Iraq and the organization of what was called the 'Political Advisory Staff' their number again went up. This staff was established in the summer of 1941 by the British ambassador, Sir Kinahan Cornwallis,[95] who in the next few years was to play an important role in shaping British policy in Iraq.

On the part of the Iraqi government, there were constant efforts throughout the period under study to reduce both the numbers of advisers and their influence. Even before independence, the minister of finance, Rustum Haidar, insisted there was no necessity for the appointment of outsiders. His argument was:

> There is no doubt that the new Adviser needs a full year ... before he studies the situation perfectly. If he is compelled to spend a few months every year in Europe [most senior Advisers spent the summer in England to escape the heat of Iraq] I do not know how the benefit from him would be complete.[96]

Iraqi resistance to the appointment of advisers persisted after 1932, taking many forms. Most governments declared that their policy was to reduce the number of foreign officials to a minimum, and some of them indeed took measures in that direction. In 1933, for instance, the government requested foreign firms working in the country to replace their foreign employees with Iraqis as far as possible. The firms were also required to provide the government with a list of their foreign employees, showing the type of work they performed.[97] In 1936 a law forbidding the engagement of non-Iraqis in many specified trades and crafts was enacted, although the government was empowered to make exceptions if no suitable Iraqis were available.[98] When the British Embassy strongly objected, Nuri as-Said explained that the law was aimed at Indians and Persians working in Iraq.[99] This law was further extended in 1940,[100] but under strong British pressure all British subjects, including Indians, were exempted from it.[101]

With the decrease in British influence during 1940–1, many contracts with advisers were not renewed, including senior ones like the adviser to the Ministry of Finance.[102] From 1942 onwards, however, the number of advisers and their influence began to increase again. The Iraqi government again tried to reverse the trend – but to no avail.

The financial crisis of 1948 and the events in Palestine further increased Iraqi antagonism to British advisers. The prime minister declared at the Chamber of Deputies that his government would not engage new British officials, and that the policy was 'to reduce as much as possible the employment of foreigners'.[103] To that end, and without consulting the Embassy, the government decided to abolish various fringe benefits to advisers, such as rent and home-leave passage, on the grounds that the country was having financial difficulties.[104] This confronted the British with an acute dilemma: whether or not to subsidize the advisers.[105] The Foreign Office opted to offer assistance to senior advisers by means of easy-term loans, but teachers and engineers were not helped, and their numbers inevitably diminished.[106]

Apart from the 'nationalistic' reason for opposing British advisers there was another, more objective one: the low level of most of the British advisers serving in Iraq.[107] The British government was quite aware of this; commenting on the Iraqi government's hestitation, in 1939, to appoint a financial adviser, Houston-Boswall of the Embassy said: 'It must be admitted that it has not infrequently happened that when they have wanted somebody, we have, after a frantic search, tried to foist on them some "antique" or, as in the case of British doctors, failed to produce candidates at all.'[108] British Embassy officials constantly reiterated to the Foreign Office that it must find suitable, experienced candidates, commenting: 'they must have real "experts". Iraq could not afford the luxury of employing Britons just because they were British ... nothing does us more harm than to inflict mediocrities on these people.'[109] Strongly pro-British Iraqis, like the regent and Nuri, also emphasized to the British government that the 'country wanted British advisers but they must be of the highest standard'.[110]

The answer from London was that neither experienced nor young experts were willing to work in Iraq (they usually preferred India or Egypt, if at all). This problem was further aggravated during the war years when young British experts wanted to be at the front.

A good example of the lack of suitable advisers was the case of Colonel Bayliss, who was appointed director-general of imports in Iraq, a position with enormous responsibilities during the war. Robert Jackson, then director of MESC, wrote of him to the British Ministry of War Transport: 'Colonel Bayliss ... is probably the best man who could be available in the Middle East at the present to deal with this problem. But again from my experience, he is not of the standard of official whom I should like to see in that appointment.'[111] Jackson was right. Bayliss, as will be seen in Chapter 3, ran into trouble not only with the Iraqis but with the British and MESC as well.

As for the advisers themselves, their situation was far from satisfactory even in their own eyes. For one thing, most realized that Iraq was a professional dead-end for them (though it should be emphasized that some were highly qualified, such as Dr Murray the statistician and Mr Haigh the irrigation expert). As one of them bluntly put it: 'lacking professional qualifications, their Iraqi experience was unmarketable. They therefore sank to the category of invertebrates.'[112] A second source of frustration was the unclear distinction between their role as British subjects on the one hand and Iraqi officials on the other. If an adviser identified with the Iraqi side, he immediately came under attack from the British. For example, when it was decided to sell gold in Iraq as a means of reducing the public's purchasing power,[113] the financial adviser, Swan, opposed the scheme on the grounds that 'it was scandalous that the Iraqi peasant should be allowed to buy gold when we knew quite well that the price would fall'.[114] For this he earned a strong rebuke from a British official at the Middle East Office in Cairo: 'Mr. Swan is a rather stupid old man who has his duty towards the Iraqis very much at heart and is at times inclined to act without regard to the general situation.'[115] A third source of frustration for the advisers was their feeling that Britain could be doing more in and for Iraq. British civil and military personnel working in close association with local Iraqi officials and the general population were often distressed by the administrative inefficiency they saw around them on all sides. They frequently wondered, and were also asked by various Iraqis, why the British government, having such strong influence, did not play a more active role in organizing better public services and stopping the more blatant malpractices which frequently discredited public life in Iraq.[116] The answer to these questions came in a most explicit elaboration of British policy in Iraq, written by Mr Chaplin of the Foreign Office:

> So far as purely British interests are concerned, I cannot see that an efficiently run Iraq is of great strategic or economic importance. We are concerned to safeguard our communications and our oil supplies, both in the country and across the Shatt al Arab. It is surely less necessary to ensure that the trains run on time, that the roads and bridges are properly maintained and that the 'fellahin' get a square deal from the 'effendis' than

that the Iraqis are friendly disposed towards us ... Conditions may be chaotic at times; there may be *coups d'état*. But temporary inconveniences are surely better than uniting effendi and fellah against us.[117]

The above quotation seems to be the key to understanding British policy in Iraq and elsewhere during the 1930s and 1940s. Britain defined its interests quite clearly, and its representatives followed them consistently. As long as the inefficiency, the continual power-struggles and the maldistribution of income did not contradict or harm basic British interests, Britain was not prepared to take action.

Interestingly, Chaplin himself was convinced that forcing British officials on the Iraqis was counter-productive in that it would unite them against Britain. However, on this issue his was a minority viewpoint.[118] Most British officials in Baghdad and London and almost all the advisers in Iraq had a different attitude: that Iraq's salvation lay in the appointment of more and more British officials. Furthermore, the advisers were bitter that the mandate had been reduced from the twenty-five years originally intended, and they were highly critical of the British ambassador and his staff, whom they accused of having an almost exclusive interest in foreign policy.[119]

At the same time, while the advisers might have genuinely believed that they, and only they, could stop the deterioration of the administration in Iraq, they also had personal reasons for defending the policy of imposing British officials on that country. Most of them had no alternative to their employment there (or in other colonial posts). Being generally mediocre to begin with, and not having advanced professionally during their tenure in Iraq, they had a strongly vested interest in maintaining the high salary, fringe benefits, prestige and responsibilities inherent in their position as advisers.[120]

Summing up the role of the advisers, it may be said that they failed to constitute a bridge between Britain and Iraq because, *inter alia*, they were constrained by the framework of British interests. But if guarding these interests was their main purpose, they fulfilled their role successfully indeed. Some of them, particularly those in technical fields (e.g. medicine, education, infrastructure), contributed significantly to Iraq's development, but on the whole their services to Britain exceeded their services to Iraq. They were the eyes and ears safeguarding Britain's military, oil and commercial interests. The benefits which accrued to Britain by virtue of its special position in Iraq and by means of these advisers were numerous, including a high proportion of Iraq's trade, oil concessions and contracts, as well as considerable military and strategic advantages.

Although not directly related to the subject of British advisers in Iraq, it is perhaps not irrelevant to note the deep prejudice and scorn with which the country and its people were perceived by certain British officials whose job it was to determine and implement British policy there. Thus, commenting on the situation in Iraq, Baggallay, a Foreign Office official, wrote:

> A point which people are apt to forget is that the Iraqis are, like many other Orientals, childish, unreasonable, vacillating and lacking in what we are pleased to call moral courage ... If the Iraqis had possessed the qualities of application and resolution of even average Europeans, they would long ago have been a great nation, and we should not be in a position today to use, more or less as if they were our own, their communications, their oil and their country generally.[121]

Another senior official at the Embassy, Thompson, reported: 'I understand there is no specific word in the Arabic language meaning "gratitude", and this *lacuna* is certainly reflected in the character of the people.'[122] And the British consul in Amara wrote on his conversations with local officials: 'One fact which always strikes me when having such conversations [with Iraqis] is the feeling of pessimism, hopelessness and despair of the persons conversed with. Running through these talks is the Muslim attitude of mind of resignation.'[123]

ANGLO-AMERICAN RELATIONS IN IRAQ

Anglo-American relations in the 1940s affected economic policy in Iraq in many ways. Unlike the 1930s, when Britain faced competition in rather limited areas (e.g. Japanese competition for the textile market), in the 1940s, and particularly the post-war period, there was strong competition from the US in almost all political and economic spheres. (Sometimes, even the mere potential of US competition forced British policy-makers to alter their course of action.) This necessitated the formulation of a detailed British economic policy in the Middle East. In order to understand the impact of the 'American factor', it is necessary to briefly examine America's interests during the 1930s, its economic entrance into the Middle East (through MESC and the Lend–Lease Act) and its economic policy there, as well as British and Iraqi reactions to that policy.

American interests in Iraq during the 1930s were limited. Apart from a quarter share in the Iraq Petroleum Company (see Ch. 6), the US conducted a small though growing trade with Iraq, and maintained a number of missionary institutions and archaeological expeditions there.[124] In 1930 the US signed a Tripartite Convention in which it waived its right with respect to consultation regarding termination of the 'special relations' between Britain and Iraq.[125] However, there were indications that the US had not in fact given up its interest in Iraq. The appointment in 1931 of one of America's most experienced consulars, Paul Knabenshue, as minister in Baghdad was not insignificant; nor was the extensive correspondence the Americans conducted with the British during 1932, in which they stressed their right to be consulted with regard to the termination of mandates in general and the conditions of such termination.[126]

After Iraq's independence, Iraqi–American relations, mainly in their commercial aspect, continued to prosper, though still on a limited scale. The fact that the gap in the balance of trade between the United States and Iraq was small and sometimes even in Iraq's favour made it easier for the Iraqis to increase that trade. In December 1938 a Treaty of Commerce and Navigation was signed between the two countries to extend the volume and nature of their trade.[127]

Prior to the outbreak of World War II there is no reference in British documents to American competition, either in Iraq or elsewhere in the Middle East. The earliest such reference appears in late 1940, in a report on Iraq by an official of the Ministry of Economic Warfare cautioning that the Americans were establishing a position in Iraq which would be very useful to them in the future.[128] But his was a voice in the wilderness. In fact, the years 1940–1 were characterized by strong political co-operation between the US and Britain, both before and during the Rashid 'Ali uprising. For example, the US government pressed Rashid 'Ali to abide by Iraq's obligations under its 1930 treaty with Britain. In December 1940 Knabenshue delivered a note to the Iraqi government (the first of its kind in the history of American–Iraqi relations) expressing American interest in Iraq's welfare, and stating that US policy was to assist Britain in its war efforts by all means available short of a declaration of war.[129] Knabenshue himself played an important role in smuggling the regent out of Baghdad to the British air base at Habbaniyya when the Rashid 'Ali revolt took place.[130]

The first attempt to increase America's involvement in Iraq came, interestingly, from the Iraqi side, particularly from Nuri as-Said. He calculated that if American interest in Iraq increased, he would be able to strengthen his position *vis-à-vis* the British. His calculation in this respect was accurate, as will be seen, for example, in the negotiations for oil concessions.

After Iraq's reoccupation in 1941 and his installation as prime minister, Nuri informed Knabenshue that he wished 'to extend American influence in Iraq', and would like more American equipment and instructors.[131] Although no response was forthcoming, the call probably left its impression on the Americans.

Meanwhile, in March 1941, the US Congress legislated the Lend–Lease Act, authorizing the president to deliver war supplies, services and technical information to those countries whose defence he found to be vital to the defence of the US. The new law became applicable to the Middle East by the end of that year.[132] Because it stipulated that all supplies should be scrutinized to prevent abuses, and since the bureaucratic procedure for such checking was very complicated, it was decided in London and Washington in 1942 that the Americans would join MESC (which had been created by the British the previous year) to facilitate the handling of Lend–Lease supplies in the region.[133] Iraq became eligible for this assistance from May 1942.[134]

There is no doubt that Lend–Lease supplies to the Middle East, as co-ordinated by MESC, helped the Allied war effort and contributed to the maintenance of the civilian economy. However, Lend–Lease and MESC also represent the beginning of Anglo-American economic competition. The clashes between the two countries began when the US authorized Middle East countries not under British control to negotiate Lend–Lease aid directly with Washington.[135] Furthermore, according to the terms of Lend–Lease, Britain was precluded from exporting goods manufactured from, or similar to, goods supplied under Lend–Lease; this gave American exporters an unrivalled opportunity to open up new markets for their products in the Middle East, an opportunity which infuriated the British. On the other hand, the Americans saw in MESC 'a thorn in the side of U.S. exporters', and a British tool to discriminate against American goods and to exploit Lend–Lease goods to strengthen Britain's own trade connections.[136]

Britain's concern over America's intentions in the Middle East began as early as 1942. In a personal despatch the Minister-Resident in the Middle East, Richard Casey, warned Prime Minister Winston Churchill that 'there are indications that U.S. is not oblivious to post-war advantages of building up their economic and political influence in this area'.[137] The clashes within MESC only increased Britain's suspicions; and when the Iraqi and Egyptian censorships, under British instructions, began intercepting correspondence between American firms and their agents in the area, they found that American diplomats in Baghdad and Cairo were helping American firms 'to increase their export trade and to gain a firm footing in Middle East territories'.[138] This discovery alarmed the British, as is reflected in a memorandum by a British official in Baghdad:

> There is one danger however of which we have so far remained almost entirely unconscious. The danger is just as threatening to our Imperial interests here and elsewhere in the Middle East as was the Nazi menace and is much more difficult to combat. The danger is the growing interest being taken in this part of the world by the U.S.A. The U.S.A. has almost everything to offer Iraq that we have, without the taint we carry of broken promises, procrastinating policies and with that most fascinating of attractions – the untried devil.[139]

Memoranda began to be written on American trade competition in Iraq and how to oppose it.[140] Ambassador Cornwallis attributed the increased trade between Iraq and the US to, *inter alia*, the revenge of the local Jewish community against the British for having stood idly by during the anti-Jewish riots of 1941.[141]

From both American and British documents it is clear that America's economic interest in the Middle East reached a turning point in 1944. An illustration of this was the despatch that year of a special economic mission, headed by William Culbertson, to study questions affecting America's foreign, economic and commercial policies *vis-à-vis* Turkey, Iran, Iraq, Syria, Lebanon, Palestine and Egypt. After a two-month tour, the mission presented to the Department of State a report covering a wide range of subjects, including financial exchange questions, oil concessions, and air and water communications. The Culbertson report became the basis for much of the thinking of the Department of State concerning these issues in the years immediately afterwards.[142] In Iraq, the mission held talks with the chamber of commerce and the Ministry of Communications and Public Works. The American minister in Baghdad, Loy Henderson, was pleased with the mission's results because it 'strengthened the impression that the United States has a friendly interest in the economic development of Iraq and has encouraged Iraqis in their hope that the United States intends to play a more active commercial role in this part of the world'.[143]

Also in 1944, a permanent representation of the US Foreign Economic Administration (FEA) was set up in Baghdad to supervise the pricing and distribution of Lend–Lease material in Iraq, but at the same time it worked unofficially to promote American trade with Iraq. The FEA representative wrote to Washington that his first year in Baghdad convinced him that the US could capture a large part of the Iraqi market.[144]

During 1945 detailed statements of American economic policy in the Middle East were prepared, based on Culbertson's findings. The policy's main aims were to increase credit facilities to the countries of the region, remove trade restrictions, revise and extend commercial treaties, strengthen diplomatic posts, conduct more economic surveys, and participate in the development of local economic life by responding to requests for technical and advisory assistance.[145] Another memorandum indicated that there were five main problems to contend with in implementing the above set of targets: Soviet ascendancy; the special British position in the area; attitudes and customs of the ruling governments and classes in the area; sociological problems such as the introduction of birth control in Egypt and elsewhere; and the dearth of commodities which could be exported to the US or elsewhere to raise local purchasing power and living standards.[146]

British reaction to the Culbertson mission and the resulting formulation of an American economic policy in the Middle East came in a memorandum prepared by Sir Ronald Campbell of the Eastern Department in the Foreign Office. Campbell took two points as axiomatic: that the British 'wish and intend to maintain a predominant political (and for that matter commercial) position', and Britain's desire that 'the United States should interest themselves in the Middle East' in order to secure American participation in world affairs and obtain American assistance in promoting peaceful conditions. The problem, in Campbell's opinion, was 'how to reconcile these two objects' since it was 'a matter of getting the mixture right'.[147]

Meanwhile, US interest in Iraq and the Middle East continued to increase. One difficulty facing the Americans in expanding their export trade to Iraq was the restrictions imposed on that country as a member of the sterling area (see Ch. 4), but they tried to ensure that the Iraqis imported up to the limit of the currency available to them. The Americans also pressed for the opening of a direct telegraphic link between the two countries, offering to provide the necessary equipment;[148] and Washington decided to participate in the development of oil resources in the area.[149] Politically, too, US interest in local developments was increasing,[150] and in November 1946 the two countries raised their respective legations to the status of embassies.[151] (This last step was the result of talks which Wallace Murray, then director of the Near Eastern Department at the

Department of State, held with Foreign Office officials in London in 1944.)[152]

The competition between the US and Britain notwithstanding, both countries were aware of the necessity of discussing mutually important issues. In Murray's conversations of April 1944, the two powers agreed to establish a more co-operative relationship, 'particularly in the economic and commercial field, and in a rather less degree in the political field'.[153] They also agreed that further exchange of ideas was in order, but it was not until 1947 that another round of talks took place.

The 1947 discussions, known as 'the Pentagon Talks of 1947', covered a wide range of subjects – military, political, economic and social – regarding all the countries of the Middle East and the Eastern Mediterranean.[154] This time, however, the two sides met on more common ground: their fear of communism and the cold war led them to reach agreement on all the basic issues. There was also another important factor creating harmony between them: by October 1947 the intentions and policies of both countries in the Middle East were well known, and Britain's weakness and America's strength were obvious to everyone. These recognitions were clearly reflected in the way the Pentagon Talks were conducted. A top-secret memorandum prepared in the Department of State underlines the fact:

> The British, it would appear, realise their inability to implement their economic policy in the Middle East without American help. They hope however that our cooperation will not preclude their retention of a certain special position in the area.
>
> It would be possible to describe the situation in terms of a simple bargain ... in view of their seriously weakened economic position, it will be necessary for us to make some sort of economic concessions .... This will be necessary in order to enable them to meet our desires in the political and strategic field.[155]

The Americans were thus ready to collaborate with the British in the Middle East under certain conditions: that there would be no division of the area into 'spheres of interest'; that both countries would pursue their economic objectives through policies of 'equal opportunity and maximum freedom of competition, avoiding preferential, discriminatory, and monopolistic arrangements'; and that both sides would recognize the right of the peoples of the area to choose their own manner of handling internal problems.[156]

On the British side, although no such 'simple bargain' was perceived, there are clear indications that London saw things in more or less the same way. An interdepartmental working party was set up in 1947, before the Pentagon Talks, to review the policy to be followed with regard to American interests in the Middle East. Minutes of its meetings show that the British decided to pursue a policy of co-operation with the US in the area, as it was obvious to them that conditions there had changed and it was necessary, for both political and economic reasons, to interest the US in Middle East affairs.[157] (The fact that the British were conducting negotiations in Washington from 1946 onwards for a loan of \$3.75 billion to boost their economy was an important incentive for reaching a *modus vivendi* with the Americans in the Middle East.)

The two countries thus reached agreement on most of the issues they discussed. With regard to Iraq, they agreed that development of the country was important to curb communism, and that they would offer it both technical and financial aid in its social and economic plans.[158]

Although America's position in the Arab world was somewhat weakened in 1948 because of the events in Palestine, its involvement in the Middle East continued to grow. Nor was there any change in Britain's policy of co-operating with the US; in fact, by the end of 1949 American advisers were even beginning to be employed by the Iraqi government, with British consent.[159]

It may be seen, therefore, that British interests in Iraq passed through two distinctive stages, facing no serious threat during the 1930s but having to contend with America's growing involvement in the Middle East after World War II. In both stages, the advisers played a significant role in implementing British policy.

NOTES

1. For a comprehensive study of British interests before World War I, see Stuart A. Cohen, *British Policy in Mesopotamia* (London, 1976).
2. Two books deal extensively with the period 1914–32: one written shortly after that period, Philip Willard Ireland's *Iraq: A Study in Political Development* (London, 1937); the other, Peter Sluglett's *Britain in Iraq, 1914–1932* (London, 1976).
3. Nachum T. Cross and Jacob Metzer, 'Public Finance in the Jewish Economy of Interwar Palestine', unpublished monograph (Jerusalem, 1977), p.82.
4. Ibid., p.83.
5. Sluglett's *Britain in Iraq* is an excellent source for understanding the procedure by which the government mechanism was developed.
6. Treaty of Alliance between Iraq and Great Britain together with Annex and Exchange of Notes (Baghdad, 1930).
7. Loy Henderson, American minister in Baghdad, to Dept. of State, 13 Mar. 1944. ACR, Reel 15.

8. Eastern Dept. (FO) to Britain's representative on the Council of the League of Nations, 21 Jan. 1932. FO 371/16030, E 369/9/93.
9. See correspondence with regard to the report, drafts and comments on it in CO 730/167/88231 and FO 371/17934, E 887/1/93. See also Sluglett, *Britain in Iraq*, pp.204–5. The full report appears in: Special Report by His Majesty's Government in the United Kingdom of Great Britain and Northern Ireland to the Council of the League of Nations, *Progress of Iraq during the period 1920–1931* (London, 1931).
10. Sluglett, *Britain in Iraq*, p.217.
11. Minutes of cabinet committee, 22 June 1932. CAB 23/71, 37(32)5.
12. Memorandum by the secretary of state for foreign affairs, 28 Sept. 1932. CAB 24/233, 48(32)6.
13. Sir Francis Humphrys, Britain's ambassador to Baghdad, to FO, 17 Nov. 1932. FO 371/16047, E 6334/2576/93.
14. For an extensive study of the political events during the period 1932–58, see Majid Khadduri, *Independent Iraq 1932–1958* (2nd edn., London, 1960).
15. 'Agreement between His Majesty, in respect of the United Kingdom and His Majesty the King of Iraq regarding the railway system of Iraq' (with exchange of notes), Baghdad 31 Mar. 1936. Cmd. 5282.
16. See for example summary of editorials in despatch from Paul Knabenshue, American minister to Baghdad, to Dept. of State, 13 Sept. 1933. ACR, Reel 7; Summary of events by director of Operations and Intelligence (Royal Air Force) to FO, 20 Feb. 1935. FO 371/18949, E 1198/464/93.
17. Khadduri, *Independent Iraq*, p.146.
18. Knabenshue to Dept. of State, 14 Nov. 1940. ACR, Reel 15.
19. *Documents on German Foreign Policy (DGFP) 1918–1945*, Series D (1937–45), xi, pp.242–3, 846–7.
20. Minute by FO, 30 Nov. 1940. FO 371/24559, E 3020/448/93.
21. American secretary of state to Knabenshue, 3 Dec. 1940. *Foreign Relations of the United States (FRUS)*, 1940, iii, pp.716–17.
22. Knabenshue to Dept. of State, 28 June 1940. *FRUS* 1940, iii, p.709.
23. Eden to Newton, 7 Feb. 1941. Anthony Eden's private papers, FO 954/12/391.
24. Cornwallis to FO, 5 Apr. 1941. FO 371/27062, E 10091/1/93.
25. Embassy (Turkey) to FO, 5 May 1941, ibid., E 1952/1/93.
26. See, for example, memorandum by the director of the Political Department at the German Foreign Ministry, 4 Feb. 1941. *DGFP* xii, pp.18–19.
27. Memorandum by the director of the Political Department, 26 Apr. 1941. *DGFP* xii, pp.641–2.
28. For a detailed survey of these events, see Khadduri, *Independent Iraq*, pp.221–34; Geoffrey Warner, *Iraq and Syria 1941* (London, 1974), pp.88–121.
29. See, for example Edith and E.F. Penrose, *Iraq: International Relations and National Development* (London, 1978), pp.95–110; Khadduri, ibid., pp.234–5.
30. Cornwallis to FO, 8 Mar. 1942. 'Annual review of Events in Iraq during 1941'. FO 371/31371, E 2596/204/93. For Nuri's relationship with the British and an analysis of his role see Wm. Roger Louis, *The British Empire in the Middle East* (Oxford, 1985), pp.307–11, 590–4.
31. *Al-'Alam al-'Arabi*, 10 Feb. 1945.
32. Kirk, *The Middle East, 1945–1950*, Survey of International Affairs (London, 1954), p.149.
33. Khadduri, *Independent Iraq*, pp.255–6.
34. Busk (British Embassy Baghdad) to FO, 1 Mar. 1946. FO 371/52401, E 2155/226/93.
35. 'Exchange of Notes Between His Majesty's Government in the United Kingdom and the Government of Iraq respecting the status of the Iraqi Diplomatic Mission in London and the Precedence of His Majesty's Ambassador at Baghdad', London, 2 Aug. 1946, Cmd. 6918.
36. Memorandum by FO, 30 July 1947. FO 624/120.
37. Although Britain officially withdrew its forces from Iraq on 26 Oct. 1947, some military bases remained. The final withdrawal took place after the monarchy was overthrown in the revolution of 1958.

38. Memorandum for ME (O) Committee, 11 July 1947. FO 371/61510, E 2589/183/65.
39. Bevin to Cripps, 15 Oct. 1947. T 236/1274.
40. Memorandum to Bevin, 3 Oct. 1947. FO 371/61594, E 9265/3/93.
41. For the development of events in Iraq at this time, see Khadduri, *Independent Iraq*, pp.262–5; 'Review of Political Events in Iraq during 1947', FO 371/68443, E 691/27/93/G.
42. FO to Baghdad (Tel. 28), 10 Jan. 1948. FO 371/68441, E 273/27/93.
43. 'Treaty of Alliance between His Majesty in respect of the United Kingdom of Great Britain and Northern Ireland and His Majesty the King of Iraq' (with Annex and Exchange of Letters), Portsmouth, 15 Jan. 1948. Cmd. 7309.
44. 'Exchange of letters signed subsequently to the Treaty which are not to be published', 15 Jan. 1948. FO 371/68442, E 651/27/93.
45. For a detailed description of the events of Al-Wathbah, see Batatu, *The Old Social Classes*, pp.545–66. Louis, *The British Empire in the Middle East 1945–1951* contains an excellent analysis of the Portsmouth Treaty and of Iraq's post-war politics (pp.315–44).
46. Iraq's Ministry of Foreign Affairs to British Embassy, 4 Feb. 1948.
47. In a secret investigation conducted by the British after the Treaty's cancellation, it was pointed out that there had been a complete breakdown of political intelligence – both British and Iraqi – and that the method of presentation of the Treaty was amateurish. See report by Major General J. M. L. Renton, head of the British Advisory Military Mission to the Iraqi Army, 5 Feb. 1948. FO 371/68446, E 2693/27/93/G.
48. Henry Mack, Britain's ambassador to Baghdad, to FO, 15 May 1948. FO 371/68449, E 6339/27/93.
49. Mack to FO, 'Review of Political Events during 1948', 4 Jan. 1949. FO 371/75125, E 6601/1018/93.
50. FO memorandum, 'A Review of Britain's Policy in Iraq', 20 Jan. 1936. FO 371/20004, E 325/325/93.
51. Ibid. Iraq's commitment to the most-favoured-nation policy will be discussed in Ch. 5.
52. Humphrys to FO, 1 Feb. 1934. FO 371/17858, E 962/190/93.
53. Minutes by Rendel, 1 Nov. 1933. FO 371/16855, E 7867/7867/65.
54. FO minute by Ward (Eastern Department), 'Policy of His Majesty's Government in Iraq', 21 Jan. 1937. FO 371/20801, E 450/450/93.
55. For the establishment of MESC, see Martin W. Wilmington, *The Middle East Supply Centre* (London, 1972), pp.32–50.
56. Its first meeting was held on 12 Nov. 1942. CAB 92/50.
57. ME (O) Committee, 7 Jan. 1943. CAB 95/1, ME(O)(43)1.
58. War Cabinet Resolutions of the ME War Council on the Political Situation in the ME, 17 June 1943. FO 371/34975.
59. Ibid.
60. Bevin to His Majesty's Representatives in the ME, Resolutions of the Conference and Annexes, 18 Oct. 1945. BT 11/2681.
61. Functions of BMEO, FO 371/61498, E 2559/44/65.
62. Ibid.
63. For a list of the technical staff, see ibid. and FO 371/68388, E 10090/120/65.
64. 'Functions of BMEO', prepared by the Joint Secretariat of ME (O) Committee for Mr J. M. Troutbeck on his appointment as head of BMEO, 27 Oct. 1947. FO 371/61501, E 10394/44/65.
65. Sir R. Hay, Persian Gulf Residency (Bahrain) to Bevin, 19 June 1948. FO 371/68388, E 8378/120/65.
66. FO to representatives in the ME, 6 Mar. 1947. FO 371/61509, E 183/183/65.
67. Memorandum by FO, 23 May 1947. FO 141/1222, 1124/5/47.
68. ME (O) Committee, 'Economic Policy in the Middle East', 15 May 1947. FO 371/61499, E 4195/44/65.
69. Ibid.
70. ME (O) Committee, FO 371/61499.
71. Memorandum by the Foreign Office, 'Economic Development in the Middle East', 12 Mar. 1949. FO 371/75083, E 3579/1103/65.
72. Meeting in London of HM's representatives in the ME, 21–28 July 1949. FO 371/75072,

E 9045/1058/65/G.
73. Ibid.
74. Ibid.
75. See note by Bevin, 25 Aug. 1949. CAB 129/36, Part 2, CP (49) 183; Memorandum by Bevin, 19 Oct. 1949. CAB 129/37, Part 1, CP (49) 209.
76. Nuri as-Said to Humphrys, 30 June 1930, Letter No. iii in the 1930 treaty.
77. Ibid.
78. United Kingdom, *Progress of Iraq*, p.25.
79. See FO to Humphrys, 8 Dec. 1932, and Humphrys to FO, 5 Jan. 1933. FO 406/71.
80. Private letter, Humphrys to Rendel, 6 Sept. 1933. FO 371/16889, E 5374/7/93.
81. Ibid.
82. Air 23/589.
83. See, for example, letter from Edmonds to Cornwallis, 10 Nov. 1943. Edmonds private papers (Middle East Centre, Oxford University).
84. Richard Gnade, third secretary of American Mission, Baghdad, to Dept. of State, 25 Feb. 1944. ACR, Reel 15.
85. Maurice Peterson, Britain's ambassador to Baghdad, to FO, 24 May 1938. FO 624/10/11.
86. Houston-Boswall to FO, 4 May 1939. FO 624/16/325.
87. FO to Baghdad, 10 May 1948. T 236/1193.
88. 1945 Conference of British Representatives in the ME. BT 11/2681.
89. FO minute, 29 Oct. 1947. FO 371/61597, E 10799/3/93/G.
90. FO minute, 7 Nov. 1947. Ibid.
91. Portsmouth Treaty of 1948, Cmd. 7309.
92. Some examples of Britain's obstruction of non-British advisers: in 1937 Italian air instructors were prevented from obtaining a contract with Iraq (Annual Report 1937 in FO 371/21856, E 794/794/93); the British officially objected to the appointment of two Egyptian agricultural specialists in 1946 (FO 371/52379, E 989/43/93); and British officials strongly objected to a suggestion in 1935 by the Iraqi government that it employ German Jewish refugees as doctors, although no British doctor was then available (FO 371/18950, E 3660/622/93).
93. Embassy to FO, 29 Apr. 1949. This information was sent, at the request of the FO, to all embassies in the ME. FO 371/75068, E 2381/1053/65.
94. Knabenshue to Dept. of State, 6 Mar. 1935. ACR, Reel 6.
95. Cornwallis to FO, 'Political Advisory Staff in Iraq', 8 June 1943. FO 371/35010, E 3554/489/93.
96. Letter from Haidar to acting High Commissioner, 24 Sept. 1931. CO 730/163/88051.
97. Knabenshue to Dept. of State, 5 Aug. 1933. ACR, Reel 3.
98. Knabenshue to Dept. of State, 15 Apr. 1936. ACR, Reel 6.
99. Bateman (British Embassy, Baghdad) to FO, 18 Apr. 1936. FO 371/18956, E 7028/6892/93.
100. Newton to FO, 30 Aug. 1940. FO 371/24562, E 2752/2428/93.
101. Newton to FO, 26 Sept. 1940. Ibid., E 2996/2428/93.
102. *Al-Bilad*, 1 Dec. 1940. Extract appears in FO 624/12/432.
103. Embassy to FO, 16 Dec. 1948. FO 371/75141, E 127/1051/93.
104. Embassy to Iraq's Ministry of Finance, 16 May 1949. Ibid., E 6626/1051/93.
105. FO to Embassy, 26 Oct. 1949. Ibid., E 7589/1051/93.
106. Ibid. See also FO 371/75150.
107. The level of the British diplomats in Iraq, particularly during the 1930s, was not much higher. Their reports reflected ignorance of local developments and poor political analysis, especially in comparison with contemporary reports on Egypt and Palestine. See H. H. Kopietz, 'The Use of German and British Archives in the Study of the Middle East: The Iraqi *Coup d'État* of 1936' in Abbas Kelidar (ed.), *The Integration of Modern Iraq*, (London, 1979), pp.46–62.
108. Houston-Boswall to FO, 4 May 1939. FO 624/16/325.
109. Thompson (British Embassy, Baghdad) to FO, 2 Aug. 1944. FO 371/40063, E 4883/280/93.
110. Stonehewer-Bird, Britain's ambassador to Baghdad, to FO, on his meeting with the

regent, 21 May 1945. FO 371/45298, E 3664/182/93.
111. Jackson to Ministry of War Transport, 22 May 1944. CAB 31/88.
112. Memorandum by Lieut.-Col. W. A. Lyon, political adviser, Kirkuk, 'British Officials in Iraq: Suggestions for the Future', 15 Jan. 1944. FO 371/40063, E 728/280/93.
113. Gold-selling as an anti-inflationary measure will be discussed in Ch. 3.
114. Meeting between W.W. France (ME Office, Cairo) and Swan, 18 Aug. 1944. FO 921/269, 81(114)/44/2.
115. Ibid.
116. Minute by Cornwallis, 25 Apr. 1943. FO 371/35020, E 2573/2573/93.
117. Minute by Chaplin, 7 Feb. 1944. FO 371/40063, E 728/280/93.
118. Ibid.
119. See Lieut.-Col. Lyon's letter. FO 371/40063.
120. See FO 371/40040, E 4306/29/93.
121. Minutes by Baggallay, 4 Dec. 1939. FO 371/23212, E 7532/374/93.
122. Thompson to FO, 2 Aug. 1944. FO 371/40063, E 4883/280/93.
123. British Consulate in 'Amara to Embassy (Baghdad), 26 Feb. 1949. FO 838/8.
124. Memorandum by Dept. of State, 31 Aug. 1934. ACR, Reel 6.
125. *FRUS*, 1930, iii, p.302.
126. *FRUS*, 1932, ii, pp.672–85.
127. *FRUS*, 1938, ii, pp.763–9. For the negotiations preceding the Treaty, see *FRUS*, 1937, ii, pp.767–84.
128. Wright (MEW) to UKCC, 13 Dec. 1940. FO 837/486, T 60/0/100.
129. Khadduri, *Independent Iraq*, pp.194–5, 373.
130. Knabenshue to Dept. of State, 2 Apr. 1931. *FRUS*, 1941, iii, pp.491–2; also pp.486–90, 493–513.
131. Knabenshue to Dept. of State, 25 Nov. 1941. *FRUS*, 1941, iii, p.514.
132. See: 'Lend–Lease in the Middle East', in *Middle East Economic and Statistical Bulletin (MEESB)* (Aug. 1944), pp.27–9.
133. F.M.H. Lloyd, *Food and Inflation in the Middle East 1940–1945* (Stanford, 1956), pp.91–2. For the US decision to participate in MESC, see *FRUS*, 1942, iv, pp.1–17.
134. Secretary of state to Farell (American chargé d'affaires in Baghdad), 1 May 1942, *FRUS*, 1942, iv, p.343.
135. Wilmington, *Middle East Supply Centre*, pp.73–4.
136. Martin W. Wilmington, 'The Middle East Supply Centre: A Reappraisal', *Middle East Journal*, vi: 2 (Spring 1952), p.163.
137. Casey to Churchill, 11 Nov. 1942. T 1332/2.
138. See FO 371/40066, E 4748/93.
139. Memorandum by J.G. Macdonald, area liaison officer, Baghdad, included in a despatch by Thompson to FO, 14 Mar. 1944. FO 624/39/574.
140. See, for example, E.R. Lingeman (first secretary, Embassy), 'American Trade Competition in Iraq', 28 Oct. 1944. FO 921/263, 81/44/9.
141. Minute by Cornwallis, 1 Nov. 1944, ibid.
142. *FRUS*, 1944, v, editor's fn., p.39. See also Phillip J. Baram, *The Department of State in the Middle East 1919–1945* (Philadelphia, 1978), p.165. For a study of the report's main points and Culbertson's general economic and political ideas, see: John DeNovo, 'The Culbertson Economic Mission and Anglo-American Tensions in the Middle East, 1944–1945', *Journal of American History*, lxiii (1977), pp.913–36.
143. DeNovo, op. cit., p.921.
144. E.M. Robinson to Dept. of State, 12 Sept. 1945. American National Archives (ANA), 890g.50/9 – Box 6963.
145. 'Aspects of Department of State thinking on political and economic policies of the United States in the Near and Middle East for the post-war period' in *FRUS*, 1945, viii, pp.33–48.
146. A. Bland Calder, first secretary at Cairo, to Loy Henderson (director of Near East Dept.), 14 July 1945. ANA, D 403 Box 1812.
147. Memorandum by Sir Ronald Campbell, 9 June 1945. FO 371/45267, E 6623/454/65.
148. BMEO, 'Activities of Major Powers in M.E. Territories', Monthly Report, Mar. 1946. FO 371/52337, E 3828/1341/65.

149. See *FRUS*, 1946, vii, pp.18–48.
150. *FRUS*, 1946, vii, pp.568–70.
151. George Wadsworth was appointed first US ambassador to Iraq, and 'Ali Jawdat first Iraqi ambassador to Washington.
152. 'Conversations with Wallace Murray', 11–28 Apr. 1944. FO 371/39985, E 2713/16/65.
153. Campbell's memorandum, FO 371/45267. Iraq did not figure prominently in these talks; the only subject discussed with regard to it was raising the status of the American minister in Baghdad to that of ambassador. See FO 371/39985.
154. For details about the Pentagon Talks, see *FRUS*, 1947, v, pp.483–626.
155. Memorandum by the Dept. of State, undated. *FRUS*, 1947, v, p.516.
156. Ibid., pp.518–19.
157. Memorandum on the creation of the working party and minutes of its meetings. BT 11/3481.
158. Summary of memorandum of informal conversations relating to social and economic affairs in the Middle East, 23–30 Oct. 1947. *FRUS*, 1947, v, p.618.
159. In early 1950, the US government began supplying Iraq with American teachers (under a Fulbright Act Agreement) and the British decided not to object, in furtherance of their policy 'to invite American cooperation in promoting development in Iraq'. See: Mack to FO, 29 Dec. 1949. FO 371/75140, E 15398/10345/93; FO to Baghdad, 17 Jan. 1950. Ibid., E 13178/10345/93.

2

IRAQI GOVERNMENT POLICY

As explained in the introduction, economic policy in Iraq was determined by two sides: the British and the Iraqi. While the first chapter examined British interests and the British advisers who played so pivotal a role in shaping that policy, the present chapter will concentrate on the Iraqi side. It will deal first with the attitudes of the various governments in Iraq towards economic policy, then with the mechanisms of formulating and implementing this policy, and finally go on to that important area of policy-making, *capital development works.*

GOVERNMENT ATTITUDES TOWARDS ECONOMIC POLICY

Iraq, during the period under study, was formally a constitutional, hereditary monarchy with a representative government. The king was the supreme head of state. He exercised power by means of royal *iradas* (decrees), issued upon the proposal of the responsible minister or ministers with the concurrence of the prime minister.[1]

The working executive, the Council of Ministers or cabinet, under the direction of the prime minister, was in theory responsible to Parliament, and its members also held seats in one or the other of the two parliamentary chambers. Theoretically, the ministers exercised the royal authority with the agreement of a majority in the Chamber of Deputies, and participated in the making of laws through their leadership of the majority. In practice, however, the executive, particularly the Council of Ministers, dominated the legislative branch, which had little real power or opportunity to call executive policy into serious question. In a real sense, then, Iraq was governed by a group of ministers, themselves usually under the domination of a strong figure like Nuri as-Said.[2] Control of elections and frequent dissolution of Parliament rendered that body completely subordinate to the cabinet, and incapable of passing a vote of no confidence in any government.[3]

Thirty governments were formed between 3 November 1932 and 5 February 1950, eight of them by Nuri as-Said, their members drawn largely from a group of about a hundred men.[4] Some of the governments did not even exist long enough to publish a declaration of policy; one lasted a mere twelve days, but the average life-span was about seven months. Most published their economic policy some weeks after being formed. We shall examine a few such programmes in order to understand Iraqi government attitudes towards the matter of economic policy.

Some of the programmes were general and short, such as that published by Nuri as-Said's government on 27 March 1939, three months after its formation:

To ensure a balanced budget.
To establish the State cadre, and to reorganise the Government departments in accordance with the needs of the country.
To reconsider the Civil Service laws and regulations so as to safeguard public interest and the rights of officials.
To improve the form of taxation.
To expand the scope of capital works.
To put in hand the important irrigation schemes required, particularly in the Middle Euphrates area; to improve road conditions and construct the state buildings required.
To organise export and import trade and to ensure the equilibrium by applying the principle of reciprocity; to organise trade and industry and increase exports, more especially in the country's chief products, such as dates, grain and tobacco.
To establish local banks and to encourage saving among the public.
To pay attention to the collection of statistics.[5]

Other programmes were very detailed and comprehensive, such as the one issued by Yasin al-Hashimi's cabinet on 5 July 1935 outlining government policy under eighteen general headings, many of which had subdivisions, calling for wide reforms in almost every sphere: labour, agriculture, industry, banking, trade, budget, education, and so on.[6]

Every programme was extremely ambitious. Commenting on al-Hashimi's statement of policy, Paul Knabenshue, then American minister in Baghdad, said, 'obviously the statement promises more than could be accomplished by any government in Iraq in a generation'. With regard to the promise made by al-Hashimi's government to drain Iraq's swamps and marshes, Knabenshue noted sarcastically that 'this could be done effectively only by an act of God'.[7]

Governments did not bother to elaborate how they would achieve their goals, neither in their statements of policy nor in any other form (such as a special paper or a press conference). The sweeping and extensive reforms promised in every programme reflected hopes and aspirations rather than capacity of achievement. They were intended to satisfy and appease every group in the country, regardless of whether or not the promises themselves were consistent with each other, or even feasible. The statements of policy all suffered from the same chronic defect: there was no provision for ensuring that machinery was established for their implementation.

Parliament, devoid of real power, could not do much to improve the policy programmes or supervise their implementation. When cabinets presented their programmes for ratification, debate focused on foreign relations or political issues. Even when a government's economic policy was specifically criticized, it was not affected thereby.[8] This state of affairs generally continued throughout the period under study; there was no change, for instance, after the 1936 *coup d'état.*

A consistent policy of development requires a measure of public tranquillity and national cohesion, both of which were absent in Iraq. Internally, the central government was almost continually preoccupied with maintaining and consolidating its own position, and dealing with secessionist movements and dissident groups. Externally, there were always the question of relations with Britain and the Palestine problem.

The frequent changes of government further hindered the formulation and implementation of a consistent policy. The reasons for these frequent changes were lack of solidarity among the members of almost every cabinet, acute competition among politicians, the absence of real political parties which could have offered legal channels for political strife, and the interference of the army in politics.[9]

Cabinet instability reflected the instability in the country as a whole. To a certain extent this was a consequence of the rivalries among individual politicians and among various political groups, the lines between which were not always clearly drawn. For instance, before Jamil al-Midfa'i's government was formed on 9 November 1933, it was agreed to start building a dam on the Gharraf, a source of the Tigris. When the minister of economics and communications, Rustum Haidar, announced the contract, the minister of finance, Nasrat al-Farsi, objected on the grounds that the money should rather be earmarked for arms purchases. On the surface it seemed a legitimate argument about government priorities, but in reality it was a manifestation of personal rivalries between the two ministers and their respective political groups. Indeed, the government split over this issue, and Midfa'i had to resign on 12 February 1934, only three months after forming his government.[10]

As a result, generally speaking, each successive government either materially changed or totally discarded its predecessor's programme and instituted its own, which was in turn changed or discarded by the succeeding government.

All this notwithstanding, it should be stressed that there were some areas of economic policy which did enjoy consistency, despite frequent changes of government. One such realm, as will be shown in Chapter 6, was oil policy, where there was a relatively fixed set of aims to which all governments adhered. Furthermore, the fact that the turnover of British advisers and senior civil servants was not as rapid as that of political ministers had a two-fold effect: it both strengthened the former's position in shaping economic policy, and led to a certain degree of consistency in government management of economic affairs.

MECHANISMS OF FORMULATING AND IMPLEMENTING ECONOMIC POLICY

General Background

Another factor which negatively affected economic policy, besides political instability, was the absence of a career civil service corps trained in the efficient administration of government and execution of policy.

After Iraq achieved independence in 1932, the central government faced many administrative problems. Growing public criticism made it begin to reduce the number of foreign officials working in government departments, and in 1933 and 1934 Iraq did not renew the contracts of a significant number of foreigners employed in various sectors of the economy.[11] Apart from nationalistic feelings against foreigners, Iraq was also unable to afford their high salaries and the allowances attached to their conditions of service.[12]

This reduction did not however lead to a meaningful decrease of British influence, since the advisers' position, as will be shown when examining the structure of Iraq's ministries and economic organizations, enabled them to safeguard and enhance British interests there.

Although the number of foreign officials was reduced, the Iraqi administration continued to be inflated. The total number of officials increased continually: a table in a confidential memorandum by Minister of Finance 'Ali Mumtaz to Prime Minister Muzahim al-Pachachi (reproduced as Table 2.1) shows that the Iraqi administration more than doubled in a twelve-year period. Mumtaz's memorandum also lists the number of appointments and the proportional increase in each ministry since 1935 (Table 2.2). However, these figures should be handled with care. That given for the Ministry of Defence, for example, is definitely wrong. (It is possible that Mumtaz did not include the military staff, but even then his figure still seems low.) Even so, it is no wonder that the government allocated so high a proportion of its budget to salaries. If the cost of pensions, the civil list and Parliament are added on, the aggregate total expenditure amounted to about 66% in 1933,[13] 42% in 1938 and 59% in 1947.[14] Indeed, general administration constituted a heavy burden on the budget throughout the period 1932–50, as will be shown in Chapter 3.[15]

TABLE 2.1 Annual Increase in Government Employment, 1935-1947

	Employment	Increase on 1935 (%)
1935	8,247	-
1936	8,789	7
1937	9,560	16
1938	9,740	18
1939	10,000	21
1940	10,754	30
1941	10,883	32
1942	11,577	40
1943	12,456	51
1944	13,947	69
1945	15,259	85
1946	-[a]	-[a]
1947	18,048	118

Source: Mumtaz to Al-Pachachi, 26 Oct. 1948. A copy appears in FO 371/68467, E 15160/112/93.

[a]No budget for government appointments.

TABLE 2.2 Increase in Government Employment by Ministry, 1935-1947

	Employment		Increase, 1935-47	
	1935	1947	No.	%
Economics	130	855	725	557
Social Affairs	531	1,539	1,008	190
Education	2,651	7,294	4,643	175
Foreign Affairs	70	167	97	138
Interior[a]	1,192	2,659	1,467	122
Justice	755	1,592	837	112
Communications and Works	1,022	1,599	577	53
Defence	178	234	56	32
Finance	1,639	1,994	355	21

Source: As for Table 2.1.

[a]Including the Directorate of Products.

Despite the huge sums allocated for salaries, almost all government officials were underpaid. This situation had its repercussions during times of crisis and high inflation. During World War II, it was reported that

> the high cost of living and the glittering profits to be gained by even small and comparatively safe departures from the paths of rectitude, have subjected the low-paid officials to almost irresistible temptation and the wide-spread corruption that has resulted has poisoned every branch of the civil service.[16]

This corruption seriously hindered the economic management of the country. The inefficiency of the government's supply organization during the war was due, *inter alia*, to the corruption of officials unable to make their salaries cover the mounting cost of living.[17] The government, aware of this fact, decided in 1945 to try to curb corruption by setting up a special committee to examine the financial affairs of its officials, and tabled a parliamentary bill for this purpose. The press welcomed the bill but, interestingly enough, there was considerable opposition to it in Parliament. Some members objected to the proposed legislation on the grounds that it did not provide for the examination of ministers' financial affairs, while others, mainly opposition MPs, were afraid it would be used politically rather than administratively. The government was not keen to amend the bill so as to include ministers or guarantee against its misuse, and in March 1945 the subject was shelved.[18]

In a memorandum on the situation in Iraq, Mr Chaplin of the Foreign Office described the administration by saying:

> In the past twenty-five years the Iraqis have not succeeded in learning how to administer their own people, whether despite or because of the considerable stiffening of British personnel in the administrative services during the mandatory period. The corruption and nepotism of the central administration in Baghdad (which controls in almost every detail the provincial administration) is only rivalled by the nepotism and corruption of the local officials.[19]

Although this statement might have been exaggerated, it definitely contained some truth and may be said to apply to the entire period under study, causing many economic decisions to be undermined.

Bodies Responsible for Formulating and Implementing Economic Policy

Ministry of Finance

At the beginning of 1930, in accordance with the plan for the further transfer of executive functions from British to Iraqi staff, the internal organization of the ministry was completely altered.[20] After Iraq's independence, the government felt the need to reorganize all the ministries dealing with economic affairs,[21] and consequently promulgated a 'Law for the Organization of Ministries' in 1933. In 1935 a regulation for the Ministry of Finance was published. According to Article 2 of this regulation, the minister was, as in the regulations of 1930, the supreme head of the ministry, responsible for all its activities, and all orders and decisions were under his authority. Some amendments were made with regard to the position of the adviser (always British) since Iraq was now formally an independent state. Article 3 provided:

> The Adviser is an advisory official. He will express his opinion on all matters referred to him by the Minister and may call for any information affecting such matters from the Directorates of the Ministry. He may also submit to the Minister proposals for the improvement of the Administration and the increase of its efficiency or the better working of financial matters.[22]

FIGURE 2.1

THE STRUCTURE OF THE MINISTRY OF FINANCE

	Director-General of Finance	Budget Section Pension Section Civil Service Section Government Press Section Correspondence Section
Minister	Director-General of Revenue	Land Revenue Section Property and Animal Section Income Tax Section Audit Section Correspondence Section
	Director-General of Accounts	Treasury Section Personal Section Foreign Transactions Section Audit and Inspection Section Correspondence Section
Adviser	Director-General of State Properties	Property Section Rights Section Land Settlement Section Correspondence Section
	Director-General of Commerce	Trade Section Statistics Section Registration Section
	Affiliated Departments	Directorate-General of Customs Directorate-General of Port of Basra

From Kerr to FO, 24 June 1935. FO 371/18945, E 4197/278/93. For comparison with the 1930 structure, see *Iraq Government Gazette*, no. 3 (2 Feb. 1930), pp.59–61.

Ministry of Economics and Communications

As with the Ministry of Finance, this ministry (called the Ministry of Communications and Works until the end of 1930) was organized at the beginning of 1930 and reorganized in 1935. The chief effect of the 1935 reorganization was to restore to independent existence the departments of Irrigation, Public Works and Surveys. Figure 2.2 shows this Ministry's structure. The powers and responsibilities of the minister and the adviser were exactly the same as in the Ministry of Finance.[23]

FIGURE 2.2
THE STRUCTURE OF THE MINISTRY OF ECONOMICS AND COMMUNICATIONS

Minister / Adviser

- Director-General of Economics
  - Financial Secretary
  - Accounts Section
  - Contracts and Concession Section
  - Personnel Section
  - Correspondence Section
  - Archives Section
- Director of Oil Affairs
  - Oil Measurement Section
- Director of Industrial Research
  - Industrial Research Section
  - Geological Section
- Director of Surveys
- Director-General of Posts and Telegraphs
- Director-General of Irrigation
- Director of Public Works
- Director of Agricultural Affairs
- Director of the Veterinary Service

Affiliated Department: The Iraqi State Railways

From Kerr to FO, 5 July 1935. FO 371/18945, E 4473/278/93. For comparison with the 1930 structure, see *Iraq Government Gazette*, no. 20 (18 May 1930), pp.263–5.

On 1 August 1939, Nuri as-Said's government decided to divide the Ministry of Economics and Communications into two separate portfolios: the Ministry of Economics, and the Ministry of Communications and Works.[24] The decision was put into effect at the end of the year. The structure of the Ministry of Economics is shown in Figure 2.3; as regards the Ministry of Communications and Works, the following departments were put under its control: Irrigation, Public Works, Survey, Posts, Telegraphs, Telephone and Wireless, and River Navigation. The ministry was also responsible for the Iraqi State Railways and the Directorate of the Port of Basra.[25]

Other Ministries Dealing with Economic Affairs

Other ministries were also involved with economic affairs. The Ministry of the Interior was responsible for land and settlement

FIGURE 2.3

THE STRUCTURE OF THE MINISTRY OF ECONOMICS

Minister

Adviser

- Secretariat
- Director-General of Economics
  - Administration and Financial Section
  - Registration Section
  - Commercial Section
  - Department of Industry
  - Principal Bureau of Statistics
  - Metallurgical Department:
    - Oil Section
    - Geology and Metals Section
- Director-General of Agriculture
  - Plant Protection Section
  - Insects and Agricultural Pests Section
  - Horticultural Section
  - Field Products and Cotton Section
  - Forestry Section
  - Fisheries Section
  - Agricultural and Co-operation Section
  - Directorate of Agricultural Districts
- Director of the Veterinary Service
  - Combating of Animal Pests Section
  - Section of Feeding and Improving Animal Genii
- Director of the Tobacco Monopoly
- Director of the Trade Board
- Director of the Cereal Organisation Board

Affiliated Institutions:
- Chamber of Commerce
- Chamber of Agriculture

From Ministry of Economics Regulations no. 91 of 1939. A copy appears in FO 371/24558, E 1411/448/93.

cases, transport (placed in May 1943 under a British director for the control of road transport, including the distribution of tyres, spare parts, etc.) and local products (set up in May 1943 under a British director to encourage local industry and control cereals and other local products).[26] The Ministry of Social Affairs was created in 1939 and made responsible for population census, town planning and village organization.[27]

The above sketch of the structures of various ministries indicates the immense problems of co-ordination faced by Iraq's decision-makers, which co-existed with the political intrigues mentioned earlier. The basic functions of each ministry were not rigidly defined, or were frequently changed by transferring a department from one ministry to another, or abolishing it altogether. The overlapping of functions and the problems of coordination constituted major obstacles to the implementation of economic policy, as will be seen throughout this book.

To this complicated structure were added numerous councils and committees handling various aspects of economic policy.

The Economic Council

Formed in May 1935, the function of the Economic Council was defined as 'thoroughly to study important development schemes'.[28] Its membership comprised the prime minister, the minister of economics and communications and his adviser, the adviser to the Ministry of Finance, the director of commerce, the director of customs and excise, and the director of industrial research.[29] This council ceased to exist with the outbreak of World War II.

Comptroller and Auditor-General's Department

Created in 1927, this department was attached directly to Parliament and, according to law, was supposed to be absolutely independent of government executive authority. (It was under the control of the Ministry of Finance only for the purpose of budget supervision.) Its functions were to examine the accounts of the state, including the railways, Port of Basra, *waqfs* (religious endowments), and the expenditure and revenue of industrial factories – to which end it was completely empowered to take cognizance of all documents and information pertaining to any government department, which it deemed necessary to peruse for the performance of its duties.[30]

The Iraqi Currency Board

Established in 1931 by Iraqi law, the Iraqi Currency Board sat in London and was independent of the central Iraqi executive. Two members were nominated by the Iraqi government, two by the British banks working in Iraq, and one by the Bank of England at the request of the Iraqi government. From 1941 onwards, the secretary of the Exchange Control Committee (usually a British official working for the Iraqi government) acted as currency officer.[31] (The duties of the board are described in full in Chapter 3.)

Apart from the above bodies, which continued to function throughout the period under study, additional economic organizations were set up after the outbreak of World War II to cope with the problems arising from the war conditions.

Ministry of Supply

The establishment of this ministry in 1944 had been advocated by the British director-general of imports, Colonel Bayliss, from his very arrival in Iraq, with a view to ensuring unified control over all supply services, previously distributed among five different ministries.[32] Cornwallis's comments on the creation of this ministry illustrate the conflicting interests and problems faced by the Iraqi administration and their impact on economic policy:

> While centralised control of all services is desirable in principle, it is in practice difficult to achieve in Iraq with its political jealousies, its shortage of trained personnel and its inexperience of controlled and centralised economy, and I fear that Colonel Bayliss has been, to some extent, animated by an ambition to bring all economic controls under his own supervision and direction and to extend them on a scale likely to prove beyond the endurance of the Administration and of the people. It is this ambition, now generally recognised, which has caused so much friction between him and Iraq Ministers, as well as the British Advisers.[33]

Cornwallis was proved right: Iraq's supply mechanism was hindered as a result of these frictions and Bayliss's ambitions of power.[34] The structure of the Ministry of Supply was never really clear. Bayliss tried to transfer to it departments functioning under other ministries, such as imports (from the Ministry of Finance) and the Tobacco Monopoly Association (from the Ministry of Economics). But the ministers in charge of the ministries affected persisted in opposing the transfers, and this struggle continued until the Ministry of Supply was abolished on 11 October 1948.[35]

Committees

Many committees were formed during the war to regulate economic life in Iraq, some of which, like the Exchange Control Committee, continued to function in the post-war period. The composition of the main committees is listed below, with the nationalities of committee members indicated as follows: B – British; BI – British official working for the Iraqi government; I – Iraqi; A – American.[36]

1. *The Central Supply Committee* (also called the High Supply Committee)

   Prime minister (I)
   Minister of finance (I)
   Minister of the interior (I)
   Colonel Bayliss – adviser to the committee (BI)
   Advisers of the Ministries of finance and economics (BI)
   Director-general of local products (BI)

   This committee was in charge of supply policy and economic controls, and two committees were directly subordinated to it:

   (a) *Price Control Committee*
   Colonel Bayliss (BI)
   Director-general of local products (BI)
   Secretary of the Exchange Control Committee (BI)

   This committee fixed the wholesale and retail prices of both imported and locally manufactured commodities.

   (b) *Export Control Committee*
   Colonel Bayliss (BI)
   Director-general of local products (BI)
   Iraqi official (I)

   This committee dealt with applications for export permits in accordance with policy laid down by the Central Supply Committee.

2. *The Joint Committee for Co-ordination of Imports* (the Anglo-Iraqi-American Committee)

   Minister of finance or his nominee (I)
   Colonel Bayliss (BI)
   Director-general of local products (BI)
   Director-general of customs (I)
   Secretary of the Exchange Control Committee (BI)
   Representative of the British Embassy (B)
   Representative of the American Legation (A)

This was an international committee outside the framework of the Iraqi government. Its function was to co-ordinate and promote action in the procurement of essential commodities from abroad.

3. *The Combined Supplies Committee, Baghdad*

Commercial secretary, British Embassy (B)
Representative of the American Legation (A)
Representative of Movements and Supply and Transport Directorates of the Persia-and-Iraq Force (PAI Force) (British Army) (B)
Representative of the Ministry of War Transport at Basra (B)
Representative of United Kingdom Commercial Corporation (B)
MESC liaison officer (B)

Although this was an Anglo-American committee, two British advisers in the service of the Iraqi government attended the meetings informally. The committee assessed and passed on essential Iraqi requirements to MESC.

4. *The Anglo-Iraqi Joint Advisory Transport Committee*

Director-general of Iraq State Railways (BI)
Director-general of Port of Basra (BI)
Deputy quartermaster-general, Persia and Iraq (PAI) Force (B)
Director-general of Ministry of Finance (I)
Adviser to Ministry of the Interior (BI)
Director-general of Ministry of Economics (I)
Commercial secretary, British Embassy (B)
Representative of UKCC (B)
Representative of Ministry of War Transport (B)

This committee met monthly to direct the use of all methods of transport in Iraq in such manner as to meet the demands of both the Allied Armed Forces and the civilian population. It had two subcommittees:

(a) The *Transport Priorities Subcommittee* allocated priorities on Iraq's railways and waterways during the war.
(b) The *Road Transport Subcommittee* examined measures of control of motor vehicles, spare parts, and so forth, and assessed the country's transport needs during the war.

5. *The Baghdad Petroleum Advisory Committee*

   This committee consisted of eight members, six British and two American. It controlled the production and distribution of all petroleum products in the Iraq–Iran Persian Gulf area.

6. *The Exchange Control Committee*

   Adviser to Ministry of Finance (BI)
   Accountant-general (I)
   Manager of Eastern Bank (B)
   President of Baghdad Chamber of Commerce (I)
   Secretary of the committee (BI)

   This committee handled the administration of foreign exchange control measures within the country.

7. *The Industrial Development Committee*

   Director-general of local products (BI)
   Director-general of agriculture (I)
   Director of chemical laboratory (BI)
   Director of industrial research (I)
   Director of factories and distribution (I)

   This committee was created in 1943 to examine industrial undertakings and consider the advisability and possibility of industrial development, in consideration of both war conditions and post-war interests.

A striking feature of the above committees is the broad influence the British had over them, and thus over Iraq's economy during the war. Table 2.3 clearly illustrates this; moreover, it shows that, with the single exception of the Industrial Development Committee, the Iraqis did not have a majority in any committee.

Other Bodies

To round out the picture of bodies dealing with economic policy, the following should also be mentioned: the chambers of commerce and agriculture, the Industrial and Agricultural Bank, the Date Monopoly Association, the Tobacco Monopoly Association etc. A brief description of their structure will be given here, while analysis of their work will be left to the relevant chapters.

The *Baghdad Chamber of Commerce* was created in 1926 as 'a public institution formed by merchants to represent and safeguard the interests of commerce in certain areas to be defined by

TABLE 2.3 Britain's Economic Influence in Iraq via Committee Membership

Committee	British	British working for Iraqi government	Iraqi	American
Iraqi Currency Board	3	1	2	-
Central Supply	-	4	3	-
Price Control	-	3	-	-
Export Control	-	2	1	-
Anglo-Iraqi-American, for co-ordination of imports	1	3	2	1
Combined supplies	5	(O) 2	-	1
Anglo-Iraqi joint advisory transport	4	3	2	-
Transport priorities	4	2	-	-
Road transport	1	3	2	1
Baghdad petroleum	6	-	-	2
Exchange control	1	2	2	-
Industrial development	-	2	3	-

Source: Gnade's memorandum, ACR, Reel 15.

the Minister of Finance'.[37] Any merchant of whatever nationality residing in Iraq, as well as Iraqi merchants not resident in Iraq, were allowed to join it. It had three standing subcommittees:[38]

1. *The Finance Committee* supervised the chamber's financial affairs.
2. *The Guarantee and Certificate Committee* certified the financial standing of guarantors and their ability to carry out
their guarantees, and granted certificates as to the origin of goods exported from Iraq.
3. *The Prices and Survey Committee* drew up a periodic register containing prices of commodities.

The *Chamber of Agriculture* was created in 1938 to 'safeguard and promote Agriculture business affairs'[39] and membership was open to every peasant. It was run by an administrative committee composed of twelve members from the capital and ten members from the provinces,[40] although the minister of economics and communications, and the *mutassarif* (governor) of every province, had the right to supervise its activities.

Both chambers of commerce were placed under the Ministry of

Economics in 1939 (Fig. 2.3). Indeed, they were never independent or able to form a lobby in any real sense.

The *Agricultural and Industrial Bank of Iraq* was inaugurated in 1936. It was administered by a board of directors appointed by the Council of Ministers and composed of a general manager (chairman) and four members: a representative of the Ministry of Finance, a representative of the Ministry of Economics and Communications, a representative of the agricultural community, and a representative of the commercial or industrial community.[41] The range of the bank's activities as set out in the law creating it was very wide, including the importation and sale of agricultural implements, the granting of loans and advances to factory owners, and so forth.[42]

In 1940 a law was passed to divide the bank into separate agricultural and industrial banks, but the tumult of war postponed the actual division until 1946. There was very little change in the machinery of the two banks, except that an additional post of manager was created, 'which seems to be the underlying motive for the action'.[43]

The *Date Monopoly Association* and the *Tobacco Monopoly Association* were formed in order to advance trade in these two commodities. Both were created under the auspices of the government and in 1939 were made the responsibility of the Ministry of Economics.[44]

In summing up the mechanism of formulating and implementing economic policy in Iraq, it is important to emphasize that the real power rested in the hands of a few politicians, mainly the ministers and the prime minister of each government, and these took their decisions under strong constraints: British influence and interests, political instability with all the implications thereof, and the lack of an experienced civil service corps to administer the country. Where the British were interested in pursuing a specific policy with regard to a certain sector or subsector of the economy, they found the weakness of the mechanism serving the Iraqi government of great advantage as it enabled them to exert that much more influence.

CAPITAL DEVELOPMENT WORKS

The Development Plans

Capital development works were one of the important areas of economic policy in Iraq during most of the period under study, particularly the 1930s. The idea of planned economic development in Iraq originated in 1927, when a separate budget was allocated for special projects. This budget provided ID 384,750 over a three-year period, mainly to construct bridges and roads.[45]

The satisfactory conclusion in March 1931, after prolonged negotiations of the revised agreement with the Iraq Petroleum Company (IPC) secured for Iraq an annual payment of £409,000. This considerably improved Iraq's financial outlook, and the government decided to earmark the revenues from this source for the furtherance of productive development schemes.[46]

The first five-year capital works programme was thus legislated, rather hurriedly, in June 1931 'in order to hypothecate the anticipated revenue from advance oil royalties and dead rent'.[47] A sum of ID 2,210,000 was allotted for expenditure on capital development works during the five-year period 1931–5, to be provided by revenues from IPC. Some 41% of the total was to be spent on irrigation schemes (mainly the Habbaniyya Project), 28% on new buildings, and 28% on roads and bridges.[48]

By 1933 the programme was lagging behind schedule. No expenditure had been incurred on the major irrigation schemes, for example, primarily because the whole of the first cash payment received in August 1931 and a large part of the payment received in January 1932 were used to finance the accumulated deficit on government accounts.[49]

It was generally agreed in government circles that the first Capital Development Works Plan needed extensive revision, and a new one was therefore prepared.[50] This decision was intimately connected with that of the policy of financing development works. In each government there were two opposing schools of thought, one arguing for the acceleration of development by means of a foreign loan, and the other calling for the development budget to be determined by the money derived from oil royalties. This question continued to occupy the minds of Iraq's decision-makers for a long time.

In May 1934 a new Law for Capital Development Works was promulgated. It designated the expenditure of ID 3,237,000 over the five-year period 1934–8. Again the government decided to pursue a policy of financing the entire expenditure from oil company royalties without recourse to a foreign loan.[51] And as in the first plan, a high proportion (58%) of the allocated sum was to be spent on irrigation – on the same irrigation schemes (Habbaniyya and Gharraf); 29% was allotted to buildings and 9% to roads and bridges.[52]

Barely had a year passed when the government decided to

abandon the second five-year plan and launch two simultaneous development programmes in its stead: a three-year plan and a five-year plan. Although the three-year plan included 1935, it was published only in March 1936. It provided ID 761,180 for expenditure during the years 1935–7 and covered projects not unlike those of the larger schemes, but on a much more modest scale.[53] Of the total allocation 42% was to be spent on buildings, 30% on roads and bridges, and 11% on minor irrigation schemes. Bateman of the British Embassy wrote at the time that 'many of the works foreseen in this programme have already begun or have been fully studied and can quickly be undertaken'.[54]

The five-year plan involved an expenditure of ID 4,120,000 over the years 1936–40. While the cost of the three-year plan was to be met from accumulated surplus held by the Iraqi government up to the end of March 1936, the five-year programme was to be financed from forthcoming IPC payments. The largest single item in the five-year plan was 'Army buildings and stores' (34% of total allocations); 24% was allotted to irrigation works, mainly the Gharraf scheme which had appeared in the previous plans (the Habbaniyya scheme, meanwhile, was dropped), and 16% was to be spent on roads and bridges. For the first time, industrial schemes were to receive a substantial sum: ID 145,000 (3.5%).[55]

During 1937 the school of thought supporting the acceleration of development by means of a foreign loan had the upper hand in the government. The General Budget Law for the financial year (FY) 1937 abolished both the three-year and five-year plans, and a new five-year capital works programme was launched based on spending ID 13,283,500 during the years 1937–41. An ambitious series of schemes was drawn up in the expectation that a loan of ID 3 million would be obtained from London. The largest item was, as in the previous five-year plan, 'Army buildings and equipment', receiving ID 2,792,000; the sum of ID 2 million was allotted to industrial schemes, reflecting the government's interest in industrialization.[56] Shortly after issuing the law, the government succeeded in raising a loan in London, but of only ID 1 million instead of the ID 3 million planned for.[57] This necessitated considerable modifications to the schemes, which in turn led to many complications. (The General Staff, for instance, opposed any reduction in the sums allotted to the army.)[58]

In less than a year, this five-year plan too was abrogated and another promulgated. The new programme allocated ID 8,230,000 to be spent during the years 1938–42. As with the immediately preceding plans, the highest proportion of total expenditure

(ID 2,650,000) was allotted for 'Army buildings and equipment'. About ID 2 million was earmarked for loans and banking organizations,[59] the main item being a loan to the railways for the purpose of retiring the unpopular British loan of ID 1 million negotiated by the previous government.[60] The railways loan was totally devoted to the extension from Baiji to Tel-Kotchek.[61] More than ID 1 million was allocated to irrigation, and the Habbaniyya scheme re-appeared after having been abandoned by the previous government. Furthermore, in this new plan the policy-makers decided to revert to the old school of thought of restricting development funds to revenues gained from the oil companies. The programme was therefore based on the expectation of some ID 6 million in royalties from IPC, ID 1.5 million from the British Oil Development Company (BOD), and ID 500,000 from the profits of the Currency Board.[62]

During FY 1938/9, the Iraqi government faced financial difficulties which, according to the British adviser to the Ministry of Finance, derived from the five-year plan:

> [the Government] produced a possibly too ambitious programme, requiring five years for its fulfilment. Oil royalties, etc., are duly earmarked for the purpose of financing this plan, but obvious difficulties arise from the fact that over 80% of the cost must be met during the first three years of the plan's course. A long term loan would ease the situation, but this Government are opposed to borrowing.[63]

A new government, formed in April 1939, announced that the five-year plan was not consistent with the cabinet's economic development and construction policy,[64] and soon (in August) replaced it by a four-year programme stipulating an expenditure of ID 11,355,000 over the years 1939–42. The chief item in the new plan was, as in previous ones, equipment and buildings for the army (21% of the total). Irrigation was the second largest item, receiving 15% (half of which was to be spent on the Habbaniyya scheme), and a state oil refinery appeared for the first time (7%). Receipts for the plan were to come mainly from oil royalties, but a loan of ID 3 million from the three oil companies (IPC, BOD, BPC) was also budgeted for.[65]

The outbreak of World War II prevented Iraq from implementing this plan. The Habbaniyya contract was again interrupted.[66] (World War I had also halted work on this scheme.) Throughout the war and until 1951 (except for 1944), the government returned to allocating funds through an annual 'Capital Works Budget', as had been done before 1931, and although 1946 press reports spoke of government intentions to formulate a ten-year plan to exploit the country's resources and raise the standard of living,[67] development plans were not adopted again until the creation of the Iraq Development Board in 1950.[68]

Implementation

Table 2.4 shows the expenditure on capital development works (not only during the period of the plans but up to 1950, in order to present a clearer picture of development in general, and the impact of plans in particular); revenues for capital works; and expenditure on capital works as a percentage of total government expenditure. A few remarks are in order with regard to this table. First, the figures are government ones and, while they may not be totally correct or exact, they do give a good indication of Iraq's economic growth during this period. Second, the table shows that army buildings and irrigation works (cols. 1 and 2) received the highest share of total investment (about 25% each), while roads and bridges received about 14%.[69] Third, although Iraq was facing financial difficulties, it is interesting to note that the revenues for capital development works (col. 8) were, for most of the period, higher than the total expenditures (col. 7). This was due mainly to lack of co-ordination and advance preparation, so that even after allotting the resources it was not feasible to start the project. Fourth, column 9 indicates that, except for the five-year period 1935–40, expenditure on capital works was quite modest as a percentage of total government expenditure. However, these works excluded development projects executed by the Basra Port Authority, the Fao Dredging Scheme, the Iraqi State Railways, the Tobacco Monopoly and other similar public institutions. Each of these was a semi-autonomous organization, had its own budget separate from the government budget, and carried out its own development programmes. Also excluded were other development projects carried out by various ministries and credited to the ordinary budget. Therefore, expenditure on capital development works did not actually reflect the government's full attempt to develop the country.

It is very difficult to reach concrete conclusions about the relative success of each of the seven plans, since no programme was carried through to termination. From Table 2.5, which summarizes, roughly, the actual spending and duration of each plan, it is obvious that one of the major shortcomings of the programmes was their continual interruption. This was due, as explained in the preceding sections, to political instability and frequent changes of government on the one hand, and to lack of an adequate mechanism to supervise implementation of the plans on the other.[70] The best example of

TABLE 2.4 Budgetary Allocations and Expenditure on Capital Development Works, 1931-1950 (Iraqi dinars)

	Army buildings and equipment	Irrigation works	Roads and bridges	Building: govt. offices, schools and hospitals	Grants to industry and other development schemes	Loans to banking and other organisations	Total	Capital development works: Revenue	Capital development works: Expenditure as % of total government expenditure
	(1)	(2)	(3)	(4)	(5)	(6)	(7)	(8)	(9)
1931	-	24,134	124,640	29,034	3,750	-	181,558	869,254	4.2
1932	1,480	84,277	133,071	79,719	34,057	-	332,604	524,398	8.4
1933	25,558	72,242	156,854	139,330	34,522	-	428,506	540,426	10.2
1934	79,027	92,932	109,462	104,900	41,901	-	428,222	1,010,304	10.1
1935	496,113	463,016	169,270	63,635	43,542	-	1,235,576	598,202	21.8
1936	556,297	433,615	314,909	130,520	80,851	886,602[a]	2,402,794	599,968	33.5
1937	1,493,332	272,994	340,428	116,567	37,680	111,739	2,372,746	730,731	31.4
1938	715,050	231,681	244,209	116,062	14,340	1,142,224	2,463,566	2,037,458	30.3
1939	708,756	275,730	365,418	118,689	15,113	749,210	2,232,916	3,114,503	26.0
1940	983,327	657,005	278,899	187,773	47,958	554,466	2,709,428	2,917,679	27.5
1941	247,473	305,090	158,305	117,619	3,411	130,716	962,614	3,166,944	11.1
1942	230,404	327,024	101,485	149,418	43,503	123,438	975,272	2,193,260	8.4
1943	474,860	513,052	132,019	245,063	64,038	225,353	1,654,385	3,704,637	10.7
1944	Ordinary and capital works budgets amalgamated				Ordinary and capital works budgets amalgamated				
1945	-	412,155	280,968	407,690	338,341	100,000	1,539,154	2,875,598	7.2
1946	-	1,004,954	325,817	652,589	388,289	678,474	3,050,123	2,386,968	11.9
1947	750,296	1,146,169	494,154	591,675	311,926	280,000	3,574,220	4,846,280	13.4
1948	1,072,206	1,319,212	598,023	503,115	96,301	340,000	3,928,857	5,511,942	12.3
1949	738,438	885,329	390,626	223,884	49,867	1,088,753	3,376,897	4,804,632	11.2
1950	952,398	905,073	629,582	218,530	238,817	657,682	3,602,081	5,342,278	12.3
Total	9,525,015	9,425,684	5,348,139	4,195,812	1,888,207	7,068,657	37,451,514	47,785,462	

Source: Wizarat al-Maliyya, Hisabat al-Dawla al-Iraqiyya lil-Sana 1950 al-Maliyya (Iraq's accounts for FY 1950) (Baghdad, 1953): Cols. 1-7, p. 61; Col. 8, p. 42; Col. 9, calculated by the author.

[a]Includes the purchase of the railways by the government.

TABLE 2.5 Actual Spending and Duration of Capital Development Works Plans

	Plan	Allotted sum (ID)	Actual spending (ID)	Approximate effective duration
1.	Five-Year Plan (1931-5)	2,210,000	942,668	3 years
2.	Five-Year Plan (1934-8)	3,237,000	428,222	1 year
3.	Three-Year Plan (1935-7)	761,000	421,415	2 years
4.	Five-Year Plan (1936-40)	4,120,000	3,216,955	2 years
5.	Five-Year Plan (1937-41)	13,283,500	2,372,745	1 year
6.	Five-Year Plan (1938-42)	8,230,000	2,463,566	1 year
7.	Four-Year Plan (1939-42)	11,355,000	2,232,916	1 year

Sources: For the years 1931-6: Wizarat al-Maliyya, Hisabat al-Dawla al-Iraqiyya lil-Sana 1936 al-Maliyya (Iraq's accounts for the financial year 1936) (Baghdad, 1938), p. 61; for the years 1937-9: Hisabat al-Dawla al-Iraqiyya lil-Sana 1950 al-Maliyya, p. 61.

the detrimental impact of frequent cancellation of plans was the Habbaniyya scheme, which continued to occupy a high priority in the list of capital projects until the end of the period under study.[71]

It must be noted that although the plans were separate from the ordinary annual budget, they were not independent from either a financial or an administrative point of view. Until 1935 there was no special organization dealing with these plans exclusively. When the 'Economic Council' was formed to study development schemes, it quickly became a consultative council whose members were politicians lacking the competence to deal with economic planning.[72] Only in 1950 was an autonomous body, the Development Board, created to plan and implement economic development plans.

Besides the many other problems facing Iraq's capital development works, one should bear in mind that the 'plans' were not plans in the real sense: there was no coherent economic policy, and the plans did not establish any system of development; all they did do was to express each government's priorities. However, while their achievements may have been modest, they nevertheless constituted the important beginning stage of economic growth in Iraq.[73]

Competition for Capital Development Works

A salient feature of Iraq's capital development works was the predominance of British firms among the recipients of contracts for development projects. And indeed, one British policy aim in Iraq was to win such contracts, and to prevent their being awarded to non-British firms.

Before independence, the Iraqi government purchased a great proportion of its supplies through the Crown Agents for the Colonies in London. American officials in Baghdad who investigated the matter learned that there was no regulation in force which compelled such a procedure. It was simply that British advisers working with the Iraqi government wanted to give the contracts to British firms.[74] In a conversation with the American chargé d'affaires, one such adviser admitted that 'any contract awarded would be given to British firms, that they (the British Advisers) preferred to work with their own people; that it was a nuisance to have foreign firms submitting bids ...'.[75]

This situation did not change after Iraq's independence. In fact, the procedure for placing orders continued exactly as it had been when Iraq was a mandate. When the issue was raised in 1944 by the Americans, the British claimed 'it was really an oversight that no change was made when Iraq acquired full independence'.[76] This statement is hard to accept, however, in view of the fact that the matter was extensively discussed in 1932 by senior representatives of Crown Agents and the Colonial and Foreign Offices.[77]

British documents clearly demonstrate how the British tried to win every possible contract. Extending loans to Iraq was linked to getting contracts, for example, as was the case when Iraq applied for a loan in 1933. When it was suggested that bonds be issued for Iraq in the City, the director of Baring Brothers and Co., who were to issue the bonds, wrote to Iraq's minister of finance, after consultations with the Treasury, that the British government would agree to sponsor such bonds provided the construction contract for the Habbaniyya scheme was placed with a British firm.[78] (In the event, the Iraqi government decided not to have recourse to a loan.)

The strong position of the British advisers in Iraq gave British firms a very considerable advantage in their competition for contracts with non-British firms. For instance, the committee appointed to consider tenders for the Habbaniyya scheme consisted of four Britons and two Iraqis.[79] Thus, it was to no avail for non-British firms to submit tenders with more advantageous terms for Iraq than those submitted by British firms.

A vivid illustration of British success in winning Iraqi contracts in the face of superior bids by non-British firms occurred in 1934 with regard to construction of the Kut Barrage. A French firm, Société Anonyme Hersent, submitted a tender which promised both cheaper and faster execution of the project than the tenders submitted by five other firms, one German and four British.[80] The British Embassy in Baghdad immediately began trying to prevent the French firm from winning the contract:

> The British technical advisers of the Iraqi Government have been urged to produce reasons for the rejection, on technical or any other grounds, of the French tender, but have been unable to do so, as the firm is financially beyond reproach and has to its credit the successful execution of many important contracts of a similar nature ...[81]

Nevertheless, despite the French firm's credentials, British pressure on the Iraqi government continued.[82] The French, meanwhile, were prepared to reduce their price even further.[83] In the end, British pressure had the upper hand, and Balfour Beatty and Co. was awarded the contract.[84] (The same company won the contract for the Habbaniyya scheme as well.)

The outbreak of World War II interrupted Iraq's capital development works, and no major contract was awarded during this period. (All communications and road construction for military purposes were executed by the British Army or by British firms on the army's behalf.)

By the end of the war the Iraqis were eager to launch many new projects, but the British were then less capable of supplying Iraq with its needs. At the same time, the British feared that most Iraqi contracts would fall into the hands of American firms. They therefore concluded an agreement with Washington in June 1945 on the procedure for dealing with major development projects, emphasizing the need to cut competition and increase consultation between the two powers.[85]

In 1947, as noted in Chapter 1, the British decided that the best means for guaranteeing that British firms continue to win Iraqi contracts was to promote the idea of creating a Central Development Board in Iraq, to consist of British, American, and Iraqi representatives. Without such a body, it was felt, most contracts would go to non-British firms.[86] British pressure on the Iraqi government persisted in this matter until Law No. 23 of 1950 creating the Development Board (*Majlis al-I'mar*) was enacted.[87]

NOTES

1. See Constitution (Organic Law of Iraq) promulgated in Mar. 1925 and amended in July 1925 and Oct. 1943 in Helen Miller Davis, *Constitutions, Electoral Laws, Treaties of State in the Near and Middle East* (2nd. edn., Durham, 1953), pp.151–75.
2. George Harris, *Iraq* (New Haven, 1958), pp.116–17.
3. Khadduri, *Independent Iraq*, pp.28–9.
4. Batatu's *The Old Social Classes* is an excellent study of the different groups that ruled Iraq.
5. *The Iraq Times*, 28 Mar. 1939. A copy appears in ACR, Reel 7. Alongside a statement on economic policy, governments usually published their policies in other areas: internal, defence, foreign relations, education. For the full text of Nuri as-Said's policy in all areas, see: 'Abd al-Razzaq al-Hasani, *Tarikh al-Wizarat al-'Iraqiyya* (History of the Iraqi ministries) (Sidon, 1953), v, pp.50–3.
6. Knabenshue to Dept. of State, 11 July 1935. ACR, Reel 7.
7. Ibid.
8. See, for example, Parliament's debate on the economic policy of Hamdi al-Pachachi's government in al-Hasani, *Tarikh al-Wizarat al-'Iraqiyya*, vi, pp.287–8. Al-Hasani's eight volumes give a clear picture of the low priority that both government and Parliament in Iraq attached to the question of economic policy.
9. Khadduri, *Independent Iraq*, p.28.
10. Al-Hasani, *Tarikh al-Wizarat al-'Iraqiyya*, iv, pp.10–11.
11. 'Current events for the period 1–15 Jan. 1934', ACR, Reel 3.
12. Ogilvie-Forbes to FO, 19 June 1933. FO 371/16906, E 3247/209/93.
13. Ogilvie-Forbes to FO, 7 June 1933. Ibid.
14. United Nations, Department of Economic Affairs, Public Finance Information Papers, *Iraq* (New York, 1951), p.16.
15. The press continually attacked this state of affairs and urged the government 'to establish a permanent and less costly corps of officials'. See: 'Current events for the period 1–15 Oct. 1933', ACR, Reel 3.
16. Cornwallis to FO, 19 Feb. 1944. FO 371/40041, E 1336/37/93.
17. Cornwallis to FO, 23 Mar. 1944, Review of Events in Iraq, Jan. to Mar. 1944. FO 371/40041, E 2113/27/93.
18. Al-Hasani, *Tarikh al-Wizarat al-'Iraqiyya*, vi, pp.216–19.
19. Memorandum on the situation in Iraq by Chaplin, FO, 12 Jan. 1944. FO 371/40041, E 245/37/93.
20. Report by His Majesty's Government in the United Kingdom of Great Britain and Northern Ireland to the Council of the League of Nations, *Administration of Iraq for the Year 1930* (London, 1931), p.60.
21. Knabenshue to Dept. of State, 21 Dec. 1932. ACR, Reel 6.
22. Ministry of Finance Regulation No. 19 of 1935. A copy appears in FO 371/18945, E 5205/278/93.
23. Ministry of Economics and Communications Regulation No. 26 of 1935. A copy appears in FO 371/23203, E 6299/78/93.
24. Newton to FO, 25 Aug. 1939. FO 371/23203, E 6299/78/93.
25. Ibid.
26. MESC, 'Economic Survey of Iraq'. FO 371/40051, E 2564/78/93. For comparison with the organization of the Ministry of the Interior in 1930, see *Iraq Government Gazette*, no. 3 (19 Jan. 1930).
27. 'Ordinance No. 59 of 1939 for the Establishment of a Ministry of Social Affairs', *Iraq Government Gazette*, no. 45 (5 Nov. 1939), pp.594–5.
28. *The Iraq Directory 1936*, p.328.
29. Ibid., pp.328–9.
30. Ibid., pp.120–1.
31. 'Iraq Currency Law No. 44 for 1931'. A copy appears in CO 813/4.

32. 'Economic Conditions in Iraq for May 1944'. FO 371/40052, E 3788/78/93.
33. Cornwallis to FO, 10 June 1944. FO 371/40057, E 3643/193/93.
34. The problems of supply will be discussed in the section on inflation and supply in Ch. 3.
35. Law No. 17 for 1948. See al-Hasani, *Tarikh al-Wazarat al-'Iraqiyya*, viii, p.14.
36. Based on: Memorandum on British Controls in Iraq by Richard Gnade (third secretary of American Mission in Iraq), 25 Feb. 1944. ACR, Reel 15; and Economic Survey of Iraq Prepared by MESC, 13 Apr. 1944. FO 371/40051, E 2564/78/93.
37. Baghdad Chamber of Commerce, *Annual Report 1935–1936* (Baghdad, 1936), p.15.
38. Ibid., pp.18–19.
39. Baghdad Chamber of Commerce, *Report for the Years 1938 and 1939* (Baghdad, 1942), p.199 (in Arabic).
40. Ibid., p.206.
41. Internal Regulations No. 23 of 1936 of the Agricultural and Industrial Bank of Iraq. A copy appears in FO 371/20012, E 6285/1182/93.
42. Bateman to FO, 22 Sept. 1936. FO 371/20012, E 6285/429/93.
43. Stonehewer to FO, 10 July 1945. FO 371/45323, E 5288/429/93.
44. Houston-Boswall to FO, 29 Apr. 1939. FO 371/23215, E 3329/1322/93; *Iraq Government Gazette*, no. 2 (14 Jan. 1940), pp.17–24.
45. Hashim al-Dabbagh, *Études statistiques sur le développement économique de l'Iraq* (Baghdad, 1960), p.283.
46. Report by His Majesty's Government in the United Kingdom of Great Britain and Northern Ireland to the Council of the League of Nations, *Administration of Iraq for the Year 1931* (London, 1932), p.38.
47. Report by His Majesty's Government in the United Kingdom of Great Britain and Northern Ireland to the Council of the League of Nations, *Administration of Iraq for the period January to October 1932* (London, 1933), p.27.
48. Law No. 79 of 1931 for Capital Development Works. A copy appears in ACR, Reel 7.
49. Annual Report on Iraq for 1933 by British Embassy. FO 371/17871, E 2204/2204/93.
50. Ibid.
51. Law No. 39 of 1934 for Capital Development Works. A copy appears in FO 624/2/10, part ii.
52. Ibid.
53. Law No. 26 of 1936 for 'Three Year Works Plan'. A copy appears in FO 624/7/399.
54. Bateman to FO, 15 Apr. 1936. FO 624/7/399.
55. Ibid.
56. General Budget Law for the Financial Year 1937, *Iraq Government Gazette*, no. 28 (11 July 1937), pp.337–48.
57. The question of raising foreign loans always had considerable political and economic implications in Iraq, and it will be discussed in detail in Ch. 3.
58. Kerr to FO, 20 July 1937. FO 371/20800, E 4476/65/93.
59. Law No. 45 of 1938 for Capital Development Works. A copy appears in FO 371/21861, E 3501/3501/93.
60. This loan was finally redeemed in 1943 (see Ch. 3).
61. Knabenshue to Dept. of State, 6 May 1938. ACR, Reel 7.
62. Law No. 45 of 1938, FO 371/21861.
63. Houston-Boswall (British Embassy, Baghdad) to FO, 31 Aug. 1938. FO 371/21859, E 5400/2000/93.
64. Newton to FO, 6 July 1939. FO 371/23209, E 4925/374/93.
65. Law No. 37 of 1939 for Capital Development Works. A copy appears in FO 371/23217, E 6090/4342/93.
66. Knabenshue to Dept. of State, 15 Nov. 1939. ACR, Reel 4.
67. Stonehewer-Bird to FO (Tel. 122), 10 July 1946. FO 371/52463, E 6756/6756/93.
68. Stanley John Habermann, 'The Iraq Development Board: Administration and Program', *Middle East Journal*, ix, (Spring 1955), pp.179–86.
69. This contradicts Ribhi el-Haj's conclusion that transport and communications had the highest share of total investment; but it should be noted that el-Haj omitted the war years, and that his calculations were based solely on foreign trade statistics. See: Ribhi Abu el-Haj, 'Capital Formation in Iraq, 1922–1957', *Economic Development and Cultural*

Change, ix, no. 4 (July 1961), pp.604–17.
70. For a list of problems of development during this period, see Fahim I. Qubain, *The Reconstruction of Iraq 1950–1957* (New York, 1958), pp.22–8.
71. A note on capital projects under consideration in 1947 appears in T 236/1185, 58/50/1.
72. Al-Dabbagh, *Études statistiques*, p.331.
73. For a detailed list of all projects undertaken during the period 1927–50, see *Hisabat al-Dawla al-Iraqiyya lil-Sana 1950 al-Maliyya*, pp.62–6 (Iraq's account for the financial year 1950).
74. Alexander Sloan (American consul) to Dept. of State, 1 Mar. 1930. ACR, Reel 6.
75. Robert Brown (chargé d'affaires) to Dept. of State on his conversation with E.B. Morgan, technical secretary of Iraq's Ministry of Economics and Communications, 26 Aug. 1931. ACR, Reel 7.
76. FO to Baghdad, 28 Dec. 1944. FO 361/40066, E 7665/346/93.
77. See CO 730/176/96497.
78. Peacock (director of Baring Brothers) to Nasrat al-Farsi (Iraq's minister of finance), 20 Jan. 1933. T 160/11883, F 131/1.
79. Embassy to DOT, 23 Feb. 1933. FO 371/16902, E 1230/85/93.
80. Embassy to FO, 7 May 1934. T 160/1188, F 1315/1.
81. Ogilvie-Forbes to FO, 8 June 1934. FO 371/17953, E 4153/16/93.
82. Ibid., E 4156 and E 4613.
83. Forbes to FO, 31 July 1934. Ibid., E 4889.
84. Forbes to FO, 7 Sept. 1934. Ibid., E 5643. France protested about Iraq's decision, but to no avail.
85. BT 11/2420.
86. Baghdad to FO, 21 Nov. 1947. T 236/1274.
87. See, for example, FO to Baghdad, 17 Oct. 1948. FO 371/68467, E 13139/112/93; Mack to FO, 11 Apr. 1949. FO 371/75150, E 5511/1103/93; and FO to Baghdad, 31 Jan. 1950. FO 371/75129, E 14936/1018/93. For details about the Development Board, its organization, powers, duties and development plans, see Qubain, *Reconstruction of Iraq*, pp.30–53.

3

FINANCE

As explained in the Introduction, one cannot speak of a particular monetary or fiscal policy in Iraq. This chapter, therefore, will deal with financial policy in general, rather than a specifically fiscal or monetary policy, and all matters relating to finance (such as budgets, taxation, banking, money supply, etc.) will be discussed without trying to categorize them according to fiscal or monetary policy.

The first part of this chapter will examine Iraq's budgets during the period 1932–50, their structure and the tax system. It will also discuss one important aspect of financial policy – internal and external borrowing; and then concentrate on the 1948 financial crisis to see how it was handled.

The second part of the chapter will deal with currency, banking and money supply. The third part will examine the factors responsible for the increase in money supply, and the problems of supply and price-controlling which stemmed from that increase, concentrating on the years 1939–45 when inflation constituted one of Iraq's major problems.

FINANCIAL POLICY

Budgets

The first budget law for the State of Iraq was issued in 1921 under the British mandate. According to a special law promulgated in 1924, the government of Iraq was obliged to present its budget to Parliament each year before the beginning of the financial year on 1 April.[1] The actual course of events, however, was somewhat different from the legal requirements, as will be seen later.

After 1927 Iraq's budgets were based on a dual system: ordinary budgets and capital works budgets. We shall concentrate here on the ordinary budgets, since the capital works budgets have been dealt with in Chapter 2. Besides ordinary receipts and expenditures, the ordinary budget usually contained supplementary budgets of independent government institutions, such as the railways, the Fao Dredging Scheme, Basra Port and the Iraq Currency Board.

As shown in Table 3.1, Iraq enjoyed a surplus for nine years of the period under study, and suffered a deficit for the other nine. Adding up the surpluses and deficits of the entire period, we get an aggregate deficit in the ordinary budgets of about ID 11 million. But there was at the same time an aggregate surplus in the capital works budgets of about ID 9.5 million, which leaves a deficit of only ID 1.5 million at the end of FY 1949.[2] The only significant deficit was that of 1948. As we shall later see, this was the consequence of harvest failures and the Palestine war.

One can say, therefore, that Iraq's financial situation was relatively sound during most of the period under discussion. This very likely stemmed from the fact that the government invariably followed the orthodox policy of budget balancing, a rather universal practice at the time which had its origins in Iraq during the mandate period.

The policy of successive governments has always aimed at the same object, and none of the various governments which held office in the country

TABLE 3.1 Ordinary Receipts and Expenditures, FY 1932-FY 1949 (Iraqi dinars)

FY	Receipts	Expenditures	Surplus or deficit
1932	3,691,053	3,586,160	+104,893
1933	3,608,189	3,736,443	-128,254
1934	4,012,777	3,794,280	+218,479
1935	4,759,300	4,413,016	+346,284
1936	5,426,808	4,756,167	+670,641
1937	6,185,966	5,169,402	+1,016,564
1938	5,801,039	5,670,738	+130,301
1939	6,093,053	6,369,148	-267,095
1940	6,800,114	7,144,910	-344,796
1941	6,988,122	7,701,178	-713,056
1942	11,633,759	10,620,823	+1,012,936
1943	14,399,911	13,749,321	+650,590
1944[a]	18,897,052	18,998,141	-101,089
1945	17,345,282	19,784,566	-2,439,284
1946	22,710,418	22,471,895	+238,523
1947	21,165,601	22,986,797	-1,821,196
1948	21,210,462	28,074,188	-6,863,726
1949	23,828,240	26,629,513	-2,801,273

Source: Wizarat al-Maliyya, Hisabat al Dawla al-Iraqiyya lil-Sana 1950 al-Maliyya.

[a]The 1944 ordinary budget included the capital works budget.

embarked on any work not in conformity with pre-determined lines of policy or any adventurous scheme likely to expose the finances of the country to danger whether immediate or remote.[3]

Budget equilibrium was indeed the main target of every government; some governments even went out of their way to augment revenues or decrease expenditures (but without jarring the basic system), as ministers would be vulnerable politically if their ministries' budgets showed a deficit.

As mentioned earlier, preparation of the budget and its presentation to parliament were supposed to take place before April of each year. But during most of the years under discussion the estimates for receipts and expenditures were in fact presented later than April. This was probably a result of the frequent changes of government and the lack of co-ordination between ministries. The delay was usually two or three months, but in one extreme case (FY 1948) the budget was not passed until the following April. During this year of delay, bi-monthly provisional budgets were produced from time to time.[4]

Many years saw additional budgets besides the regular annual budget. For example, Iraq's budget for the financial year 1940 was approved only in June, but in August of that year another budget was added to meet expenditures not taken into account previously.[5] After 1944 there were also additional emergency expenditure budgets for the Ministry of Supply.

Another aspect of budget preparation was the differences between planned and actual estimates. During the period 1932–9, there was a tendency to plan for less revenue and more expenditure than anticipated,[6] probably due to the desire to show a surplus at the end of the year. During World War II, inflationary trends played havoc with attempts at budgetary planning, and throughout most of the 1940s actual expenditure exceeded that planned for. As expenditures continued to rise during the war and immediately after it (in current prices), the government was forced to plan for budget deficits in certain financial years (e.g. 1944 and 1945), to be covered by transfer of surplus revenue from the capital works budget or from oil revenues.[7] In FY 1945, the actual deficit of about ID 2.5 million exceeded that planned for by about ID 0.8 million.

One should not, however, pay too much attention to these differences between planned and actual spending. It should be remembered that the government exercised broad authorities, and because of the weakness of Parliament, the minister of finance could always bring additional budgets without fear of undue repercussions.[7] 'The debates, although absorbing a good deal of the time of both Houses, did not arouse much interest either in Parliament or in the press.'[9]

Some ministers of finance lacked expertise in financial affairs. When a new government was formed at the end of October 1936, it informed the British ambassador that it found the treasury empty. Reinforced by a memorandum from the British adviser to Iraq's Ministry of Finance, the ambassador's perception of the situation was different from that of the Iraqi government's: 'I had two long talks with the new Minister for Finance [Ja'far Abu Timman], and my impression is that he is needlessly anxious. He has not had much experience of high finance and his idea of financial stability is, I suspect, a large cellar full of sacks of gold.'[10]

Not only British advisers and ambassadors had a low opinion of some Iraqi ministers of finance; Ibrahim al-Kabir, who held such important positions in the Ministry of Finance as director-general and accountant-general, summed up his twenty-five years of service by saying: 'I served under twenty-five different ministers. Some of them held the post for only a few weeks, others for quite a long period. ... Some of them knew nothing of finance and had no qualifications at all for such a high office.'[11] In al-Kabir's opinion, Iraq's best ministers of finance were Sassoon Heskail and Rustum Haidar.

> Nearly all the others did nothing of importance except deal with routine matters, mostly the appointment of personnel, as submitted to them by the director general or the adviser. Some did nothing but make mischief by pursuing a sectarian policy which slowly undermined the solid structure of the country's finance and stable administration.[12]

The above factors combined to create a situation where the main aim was balancing the budget, and there was consequently strong reluctance to change its structure.[13]

Expenditures

Table 3.2 shows government expenditures by category from FY 1932 to FY 1949. Again, although one should be cautious with these official figures, they nevertheless do give an indication of the pattern of expenditure in Iraq. The system of allocating expenditure in the budget was according to ministries – usually thirteen or fourteen in number – with sub-allocations according to departments and government institutions. The table shows actual spending by the ministries and the more important departments, while expenditures of less important departments are included within the relevant ministries. Ministries or departments were sometimes abolished, which is the reason for the non-continuation of the sums of expenditure in certain columns of the table. (For example, the Public Health Department became part of the Ministry of Social Affairs.)

The table indicates a major increase in expenditure between 1939 and 1946, but it should be noted that this was a period of high inflation; a United Nations study indicates that government expenditures in fact showed a considerable reduction in terms of pre-war prices. In current prices, taking FY 1938 as 100, government expenditures reached 240 in 1945 and 347 in 1949, but in real terms (at 1938 prices) they dropped from 100 in 1938 to 30 in 1942, to 46 in 1946, and even at the end of the period reached only 75.[14]

It can be seen from Table 3.2 that throughout the period the Ministry of Defence received the highest allocation: about 30% of total ordinary expenditures during most of the 1930s and 1940s. If we add to these sums the expenditures for internal security (Ministry of the Interior and Police), allocations for defence and internal security were between 40% and 50% of total ordinary expenditures. The British warned the Iraqis time and again about the rise in defence expenditures without due regard to the country's financial resources.[15] It is interesting to note, however, that these warnings were not coupled with any pressure, except when Iraq turned to non-sterling countries, particularly the United States, for military supplies.

It should also be remembered that the figures for internal security and defence include the salaries paid to ministry officials. In fact, as noted in Chapter 2, salaries in general constituted the major item of expenditure. In some years, salaries (including pensions, Parliament and the civil list) amounted to about 66% of total ordinary expenditures. The Parliamentary Financial Committee continually asked the government to reduce the high proportion of salaries in the budget, but in vain.[16] The cost of living allowance, which began to be paid to compensate for inflation (included in Table 3.2 under the Ministry of Supply), only added to the burden on the budget imposed by salaries.

Expenditures for various social services, such as education, public health and social welfare, accounted for 13.4% of total ordinary expenditures in the FY 1932, 18.7% in 1939, 14.5% in 1945, and 16% in 1949. Taking inflation into consideration, this meant that in real terms allocations for social services did not increase, or increased only slightly between the beginning and end of the period. In addition, it should be noted that the financial

TABLE 3.2 Government Expenditure by Main Categories, FY 1932-FY 1949 (Iraqi dinars)

	1932	1933	1934	1935	1936	1937	1938	1939	1940
Pensions and grants	196,580	205,244	199,883	214,855	197,931	193,421	190,254	245,405	229,526
Public debt	63,649	63,649	-	-	-	-	-	-	-
King's civil list	58,392	58,901	57,279	60,350	59,152	57,978	58,058	53,104	54,646
Parliament	34,954	69,257	38,577	70,066	26,478	69,828	41,738	69,317	65,531
Comptroller and auditor general	9,175	9,127	9,187	6,780	8,518	7,740	8,668	8,690	9,021
Office of the council of ministers	20,362	38,489	13,554	18,521	19,356	29,989	12,586	18,580	19,383
Ministry of Foreign Affairs	29,906	40,725	48,559	61,610	75,870	85,715	79,152	92,272	92,328
Ministry of Finance	253,190	271,859	294,335	291,633	297,920	335,520	363,282	345,622	473,418
Customs and Excise	166,670	158,791	165,023	170,337	167,563	174,039	184,979	198,543	200,616
Ministry of the Interior	291,214	298,760	325,383	386,347	339,530	425,780	495,916	493,379	451,095
Police	541,759	567,568	573,864	644,643	622,261	658,913	674,575	685,950	726,744
Ministry of Social Affairs	-	-	-	-	-	-	-	1,835	98,859
Public health	176,292	187,640	219,130	243,039	286,813	372,836	357,999	362,323	457,541

Ministry of Defence	801,442	789,208	860,233	1,041,099	1,253,612	1,215,083	1,620,030	1,969,167	2,215,615
Ministry of Justice	105,422	116,768	130,297	129,067	127,444	145,146	149,738	148,240	153,754
Tapu and Land Settlement Depts.	28,383	32,938	36,003	34,056	34,341	36,967	39,299	71,899	79,480
Ministry of Education	306,994	348,559	379,355	428,034	523,505	626,103	718,100	828,465	865,954
Ministry of Economics	-	-	-	-	-	-	-	29,024	33,336
Agricultural and veterinary services	56,693	69,746	55,241	87,553	90,347	101,514	96,266	117,711	146,439
Ministry of Communications and Works	194,808	176,803	133,590	59,793	66,104	59,428	70,348	69,985	66,312
Tobacco Monopoly	-	-	-	-	-	-	-	-	-
Irrigation Dept.	87,005	72,102	105,003	304,238	359,060	354,565	304,893	331,568	453,998
Posts and Telegraphs	163,212	160,309	149,804	160,995	200,362	218,837	204,857	227,969	252,317
Ministry of Supply[a]	-	-	-	-	-	-	-	-	-
Total ordinary expenditure	3,586,160	3,736,443	3,794,280	4,413,016	4,756,167	5,169,402	5,670,738	6,372,048	7,145,913
Capital development works	332,604	428,506	428,222	1,235,576	2,402,794	2,373,746	2,463,566	2,232,916	2,709,428
Total	3,918,764	4,164,949	4,222,502	5,648,592	7,158,961	7,542,148	8,134,304	8,604,964	9,855,341

[a]Includes cost-of-living allowance and Directorate General of Imported Goods.

TABLE 3.2 - continued

	1941	1942	1943	1944	1945	1946	1947	1948	1949
Pensions and grants	275,018	302,965	367 377	302,639	327,120	338,014	352,542	384,229	426,876
Public debt	-	-	-	-	-	-	-	-	-
King's civil list	55,481	58,414	62,576	72,904	79,048	77,613	84,594	84,029	91,537
Parliament	41,089	58,989	68,994	76,531	86,616	65,147	142,188	84,703	98,837
Comptroller and auditor general	10,199	11,831	14,029	11,913	13,429	12,453	13,914	13,080	13,820
Office of the council of ministers	34,462	16,990	34,416	22,317	33,588	31,329	27,585	29,279	38,411
Ministry of Foreign Affairs	88,939	122,261	141,120	160,669	455,443	487,700	743,893	527,507	453,740
Ministry of Finance	724,651	584,356	1,215,144	1,424,742	776,754	1,440,206	1,306,920	1,369,634	1,183,675
Customs and Excise	215,575	805,334	771,604	540,613	433,307	441,799	399,383	433,482	530,379
Ministry of the Interior	507,329	572,892	811,152	590,003	788,982	1,539,554	1,151,509	1,006,901	1,445,550
Police	837,357	1,395,301	1,840,536	1,441,079	2,088,450	2,576,681	2,573,791	2,835,603	2,571,869
Ministry of Social Affairs	137,315	908,243	1,115,166	1,188,882	1,261,096	1,389,597	1,995,574	1,983,926	1,706,404
Public health	418,544	-	-	-	-	-	-	-	-
Ministry of Defence	2,306,166	3,059,289	3,719,615	4,436,025	5,362,808	5,279,897	4,360,735	6,745,941	6,585,023

Ministry of Justice	161,035	206,070	256,133	217,358	268,478	275,635	306,636	339,979	335,285
Tapu and and Settlement Depts	78,757	103,785	140,961	119,556	149,191	193,335	220,683	220,549	199,596
Ministry of Education	873,257	1,152,833	1,515,542	1,335,475	1,611,843	1,737,604	2,157,315	2,572,625	2,597,048
Ministry of Economics	31,067	39,496	87,144	139,865	200,061	134,026	183,217	196,148	228,895
Agricultural and veterinary services	161,060	299,992	321,480	486,279	567,017	680,925	926,177	1,159,962	660,769
Ministry of Communications and Works	67,069	82,044	108,498	94,005	141,393	136,006	176,800	191,590	202,656
Tobacco Monopoly	-	-	-	37,134	48,730	60,834	48,531	54,381	40,272
Irrigation Dept.	357,821	480,957	702,203	1,924,290	662,228	881,439	842,675	910,305	713,839
Posts and Telegraphs	303,961	358,781	455,631	397,810	471,670	562,699	644,494	804,141	595,707
Ministry of Supply[a]	-	-	-	3,977,052	3,957,305	4,129,351	4,327,572	6,126,193	5,909,325
Total ordinary expenditure	7,704,152	10,620,823	13,749,321	18,998,141	19,784,557	22,468,844	22,986,728	28,074,187	26,629,513
Capital development works	962,614	975,272	1,654,385	-	1,539,153	3,050,123	3,574,220	3,928,857	3,376,897
Total	8,666,766	11,596,095	15,403,706	18,998,141	21,323,710	25,518,967	26,560,948	32,003,044	30,006,410

Source: Various editions of Wizarat al-Maliyya, Hisabat al-Dawla al-Iraqiyya al Maliyya, as follows: for FY 1932-FY 1936, report for 1936 (Baghdad, 1938), pp. 10, 60; for 1937-41, report for 1941 (Baghdad, 1944), pp. 12, 65; for 1942-5, report for 1945 (Baghdad, 1947), p. 16, for 1946-9, report for 1950 (Baghdad, 1953), pp. 13, 59.

[a]Includes cost-of-living allowance and Directorate General of Imported Goods.

burden of these services was carried almost entirely by the central government, since privately sponsored schools and hospitals were not numerous.

Communications and irrigation received a very low share of the ordinary expenditure: 7.8% in FY 1932, 6.3% in 1939, 4% in 1945, and 3.4% in 1949. But these sums were mainly earmarked for paying salaries and local administration costs, since the bulk of investment in these two areas was done within the framework of capital development works.

The structure of government expenditures did not change radically during the period 1932–50. Priorities were, in order of allocation: local administration and salaries; defence and internal security; social services; and communications and irrigation (see Table 2.4).

Receipts

As with expenditures, government receipts increased considerably between 1932 and 1950, mainly during the war (see Table 3.3). But again, this increase was in current prices. The United Nations study shows that if FY 1938 is taken as a base (index 100), then at current prices, receipts reached 270 in 1945, and 345 at the end of the period under discussion. In 1938 prices (1938 = 100), however, receipts (like expenditures) decreased to 52 in 1945, and to 75 in 1949.

Oil royalties were a further major source of revenues. The sums received from this source along with such other sources as internal loans or contributions from the Iraq Currency Board, were channelled to capital development works.

With regard to the different sources of ordinary receipts, it may be appropriate to describe Iraq's revenue system by examining the structure of each tax and its contribution to total ordinary receipts. The main tax sources of revenue were the following:

1. Taxes on agricultural land and its natural produce
2. Tax on sheep, cattle and produce thereof brought to market
3. Tax on fish brought to market
4. Income tax
5. Property tax
6. Customs duties
7. Excise duties
8. Stamp duties

Agricultural Taxes

One important feature of the revenue from agricultural taxes was that it was quite low, notwithstanding the fact that the majority of Iraq's population earned their living from agriculture. An even more striking feature was the virtual absence of direct taxation in this sector.

The basic tax was that on agricultural crops, the *istihlak* tax. This was a development of the traditional tithe, called *ushur*, which became the land tax in 1929 and was established as the *istihlak* tax in 1933.[17] The development of this tax in the 1930s and 1940s had significant implications for agricultural policy in Iraq; this and other issues relating to agricultural taxes will be dealt with in Chapter 4.

As Table 3.3 indicates, taxes on land and land produce constituted 16.5% of total ordinary receipts in FY 1932, 13.8% in 1939, 21.2% in 1945, and 17% in 1949. The vulnerability of indirect agricultural taxes is obvious: bad harvests lead to serious shrinkage of revenue.[18] This, for instance, was one of the major reasons for the deterioration in Iraq's financial position in 1940. [19] The financial crisis of 1948 also stemmed from a bad harvest.

Income Tax

Income tax was first introduced in Iraq with effect from 1 April 1927. It was levied on incomes which were not subject to any other tax, so that incomes derived from agriculture, buildings and the possession of animals were exempted. The 1927 law and a subsequent one (Law No. 36 of 1939) defined the categories of taxable income as follows:[20]

1. Profits arising from trade, business, vocation or any other work.
2. Incomes arising from employment.
3. Interest, discounts and dividends.
4. Pensions and annuities.
5. Other incomes not liable to any other tax in Iraq.

The income tax was assessed on the basis of returns where books were kept, and otherwise on the basis of a comparison with similar activities. Taxes on wages were withheld by employers. The rate progressed from 6% for annual incomes below ID 150, to 9% for incomes of ID 150–500, to 15% for incomes exceeding ID 1,200 per year.[21]

Assessment of income tax was difficult because many merchants either did not keep books or were reluctant to produce them.[22] In

TABLE 3.3 Government Receipts by Main Headings, FY 1932-FY 1949 (Iraqi dinars)

	1932	1933	1934	1935	1936	1937	1938	1939
Direct Taxes:								
Income and excess profits taxes	112,544	123,275	114,288	248,613	268,734	267,551	315,977	370,013
Property taxes	112,370	105,449	116,484	112,792	121,625	115,244	132,177	155,697
Total direct taxes	224,914	228,724	230,772	361,405	390,359	382,795	448,154	525,710
Indirect Taxes:								
Taxes on land and land produce	607,888	603,156	662,350	658,435	864,104	885,928	852,030	842,059
Customs and Excise	1,932,867	2,047,005	2,305,092	2,543,206	2,823,101	3,310,767	3,262,269	3,387,644
Stamp duties	104,354	103,273	106,313	116,634	132,940	146,735	149,883	145,970
Tobacco monopoly	-	-	-	-	-	-	-	-
Total indirect taxes	2,645,109	2,753,434	3,073,755	3,318,275	3,820,145	4,343,430	4,264,182	4,375,673
Total revenue from taxes	2,870,023	2,982,158	3,304,527	3,679,680	4,210,504	4,726,225	4,712,336	4,901,383
Posts and telegraphs	205,798	199,555	204,232	220,855	243,658	260,193	285,404	338,349
Other receipts[a]	615,232	426,476	504,018	858,744	972,646	1,199,548	803,299	853,321
Total ordinary receipts	3,691,053	3,608,189	4,012,777	4,759,279	5,426,808	6,185,966	5,801,039	6,093,053
Oil royalties	524,398	540,426	995,304	598,202	599,968	730,731	1,977,458	2,014,088
Advance from the three petroleum companies	-	-	-	-	-	-	-	1,000,000
Contribution by currency board	-	-	15,000	40,000	81,000	110,000	60,000	60,000
Loan recoveries from railways	-	-	-	-	-	-	-	-
Foreign credit accounts	-	-	-	-	-	-	-	40,415
Iraqi advance (internal loan)	-	-	-	-	-	-	-	-
Total receipts	4,215,451	4,148,615	5,023,081	5,397,481	6,107,776	7,026,697	7,838,497	9,207,556

Sources: Various editions of Wizarat al-Maliyya, Hisabat al-Dawla al-Iraqiyya al Maliyya, as follows: for FY 1932-FY 1940, report for 1941 (Baghdad, 1944), p. 64; for 1941-9, report for 1950 (Baghdad, 1953), p. 58. Also from Iraq, Principal Bureau of Statistics, Statistical Abstract 1944 and 1945 (Baghdad, 1946), p. 119; and Statistical Abstract 1950 (Baghdad, 1952), p. 238.

[a] Includes court dues and fines, tapu fees and registration; proceeds from sale of sugar, rents, tolls and receipts of other government departments.

1940	1941	1942	1943	1944	1945	1946	1947	1948	1949
553,122	640,105	992,108	1,701,616	2,286,315	1,946,613	1,752,637	1,790,968	2,157,320	2,373,505
188,409	193,204	201,424	243,460	350,182	398,673	418,169	477,109	582,558	783,706
741,531	833,369	1,193,532	1,945,076	2,636,497	2,345,286	2,170,806	2,268,077	2,739,878	3,157,211
1,060,236	1,106,040	2,128,694	3,880,643	4,101,651	3,678,517	4,349,208	3,545,053	3,836,203	4,035,887
3,465,853	3,488,402	4,505,441	4,320,901	4,619,520	4,674,627	7,180,157	8,851,113	9,800,513	11,296,355
143,484	147,516	204,214	262,845	312,887	341,893	382,785	357,837	464,843	507,171
-	186,497	468,979	121,020	843,105	1,235,031	3,489,650	1,861,358	342,643	424,293
4,669,573	4,928,455	7,307,328	8,585,409	9,877,163	9,930,068	15,401,800	14,615,361	14,444,202	16,263,706
5,411,104	5,761,824	8,500,860	10,530,485	12,513,600	12,275,354	17,572,606	16,883,438	17,184,080	19,420,917
434,979	481,809	626,356	669,057	712,865	748,110	857,200	991,740	992,049	1,119,478
954,031	744,489	2,506,543	3,200,369	3,373,838	4,321,818	4,280,612	3,290,423	3,034,333	3,287,845
6,800,114	6,988,122	11,633,759	14,399,911	16,600,363	17,345,282	22,710,601	21,165,601	21,210,462	23,828,240
1,575,915	1,463,371	1,463,371	2,794,245	2,224,730	2,315,598	2,326,968	2,346,280	2,011,942	3,237,965
1,000,000	1,000,000	-	-	-	500,000	-	-	-	-
60,000	60,000	60,000	60,000	60,000	60,000	60,000	500,000	500,000	500,000
-	550,000	660,000	790,000	-	-	-	-	-	66,667
281,764	93,573	9,889	60,392	11,959	-	-	-	-	-
-	-	-	-	-	-	-	2,000,000	3,000,000	1,000,000
9,717,793	10,155,066	13,827,019	18,104,548	18,897,052	20,220,880	25,097,386	26,011,880	26,722,404	28,632,872

such cases the Income Tax Department was compelled to make arbitrary assessments, and this created scope for tax evasion. There was also the possibility of appeal against department assessments to an Appellate Committee, which was composed of both officials and non-officials. Although committee sessions were presided over by the senior official member, assessments were frequently reduced, and the decision of the committee was final.[23]

An excess profits tax was added in March 1940, as a levy on all income other than that derived from professional or salaried employment, which was subject to the income tax. 'Excess profits' were defined as income exceeding the average income of the three preceding years. The rate of tax varied from 20% for the first ID 1,000 of excess profits to 30% on ID 3,000 and above.[24] A 1941 amendment made the excess profits tax applicable to *all* income subject to the income tax, regardless of source, while reducing the rates to a range of 5–20%.[25]

The government, finding it difficult to apply the excess profits tax, decided to replace it in 1943 by an income surtax. This constituted a simplification of the system by defining as liable to surtax all income above ID 1,500. The rates for individuals varied from 5% for the first ID 1,000 to 45% on incomes of over ID 8,000. Companies had to pay from 10% for the first ID 1,000 to 25% on incomes above ID 3,000.[26]

Table 3.4 shows that the number of taxpayers of both income tax and surtax was very small in proportion to the size of the population, but it must be remembered that Iraq was mainly an agricultural country, and that agricultural incomes were not subject to these taxes. It is obvious, however, that tax evasion and poor tax collection were prime reasons for the small number of taxpayers. It should also be noted that the three principal oil companies working in Iraq were not required to pay income taxes – and that in return for annual payments in commutation of all taxes.[27]

Data for the 1930s are less reliable than those of the 1940s but they do indicate that the number of taxpayers was much smaller: in FY 1933 there were only 4,081 taxpayers; in 1935, 4,785; and in 1938, 4,578.[28]

Income and surtaxes were thus borne primarily by salaried employees, and by individuals and companies engaged in commerce. In FY 1947 Iraqi companies paid a total of ID 258,596 in income and surtaxes, as compared with ID 487,683 paid by foreign companies (Table 3.4).

Another feature of the income tax system was its 'concentration': about 80% of all income taxes paid by individuals came from

TABLE 3.4 Returns from Income Tax and Surtax, FY 1944 and FY 1947

	1944				1947			
	Income tax		Surtax		Income tax		Surtax	
	No. of payers	Amount (ID)	No. of payers	Amount (ID)	No. of payers	Amount (ID)	No. of payers	Amount (ID)
Individual (self-employed)	6,297	308,419	497	177,746	18,170	454,331	992	224,951
Government officials and employees	5,677	63,401	35	1,959	7,194	99,977	40	3,307
Employees of private firms and companies	2,024	51,351	72	4,833	2,440	116,555	160	3,893
Iraqi companies	40	90,370	36	122,718	34	121,640	27	136,956
Foreign companies	66	236,981	39	365,541	94	178,028	59	309,655
Total	14,103	750,522	679	672,797	27,932	970,531	1,278	678,762

Sources: For FY 1944: Iraq, Principal Bureau of Statistics, Statistical Abstract 1947 (Baghdad, 1949), p. 210. For FY 1947: Iraq, Principal Bureau of Statistics, Statistical Abstract 1948 (Baghdad, 1950), p. 232.

taxpayers residing in the district of Baghdad, while the Basra district accounted for another 10% or more.[29] This too reflected the fact that farmers were not subject to these taxes.

The contribution of revenues from income and excess profits tax to the government's total ordinary receipts was, not surprisingly in light of the above, quite modest: in FY 1932 it constituted only 3%; in 1939, 6%; in 1945, 11.2%; and in 1949, 10% (Table 3.3). The actual receipts of income tax were disappointing to the government throughout the period 1932–50,[30] but it would seem that the government was not prepared to introduce drastic change in the laws, lest certain sectors of the population be antagonized. For instance, in 1942 the British Embassy in Iraq reported that merchants, contractors and the like were making large profits from the British forces there, but that the Iraqi government was somewhat reluctant to tax them appropriately.[31]

Undertaxation of the rich was indeed one of the basic aspects of the tax system in Iraq, where wealth was very concentrated: by 1958 the Iraqi bourgeois families worth ID 1 million or more appeared to number but twenty-three.[32] Even if the real number was higher, it still represented an extremely small proportion of the country's population.

Property Tax

The property tax was really a form of income tax, levied at the rate of 10% of annual rental value throughout the 1930s and 1940s, and increased in 1948 to 12.5%.[33] It applied to owners of non-agricultural land and of dwelling houses and commercial buildings above a certain minimum value. Revenues from this tax constituted 3% of total ordinary receipts in FY 1932, 2.5% in 1939, 2.3% in 1945, and 3.3% in 1949 (Table 3.3). From time to time there were suggestions that this tax should be abolished and the revenue from property be defined as income and made liable to income tax, but there were political difficulties in the introduction of such a measure.[34]

Customs and Excise Duties

The principal source of revenue throughout the period 1932–50 was customs and excise receipts. In FY 1932 they comprised 52.3% of total ordinary receipts; in 1939, 55.6%; in 1945, 27%; and in 1949, 47.4% (Table 3.3). The relative decline of this source with respect to total ordinary receipts during the war period was due to the decrease in the volume of imports. In the post-war years, receipts from this source gradually increased as more goods were imported, although the import of non-essential goods was still restricted and a large number of essential items (e.g. agricultural machinery, capital goods) were exempted from duty.

In general, customs duties were devised with the object of producing as much revenue as possible; at the same time, the scale of duty varied according to whether the goods were considered necessities, semi-luxuries or luxuries. There were two notable exceptions to this classification of goods, namely sugar and tea, duties on which were periodically raised in order to bring in more revenue. The range of duties, usually valued at 'wholesale cash prices', was from 8% to 50%; while the average import tax rate in FY 1946 was 13.5%.[35] No duty was imposed on agricultural machinery, but a 5% duty was levied on some industrial machinery. In 1948 and 1949 customs duties were increased substantially. (The policy of imposing and increasing duties will be examined in Ch. 5.)

From a financial point of view, there were many reasons for such a heavy reliance on import duties. Revenues could be easily assessed and collected from importers at a few designated points of entry. Protection of local infant industries was another motive. Finally, from a political point of view it was simpler to impose these duties than direct taxation.

One of the major defects in the application of customs duties was that most imports were taxed on a specific rather than an *ad valorem* basis. Thus, although the price of imports rose throughout most of the period under study, the increase was not reflected in the tax yield.[36]

Excise duties were imposed on petrol, salt, tobacco, and other products, and they yielded a relatively substantial amount of revenue. In 1940 an emergency tax was added to the existing levies.[37]

Stamp Duties

Stamp duties were another form of indirect taxation, and were levied on contracts, licences, commercial agreements, foreign currency exchanges, etc.[38] Receipts from stamp duties did not exceed 3% in the period 1932–50: 2.8% in 1932, 2.4% in 1939, 2% in 1945, and 2.1% in 1949 (Table 3.3).

Other Sources of Revenue

The Tobacco Monopoly was established in 1939 but put into effect only in 1941. It gave the Government exclusive rights to the purchase, storage and wholesale marketing of all tobacco cultivated in Iraq or imported from abroad.[39] Revenues from this source increased from 2.6% in 1941 to 7% in 1945, then decreased again after 1946, constituting only 1.8% of total ordinary receipts in FY 1949 (Table 3.3).

Receipts from non-tax sources – for example, revenues from posts and telegraphs, *tapu* fees and supply revenue – increased throughout the period. The substantial increase in the item 'other receipts' in Table 3.3 was due mainly to the sale proceeds from sugar, particularly during the years 1942–6. (Again, one should be cautious here with regard to current and real prices.)

Concluding Remarks

Two concluding remarks may be added about the revenue system in Iraq during the years 1932–50. First, it was dominated by indirect taxes (customs and excises, agricultural taxes, stamp duties, etc.): in FY 1932, 73% of total ordinary receipts came from this category of taxes, 72.5% in 1939, 57.7% in 1945, and 68.4% in 1949 (Table 3.3). The decrease in importance of indirect taxes during the war years was due, as explained before, to the shrinkage of imports. Second, throughout the period many suggestions were put to the Iraqi government for altering its revenue system, mainly by expanding direct taxes (income taxes, property taxes), but although the government recognized the merit of these suggestions, it was inhibited both administratively and, more importantly, politically from implementing them.[40] Thus, Iraq's taxation system was a regressive one, and did not contribute to a reduction of the immense gap between the small minority of rich Iraqis and the large majority of poor ones.

Public Debt and Loans

As we have seen in Chapter 2, the questions of raising loans abroad, issuing internal loans and receiving advances from the oil companies all had political and economic implications in Iraq. The first two of these questions will be examined here; that of receiving advances from the oil companies will be left to Chapter 6.

Ottoman Public Debt

With the dismemberment of the Ottoman empire and the division of its public debt among the detached territories, Iraq's share was put at 7 million Turkish pounds, plus about 2.5 million Turkish pounds for accumulated interest and amortization charges. In 1928, in a special redemption operation, the Iraqi government bought (at current market prices and through agents) Ottoman debt securities to the value of £1.2 million. This left outstanding a sum of £383,000, which was paid off in seven instalments;[41] as early as FY 1934, no provision for public debt was necessary (Table 3.2).

Foreign Loans

Having rid themselves of the Ottoman debt burden, for some years thereafter the Iraqis were not eager to incur new debts. When Iraq's minister of finance, Yasin al-Hashimi, declared in London in 1933 that financial assistance was easily obtained on the London market, there was outrage in Baghdad. The press launched a campaign demanding that the government refrain from raising loans abroad since that would lead to foreign interference in Iraq's financial and economic affairs. The American minister in Baghdad summed up the situation by saying: 'These editorials are indicative of the public's antipathy to a foreign loan, particularly to a loan raised in London at a time when public opinion insists upon the Government becoming still further divorced from compacts with Great Britain.'[42]

In spite of the urgent need for money to finance development plans, the Iraqi government knew that raising a loan in London would give the British important leverage in any political dealings between the two countries. The British themselves were also alert to that possibility. Commenting on the political disagreements between Iraq and Britain in 1933, Hull of the Foreign Office wrote that threatening to withhold credit facilities which Iraq needed for development works might bring Iraqi politicians 'to a more satisfactory frame of mind, and [contribute to reaching] agreement on some at least of the outstanding issues'.[43] Rendel, also of the Foreign Office, agreed that 'probably the only lever we possess is that of financial facilities'.[44]

As we saw in Chapter 2, there were two opposing schools of thought in Iraqi government circles, one arguing for the acceleration of development with the help of foreign loans and the other insisting on restricting development programmes to the money derived annually from oil royalties. The desirability of foreign loans was mooted as early as 1930 by E. Hilton Young in his report to the Iraqi prime minister on loan policy. Young rejected Iraq's reluctance to incur debts for political reasons because such reluctance was based 'upon the experience of conditions in the past which have ceased'.[45] His recommendation was straightforward: 'that it should be the policy of the Government to undertake approved productive works of development out of loan funds'.[46] By this he meant foreign loans because 'it is not possible at the present time to raise internal loans for the amount needed, or perhaps indeed, for any amount at all'.[47]

Towards the end of 1936 this debate was renewed. The government which came to power in October 1936 wanted to launch an ambitious plan of development (mainly a railway extension scheme) and began exploring the London market. The Iraqis knew that the British were anxious about foreign competition in Iraq, and that this concern could be exploited. The Iraqi prime minister informed the British that the French and Germans were tempting him to borrow from their respective countries,[48] upon which the Foreign Office immediately cabled its representative in Baghdad emphasizing the 'desirability of making every effort to meet French and German competition'.[49] Soon after that, tentative negotiations were opened with Baring Brothers and Co. in London, continuing in 1937 with the approval and encouragement of the British government.

By April general agreement was reached for a loan of £3 million at 4%, to be issued in instalments and secured on the oil royalties received from IPC.[50] Correspondence between Baring and Iraq's Ministry of Finance proceeded so satisfactorily that by June 1937 all important points were settled; a 4% loan to be issued at 97½ and purchasable by Baring's at 94¼ was to be announced shortly thereafter. At the last moment, however, serious difficulty arose over the manner in which the royalties should be assigned.[51] IPC indicated that they could not accept a letter which it had been proposed that the Iraqi government should write, instructing them to pay Baring each year from the royalties due to the Iraqi government the sum required for the interest and redemption charges of the loan.

The Iraqis were very upset by IPC's decision. They suspected that it was a manoeuvre to force the Iraqi government to give the company a concession for south Iraq.[52] The Foreign Office, meanwhile, began to argue that Iraq's proposal that IPC become responsible for paying royalties direct to representatives of bondholders, regardless of any possible political changes in Iraq or subsequent instructions to the contrary by a future government, was in fact dangerous.[53] The Foreign Office also asked its representative in Iraq to do everything possible in order to prevent the Iraqi government from penalizing IPC.[54]

It became obvious that the loan negotiations had proceeded on a basis of complete misunderstanding, but no one was prepared to take responsibility for this development. Sir L. Oliphant of the Foreign Office wrote privately to Ambassador Kerr that 'both you and the Iraqis must really put out of your minds any illegal action by the IPC'.[55] (By 'illegal action', Oliphant was referring to the suggestion that IPC should pay royalties, or commit itself to paying royalties, to Baring rather than to the Iraqi government.) The ambassador replied that when Iraq's prime minister had raised the question of arrangements for the security of the loans, he had not understood that IPC was being asked to act illegally.[56]

Urgent presentations were made by Iraq to Britain for assistance in finding a solution to the problem. The British government, aware that 'the political consequences might be disastrous if the Loan were not obtained', pressed Baring to issue the loan without delay.[57] On 20 July, Baring offered to issue bonds immediately for only £1 million and at 4½%, which they would themselves buy at 87½ and issue at 93.[58] At its meeting of 21 July the British cabinet discussed this subject and, fearing that 'further postponement could not be made without bringing about the fall of the Iraqi government', decided to approve in principle the issue of the loan.[59] The Iraqi government was given only three days in which to decide whether to accept or reject the offer. 'Their heavy commitments really left them little choice and they accepted, though protesting bitterly against the unfavourable terms offered.'[60]

In the end, market conditions in the City improved slightly, and Baring were able to put the bonds on the market at 94 and to increase their price to the Iraqi government to 90½, the interest remaining at 4½%.[61] The difficulty with IPC was overcome by a clause in the general agreement which provided that the Iraqi government should inform the company that the bonds had been secured by a first charge on the royalties payable to the government, but that no acknowledgement was required of the company.[62]

This experience of borrowing from Britain left the Iraqi government deeply disappointed, and any idea of raising the remaining £2 million of the loan of £3 million originally contemplated was at once dropped; in any case, because of internal problems, the Iraqi government had to resign in August of that year.[63] As Table 3.5 shows, by 1943 Iraq had exercised its right to redeem the loan totally, although the original date of redemption was not until 1952.

In 1938 the acceleration of the public works programme and the expansion of the army created serious financial difficulties.[64] Despite the experience of the 1937 loan, the Iraqi government again turned to IPC and the British government for help. In May 1939 an agreement was reached with the oil companies which provided for an advance against future oil royalties of £3 million over three years without interest.[65] (As Table 3.5 shows, the net advances from the oil companies reached £4.1 million in 1950.) In addition to this advance from the oil companies, another series of negotiations between Iraq and Britain got underway in April 1939. Once again,

TABLE 3.5 Iraq's Public Debt Outstanding on 1 January 1950 (ID million)

	Amount	Repayment	Interest	Redemption
Foreign loans				
1937	1.000		4½%	Planned: 1952
1938		0.038		
1939		0.095		
1940		0.095		
1941		0.095		
1942		0.095		
1943		0.582		Totally redeemed in 1943
	1.000	1.000		
1939	Credit opened: 3.7		4%	From July 1941: ID 200,000 twice yearly
1944	Credit used: 0.7			
1945		0.7		Totally redeemed in 1945
	0.7	0.7		

Total debit: 0

Advances from oil companies (against royalties)				
1939	1.000		0%	To be repaid in annual instalments not exceeding 20% of Iraqi government's revenue from oil
1940	1.000			
1941	1.000			
1943	1.000			
1945	0.500			
1946		0.116		
1947		0.144		
1948		0.127		
	4.500	0.387		
Total debt: 4.113				
Internal loans[a]				
1944[b]	1.000	1.000 (1947)	3%	Maturity: 3 years
1944[b]	1.000		4%[c]	20
1947	1.000		3%	5
1948	1.000		3½%	10
1948	3.000		4%	20
	7.000	1.000		
Total debt: 6.000				

Sources: FO 371/40053, E 3370/79/93; FO 371/68461, E 6110/112/93. Iversen, *Monetary Policy in Iraq*, p. 67 UN, *Iraq*, p. 29.

[a]Repayable in full on the date of maturity.

[b]Sold only in January 1945.

[c]Two per cent interest and 2% prizes.

anxiety about foreign competition played an important role in British decision-making. With the increasing international tension that year, the Foreign Office recommended that the Iraqi request for assistance in the purchase of armaments be dealt with as sympathetically as possible.[66] This recommendation came as a result of news reaching the British Embassy in Baghdad that the Germans were offering to supply on extended terms more munitions than what was considered essential for Iraq's defence.[67]

Apart from foreign competition, there was an additional consideration making the British more amenable to giving Iraq financial aid. This was the Palestine question. In a letter to the Export Credits Guarantee Department (ECGD), encouraging it to be more receptive to Iraq's demand, Britain's secretary of state for foreign affairs, Lord Halifax wrote:

> His Majesty's Government are at present making serious efforts, partly at any rate because of the international situation, to satisfy the Arab States as to the policy to be adopted in Palestine. It would be paradoxical if His Majesty's Government were to fail to gain the full benefit of these efforts by not doing everything in their power to meet these States in other directions.[68]

In June 1939 the British were ready to offer substantial credits for military and quasi-military purposes, but the Iraqis were not entirely satisfied with the rate of interest suggested by ECGD. Lord Halifax urged the chancellor of the Exchequer to agree to give Iraq non-military credits as well,[69] while the British ambassador in Baghdad was also pressing the Foreign Office to hasten the granting of credits to Iraq.[70]

In November 1939 it was proposed to conclude an intergovernment agreement with Iraq in lieu of an agreement with ECGD. The reason for this change was that, under the international conditions then prevailing, the British government was prepared not to insist on an elaborate procedure of guaranteed bond issue.[71] Thus, on 1 December 1939 an agreement between the two countries was signed, according to which the British government undertook to advance by way of a loan the sum of £3,710,000 for the purchase of defence materials (£3,250,000) and the development and maintenance of the Iraqi State Railways (£460,000). Repayment of the principal and interest (at 4%) was to be in instalments of £200,000 twice yearly, starting from July 1941.[72]

The British government very much wanted to keep this agreement secret:

> it would undoubtedly put us [the British] in an awkward position towards

the other foreign countries to whom we have given credits at 5% if the rate of interest charged to the Iraqis [4%] became known. Nor do we wish it to be generally realised at this stage that it is possible for us to give credits without an issue of bonds.[73]

It was not an easy decision for the Foreign Office to make:

For other reasons we should, of course, like to make some play with the generosity of our terms. But, although it is rather ironical that when we have for once been able to do something handsome by the Iraqis we cannot make public use of the fact, we have had to resign ourselves to this as the lesser evil.[74]

Iraq's minister of finance decided it was not necessary to submit the Credits Agreement to Parliament. He made only indirect reference to it by telling Parliament that the capital works programme was to be financed from, *inter alia*, 'credits which he hoped to secure very shortly from His Majesty's Government'.[75]

It took another four months for the detailed arrangements of the agreement to be settled.[76] In April 1940 the Iraqi government published 'The Law for the Purchase of Materials against the Issue of Bonds', which authorized the minister of finance to purchase war stores and munitions to the sum of ID3,250,000, and to purchase stores for the purpose of completing the Baiji-Tel Kotchek railway line up to a total value of ID560,000. (It seems the government had decided to add ID100,000 from its own budget to the ID460,000 allocated to the railways in the agreement.) There was no mention in the new law of the Anglo-Iraqi Credits Agreement.[77]

Owing to supply difficulties after the outbreak of war, only a small proportion of the British credit was utilized. Nevertheless, when repayment came due in July 1941, the Iraqi government, finding itself in financial difficulties, deferred payment of the credit used, though it commenced payment of interest and continued to pay interest regularly.[78]

By 1944 the Iraqis were found by the British Treasury to be using most of the credit for military supplies of a purely maintenance nature (probably mainly because the British were in no position, in the years 1940–4, to supply Iraq with war stores and munitions), while requesting permission to apply the remainder to their capital works programme, reduction of the rate of interest and revision of the terms of repayment. At this stage the British decided that all future supplies of military stores should be paid for in cash, and not charged against the credit.[79] They informed the Iraqis that credit loans could not be used for post-war development in the case of countries, like Iraq, which accumulated large sterling balances during the war. The British also suggested that since Iraq could no longer derive much benefit from the credit, the capital utilized should be repaid.[80]

Eventually, Iraq agreed to wind up the credit account by payment of a lump sum of £708,426 against capital used.[81] A letter from ECGD three months later stated that all the advances had been repaid with interest.[82]

This episode of Iraq's second loan from Britain shows that the British were prepared to come to Iraq's aid if their own political or economic interests were in jeopardy. While they had no such motive in 1937 (except perhaps the fear of foreign competition), the threat to their interests at the end of 1939 was imminent indeed.

World War II ended and Britain was now a weaker country. As mentioned in Chapter 2, there was an urgent need in Iraq after the war for development plans, and consequently the need for financial aid re-emerged towards the end of 1947 – a time when the British could not help even if they wanted to. As a note by the Foreign Office on British economic policy in the Middle East stated:

> In the Middle East, as elsewhere, it is no longer possible for us in general to grant loans to foreign countries ... Since, however, the whole area is of political, strategic and economic importance to the United Kingdom we must endeavour to secure that where we ourselves are unable to provide assistance, it is supplied by countries or institutions whose basic interests are broadly the same as ours.[83]

The most important such country was the United States, and the most important such institution was the International Bank for Reconstruction and Development (IBRD). However the Iraqis, at that time, had no wish for American assistance because of the US role in Palestine.[84] The British themselves preferred that Iraq borrow from IBRD rather than from the Americans, since this was the lesser evil for them: 'Every effort must therefore be made to persuade the Iraqi Government to turn to the International Bank in order to safeguard the interests of our contractors and manufacturers [from American competition].'[85]

The Foreign Office began persuading the Iraqis that IBRD was not an American concern but rather truly international, and there was therefore no political reason to prevent their turning to this institution.[86] Furthermore, Britain informed Iraq officially that it would support any application to IBRD for financial help, and would use its influence with the United States to gain that country's approval for Iraq's request.[87]

Conscious that the Iraqis would not ask for a US loan because of political circumstances in the area, the State Department began in 1948 to encourage Iraq to approach IBRD and to see that institution as a logical source of financial assistance.[88] Negotiations between Iraq and IBRD started in 1949, and in July 1950 an agreement was signed according to which Iraq was to receive $12.8 million.[89]

Internal Loans

The idea of floating domestic loans in Iraq originated in late 1942, when the British government and its organizations in the area (e.g. MESC) were trying to decrease Iraq's inflation rate. But while the concept of floating loans to reduce the population's purchasing power was raised, for administrative and political reasons it was never implemented.[90]

The idea re-emerged when the problem of currency expansion became acute,[91] at which point the Iraqis, with British encouragement, began to examine it seriously. The Foreign Office saw the floating of such loans as 'an immediate anti-inflationary measure and as a preparation for reasonable post-war development'.[92]

In June 1944 a law was published authorizing the minister of finance to make two loans from the public of ID1 million each.[93] Issued only in January 1945, the first was a three-year loan at 3% interest, while the second was a twenty-year loan carrying 4% interest (2% prizes and 2% interest).[94] Public response to the issuing of the loans was more than enthusiastic; the bonds were sold out in a short time.[95]

This was definitely a new phenomenon in Iraq's economic history. It showed that the government could use such a method not merely to meet the needs of the treasury, but also in order to influence economic activity in general. Nevertheless, no one had great expectations of these loans. Immediately after they were issued, the British currency officer, C.E. Loombe, wrote that 'bonds amounting to 2 millions would have little result from the deflationary aspect'. Loombe rightly felt that 'the most important role of the two loans would be in the nature of educating the public and preparing the way for future issues'.[96]

Frequent political changes made it impossible to develop this new policy. No further loans were issued until October 1947, when a loan of ID1 million bearing interest at 3% for a period of five years was sold to the public. But unlike the earlier issues, this one was not meant as an anti-inflationary measure but rather as a source of finance for government-funded development projects. Preference in the sale of the 1947 bonds was given to holders of the 3% loan of 1944, which matured in December 1947.[97]

The 1947 loan was not received as favourably as the 1944 loan had been, for a number of reasons: the public was disappointed at the rate of interest, and the issue was somewhat ill-timed in that it coincided with a succession of Jewish holidays which delayed its sale, and created the impression that it was not worthwhile (most of the bankers in Iraq at the time were Jews).[98] But the main reason was probably that the domestic money market, which had absorbed the earlier issues, had quickly reached its saturation point.

Two further loans were issued in 1948, one for ID1 million bearing interest at 3½% for a period of ten years, the other a twenty-year loan for ID3 million carrying an interest of 4%.[99] But public interest in such loans had by this time waned, and the bonds were taken up only slowly.[100]

Iraq's experience with domestic loans was short-lived. They did not help decrease inflation to any substantial degree, nor did they create the required finances for development plans. But they proved to be an educational experiment for both the government and the public, paving the way for a later attempt at the idea in the 1950s.

To sum up this aspect of Iraqi finance, it may be said that due to a conservative financial policy the public debt in the 1930s and 1940s remained small and did not constitute a heavy burden on the budget. (As Table 3.5 indicates, in 1950 Iraq's total foreign debt – entirely from oil company advances – was ID4,113,000, and its total domestic debt was ID6,000,000.)

The 1948 Financial Crisis: A Case Study of Crisis Management in Iraq

During the period 1932–50, Iraq's economy faced a number of severe financial crises, of which the 1948 crisis was the most serious. We will examine how such a crisis developed, how the Iraqi government handled it, and what British policy was towards such crises.

Salih Jabr's government (29 March 1947 to 27 January 1948) faced many serious difficulties, among them a deterioration of the administration. The political arena was also in tumult, partially as a result of the signing in January 1948 of the Portsmouth Treaty (see Ch. 1). Riots erupted in Baghdad in protest, and at the end of January Salih Jabr resigned, later fleeing to Trans-Jordan. To the tension in Iraqi-British relations was added the complicated issue of Palestine, which preoccupied the Iraqis during this period.

These developments also detracted from the stability of Iraq's finances and administration. Indeed, the worsening financial situation was the most pressing difficulty: receipts were not increasing in proportion to the increase in expenditures; there was a shortage of hard currency; the harvest was so far below average that it was necessary to consider importing grain; and hoarding and unplanned exporting had by the later months of 1947 already led to a serious deficiency in food stocks.[101]

Thus, the fall of Jabr's government and the development of the 1948 crisis were due not so much to political as to economic factors. These included the bad harvest and the consequent deterioration in the quality and supply of bread;[102] the reduction in tax income from agricultural produce due to the poor harvest, and the adamant refusal of the land-owning members of Parliament to consider any taxation that would seriously affect their own incomes; contributions to the Arab Fund for Palestine totalling ID1 million (the subsequent war in Palestine was a further burden on the budget);[103] a substantial increase in the cost of secret service and diplomatic missions abroad; and finally, a decrease in customs revenue (despite increased imports) which led the government to order an investigation of administrative malpractice in the Customs and Excises Department.[104]

By April 1948 the financial crisis was so aggravated that Iraq's prime minister (Mohammad as-Sadr) informed the British ambassador Sir Henry Mack that his government would not be able to pay the salaries of officials, including the police, at the end of that month.[105]

From that point on, the Iraqi government tried to handle the crisis in the easiest way possible: by borrowing from every available source, one of the main sources being, of course, the British government. Half a million dinars had already been borrowed from the Basra Port Directorate.[106]

The food shortage and high prices led to almost daily industrial strikes and demonstrations in the streets of Baghdad and other big cities.[107] The main themes of the demonstrators' slogans were 'bread' and 'Palestine'.[108] The flooding of the Tigris and the Euphrates towards the end of April further worsened the situation.[109]

In May the British position *vis à vis* the crisis in Iraq was articulated in a telegram to the British ambassador in Baghdad:

> We have very carefully considered all your telegrams on the financial crisis in Iraq and we remain unconvinced that it is more than a temporary shortage of cash due to lack of confidence in the administration ... It is not a situation which could properly be dealt with by an external loan ... His

Majesty's Government is in any case in no position at present to give foreign loans ...[110]

Although it was clear that the British had no intention of granting Iraq a loan at that point, the Foreign Office nevertheless began to consider what conditions it might try to impose on the Iraqis should financial aid eventually be extended. These conditions were stated in a Foreign Office meeting as a possible opening position in any negotiations which might take place between the two sides: they would expect the Iraqis to

(i) accept a British Financial Adviser [the Iraqi government had been without a British financial adviser for a year, and the Foreign Office had emphasized time and again that this was an unbearable situation];
(ii) undertake certain administrative reforms and tighten up financial control;
(iii) grant concessions to the Oil Companies.[111]

Meanwhile Iraq's political and financial situation continued to deteriorate. The Palestine war began and martial law was declared in Iraq on 15 May.[112] British reports went on describing the financial situation as desperate.[113] There was no change, however, in the Iraqis' attempts to deal with the crisis: in August the minister of finance asked the British for an immediate loan of ID 3 million to enable Iraq to buy wheat and barley.[114]

As a result of these developments, the Foreign Office began to change its attitude. In a minute, a senior Foreign Office official recommended a straight loan from government to government.[115] The new position taken by the Foreign Office was elaborated in a telegram to Baghdad:

There is clearly no financial case to be made; all we can do is to justify it [the loan] on purely political grounds ... A breakdown of the bread supplies in the principal towns of Iraq might well, as nearly happened earlier this year, lead to complete administrative collapse and the emergence of a regime fundamentally hostile to us.[116]

The Foreign Office now decided to approach the Treasury for a loan to Iraq for certain supplies. The problem was complicated, however, by the fact that the Iraqis were simultaneously asking permission to float a ID 5 million loan in London for their railways.[117] (These requests were being made concurrently with the tough negotiations between the two governments over hard currency agreements.)

In September the Iraqi government began negotiating with the Egyptian government for a loan of ID 3 million to undertake the

Wadi Tharthar flood control scheme. At one point the Iraqis were so sure of their success that they even informed the British that Egypt had agreed to lend them this sum,[118] but the loan in fact never materialized; in fact, the matter of a loan from Egypt was dropped totally and not mentioned in any subsequent correspondence.

In October London decided to refuse to float the railways loan, the main reason given being that 'there is a long queue of colonies waiting to do the same and we could not possibly let Iraq in ahead of them'.[119] At the same time, the Treasury informed the Foreign Office that it could not agree to a direct loan to Iraq to meet its temporary internal shortage, because that would be a precedent which might invite similar requests from other countries.[120]

The Iraqi government's reaction to these two refusals was unequivocal: the minister of finance threatened that he would resign, that no salaries would be paid to officials the following month, that all orders outside Iraq would be cancelled, that all development works would be stopped, and so on.[121]

At this point, the Foreign Office decided to press the oil companies to make advance payments to Iraq. Bevin thought 'it would be politically a very bad thing if Iraq disintegrated', and everything should therefore be done to help its government.[122] Negotiations with the oil companies had begun, however, even before the Foreign Office's decision. IPC expressed its readiness to advance ID 1 million on account of three separate payments it was due to make to the Iraqi government on 1 January 1949. The Anglo-Iranian Oil Company was approached to make an advance of ID 120,000, but was very reluctant to do so.[123] At the same time, the British began to press the Iraqis to resume pumping of their oil through the pipeline to Haifa, which had been halted after the outbreak of war in Palestine, in return for any advance the oil companies might make.[124]

At the end of October, Iraq's minister of finance, 'Ali Mumtaz, resigned because of the government's financial difficulties and his own inability to solve them.[125] But after the cabinet had decided to set up a committee to consider the financial situation and the report he had attached to his letter of resignation, the prime minister, Muzahim al-Pachachi, convinced him to remain at his post.[126] In analysing the problem and suggesting remedies, Mumtaz recommended cutting expenditures, obtaining ID 6 million in loans (without suggesting how or where), increasing taxes, and creating a government monopoly for the import of cars, agricultural machinery, tea and sugar.[127] But, as al-Pachachi told the British ambassador, 'the report was excellent but it would be impossible to put its recommendations into force in time to relieve the present situation'.[128]

Meanwhile, the Iraqi government received ID 1.5 million from the Currency Board, which presumably enabled it to meet its obligations for a short period.[129] Moreover, negotiations with the oil companies continued (the companies making any loan conditional on the reopening of the Haifa pipeline),[130] while the three British banks operating in Iraq were approached for a loan of ID 750,000.[131]

Discussions continued on the seriousness of the situation, conditions for loans, and so on, but talk alone could not ameliorate Iraq's position. In January 1949 the Foreign Office again decided to ask IPC to lend Iraq ID 5 million, and presented Baghdad with conditions (even before receiving IPC's agreement) which included the appointment of a British deputy-governor or other high official to the National Bank, and of British customs collectors at Baghdad and Basra; the constitution of a politically independent Development Board with a British secretary; introduction of measures to improve the administration of existing legislation, and the like.[132] However, IPC perceived the situation in Iraq differently, and in the event no loan was extended.[133]

The financial situation in Iraq finally began looking up in 1949 – not because of British help but due to a good harvest, the cutting of expenditures, an increase in oil royalties, and relative improvement in the revenue system. By 1950 the government was able to announce that the bad times were over, thanks to substantial rises in oil royalties.[134]

The 1948 events show how easily a crisis in Iraq in the pre-oil period could begin as a result of a bad harvest (even if for a single season) or extra unexpected expenditures (such as the Palestine war).

Iraq's handling of the crisis – trying to borrow from every possible source – was too simplistic. However, because governments in Iraq, in an attempt to ensure their own longevity, wanted to solve problems in an easy fashion without antagonizing any political groupings, they were not prepared to introduce tax or administrative reforms.

The British attitude towards the crisis was dictated, as usual, by their own economic and political interests in Iraq. While it is true that the British government was itself facing hard times in 1948, it could have nevertheless, had it wanted to, really pressed the oil companies or the British banks to grant Iraq the loans it needed. Instead, the British tried to exploit the crisis to improve their own position in the country, and only when matters became very severe indeed (and might therefore negatively affect their interests) did they begin seriously to consider ways of helping Iraq.

CURRENCY AND BANKING

Before embarking on a discussion of currency and banking in Iraq in the period under review, it is perhaps necessary to say something about the role of money in Iraq. A considerable segment of the Iraqi population was completely outside the institutionalized money economy. Hoarding – especially of bank notes, and sometimes of gold – was relatively widespread as a form of saving. The main reason for this was unfamiliarity with and distrust of other, more profitable ways of utilizing money and, as Iversen put it:

> With only about 45 bank branches scattered over the country people would often have to travel a long distance to deposit their savings with them, and many people may not even have heard of the existence of banks, or if they have, they may fear to get their money back if they part with it against a mere receipt or an entry in a book.[135]

The factor of distrust must be emphasized. The population's distrust of central government pre-dated independence, hailing back to the Ottoman Empire, when the administration's main target was collecting as much money as possible from the population.

The fact that, for the majority of Iraqis, incomes were too low to permit saving should also be taken into consideration. Those who could save, such as the middle class (albeit on a small scale) and the wealthy, chose to invest in goods or property, or simply to hoard their money.

Investment in stocks and shares was unknown. After 1941, however, certain groups began to invest in British government and other securities, taking particular interest in industrial shares, mainly of oil and rubber companies. In 1944 these investments reached £256,111 in British government securities, and £560,288 in British and other sterling area industrial shares.[136] Relatively speaking, these were high sums, especially if compared with saving deposits in post offices (about ID 450,000) and banks (about ID 2.6 million) at the time (Table 3.6). (Saving in post office accounts was generally on a more limited scale, as will be seen below.) This interest in foreign investment was mainly due to the encouragement given by the banks in Iraq, which co-operated with the British authorities in providing information to potential investors; a London Stock Exchange price list was even published in the local press from time to time.[137]

TABLE 3.6 Bank and Post Office Deposits, 1936-1950 (ID thousand)

End of year (December)	Bank deposits				Post Office deposits
	Fixed deposits	Current deposits	Saving deposits	Total	
1936	688	1,205	421	2,314	24
1937	709	1,275	438	2,422	50
1938	615	1,231	387	2,233	67
1939	522	1,182	314	2,018	66
1940	309	1,689	180	2,178	64
1941	274	2,983	254	3,511	45
1942	423	6,411	566	7,400	91
1943	1,015	12,759	1,694	15,468	215
1944	2,458	15,493	2,605	20,556	451
1945	3,764	13,276	3,011	20,051	791
1946	3,415	13,614	2,966	19,995	926
1947	2,799	12,543	2,719	18,061	954
1948	1,421	12,254	2,303	15,977	822
1949	1,322	12,272	2,390	15,984	866
1950	795	12,994	1,980	15,769	903

Sources: For 1936-9: Statistical Abstract 1939 p. 173, 174. For 1940-3: 'Banking in Iraq', paper A5. Middle East Financial Conference FO 371/40053, E 3383/79/93; Statistical Abstract 1944 and 1945, p. 225. For 1944-6: Statistical Abstract 1946 (Baghdad, 1948), p. 193; Statistical Abstract 1948, p. 264. For 1947-1950: Statistical Abstract 1950, p. 281, 318.

Note: To 1945, banks included Eastern Bank, Ottoman Bank, Imperial Bank of Iran and Zelkha House; from 1946, also Agricultural, Rafidain and Arab Banks.

The interest in the London Stock Exchange was in great contrast to the failure of Iraq's own stock exchange. Created in 1936 to deal with the trade of commodities, but not with bonds and shares, it began to register daily prices of commodities on 1 July 1937. However, all export and import transactions continued to take place outside this institution, in spite of the fact that the stock exchange law clearly stated that trade in principal commodities must occur within the framework of the exchange.[138] The acting controller of the exchange attributed its failure to the big merchants' refusal to co-operate with it. Since the law stipulated registration of commodity prices in the stock exchange centre (i.e. Baghdad), big merchants began to conduct their commercial dealings outside Baghdad, in nearby provinces like Hilla, in order to evade exchange supervision. Thus, while the initial intention had been that the exchange would establish itself firmly in Baghdad and then open branches in other provinces, the merchants' opposition made this impossible.[139]

A year later, the Ministry of Finance, in consultation with the chamber of commerce, reached the conclusion that creation of the stock exchange had been premature, and that financial and trade conditions would have to change before such an institution could succeed. In May 1938 a law abolishing the stock exchange and transferring its duties to the chamber of commerce was put into effect.[140]

Raising capital in Iraq, particularly for long-term periods, was indeed difficult. Commercial (foreign) banks were engaged in financing foreign trade, while local bankers undertook only short-term advances against property and bullion. The government therefore had to intervene by establishing banks which would extend long-term advances, such as the Agricultural and Industrial Bank and the *Iqari* Bank, as will be seen in the section on banking.

The Currency Board and the National Bank

When the British captured Iraq from the Turks during World War I they introduced the Indian rupee, but with the establishment of the new State of Iraq in 1921 there were many efforts by the nationalists to replace the rupee with a national currency. These efforts culminated in the passing of the Iraqi Currency Law in 1931,[141] which, due to international monetary conditions, went into effect only on 1 April 1932.[142] It provided for a gold value of the Iraqi dinar equal to that of the pound sterling (by the time the law was put into effect, however, the dinar's gold parity was dropped because Britain had abandoned the gold standard at the end of 1931); guaranteed convertibility of the dinar into sterling at the rate of one to one (the implications of this are discussed in Ch. 5); and required the investment of the currency cover in gold and/or foreign exchange and securities of (or guaranteed by) states whose currencies were convertible into gold or sterling.[143]

The Iraqi currency was controlled by a Currency Board sitting in London, the majority of whose members were British (see Ch. 2). Throughout the period under study, the Iraqis made many efforts to transfer the board to Baghdad, but in vain. Iraqi feelings on this subject were well expressed by Iraq's accountant-general, Ibrahim al-Kabir, who regarded it 'as derogatory to the status of Iraq as an independent sovereign state that the control of its currency should be in the hands of an exotic body functioning elsewhere than in the capital of the country'.[144]

The Currency Board was formally a government agency subject to the laws and regulations of Iraq. It was, however, given authority to act independently in a number of matters. The board's duties fell into four categories from the standpoint of government control:

1. Duties carried out in *consultation* with the government, such as the supply and control of currency, and arrangements for minting coins and printing notes (Article 16*a* and *b*).
2. Duties requiring the *approval* of the government, such as appointment of currency officers and determination of the rates charged for transfers between Iraq and London (Articles 15, 17 and 18).
3. Duties requiring Government *supervision*, mainly in administrative matters (Articles 20 and 21).
4. Actions taken *independently* by the Board:
   (*a*) minting of certain coins (Article 5);
   (*b*) appointment of the currency agent in Iraq (the Eastern Bank was appointed) (Article 15);
   (*c*) issuing, reissuing, cancelling and destroying unfit notes (Article 16*c*);
   (*d*) managing the revenues to and expenditures from the Currency Reserve Fund, including the contributions made to the Iraqi government (Article 16*f*);
   (*e*) appointing officers and increasing expenditure as might be necessary for the performance of its duties (Article 23).[145]

The most important independent duty of the board was 'to invest its assets in securities ... etc.'[146] In this realm, the board had absolute authority to select both short and long-term securities for investment. Its choice of securities proved, throughout the period, to be sound and profitable.[147]

As noted above, contributions to the Iraqi government were made at the board's discretion. The first such contribution (ID 15,000) was made in FY 1934 as a result of the improvement in the board's financial position.[148] From Table 3.3 it can be seen that the total contribution by the Currency Board during the period under study was ID 2,286,000.

The amount of currency in circulation, which of course was the most important aspect of currency management, was determined by neither the government nor the board, but rather by Iraq's foreign exchange reserves. As Table 3.7 shows, the general trend was that when these reserves increased (usually as a result of a favourable

TABLE 3.7 Iraqi Currency Circulation and Reserves, FY 1933-FY 1950

FY to 31 March	Circulation of notes and coins (ID)	Reserves (£ sterling)
1933	2,248,185	2,191,446
1934	3,084,365	3,087,926
1935	3,604,321	3,683,258
1936	3,760,313	3,901,878
1937	4,868,312	4,974,060
1938	4,838,301	5,011,315
1939	4,773,296	4,820,832
1940	6,183,293	6,462,113
1941	6,623,291	7,052,989
1942	12,760,789	13,183,517
1943	26,290,808	26,677,712
1944	38,965,831	39,920,107
1945	41,905,622	44,093,779
1946	41,505,588	44,727,743
1947	39,145,722	43,754,234
1948	34,899,272	39,326,125
1949	34,526,390	34,655,458
1950	40,165,079	40,165,078

Sources: FY 1933-FY 1936: Iraq, Principal Bureau of Statistics, Statistical Abstract 1927/28-1937/38 (Baghdad, 1939), p. 145. FY 1937-FY 1945: Statistical Abstract 1944 & 1945, p. 226. FY 1946-FY 1950: Statistical Abstract 1950, p. 282.

balance of trade, a foreign loan, Allied army expenditure, etc.), it caused an increase of currency in circulation, while a decline in the reserves caused a contraction of currency. For instance, the prodigious expansion of currency between 1942 and 1943 (by about 117%) was attributed by the acting currency officer to

> Allied Army expenditure accompanied by the high cost of living and a tendency to hoard currency on the part of the public. This excessive latent purchasing power together with the curtailment of import trade resulted in acute speculation in available goods, property, etc., and this no doubt contributed to the accelerated pace of currency expansion ...[149]

It can be said, therefore, that the board's role was a purely passive one. Although other factors, such as withdrawal of bank deposits or higher prices, affected currency in circulation, the fact remained that foreign exchange reserves were the main determinant of the volume of currency. As Iversen put it:

There was no scope for a monetary policy aiming at influencing domestic economic activity by varying the volume of money in circulation at the expense of variations in the rate of cover. It was the foreign exchange situation as it presented itself to the Currency Board which solely and mechanically determined the volume of currency in circulation.[150]

The National Bank

Termination of the Currency Board's activities was visualized in the Currency Law of 1931. Article 24 stated that the board was to cease functioning on the formation of a National Bank of Iraq, or any other bank which would have an exclusive right of note issue.[151]

In 1938 it was reported that the Iraqi government would proceed with the idea of establishing a national bank, because of its lack of satisfaction with the policy of the Eastern Bank (which was the currency agent in Iraq) and the refusal of the Ottoman Bank to take over the government's accounts.[152] At the time, the British thought that creation of a central bank was a natural development, and the proper policy was therefore not to try to prevent it but rather to strive to have British elements included within it.[153]

A law was passed in 1939 providing for government participation in the establishment of a national bank.[154] The intention was to create a joint private–governmental institution with the exclusive right of issuing currency in Iraq, in addition to normal commercial transactions. This law was not put into effect, however, because upon reconsideration the government decided to separate currency issue from commercial banking activities. In 1941 the entirely state-owned Rafidain Bank was established to handle the government's accounts, while the task of currency issue was left to a central bank to be established after the war.[155]

Only with the enactment of Laws Nos. 42 and 43 in 1947 were the Currency Board's activities officially terminated. These two laws authorized the government to establish a national bank and entrust it with the duties and powers previously given to the board.[156] However, the actual transfer did not take place until 1 July 1949.

During the period under study (i.e. until February 1950), the impact of the National Bank on economic policy in Iraq was non-existent because, *inter alia*, it had no legal power to control commercial banks, and therefore was not able to affect the quantity of money.[157] (Even after that period, in the early 1950s, the National Bank did not fulfil all its functions.)

In summing up this section, it may be said that neither the Currency Board nor the National Bank determined money supply in Iraq. It was rather three other factors which had this effect during the period 1932–50: the government's cash position, the balance of payments, and the credits extended by commercial banks to the private sector.

Banking

Banks in Iraq in the years 1932–50 can be divided into three categories: local, commercial and state-owned.

Local Banks

There were two types of local banks in this category: discount houses and *sarrafs*, which engaged mainly in domestic banking transactions. Both types undertook the acceptance of deposits, the discounting of bills, short-term advances, and advances against property and bullion. Discount houses also acted as intermediaries between businessmen and commercial banks. According to a government publication, there were forty-eight local bankers in Iraq in 1936 (thirty-nine in Baghdad, five in Mosul and four in Basra).[158] The main characteristics of these discount houses were that their structure was that of a one-family operation, occasionally with one or two partners, but never a joint-stock company; their capital was limited and rarely exceeded ID 100,000; they had no branches, except for the Khedhouri Zelkha, which had two branches outside Iraq (in Beirut and Damascus); the bankers generally operated in the spheres of finance and commerce; and some of them were landowners.[159] Such discount houses attracted a considerable amount of business, as they were well known to the local population and did not observe the strict rules and regulations practised by banks.[160]

The structure of the interest rate was usually determined by the bankers among themselves. The law fixed only the maximum rate: until 1935 it was 9%,[161] and in 1936 a law provided that it should not exceed 7%.[162] (In 1939 the interest rate was raised to 9% because of the world financial situation, but this was repealed six weeks later.)[163]

The above description refers only to 'legal' bankers registered with the government; in addition there were a number of *sarrafs* and money lenders working in small towns and villages. Some (mainly those in towns) were professional money lenders, while others were merchants and landowners who saw in lending a form of investment. No figures were kept about them or their loans. It is known, however, that the (illegal) rates of interest they charged on loans and advances ranged between 15% and 50%.[164] Professional money lenders gave credit in return for a promissory note, against bullion and property. Merchant money lenders usually lent money to retail traders or sold goods to shopkeepers in villages and towns, receiving the price of these goods in addition to interest after a period of not more than six months, while land-owning money lenders usually extended credits to their tenants, who did not have private capital.[165]

Local bankers constituted an important factor in raising capital for domestic economic activities, and a limited factor in financing foreign trade. Their role declined substantially in the years 1949–50 due to two main factors: the exodus of Iraqi Jews, who comprised the majority of local bankers (about 85% of discount houses were owned by Jews), and the enactment of the 1950 Law for the Control of Banking.[166] This law imposed a number of requirements on local bankers, and subjected their operations to the supervision and control of the National Bank. The 'illegal' money lenders (i.e. merchants and landowners) were affected only by the first factor, since they themselves had dealings with the registered bankers, but it can be assumed that they eventually resumed their activities after finding new sources of local money. The impact of this category of bankers on money in Iraq in the early 1950s is estimated to have been very limited.[167]

Commercial (Foreign) Banks

The commercial banks were branches of large foreign establishments. Their main activities were financing imports and exports and other foreign exchange transactions. Some of them were also, at one time or another, official bankers for the government or the governing authorities. The three main foreign banks, all of them British, operating in Iraq were:

1. *Ottoman Bank* (up to 1925, the 'Imperial Ottoman Bank'): A branch was opened in Baghdad in 1890; for a long time this was the leading bank not only in Iraq but in the whole Middle East.[168]
2. *Eastern Bank*: A branch was opened in 1912, only to be closed immediately after World War I was declared. However, when British forces were landed in Basra in 1915, the bank opened a branch there;[169] in 1917 a branch was opened in Baghdad and in 1919 another in Mosul. The Eastern Bank became the official bank for the Iraqi government and remained so until 1941.
3. *Imperial Bank of Iran* (later known as 'British Bank of Iran and the Middle East'): A branch was opened in Baghdad in 1918, followed by another in Basra.[170]

Up to 1936 these were the only commercial banks operating in

Iraq. The Agricultural and Industrial Bank was created that year, but as will be shown below, this was a state bank established to serve special sectors.

At the beginning of 1938, the Banco di Roma opened a branch in Baghdad. At the end of that year it was reported to be making little progress and operating at a loss, although it offered $4\frac{1}{2}\%$ interest to depositors as against the 2% then offered by all other banks, and although (according to the British) it used dubious methods to attract clients.[171] The bank was closed in mid-1941 following the imposition of exchange control on 'enemy' funds.[172]

The fact that these banks were branches of foreign banks had considerable influence on economic policy in Iraq. Since the local managers were not expected to enter into new ventures without the approval of their boards of directors abroad, loan policy, liquidity and all other such matters were decided not according to Iraq's interests but rather according to the banks' interests. This meant, in effect, that these banks were more or less independent of the Iraqi government (and later of the National Bank).[173]

The best example illustrating this phenomenon was the law for the control of banking which was put into effect in May 1938,[174] reflecting as it did the growing process of 'Iraqization' of foreign firms and ventures in the country, a process which began immediately after independence and was supported by Iraq's politicians and civil servants. Until that year, neither foreign banks nor local Iraqi bankers were under legal supervision. They were free to vary their credit and reserve policies in any direction they desired. The new law limited the deposits a bank might receive in proportion to its capital; provided that banks had to keep cover reserves against their deposits; prohibited banks from buying real estate, and required them to submit semi-annual balance sheets to the minister of finance; and appointed controllers 'for the purpose of supervising and inspecting the transactions of the Bank so as to ensure that its operations conform to the provisions of this law'.[175]

The British banks did not receive the law with much enthusiasm, especially the provisions for supervision in Article 15. They considered this to constitute interference in their affairs, and began pressing for 'a liberal interpretation of the more onerous provisions of the law'.[176] The Iraqi government allowed one year for compliance, but in fact was in a weak position *vis à vis* the British banks and unable to exert much influence. Besides, the banks were so liquid and financially sound that enactment of the law did not affect them. The law remained, therefore, on paper only.[177]

Even after the National Bank Law was enacted in 1947 and put into effect in 1949, the situation did not change. In his report, Iversen emphasizes that the banks continued to follow policies independent of the National Bank's regulations.[178] Nor did they rely on the National Bank for funds, since their connections were really with the London market, which they regarded as their natural banking centre.

The British banks were an important tool in implementing British policy – economic and political – in Iraq. Thus when the British complained in 1940 that foreign exchange restrictions were not complied with in Iraq,[179] British banks there were instructed by their head offices in London to refuse all applications for dollar exchange,[180] even before the Iraqi government decided to take that step itself.

The banks were also used for political purposes. In April 1941, when an anti-British regime was in power in Iraq, London asked the Eastern Bank to block all the Iraqi government's accounts (which it managed), in order to undermine the regime's internal situation.[181]

Iraq's minister of supply, Mohammad Mahdi Kubbah, relates in his memoirs that when his country was facing a sugar shortage in 1948, the British insisted that it buy from London markets, at high prices. Kubbah refused to do this and asked some Iraqi merchants to find a new source. When the merchants made an agreement with a Polish firm to import sugar at lower prices than those obtaining in London, the British banks refused to open credit for the deal. Kubbah adds that the agreement with Poland was nevertheless implemented when the Arab Bank undertook to open the necessary credit.[182] (The Arab Bank, whose head offices were in Amman, opened a branch in Baghdad in 1945, but its position there was weak because it was small in comparison with the British banks.[183])

Throughout the period under study, the British banks kept close contact with the British Embassy in Baghdad and with the Foreign Office. It was, in fact, quite a normal occurrence for copies of letters from the local bank managers to their headquarters in London to be sent to the Embassy or the Foreign Office.[184]

It is very hard to determine the exact impact of the commercial banks on Iraq's economy, as they published no annual statements. Some insight into banking development, however, can be obtained by studying bank deposits between 1936, the earliest year for which data are available, and 1950. Table 3.6 shows that total bank deposits remained more or less the same during the years 1936–40. The impact of World War II on Iraq's economy became tangible in 1941, and this was reflected in the deposits. With the increase in currency circulation, bank deposits increased more than six-fold between 1941 and 1945. But even in the peak years, like 1945 when currency circulation reached some ID 40 million, bank deposits never exceeded half the amount in circulation (see Tables 3.6 and 3.7). This gap between currency circulation and bank deposits may be explained by the tendency to hoard money notes as a means of saving. Deposits began to decrease from 1946 as the effects of the war started to disappear, which in turn led to a decline in currency circulation.

Saving deposits also increased substantially after the war began, but on the whole they continued to be low relative to total deposits. One reason for the low saving rate was the fact that banking facilities were concentrated in the three main cities – Baghdad, Basra and Mosul – whereas the rest of the country was only scantily supplied with such facilities, making hoarding a more common method of saving. The low interest rates were an additional factor discouraging potential depositors. Interest rates usually ranged from $\frac{1}{4}$% to 2% on the first ID 100–500, and no interest was paid on amounts exceeding ID 500.

Another indicator of a bank's activities and policy, besides deposits, is its consolidated balance. The earliest information of this sort is from February 1950, in the National Bank's first annual report. It shows the banks' most conspicuous characteristic to have been their high degree of liquidity. (No breakdown of the balances for individual banks was given.) In February 1950 the commercial banks held about 22% of their deposits with other banks in Iraq or with the National Bank. Furthermore, almost 30% of their assets consisted of 'deposits and investments abroad'. These may also be considered very liquid. On the other hand, less than 7% was invested in Iraqi government bonds and treasury bills.[185] This illustrates the banks' traditional policy of playing a passive role in affecting money supply, as well as the statement above about the London money market being their main outlet. This high liquidity also explains what was emphasized above about the banks' independence and lack of need to resort to the National Bank for borrowing.

In order to correct the banking situation and increase the control of commercial banks, a special law was promulgated in May 1950 to annul the law of 1938.[186]

State-owned Banks

Besides local and foreign banks, Iraq also had state banks which were established for specific purposes. The first bank created by the Iraqi government was the Post Office Savings Bank. Aware of the importance of savings, especially among low-income groups, the government passed a special law in 1935 establishing this bank.[187] The decision to establish a saving system as part of the Post Office was based on the fact that post offices were scattered around the country in large number, while banks concentrated their activities in big cities.

The law imposed limitations on the amounts of deposits accepted by the bank and the interest rate paid thereon. At first the maximum deposit accepted was only ID 100, exclusive of interest. In 1938, this ceiling was raised to ID 500.[188] The interest rate was fixed at 3% per annum (higher than the $1\frac{1}{4}$% commercial banks were paying at the time), but this was hardly encouraging, especially when savers could get interest ranging from 10% to 20% per annum on the 'free' market.[189]

As Table 3.6 shows, post office deposits increased (slowly) until 1941, when this tendency was reversed. The explanation for the reversal is that with the uncertainty of war, people in small towns preferred to hold on to their cash. (There was no corresponding decline of saving deposits with the commercial banks.) This tendency did not persist long, and in 1944 a substantial increase occurred, continuing steadily until 1947. This was followed by a mild decline which probably reflected the general economic conditions of the country in 1948.

On the whole, post office deposits were relatively low since most of the rural population was unaccustomed to saving and the city dwellers were inclined to place their money in banks rather than post offices, possibly because they knew more about saving plans with banks and trusted them more.[190] However, the number of post-office depositors increased from 2,590 in 1936, to 9,428 in 1939, 18,567 in 1944, and 38,066 in 1949.[191]

In 1936 another state bank was created, the Agricultural and Industrial Bank. The main reason for its establishment was that commercial banks were giving only short-term credit to finance foreign trade transactions. The new bank, which was divided in 1940 into the Agricultural Bank and the Industrial Bank, was supposed to fill this gap in banking activities by providing long-term credit. An analysis of its activities and the extent of its success in accomplishing its purpose will be left to the chapters on agriculture and industry.

The need for a bank controlled by the government had long been felt vital to the 'Iraqization' of foreign firms, and especially in 1940–1 when the role of British banks in serving British interests became so obvious. It having been decided, as explained above, to temporarily drop the idea of a national bank which would issue currency, the new institution was limited to the status of state-owned commercial bank. Thus, in 1941 the Rafidain Bank was opened, designed to operate on purely commercial lines – in other words, to obtain the largest possible profits.[192]

In its first few years, the Rafidain's activities were restricted; its authorized capital was ID 500,000 but the paid-up capital was merely ID 50,000. From 1943 on, the bank's operations expanded; no loss was incurred for the years 1943–50, and new branches were opened in Basra, Mosul, Kirkuk, Hillah and, in 1948, Beirut.[193]

Prior to the establishment of the Rafidain Bank, the government's accounts and other financial transactions were handled by the Eastern Bank. In 1942 government deposits were transferred to the Rafidain where, except for the recession in the financial years 1947–9, they grew steadily.[194] The transfer of government accounts to a local bank was the main object of establishing the Rafidain, since that would reduce Iraq's independence on foreign banks. Even after the National Bank was established in 1949 (and until 1956), the Rafidain continued to handle government accounts and banking facilities. Another way in which the Rafidain served the government was by issuing and administering internal loans.

It is interesting to note that at the end of FY 1949 the Rafidain Bank was holding about 20% of its assets in liquid form,[195] thus following the foreign banks' policy of high liquidity instead of trying to increase its investments in and loans to the domestic market.

The *Iqari* Bank (literally, the 'Estate Bank', or mortgage bank) was established in 1948 with a capital of ID 1 million, to provide owners of dwelling houses with an opportunity to convert high-interest loans secured by mortgages on their properties into government loans bearing more reasonable interest.[196]

The need for a mortgage bank did not become pressing until World War II, when the growth of population and the scarcity of building materials created a severe housing shortage. Rents became exorbitant and the rate of interest on mortgages ranged between 10% and 15% per annum.[197] By FY 1950, the average loan advanced amounted to approximately ID 420. Most of the borrowers were of the middle or upper class.[198]

The preceding discussion has illustrated how Iraq's monetary organization was deficient in many ways. Management and control of the national currency was, for most of the period under study, in foreign hands, and the government was thus unable to affect money supply. Banking facilities were few and unevenly distributed. The structure of interest rates was unintegrated, and financial mobility was lacking. Knowledge about securities was not widespread and raising capital was very difficult, particularly because local and commercial banks extended only short-term advances.

INFLATION AND SUPPLY

The first two parts of this chapter sketched a general picture of Iraq's financial and monetary structure. This last part will deal with two specific problems, inflation and supply, and will examine how the economic mechanism reacted to them.

Causes of Inflation

The outbreak of World War II in September 1939 led, in Iraq's big cities, to a period of financial and commercial panic: credits were restricted, the prices of most commodities rose, food was bought up in large quantities and hoarded, and there was a general disruption of the normal channels of trade due to lack of shipping facilities.[199] The situation, however, soon returned to normal, if only briefly, and the market was well supplied with imported goods, mainly from the United States and Japan, which offset the cessation of imports from Germany and the fall in supplies from the United Kingdom.[200] However, the collapse of France in June 1940 and Italy's entry into the war and the subsequent closing of the Mediterranean to sea transport, led to a serious disturbance of supplies, causing the prices of both local and imported goods to increase.[201]

Other factors also led to an increase in prices. First, Rashid 'Ali's uprising in May 1941 brought trade almost to a standstill and it took several months for commercial life to recover. Meanwhile, British troops were arriving in increasing numbers and their purchases boosted the local market, which was by then suffering from aggravated shipping and supply difficulties. Another important stimulant to prices occurred with Japan's entry into the war, when prices immediately soared to unprecedented heights – the wholesale price index jumped from 179 to 382 (see Table 3.8)[202] – and inflation became an everyday fact of life.[203] The situation was exacerbated by a bad wheat harvest, restriction of imports in general, and the large increase in purchasing power resulting from local expenditure by the British forces. All this led to a great rise in the price of almost every commodity.[204]

Some writers attribute this inflation in Iraq mainly to the fact that the Currency Board could not refuse to issue local currency on the receipt of pounds sterling. However this argument seems simplistic. Although it may be true that the Currency Board's automatic and

TABLE 3.8 Wholesale Price Index, 1939-1950 (base = 1939)

Average for year[a]	Food, vegetable and animal products				Industrial materials				General index number
	Grain and dates	Meat and milk products	Other foods	Other products	Building materials	Textiles	Fuels	Other goods	
1939	100.0	100.0	100.0	100.0	100.0	100.0	100.0	100.0	100.0
1940	148.4	128.7	134.8	144.7	153.6	136.8	103.5	150.3	137.7
1941	193.0	144.5	178.0	173.4	225.4	228.2	108.8	189.7	179.1
1942	460.8	313.7	420.8	211.0	520.9	577.8	123.6	366.0	382.6
1943	773.6	639.0	496.9	284.2	609.3	1,287.6	131.1	680.6	590.0
1944	617.5	785.9	334.7	385.0	649.7	1,212.0	142.3	590.9	534.2
1945	592.9	665.2	309.6	412.9	634.5	944.0	138.7	535.0	494.3
1946	595.7	680.9	302.7	424.5	517.2	919.5	140.4	482.5	481.9
1947	714.2	709.1	285.5	393.4	617.3	1,003.7	136.0	454.6	527.0
1948	851.0	641.9	266.4	434.5	568.4	972.8	148.3	477.4	557.8
1949	538.0	642.3	304.9	469.9	528.2	831.8	156.1	471.9	463.3
1950	530.0	627.7	346.0	615.3	488.8	792.5	149.0	428.6	475.1

Source: Iraq, Ministry of Economics, Statistical Abstract 1951 (Baghdad, 1954), p. 327.

Note: Figures for the post-war period are included to give a better perspective.

[a] Figures for 1939 are the average from December to August. For other years, figures are the mean monthly average.

dependent mechanism played a role in firing inflation,[205] it is hard to agree that it constituted the major factor. From mid-1941 to 1942, the main cause was probably the drastic shrinkage of imports, particularly in 1941. This was complicated by the inadequate machinery for handling the supply problem, as will be seen below. From the last six months of 1942 and for eighteen months thereafter, the crucial factor leading to Iraq's worsening inflation was the expenditure by the British forces there, which reached its peak in 1943 when net military expenditure (British Army and Royal Air Force) totalled ID 30 million;[206] and as Table 3.8 shows, during the same year, 1943, the general index also reached its climax (590). It was no coincidence that in 1943, currency in circulation increased by 206% and total bank deposits by 209%, relative to 1942 (see Tables 3.6 and 3.7).

Besides the two major causes of inflation already mentioned, shrinkage of imports and British military expenditure, there were other minor causes which aggravated the situation. These were restricted shipping to Iraq, and internal transport difficulties; the rise in price levels in neighbouring countries, especially Iran; and the increased cost of imported goods from certain sources of supply.[207]

Impact of Inflation

The effects of inflation were felt in all sectors of Iraq's economy. Some of these effects will be examined here; others (for example, those on foreign trade and industry) will be discussed in later chapters.

Most notable of the financial effects were the drastic changes in wholesale prices, as shown in Table 3.8. The index covered 57 commodities: 22 foodstuffs, 10 other animal and vegetable products, 10 building materials, 2 forms of textiles, 7 types of fuel, and 6 other industrial products. Prices were collected weekly from leading wholesale merchants by the Baghdad Chamber of Commerce, and were weighted and compared with the price of the base period (December 1938–August 1939).[208] Owing to the inadequacy of many rationing and distribution arrangements, however, black-market rather than controlled prices (which the wholesale index was based on) were far more the rule than the exception. Furthermore, the price index hid enormous disparities in the extents to which prices of individual commodities rose.[209] Nevertheless the wholesale price index was one of the soundest statistical calculations produced in Iraq.[210]

Table 3.9 shows the relation between wholesale prices and the supply of money during the war period. It indicates that there was a general tendency for wholesale prices to increase faster than the supply of money up to the end of 1942. The reasons for this were the

TABLE 3.9 Indexes of Money Supply and Wholesale Price Index during World War II (base = August 1939)

	Money supply		Wholesale price index
	Index of notes in circulation	Index of total bank deposits	
Aug. 1939	100	100	100
Dec. 1939	111	103	121
June 1940	121	107	136
Dec. 1940	123	111	152
June 1941	128	94	158
Dec. 1941	217	180	284
June 1942	302	252	359
Dec. 1942	442	378	533
June 1943	612	529	581
Dec. 1943	725	790	636
June 1944	845	1010	568
Dec. 1944	825	1050	521
June 1945	858	1047	488

Sources: For index of notes in circulation: Iraq Currency Board, Annual Reports of the Iraq Currency Board. For index of total bank deposits, see Table 3.7. For wholesale price index: Statistical Abstract 1944 and 1945, p. 223.

uprising of May 1941, which created an unstable economic situation, and lack of public confidence, which led in turn to a movement into goods of all kinds; the rise in c.i.f. import prices of dollar-area goods; the succession of Allied defeats; the bad harvests in Iraq (and throughout the Middle East) in 1941; and the persistent speculative hoarding of commodities in the hope of rising prices.[211] After 1942 the political situation stabilized and British military expenditure increased, as did currency in circulation and with it bank deposits.

The main impact of the rise in money supply and wholesale prices was on the distribution of income. Although little information is available on income changes in Iraq, there is no doubt that certain groups in the society benefited greatly from the inflation. At one extreme were the merchants, army contractors, and landowners with crops to sell. In the middle, and not unprosperous, were those cultivators receiving high prices for their produce, shopkeepers and transport operators serving mainly the British Army, and skilled labourers. The poor were those, like government officials, tied to fixed incomes.

The government was aware of the fact that the big landowners were making huge profits, while no real benefit was accruing to the small cultivator. This awareness was expressed in November 1942 in a special report by the inflation committee appointed by the minister of finance: 'Farmers throughout the country are making very high profits and it is most desirable that they should in some way bear their share of taxation, quite apart from the necessity of draining off surplus purchasing power.'[212]

The disparity of incomes among the different segments of Iraqi society was reflected in the pattern of consumption. The distribution arrangements for scarce commodities involved many inequities. Rationing schemes seem to have favoured towns rather than villages, and even in rural areas some districts suffered more than others. (For example, some Kurdish villages received less than the rest of the rural population.)[213]

The overwhelming factor determining the changes in consumption patterns was the substantial reduction in the volume of nearly all types of imports, as will be seen in Chapter 5. This reduced the total consumption of sugar, tea and soap; but probably the most acute shortage of all was in textiles (especially after Japan's entrance into the war).

The sharp contraction of imports also affected public works and major building activity. Many vital schemes, such as the Habbaniyya project, had to be suspended.[214]

Little development took place during the war in Iraq's manufacturing industries, but as will be shown in Chapter 6, the war stimulated entrepreneurial interest in industry as a means of investment, and this eventually constituted an important stimulus for that sector. Another sector that benefited from the war was communications, which were developed for military purposes but in the post-war period served the economy as a whole.

It is important, however, to note that the majority of the population was not seriously affected by the inflationary tendencies, at least until mid-1942. The only group which suffered hardship was the fixed-income class, and even they received salary increments from time to time.[215] This fact is the key to our understanding of the government's reluctance to take any drastic anti-inflationary measures until the end of 1942.

Anti-Inflationary Measures

Since the bulk of Iraq's population – and particularly those groups which constituted the political basis of every government – were better off than before the war, the government, while recognizing the gravity of the inflation problem, had no real incentive to take radical and unpopular measures to check rising prices.[216]

The British, however, began in 1941 to press for such measures, feeling troubled by the Iraqi government's failure to take the necessary steps to fight inflation.[217] The reason for this pressure and apprehension on the part of the British was not concern about Iraq's economic position; rather, they saw in inflation a destabilizing factor which might imperil their political and economic interests in the area. As M. H. Lloyd, who served in 1943 and 1944 as economic adviser to the British minister of state in the Middle East, put it: 'prevention of civil unrest and bread riots was recognised to be of the highest political and strategic importance'.[218]

The American representative in Baghdad described the situation thus:

> Iraqi politicians are so loath to impose unpopular measures, and the measures to control hoarding of supplies, for which there now exists such a crying need, are bound to be extremely distasteful to the Iraqi public – that the typical politician would by far prefer to throw in his hand rather than risk his political career. The British are thus compelled to play a very delicate game, endeavoring on the one hand to induce the Government to impose those strict economic measures ..., while not going so far as to ... assume administration of the country's affairs.[219]

The British were also aware that even if the Iraqis were to decide to take anti-inflationary measures, they would face immense difficulties because of lack of experience, inefficiency of the country's economic mechanism, and lack of government authority.[220] Nevertheless, British pressure increased with the continued soaring of prices.

Meanwhile, from mid-1942, the Iraqi government was becoming conscious that the situation was indeed deteriorating, and that bitterness was growing among certain sectors of the public. The measures it finally adopted for checking inflation can be divided into two categories: an 'active' policy based on introducing deflationary methods, and a 'passive' policy based on rationing, supply and control measures.

The deflationary steps taken between 1941 and 1945 included the sale of diamonds and government real estate,[221] as well as increasing income tax, floating internal loans, encouraging savings and increasing facilities for investment in sterling area securities as discussed earlier in this chapter. We will concentrate here on one particular deflationary measure, gold-selling.

* * *

At the Anti-Inflation Conference held in Cairo in September 1942, which was attended by British representatives in Middle East countries and by two US observers, a resolution was passed advocating the import of gold for sale on the open market in the Middle East. The conference, however, qualified its recommendation by the provision that the gold would have to be obtained from other than British sources (mainly from the United States), since the British Treasury stated that gold could not be made available at that time.[222]

The recommendation was given on the basis of three factors: that fresh supplies of gold would be likely to absorb surplus purchasing power which might otherwise be diverted to buying commodities; that selling gold would make it possible to procure some of the currency required for British military expenditure at favourable rates, and thus slow down the rate of expansion of the note issue; and that a fall in the price of gold might bring down other prices in sympathy.[223]

On the other hand, it was feared in some quarters in London, particularly the Bank of England, that importing gold, especially coins, might undermine confidence in local currency and lead to demands for payment in gold for all purposes, in which case it might be impossible to meet demand. The chancellor of the Exchequer felt that 'it would be a fatal mistake to begin selling gold and then to have to stop because our sources have dried up'.[224] In addition, it was feared that governments in the Middle East might refuse to accept sterling in exchange for local currency and might demand shipment of gold up to the full amount of their sterling balances.[225] Another factor which deferred gold-selling as an anti-inflationary measure in the Middle East was the strong objection expressed by the government of India, which feared the sale of gold might strengthen demands for convertibility of sterling and rupees into gold at the official rate.[226]

After discussions with the government of India, and realising that the threat of inflation was much more imminent than problems such as the post-war balance of payments and the rate at which sterling balances were piling up, it was decided in London in April 1943 to start selling gold in India and the Middle East.[227] Still feeling that Iraq's measures of supply and control policy were inadequate,[228] the British decided to start selling gold in Iraq as well.[229] This began in August 1943 and ended in June 1944. Sales policy was based on selling at best price and thus absorbing the maximum amount of purchasing power.[230] In Baghdad sales were made only to a few brokers or dealers at the head office of the Eastern Bank, and though the public was free to buy in small quantities, no steps were taken to encourage them to do so. There was no fixed price in Baghdad; for each individual deal the bank manager negotiated the best price.[231]

Despite initial apprehension regarding the effect of gold sales, no adverse repercussions occurred: confidence in local currency was not undermined, and no government refused to take sterling in payment for exports or in exchange for local currency.[232] But although there were no negative effects, it is more difficult to draw conclusions about positive results.

The significance of gold sales can best be measured by comparing the proceeds thereof with net military expenditure and increase in note circulation during the same period (August 1943 to June 1944). Table 3.10 shows that gold sales in Iraq amounted to only 28.5% of the note increase, and constituted 18% of military expenditure. (Iraq's figures were the lowest in the Middle East except for Persia.) These comparatively low figures can perhaps be explained by the large extent of gold smuggling from Persia to Iraq. Even when gold prices were approximately the same in Baghdad and Tehran, it was still cheaper to transport gold from Tehran to southern Iraq than from Baghdad.[233]

Indeed, it is quite difficult to gauge the exact effect of gold sales in Iraq. British military expenditure was decreasing during the same period, and prices began falling from the beginning of 1944. On the whole, the experiment proved satisfactory, at least from the British point of view;[234] it provided local currency for Allied armies at a

TABLE 3.10 Impact of Gold Sales in Iraq, Persia and Egypt, August, 1943 - June 1944

	Gold sales (£ million)	Allied military expenditure	Gold sales as % of allied expenditure	Note increase (£ million)	Gold sales as % of note increase
Iraq	2.9	16.2	18.0	10.2	28.5
Persia	3.8	20.7	18.5	14.7	25.5
Egypt[a]	4.0	38.8	10.5	3.5	114.5

Sources: Middle East Economic and Statistical Bulletin, August 1944, p. 32.

[a]Gold sales in Egypt began only in November 1943 and the figures are therefore for seven months only

cheaper rate than through the sale of sterling or dollars, and it probably did contribute, albeit on a limited scale, to the slowing down of the rate of inflation.[235]

Supply Policy

Government supply policy during World War II fell under three main headings:

1. the control by licence of all imports and exports;
2. the price and distribution control of commodities;
3. the rationing by coupons of essential goods.

This section will examine each of these policies, discussing what organizations and committees shaped them, how they were put into effect, and what problems faced their implementation.

During the first two years of the war, little attention was paid in the Middle East to questions of supply,[236] although the supply problem had in fact begun in June 1940 with France's defeat, Italy's joining the war, and Britain's expulsion from Greece. Mediterranean ports were temporarily closed and shipping became increasingly difficult (due to submarine warfare), thus making supply of the important strategic area of the Middle East a major problem for the British.[237] However in April 1941 MESC was set up with the aim of controlling all imports to the area, and its representatives were to play a crucial role in the supply policy of the countries in the region.[238]

With the exacerbation of the shipping crisis towards the end of 1941, MESC found that not only luxuries and semi-luxuries had to be restricted, but that it was necessary to reduce the volume of essential imports as well. In collaboration with the Foreign Office, MESC began pressing Middle East governments to take action in that direction.[239]

In Iraq, as noted above, the government was not keen to introduce drastic measures to counter inflation or tackle the supply problems that were beginning to appear on the horizon. Though it had formed the Iraqi Central Supply Committee as early as October 1939,[240] no concrete targets were set and the committee's members had to grope in the dark.[241]

The first turning point came in mid-1941 when, due to the bad harvest and widespread pest damage, local wheat shortages were reported. Up to and including 1940 Iraq had been a wheat-exporting country, but in November 1941 the Minister of Economics had to urge UKCC to help Iraq obtain about 15,000 tons of wheat from India.[242] The government of India, however, had meanwhile prohibited export of wheat, and at the end of 1941 Iraq's wheat shortage became very acute.[243]

By then the Iraqi government had become aware of the population's growing bitterness at the soaring prices and shortages of certain goods. It passed laws providing cost of living allowances to all state employees and pensioners, and giving the government powers to take the necessary steps in dealing with the hoarding of essential commodities.[244] The Exchange Control Law was also promulgated, prohibiting all dealings in foreign exchange except through licensed banks.[245]

The British considered these laws too mild, argued that they were not effectively enforced after the first week, and continued to press for stronger measures.[246] The Iraqis agreed to the formation of a number of committees, such as the Central Imports Committee established in December 1941 to deal with import licences, but it took some months for these committees to start functioning.[247]

A second turning point in the supply history of Iraq came in March 1942 with the promulgation of the law regulating economic life.[248] It empowered the government to carry out the following measures:

1. prevent monopolization, profiteering and hoarding;
2. control the export of certain commodities;
3. regulate imports;
4. fix prices and organize distribution;
5. requisition goods, factories, machinery and means of transport;
6. regulate industry;
7. control labour and wages.

These measures were necessarily wide, but for administrative reasons it was possible to introduce them only piecemeal. The first step was the establishment of the Directorate-General of Supply in March 1942, and sugar rationing was introduced in urban districts (sugar was the only rationed commodity until 1944).

Subsequently, an Exports Committee was established to prevent essential commodities from leaving the country, and efforts were made to control the internal movement of goods prohibited from export. The work of this committee was not very effective, however, since smuggling did much to nullify its efforts.[249] But the main problem was a political one. The creation of these 'powerful committees' (in the legal sense, at least) led to conflicts among ministers, each wanting them to be under his own influence. An illustrative example of such conflicts, described for the Foreign Office by Cornwallis, was the publication by the minister of finance, Salih Jabr, of a notice declaring that 50% of the barley in *istihlak* centres would be taken over by the government: 'He [the Minister of Finance] said that he had consulted none of his colleagues, not even the Prime Minister, as he preferred to present them with a fait accompli than with a proposal which they would certainly hesitate to approve.'[250]

Nepotism was another important factor contributing to the ineffectiveness of these committees, as high officials continued to obtain export licences, and the like, for relatives, friends and influential persons.[251]

In May 1942 the registration of certain essential goods (tyres, cement, etc.) was required in order to prevent profiteering by selling from one dealer to another at enhanced prices, and by June 1942 supply shortages, profiteering and hoarding made it necessary to requisition certain commodities, like tyres and newsprint. However, these measures were far from adequate in view of the large black market which developed in response to the inflationary prices.[252] But here again the real difficulty was political; the British adviser to the Ministry of the Interior reported that Minister of Finance 'Ali Mumtaz had told him that 'with every commodity brought under control he came up against fresh vested interests'.[253] These vested interests were represented by merchants, contractors and landowners who saw in the system of price control and licensing an impediment to profiteering.

> This system has been under constant attack by merchants whose profits have been curtailed, by certain Iraqi politicians and members of the wealthy Iraqi classes who have been disgruntled because of their difficulty in obtaining their accustomed disproportionate share of imported goods, and by some Iraqi officials who have taken the position that a system of so complex a nature is unworkable in a backward country like Iraq.[254]

After Iraq's declaration of war against the Axis powers in January 1943, it was urged to do everything in its power to assist the common war effort by instituting control of supplies and prices. On 13 January the government decided to fix barley prices and establish its control over all sales of that commodity. As Cornwallis reported, 'The notification was the Government's first important endeavour to co-operate more fully on the economic front and represented a major step towards control of cereals and stabilisation of cereal prices.'[255]

Indeed, the first half of 1943 was the third turning point in Iraq's supply policy. In April of that year a revised law for the organization of economic life was put into effect, providing for extensive powers to achieve the objects set out in the earlier 1942 law.[256] Shortly afterwards, two important measures were taken: the establishment of a Directorate of Transport and a Directorate of Local Products. (Also, by the beginning of that year the Lend–Lease assistance which Iraq had begun to receive from the United States in May 1942 became significant and helped solve certain problems of supply.)[257]

Until this turning point occurred, government policy was largely limited to the control by licence of all imports and exports. With the promulgation of the new law and the creation of the two above-mentioned directorates, policy was now geared towards price and distribution control of commodities. The objectives of the Directorate of Transport were to control mechanical transport, tyres, tubes and spares, to fix prices and to arrange distribution. The objectives of the Directorate of Local Products were the control of factories and their production, the control and distribution of grains and other food commodities produced locally, and supervision of retail sales of all kinds.[258]

Basing itself on the 1943 law for organizing economic life, the government began a scheme for the collection of cereals, according to which all growers were to hand over one-half of their wheat crop and one-third of their barley crop at a fixed price.[259] The way in which this was implemented with regard to barley in 1943 illustrates how the conflicting objectives of various British organizations affected Iraq. In this case, the views of MESC, backed by the minister of state in Cairo, clashed with those of UKCC and the British Treasury in London. The latter's concern was to avoid losses on commercial transactions, while the former was primarily interested in encouraging home production of grain and in saving shipping, considering financial loss as of secondary importance.[260]

These conflicts produced a harmful effect on Iraq's economy. Furthermore, the British parties all wanted to increase production, while the Iraqi government had to bear in mind the interests of the consumers and the need to check inflation, both of which could have been done by limiting exports and allowing a free internal market.

Although the cereal collection scheme proceeded satisfactorily,[261] except in northern Iraq,[262] the participation of UKCC and three British firms (acting as UKCC's purchasing agents) was never popular in Iraq and was only reluctantly accepted by the Iraqi government.

The fourth turning point in Iraq's supply policy came in late 1943 and early 1944. In November 1943 the Directorate-General of Supply was abolished and a new Directorate of Imported Goods established, together with the necessary administrative machinery for putting into operation many of the measures required to control prices and embark on rationing. The new directorate immediately extended the import licensing system to cover all imported goods.[263]

Before considering the rationing policy, a few words should be said about the mechanism that handled it. On 1 December 1943 the Iraqi government announced that Colonel Bayliss had been appointed economic adviser to the High Supply Committee of the Iraqi government and director-general of imports. In his new capacity, Colonel Bayliss began to advocate the concentration of all supply and control mechanisms in a single ministry which would be under his control.[264]

On 1 May 1944 the Ministry of Supply was created but much to Bayliss's disappointment he was not appointed director-general. As mentioned earlier, he did not get along with either his Iraqi colleagues or the other British representatives in Iraq,[265] and the Americans complained that he was waging anti-American propaganda in Iraqi circles.[266] At this point he was, in fact, beginning to lose ground: his conflicts with various Iraqi officials, especially Arshad al-'Umari, the acting minister of supply, were deepening,[267] and the British decided not to support him any longer because he was not consulting them and because, as Cornwallis put it, 'since it is widely believed that we forced him on the Iraqi Government, criticism engendered by his exuberant tactics is directed largely against ourselves. This is reaching disturbing proportions.'[268] In consequence, on 26 July 1944, ten months after his appointment, Colonel Bayliss was asked to hand over his duties to Colonel LeBlanc, director-general of transport.[269]

Rationing

As noted above, sugar was the only commodity rationed in Iraq prior to 1944. The new policy which brought in rationing for additional commodities was a direct result of the Middle East Conference on Control of Distribution and Rationing, which met in Cairo in August 1943.[270] On 1 January 1944 tea and coffee rationing was introduced.[271] This new measure made fairly good progress in Baghdad and one or two other large towns, but was hampered by administrative difficulties and the fierce opposition of merchants in rural districts.[272]

Rationing of textiles was initiated in March of the same year, but did not proceed as smoothly as the rationing of tea and coffee. Rural areas were discriminated against in these rationing measures:

> The main supply problem remains the shortage of cotton piece-goods, which is causing widespread anxiety and growing discontent, particularly

in rural areas. The latter have so far received no cloth under the rationing scheme which, owing to the reduced supplies, has hitherto been limited to urban areas.[273]

There was relative improvement in the distribution of textiles after the number of distributors was increased to about two hundred, located in both big cities and villages (until September 1944 there were only twenty-five distributors, most of whom were located in Baghdad). The issue of textile ration books also helped somewhat, but all these measures combined did not in fact change the situation drastically. The shortage finally began to decrease at the end of 1944 with the arrival of large supplies from India and the United States.

Meanwhile, a more liberal policy was being adopted by Colonel Bayliss's successor, resulting in a wide variety of articles being decontrolled 'to the general satisfaction of merchants and public'.[274] Goods arriving by land were no longer subject to import licences. The policy of decontrol continued throughout 1945, helped by the downward trend of local prices; by June 1946 most commodities were released from all control and sales restrictions.

The Iraqi government's policy with regard to the two problems of inflation and supply came under harsh attack during and after the war period. Before discussing the validity of this criticism, however, a few points should be emphasized. First and foremost were the objective problems, such as the lack of accurate census statistics and identity cards. This hindered the application of certain supply measures which were based on the use of census cards; it also made it difficult for the government to plan its rationing schemes realistically.[275]

There is no doubt that during the years of high inflation, financial and fiscal measures were necessary. However, some of these measures were not available to Iraq. It was not possible, for example, to change the discount rate for credit control, since this is normally the function of a central bank, which Iraq did not have at the time. On the other hand, governments in Iraq were not prepared to use some of the measures which were available, such as reform of the tax system, primarily because of various local pressure groups.

Within the above mentioned constraints, however, Iraq succeeded in preventing the situation from deteriorating to the extent where it would have hampered post-war development. And although it is true that certain groups in Iraqi society benefited unjustly from the inflation, the problem of food for the masses did not reach the critical point it did in other countries during those immensely difficult years.

The four years of controlled economy proved invaluable to Iraq in a number of ways. The new mechanisms provided training for a cadre of officials, and MESC's constant demands for information and data led to improved statistics. Iraq also benefited from the study and research carried out by British and American experts sent there to examine various sectors of the economy.

The British also benefited, in that their predominant objective – the prevention of civil unrest and bread riots throughout the war period – was achieved. Further, the supply control measures also immensely reduced calls on shipping space, materials and labour to supply the civil requirements of Iraq (and elsewhere in the Middle East).[276] At the same time, the fact that they also dominated most of Iraq's supply and control committees meant that their involvement in Iraq increased substantially, and despite the friction and competition between various British organizations (such as plagued the wheat collection scheme), the unpopularity of MESC,[277] and ongoing friction between the British and American representatives in the Middle East, by the end of the war the British had succeeded in deepening their control over Iraq, and those who supported them there had gained in power.

NOTES

1. Ahmad 'Abd al-Baqi, *Mizaniyyat al-Dawla al-Iraqiyya Tahdiruha wa-Tahliluha*, (The Iraq State Budget: Its Preparation and Analysis) (Baghdad, 1947), p. 24.
2. The 1950–1 budget showed a surplus amounting to ID 5.4 million, mainly on account of increased revenues from customs and excises, and high oil royalties. See 'Facts and Figures: Iraq', *Middle Eastern Affairs* iii, no.12 (Dec. 1952), p. 394.
3. Iraq's Ministry of Foreign Affairs to British Embassy, 'Memorandum on Iraq's Financial Position', 15 Jan. 1942. FO 624/28.
4. Board of Trade, Department of Overseas Trade, *Economic and Commercial Conditions in Iraq 1949*, by F. H. Gamble (London, 1950), p. 3.
5. Newton to FO, 14 Aug. 1940. FO 371/24556, E 2730/203/93.
6. From a comparison of the planned receipts and expenditures appearing in budget laws with the actual figures given in Table 3.1.
7. A copy of the budget for FY 1945 appears in FO 371/45321, E 5383/427/93.
8. Baqi, *Mizaniyyat al-Dawla al-Iraqiyya*, pp. 125–39.
9. Humphrys to FO, 8 May 1934. FO 371/17862, E 3369/326/93.
10. Kerr to FO, 16 Nov.1936. FO 371/20013, E 7480/1393.
11. Ibrahim al-Kabir memoirs (unpublished) *Moreshet Yehudei Bavel* (Iraqi Jewish Heritage Foundation, Tel Aviv), iii, pp. 172–3.
12. *Ibid.*
13. See, for example, comments on the 1935 budget in FO 371/18948, E 1452/432/93 and on the 1936 budget in FO 371/20012, E 2467/1393/93.
14. UN, *Iraq*, p. 11.
15. Newton to FO, 19 Oct. 1940. FO 371/24556, E 2913/203/93.
16. Baqi, *Mizaniyyat al-Dawla al-Iraqiyya*, pp. 46–8.
17. Law No. 59 of 1933 was a modification of Law No. 83 of 1931. Both laws will be discussed in Ch.4.

18. Newton to FO, 19 Oct. 1940. FO 371/24556, E 2913/203/93.
19. Unable to replace the lost agricultural taxes to cover its expenditures, the government felt compelled to introduce new measures, such as an emergency tax increasing duties on local cigarettes, spirits and other consumer goods, and another tax on urban land on which no buildings were erected. Newton to FO, 10 June 1940. FO 371/24556, E 2198/203/93. 'Emergency Tax Law No. 7 of 1940', *Iraq Government Gazette*, no. 15 (14 Apr. 1940), 173–4.
20. 'Iraq Income Tax Law No. 36 of 1939'. A copy appears in FO 371/23203, E 6605/78/93.
21. *Ibid.*
22. Batatu quotes a merchant as saying that merchants kept three different books: one for themselves, one for their partners, and one for the government. See Batatu, *The Old Social Classes*, p. 265.
23. 'Taxation in Iraq', Paper B5, Middle East Financial Conference 1944. FO 371/40053, E 3818/79/93.
24. 'Excess Profits Tax Law No. 14 of 1940', *Iraq Government Gazette*, no. 13 (31 Mar. 1940), pp. 155–6.
25. UN, *Iraq*, p. 22.
26. Income Surtax Law No. 63 of 1943. A copy appears in FO 371/40053, E 3621/79/63.
27. IBRD, *The Economic Development of Iraq* (Baltimore, 1952), pp. 173–4.
28. Iraq, Principal Bureau of Statistics, *Statistical Abstract of Iraq, 1939* (Baghdad, 1941), p. 183.
29. *Statistical Abstract 1948*, p. 233.
30. See, for example, letter from Ogilvie-Forbes to FO, 19 June 1933. FO 371/16906, E 3247/209/93.
31. Comment on memorandum by Iraq's Foreign Ministry on 'Financial position in Iraq', Feb. 1942. FO 624/28/221.
32. Batatu, *The Old Social Classes*, p. 274. Batatu brings a list of the names of these families, their ethnic origin (15 were Moslems and the rest members of minority groups), main place of activity (17 were Baghdadis), and the nature of their business. *Ibid* pp. 276–81.
33. UN, *Iraq*, p. 26.
34. 'Taxation in Iraq', FO 371/40053, E 3818/79/93.
35. UN, *Iraq*, p. 26.
36. Abbas al-Nasrawi, *Financing Economic Development in Iraq* (New York, 1967), p. 13.
37. Newton to FO, 10 June 1940. FO 371/24556, E 2198/203/93.
38. Baqi, *Mizaniyyat al-Dawla al-Iraqiyya*, pp. 77–8.
39. 'Tobacco Monopoly and Improvement Law No. 35 of 1939', *Iraq Government Gazette*, no. 2 (14 Jan. 1940), pp. 17–24.
40. See, for example, Sir E. Hilton Young's memorandum, 'Credit Policy in Iraq', July 1931. FO 371/16050, E 5646/4680/93; and suggestions by Mr Swan, British adviser to the Ministry of Finance, 1942. FO 624/28/221.
41. The seven instalments were paid between 1928 and 1933 (two in 1929) and totalled about £445,000 (including interest). See: United Kingdom, *Progress of Iraq*, p. 127; *Hisabat al-Dawla al-Iraqiyya lil-Sana 1936 al-Maliyya*, p. 60.
42. Knabenshue to Dept. of State, 10 Aug. 1933. ACR, Reel 10. It should be noted that Iraq lacked the expertise or the contacts to raise money in America or anywhere else outside Britain.
43. Minutes by Hull, 30 May 1933. FO 371/16918, E 2977/870/93.
44. Minutes by Rendel, ibid.
45. Report on 'Loan Policy' by E. Hilton Young to prime minister, 15 June 1930. A copy appears in appendix 2 of *Administration of Iraq for the Year 1930*, p. 181.
46. Ibid., p. 184.
47. Ibid., p. 180.
48. Note by Treasury, 9 Dec. 1936. T 160/1188 /F 13151/2.
49. FO to Kerr (Tel. 285), 9 Dec. 1936. Ibid.
50. Morgan to FO, Annual Report 1937, 25 Jan. 1937. FO 371/21856, E 794/794/93.
51. Ibid.
52. Kerr to FO (Tel. 128), 24 June 1937. T 160/1188/13151/2.
53. FO to Kerr (Tel. 131), 14 July 1937. Ibid.

54. Ibid.
55. Oliphant to Kerr, 15 July 1937. Private papers of Baron Inverchapel (formerly Kerr). FO 800/298/37/23.
56. Kerr to Oliphant, 30 July 1937. Ibid.
57. CAB 23/89, 31(37)4.
58. Annual Report 1937.
59. CAB 23/89, 31(37)4.
60. Annual Report 1937.
61. Satterthwaite (American Legation, Baghdad) to Dept. of State, 5 Aug. 1937. ACR, Reel 10.
62. Annual Report 1937.
63. Houstoun-Boswall to FO, 'Annual Report, Economic (A) for 1938', 10 May 1939. FO 624/14/78.
64. See memorandum sent by Iraqi government to British Embassy on the financial situation, 13 April 1939. FO 371/23208, E 2821/374/93.
65. Newton to FO Annual Report, Economic (B) for 1939, 14 Dec. 1939. FO 371/23204, E 8084/78/93.
66. Comments by FO, 21 Apr. 1939. FO 371/23208, E 2821/374/93.
67. Houstoun-Boswall to FO, 13 Apr. 1939. Ibid.
68. FO to ECGD, 4 May 1939. FO 371/23208, E 2959/374/93.
69. Minutes by Baggallay (FO), 10 June 1939. FO 371/23194, E 4309/4309/65.
70. Newton to FO (Tel. 250), 20 July 1939. FO 371/23209, E 5195/374/93.
71. FO to Newton, 3 Nov. 1939. FO 371/23209, E 7312/374/93.
72. Anglo-Iraqi Credit Agreement, 1 Dec. 1939. FO 371/23209, E 7842/374/93.
73. FO to Newton, 16 Dec. 1939. FO 371/23209, E 7807/374/93.
74. Ibid.
75. Newton to FO, 13 Jan. 1940. FO 371/24555, E 330/202/93.
76. Somerville (British Embassy, Baghdad) to FO, 11 Apr. 1940. FO 371/24556, E 1624/202/93.
77. Law No. 39 of 1939. A copy of this law appears in FO 371/24556, E 1824/202/93. To the best of my knowledge, this agreement was never made public.
78. Note by Treasury to FO, 'Iraq: Grants and Credits Advanced', 20 Apr. 1948. FO 371/68461, E 6110/112/93.
79. Note by ECGD to FO, 28 Mar. 1944. FO 371/40067, E 2009/347/93.
80. Thompson to FO, 25 Aug. 1944. FO 371/40067, E 5630/347/93.
81. Iraq's Ministry of Affairs to British Embassy, 21 Feb. 1945. FO 371/45317, E 1706/287/93.
82. Note by ECGD, 24 May 1945. FO 371/45317, E 3120/287/93.
83. Note by FO to Middle East (Official) Committee, 'Economic Policy in the Middle East', 15 May 1947. FO 371/61499, E 4195/44/65.
84. Record of a conversation between Wright (FO) and Iraq's foreign minister, 22 Dec. 1947. FO 371/62351, UE 12662/44/53.
85. Note on 'Economic Policy in the Middle East'.
86. Record of conversation, op. cit.
87. Minutes of Middle East (Official) Committee, 18 Dec. 1947. FO 371/61502, E 11807/44/65.
88. *FRUS* 1948, V, p. 207.
89. Project Funds Agreement between Government of Iraq and National Bank of Iraq and IBRD (Washington, 15 June 1950). The impact of this agreement on Iraq's economy is outside the scope of this book. However, until the end of 1953 only $5.9 million was actually drawn. See Carl Iversen, *Monetary Policy in Iraq* (Copenhagen, 1954), p. 67, fn. 3.
90. British Embassy to Iraq's Ministry of Foreign Affairs, 13 Oct. 1942. FO 371/31361, E 6634/31/93.
91. Cornwallis to FO (Tel. 59), 21 Jan. 1944. FO 371/40053, E 500/79/93.
92. FO to Embassy (Tel. 131), 17 Mar. 1944. FO 371/40053, E 1535/79/93.
93. Law No. 22 of 1944. A copy appears in FO 371/40053, E 3528/79/93.
94. Cornwallis to FO, 16 Jan. 1945. FO 371/45321, E 625/427/93.

95. Meer Basri, *Mabahith fi al-Iqtisad al-'Iraqi* (Essays on the Iraqi ecomony) (Baghdad, 1948), p. 190.
96. Included in Cornwallis's despatch to FO, op. cit.
97. Law No. 40 of 1947. FO 371/61654, E 9917/453/93.
98. Report on Economic Conditions in Iraq for Oct. 1947. FO 371/61661, E 10869/641/ 93.
99. Pelham (British Embassy, Baghdad) to FO, 20 Jan. 1948. FO 371/68460, E 1199/112/93.
100. United Kingdom, *Economic and Commercial Conditions*, p. 3.
101. S. H. Longrigg, *Iraq, 1900–1950* (London, 1953), p. 341.
102. Buck to FO, 6 Feb. 1948. T 225/24.
103. Gabriel Baer, 'Ha-Mashber ha-Kaspi be-Iraq' (The monetary crisis in Iraq), *Ha-Mizrah He-Hadash*, 1 (January 1950), p. 126.
104. Mack to FO (Tel. 403), 14 Apr. 1948. T 225/24. See also: 'Iraq's Empty Exchequer', *The Economist* (8 Jan. 1949), p. 60.
105. Mack to FO (Tel. 397), 13 Apr. 1948. T 225/24.
106. Mack to FO (Tel. 401), 14 Apr. 1948. T 225/24.
107. Embassy to FO, 'Report on Economic Conditions in Iraq for March 1948', 14 Apr. 1948. FO 371/68458, E 5179/77/93.
108. Mack to FO (Tel. 408), 15 Apr. 1948. CO 537/3985.
109. Embassy to FO, 'Report on Economic Conditions in Iraq for April 1948', 13 May 1948. FO 371/68458, E 6537/77/93.
110. FO to Mack (Tel. 468), 11 May 1948. T 236/1193.
111. Record of a meeting held at the Foreign Office to consider Iraq's financial crisis, 18 May 1948. FO 371/68462, E 6664/112/93.
112. Mack to FO 15 May 1948. FO 371/68449, E 6339/27/93.
113. Embassy to FO, 7 July 1948. FO 371/68464, E 9486/112/93.
114. Richmond to FO (Tel. 834), 4 Aug. 1948. FO 371/68464, E 10384/112/93.
115. FO minute by Dundas, 12 Aug. 1948. FO 371/68464, E 10775/112/93.
116. FO to Baghdad (Tel. 869), 13 Aug. 1948. FO 371/68464, E 10764/112/93.
117. Ibid.
118. Mack to FO (Tel. 935), 20 Sept. 1948. FO 371/68465, E 12270/112/93.
119. FO to Baghdad (Tel. 1037), 1 Oct. 1948. FO 371/68465, E 12653/112/93.
120. Sir E. Bridges (Treasury) to Sir O. Sargent (FO), 1 Oct. 1948. FO 371/68466, E 12839/112/93.
121. Mack to FO (Tel. 989), 2 Oct. 1948. FO 371/68465, E 12810/112/93.
122. Record of a meeting held at the Foreign Office, 6 Oct. 1948. FO 371/68466, E 13038/112/93.
123. Record of a meeting between FO officials and representatives of IPC and the Anglo-Iranian Oil Company, 5 Oct. 1948. FO 371/68466, E 13064/112/93.
124. FO to Baghdad (Tel. 1054), 6 Oct. 1948. FO 371/68466, E 12978/112/93.
125. Mack to FO (Tel. 1070), 30 Oct. 1948. FO 371/68453, E 14021/27/93.
126. Mack to FO (Tel. 1100), 11 Nov. 1948. FO 371/68467, E 14510/112/93.
127. Mack to FO, 'Report by 'Ali Mumtaz on the Iraqi Financial Situation: Measures to Overcome the Difficulties', 19 Nov. 1948. FO 371/68467, E 15160/112/93. (See also Ch. 2.)
128. Mack to FO (Tel. 1100), 11 Nov. 1948. FO 371/68467, E 14510/112/93. 'Ali Mumtaz resigned once again on 15 Nov., and this time his resignation was accepted.
129. Mack to FO (Tel. 1106), 12 Nov. 1948. FO 371/68467, E 14557/112/93.
130. British Middle East Office (Cairo) to FO, 23 Nov. 1948. FO 624/141, vol. iv. This point will be further elaborated in Ch. 6.
131. Embassy to FO, 'Report on Economic Conditions in Iraq for November 1948', 13 Dec. 1948. FO 371/68458, E 16124/77/93.
132. FO to Embassy, Baghdad (Tel. 36), 8 Jan. 1949. FO 371/68467, E 1588/112/93.
133. See p. 252.
134. Longrigg, *Iraq: 1900 to 1950*, p. 360.
135. Iversen, *Monetary Policy in Iraq*, p. 41.
136. 'Loans and Savings in Iraq', paper G5, Middle East Financial Conference 1944. FO 921/300.
137. Ibid.

138. Baghdad Chamber of Commerce, *Annual Report 1937–8* (in Arabic) (Baghdad, 1939), pp. 52–3.
139. Conversation with Meer Basri, 27 Aug. 1979.
140. Baghdad Chamber of Commerce, *Report for the years 1938 and 1939*, pp. 63–4.
141. For the efforts and debates surrounding issuance of currency during the period 1921–31, see Edward Abdul Kareem Kalian, 'Money and Banking in Iraq, 1914–1958: A Study in Economic History' (Columbia University Ph.D. thesis, 1966), pp. 35–57.
142. United Kingdom, *Administration of Iraq for the period January to October 1932*, pp. 25–6.
143. Iraqi Currency Law No. 44 for the year 1931. A copy appears in CO 813/4.
144. Illif (BMEO) to Young (Treasury), 'Record of a conversation with al-Kabir in Baghdad', 13 Dec. 1946. T 236/1186.
145. Law No. 44 of 1931.
146. Ibid, Article 16g.
147. Kalian, 'Money and Banking in Iraq', p. 65. Kalian, however, criticized the Board for investing in securities of sterling area countries only, and in long-term securities. The former, according to Kalian, led to the deprivation of foreign exchange which Iraq badly needed afterwards, while the latter was at the expense of 'liquidity' of reserves. Ibid., pp. 81–3.
148. 'Annual Report of the Iraq Currency Board for the Financial Year 1934'. A copy appears in FO 371/18948, E 4815/432/93.
149. Embassy to FO, 'Report by CE Loombe, Acting Currency Officer', 8 June 1943. FO 371/34984, E 3265/9/93. The correlation between currency expansion and inflation during World War II is discussed in detail in the section on inflation.
150. Iversen, *Monetary Policy in Iraq*, pp. 5–6.
151. Law No. 44 of 1931.
152. Peterson to FO, 15 May 1938. FO 371/21859, E 3053/2000/93.
153. Hogg (adviser, Ministry of Finance) to Waley (Treasury), 10 June 1938. Ibid.
154. Law No. 27 of 1939. A copy appears in FO 371/23217/, E 58914/2564/93.
155. National Bank of Iraq, *Annual Report 1st July 1949 – 31st December 1950* (in Arabic) (Baghdad, 1951), pp. 6–7. See also next section.
156. Law No. 42 of 1947, 'Amending the Iraq Currency Law No. 44 of 1931'; a copy appears in FO 371/61654, E 9915/453/93. Law No. 43 of 1947, 'National Bank of Iraq'; a copy appears in FO 371/61652, E 9914/453/93.
157. For a detailed analysis of the National Bank's activities in the first few years after its establishment, see Iversen, *Monetary Policy in Iraq*, pp. 6–16, 39–54; 'Abdul Munim 'Ali, 'A Study of the Banking System and its Role in the Economic Development of Iraq' (George Washington University Ph.D. thesis, 1958), pp. 227–68.
158. *Iraq Directory 1936*, Commercial Section, pp. 131, and 135.
159. 'Banking in Iraq', Paper A5, part ii. Middle East Financial Conference 1944. FO 371/40053, E 3383/79/93. See also Sa'id Himadeh, *Al-Nizam al-Iqtisadi fi al-Iraq* (The economic structure in Iraq) (Beirut, 1938), pp. 446–8.
160. Ibid.
161. Baghdad Chamber of Commerce, *Annual Report 1935–1936*, p. 36.
162. *Iraq Government Gazette*, no. 13 (29 Mar. 1936), p. 180.
163. *Iraq Government Gazette*, no. 47 (19 Nov. 1939), p. 631; no. 53 (31 Dec. 1939), p. 731.
164. According to the Chamber of Commerce Report of 1935–6 it was 24%, but Himadeh, op. cit., p. 448 reports higher rates.
165. Himadeh, op. cit., pp. 448–9.
166. Law for the Control of Banking No. 34 of 1950, 20 May 1950 (Pamphlet), n.d. See also next section.
167. Iversen, *Monetary Policy in Iraq*, p. 29.
168. Kalian, 'Money and Banking in Iraq', p. 31.
169. Arnold T. Wilson, *Loyalties: Mesopotamia 1914–1917* (London, 1930), p. 283.
170. Kalian, op. cit., p. 33.
171. 'Annual Report, Economic (A) for 1938'. FO 371/23203, E 3556/78/93.
172. Kalian, op. cit., p. 208.
173. Iversen, op. cit., p. 18.

174. Law for the Control of Banking No. 61 of 1938. A copy appears in ACR, Reel 6.
175. Ibid., Article 15.
176. 'Annual Report, Economic (A) for 1938'. FO 371/23203, E 3556/78/93.
177. 'Ali, 'Study of the Banking System', p. 85.
178. Iversen, *Monetary Policy in Iraq*, p. 18.
179. Newton to FO, 18 May 1940. T 231/342.
180. Knabenshue to Dept. of State, 18 Dec. 1940. ACR, Reel 18.
181. Grant (Treasury) to Crosthwaite (FO), 9 May 1941. FO 371/27069, E 2131/1/9.
182. Mohammad Mahdi Kubbah, *Mudhakkarati fi Samim al-Ahdath, 1918–1958* (My memoirs in the core of the events, 1918–1958) (Beirut, 1965), p. 240.
183. 'Ali, op. cit., p. 96.
184. See, for example, a copy of a letter from the local manager of the Eastern Bank to his head office in London about financial support for the regent of Iraq. FO 371/45293, E 4686/89/93/G. This affair will be elaborated in the section on the sterling area in Chap. 5. See also Mack to FO, 25 Nov. 1948. FO 371/68467, E 15586/112/93.
185. National Bank of Iraq, *Annual Report 1st July 1949 – 31st December 1950*, p. 81.
186. Law No. 34 of 1950 for the Control of Banking. For a thorough analysis, see Iversen, *Monetary Policy in Iraq*, pp. 20–5.
187. Law No. 48 of 1935 of Post Office Savings Bank, *Iraq Government Gazette*, no. 13 (29 Mar. 1936), pp. 185–6.
188. Law No. 50 of 1938 Amending Law No. 40 of 1935. See Iraq, Ministry of Justice, *Compilation of Laws and Regulations for the Year 1938* (in Arabic) (Baghdad, 1939), p. 351.
189. Kalian, 'Money and Banking in Iraq', p. 186.
190. 'Loans and Savings in Iraq', paper C5, Middle East Financial Conference 1944. FO 921/300.
191. Iraq, *Statistical Abstract 1943* (Baghdad, 1945), p. 183; *Statistical Abstract 1948*, p. 264; *Statistical Abstract 1950*, p. 318.
192. Iversen criticized the fact that this government bank operated on commercial lines, arguing that it should undertake projects benefiting the country as a whole even if they resulted in some loss to the bank. Iversen, *Monetary Policy in Iraq*, p. 19.
193. Rafidain Bank, 'The Rafidain Bank in Twenty Years' in *Annual Report and Balance Sheet for 1961* (Baghdad, 1961).
194. Ibid.
195. Rafidain Bank, *Balance Sheet and Profit and Loss Account at the End of March 1950*.
196. Law No. 18 of 1948 for the Iqari Bank. See Iqari Bank, *Annual Report for the Financial Year 1949/1950* (in Arabic) (Baghdad, 1950).
197. Ibid.
198. Iversen, *Monetary Policy in Iraq*, p. 35.
199. Knabenshue to Dept. of State, 18 Oct. 1939. ACR, Reel 9.
200. Board of Trade, DOT, *Iraq, Review of Commercial Conditions* (London, 1945), p. 12.
201. Ibid.
202. The cost of living index was prepared only after the war, 1939 being the base year (100) while 1945 was put at 590.
203. British Embassy to FO, 'Report for week ending 14 December 1941' (prepared by political adviser of Central Area). FO 838/1.
204. Cornwallis to FO, 'Review of Events in Iraq during 1942', 8 Mar. 1942. FO 371/31371, E 2596/204/93.
205. 'Abdul Hasan Zalzalah, 'Iraq in the Sterling Area 1932–1954' (Indiana University Ph.D. thesis, 1957), p. 227.
206. *MEESB* (Jan. 1945), p. 33. In a note on Allied military expenditure in the Middle East, it was emphasized that the figures were only a very rough calculation of the financial impact of the war on the Middle East economy. See Meeting of Economic Advisory Bureau in Cairo, 14 Oct. 1941. FO 921/239.
207. 'General Economic Position', Paper A5, Middle East Financial Conference 1944. FO 371/40053, E 3383/79/93.
208. 'Notes on Statistics Relating to Inflation in the Middle East', Middle East Financial Conference 1944. FO 921/235, 79(1)/44/24.

209. A. R. Prest, *War Economies of Primary Producing Countries* (Cambridge, 1948), pp. 205–6.
210. John Murray, *A Report on Statistical Organization in the Government of the Kingdom of Iraq* (Baghdad, 1948), p. 159.
211. Ibid., pp. 206–7.
212. Cornwallis to FO, 'Report of the Inflation Committee', 19 January 1943. FO 371/34983, E 991/9/93. The committee was comprised of: L. Swan, adviser to Ministry of Finance; Ibrahim al-Kabir, accountant-general; Kamil al-Khedhery, chairman of Baghdad Chamber of Commerce; and F. Harris, regional manager of Ottoman Bank in Baghdad.
213. Prest, *War Economies*, p. 204.
214. Board of Trade, *Iraq 1945*, p. 16.
215. See for example Cornwallis to FO, 'Review of Chief Events during 1942', 21 Feb. 1943. FO 371/35010, E 1667/489/93.
216. Thompson to FO, 'Memorandum on the Economic Situation in Iraq', 22 Oct. 1942. FO 371/31361, E 6607/31/93.
217. Cornwallis to FO, 3 Dec. 1942. FO 371/31371, E 7097/204/93.
218. Lloyd, *Food and Inflation*, pp. 210–11.
219. Wilson (American Legation, Baghdad) to Dept. of State, 22 Oct. 1942. ACR, Reel 15.
220. Minutes of meeting on supply and finance held at the British Embassy in Baghdad, 18 Oct. 1942. FO 371/31361, E 6607/31/93.
221. 'General Economic Position', Paper A5, Middle East Financial Conference 1944, FO 371/40053, E 3383/79/93.
222. Resolution (7) of Anti-Inflation Conference, Cairo, 26 Sept. 1942. FO 921/91, 45(15)/43/8.
223. Memorandum on 'Gold Policy', 31 Mar. 1943. FO 921/91, 45(15)/43/8.
224. Chancellor of Exchequer to Washington (Tel. 2657), 22 Apr. 1943. FO 371/34970, E 2235/1858/65.
225. 'Gold Policy', op. cit.
226. FO to minister of state (Cairo), 14 Apr. 1943. FO 921/91, 45(15)/43/29.
227. 'Arguments for and against the Sale of Gold in the Middle East', 1 Apr. 1943. FO 921/91, 45(15)/43/8.
228. Casey (minister of state, Cairo), to FO, 9 June 1943. FO 371/34971, E 3522/1858/65.
229. Conclusions of a meeting concerning the sale of gold held at the office of the minister of state, Cairo, 29 July 1943. FO 921/128, 143/40/68.
230. The price of an ounce of gold ranged around $57. FO 921/254.
231. *MEESB*, (Aug. 1944), pp. 34–5.
232. See: 'Report on Gold Sales in Iraq during the period August–October 1943'. FO 921/130, 143/43/250; and 'Report on Gold Sales in Iraq for the Three Months November 1943–January 1944'. FO 921/254, 79(22)/44/1.
233. Ibid.
234. See Lloyd, *Food and Inflation*, pp. 216–17.
235. The question of gold sales re-emerged in 1945, when the Iraqi authorities tried to make the Eastern Bank pay income tax on its profits from gold sales. The bank, however, supported by the British Treasury and the Embassy, refused to pay anything, claiming that it had only been acting as an agent of the British government. See T 236/1192 and T 236/1183. The issue was raised again in 1949 and negotiations between the Iraqi government and the Eastern Bank resumed. But up to the end of the period under study, no agreement was reached. See FO 371/75155, E 7223/112/93.
236. Lloyd, *Food and Inflation*, p. 179.
237. Wilmington, *Middle East Supply Centre*, pp. 15–19.
238. For more details about MESC's mechanism and supply policy see Wilmington, ibid.; and Guy Hunter, 'Economic Problems: The Middle East Supply Centre' in George Kirk, *The Middle East in the War* (London, 1952), pp. 169–93.
239. Wilmington, 'Reappraisal', p. 146.
240. Ordinance No. 58 of 1939 for Regulating Economic Life during the International Crisis', *Iraq Government Gazette*, no. 40 (1 Oct. 1939), pp. 511–12. For the structure of the committee, see Ch. 2.

241. Newton to FO, 3 Oct. 1939. FO 371/23203, E 6899/78/93.
242. Cornwallis to FO (Tel. 1248), 7 Nov. 1941. FO 371/27119, E 7323/7323/93.
243. Cornwallis to FO (Tel. 1405), 27 Dec. 1941. FO 371/27119, E 8573/7323/93.
244. Cornwallis to FO, 14 Dec. 1941. FO 371/31371, E 258/204/93.
245. This law and its implications will be examined in the section on sterling area in Ch. 5.
246. Cornwallis to FO, 'Review of Events in Iraq during 1941', 8 Mar. 1942, FO 371/31371, E 2596/204/93.
247. Cornwallis to MESC, 20 May 1942. FO 371/31339, E 3242/52/65.
248. Law No. 11 of 1942. A copy appears in FO 371/31360, E 3292/17/93.
249. 'General Economic Position', Paper A5, Middle East Financial Conference 1944. FO 371/40053, E 3383/79/93.
250. Cornwallis to FO (Tel. 27), 8 Jan. 1943. FO 371/35483, UE 52/37/71. On the absence of co-operation between the various government departments, see *Saut al-Ahali*, 3 Feb. 1943. A copy of the article appears in ACR, Reel 17.
251. Edmonds (British adviser to Ministry of the Interior) to Thompson (Embassy), 28 Sep. 1942. Edmonds private papers.
252. 'General Economic Position', Paper A5, Middle East Financial Conference 1944. FO 371/40053, E 3383/79/93.
253. Edmonds private papers, op. cit.
254. Loy Henderson (America's minister in Baghdad) to Dept. of State, 3 July 1944. ACR, Reel 17.
255. Cornwallis to FO, 28 Mar. 1943. FO 371/35010, E 2239/489/93.
256. Cornwallis to FO, 5 June 1943. FO 371/35010, E 3585/489/93. A draft of the law was handed to Edmonds for comment, and he directed his remarks mainly to the appointment of directors of committees and directorates. See Edmonds to Ambassador Kerr, 24 Feb. 1943. Edmonds private papers.
257. Dept. of State to Legation, Baghdad, 1 May 1942. *FRUS* 1942, iv, p. 343. The question of Lend–Lease was dealt with in Ch. 1.
258. 'General Economic Position', Paper A5, Middle East Financial Conference 1944. FO 371/40053, E 3383/79/93.
259. Cornwallis to FO, 5 June 1943. FO 371/35010, E 3584/480/93.
260. Lloyd, *Food and Inflation*, pp. 113–14. This work contains a detailed description of the cereal collection scheme. See also Ch. 4.
261. See for example 'Report on Economic Conditions in Iraq for August and September, 1943'. FO 371/35022, E 6283/3137/93.
262. 'Report on Economic Conditions in Iraq for the Month of November, 1943'. FO 371/35022, E 8108/3137/93.
263. *MEESB* (Jan. 1944), p. 14.
264. Henderson to Dept. of State, 3 Jan. 1944. ACR, Reel 17.
265. See for example Tel. 441 from Cornwallis to FO, 29 May 1944. FO 371/40057, E 3245/193/93.
266. Henderson to Dept. of State, 21 Feb. 1944. ACR, Reel 17.
267. Henderson to Dept. of State, 3 July 1944. ACR, Reel 17.
268. Cornwallis to FO (Tel. 441), 28 May 1944. FO 371/40057, E 3245/193/93.
269. *MEESB* (Aug. 1944), p. 17. The following month, LeBlanc was asked to stand down in favour of C. R. Grice, director-general of Local Products.
270. Lloyd, *Food and Inflation*, pp. 218–24.
271. *MEESB* (Feb. 1944), p. 15.
272. Col. Bayliss, 'Report on Supply Control in Iraq, 6 Oct. 1943 to 15 June 1944'. FO 922/317.
273. Cornwallis to FO, 'Review of Events, March–June 1944', 8 June 1944. FO 371/40042, E 3640/37/93.
274. *MEESB* (Oct. 1944), p. 16.
275. See for example 'Intelligence Report by Air Headquarters of Iraq and Persia for the period January–February 1944'. Air 24/851.
276. *MEESB* (July 1945), pp. 15–16.
277. There was constant suspicion and friction between MESC and the Middle East

governments due to the fact that 'the people of the Middle East had no representative of policy-making status with the Supply Centre, so that its decisions inevitably looked like a foreign dictate, no matter how much local interests had been consulted.' Wilmington, p. 155. MESC was dissolved on 1 Sept. 1945.

4

AGRICULTURE

EXISTING CONDITIONS

Iraq consists mainly of a basin or syncline, which lies between an arch of mountains to the north and east and the Syrian desert to the west and south. The land descends from the mountains to the desert in a series of hills and steppes, cut by rivers and wadis which carry the winter rainfall and melted snow to the Tigris and Euphrates river valleys, which run through the basin, from north-west to south-east across the Iraqi desert. This desert stretches from the west bank of the Euphrates to the western frontier and constitutes about 47% of Iraq's total area.

The productive core of Iraq – an oasis amounting to about 20% of the total land surface of the country – divides into two regions:

> The northern region is fed by rainfall supplemented by perennial streams arising in the mountains and, to a limited extent, by lift from the rivers. The southern region largely depends upon irrigation, supplied by canals drawn from the river system, following winter rainfall. The former may be appropriately called the Rainfall Zone, and the latter the Irrigation Zone.[1]

Accurate statistics on the total cultivable area are lacking. In 1930 Dowson estimated the area of the Rainfall Zone at 16.4 million donums, and that of the Irrigation Zone at about 20.4 million donums.[2] These figures represent 9% and 11% respectively of the total area of the country. According to Dowson, only a fraction of these zones, 'possibly from a fifth to a tenth, appears to be actually cultivated in any given year'.[3]

The Agricultural Census of 1952–3, the first census of its kind to be taken in Iraq, surveyed 125,045 agricultural holdings covering an area of 25.5 million donums, which constituted 28% of the total area of the fourteen provinces. Of this, the land planted with winter or summer crops amounted to over 10 million donums (about 40% of the total area of holdings); some 11 million donums (44%) were lying fallow that year; 2.6 million donums (10%) were classified as uncultivable; and the remainder was in orchards, date gardens, vineyards and woodlands.[4]

According to an IBRD report published in 1952, the cultivable area was put at 48.1 million donums, of which 32.1 million were in the Irrigation Zone and 16 million in the Rainfall Zone. The report estimated the area under cultivation at 17.5 million donums, and the area actually in crops at 11.1 million donums.[5]

In addition to the area which was utilized, there were large expanses of cultivable land which could be brought under cultivation if water were stored for irrigation. Estimates of the potential area varied according to what assumptions were made as to capacity for water storage.[6]

Iraq was sparsely populated during the period under study. According to the 1947 census the total population was 4.82 million, with 57–60% of the active population working in the agricultural sector. The Agricultural Census of 1952–3 gave a total of 1,400,152 agricultural labourers, but this figure did not include non-working family members like young children, those engaged in pastoral farming without fixed land holdings of their own, nomadic tribes, and so on.[7] In relation to this small population, the area utilized for agriculture was large. The density of the rural population, according to the 1947 census, was fourteen per square kilometre. (Man–land ratios were higher in central and southern Iraq than in the north.[8])

Annual income per capita in the agricultural sector was minimal: in 1950 it was ID 17, as compared with ID 75 in the non-agricultural and non-oil sectors.[9] The fundamental reasons for this were low productivity and low output. Most of the manpower on the land was underemployed for a large part of the year, and primitive methods were used in cultivating, irrigating and harvesting. Agricultural yields were poor in comparison not only with developed countries but with other Middle East countries as well (e.g. Egypt, Iran and Syria).[10] The low level of mechanization and limited use of chemical fertilizers was one of the important reasons for Iraq's poor productivity. This problem was aggravated during World War II due to the almost total cessation of fertilizer imports and the wearing out of agricultural machines, such as irrigation pumps, which could not be replaced during the war. (Only in 1945 did the number return to its 1940 level.) In 1950 an IBRD mission found that only 170 combines and 549 tractors, exclusive of government-owned machines, were in operation (five provinces had no combines and three provinces had no tractors).[11]

Other problems associated with the low productivity of Iraq's agricultural sector, such as water control and soil conservation, will be dealt with below. First we will concentrate on the problems of restricted crop range and insufficient crop rotation.

As Table 4.1 indicates, barley and wheat were by far the most important crops. According to the Agricultural Census of 1952–3, these crops covered between them over 88% of the total area under cultivation, while rice accounted for about 5% and maize for a little over 2%.[12] During most of the period under study, barley was Iraq's most valuable export.

Iraq's agricultural production (and consequent foreign trade) fluctuated from year to year, mainly because of adverse weather conditions. In years when the output of wheat and barley decreased substantially, Iraq faced immense financial difficulties. For example, the 1948 financial crisis was due, *inter alia*, to the fact that the previous year's wheat and barley production had fallen to a very low level (300,000 tons of wheat and 570,000 tons of barley).[13]

It is very hard to draw conclusions from Table 4.1 since data about crop area and production in the 1930s are incomplete, and information about the 1940s is probably also inaccurate. But from the available data it would seem that wheat production reached 580,000 tons in 1937 and decreased to 520,000 in 1949, while barley production increased from the 500,000-ton range in the 1930s to the 800,000-ton range in the 1940s. With regard to summer crops, both the area and production of cotton decreased steadily throughout the

TABLE 4.1 Area and Production of Major Crops in Iraq, Selected Years

	Area (1,000 donums)					Production (1,000 tons)				
	1933	1937	1941	1945	1949	1933	1937	1941	1945	1949
Winter crops										
Wheat	...	3,180	3,600	3,480	,3800	338	580	532	370	520
Barley	...	3,226	3,497	4,875	4,000	240	570	859	895	851
Lentils	...	...	25	39	44	...	...	3	4	6
Summer crops										
Rice	...	484	587	838	890	...	150	196	329	212
Sesame	...	61	75	120	175	...	20	6	8	9
Maize	...	...	650	81	61	...	...	10	12	10
Cotton[a]	...	108	372	51	42	...	4	4	1	2
Tobacco	...	16	25	25	28	...	5	3	13	6
Millet	...	...	175	244	165	...	...	11	10	18

Sources: For 1933: League of Nations, Statistical Yearbook 1936/37 (Geneva, 1937), p. 84, 86. For 1937: MESC, 'Economic Survey of Iraq', FO 371/40051, E 2564/78/93; League of Nations, Statistical Yearbook 1940/41 (Geneva, 1941), p. 90, 92, 98. For 1941: Statistical Abstract 1948, Appendix, p. 3. For 1945 and 1949: Statistical Abstract 1950, p. 121, 123, 130.

... Data not available.

[a] Bale-equivalents for cotton production figures are as follows: 1933, 512 bales; 1937 and 1941, 20,000 bales; 1945, 5,770 bales; 1949, 10,000 bales.

period under study, while crops such as rice and maize fluctuated from one period to another.

Wheat was cultivated mainly in the northern area of natural rainfall, while barley was grown in both the rainfall and irrigation areas. Rice was grown in the southern irrigated provinces (mainly 'Amara and Muntafiq), but its cultivation was restricted by a 1932 law because of the large amount of water required.

The main cotton-growing areas were around Baghdad and Deyala. Cotton production reached its peak (about 4,700 tons) in FY 1940 with the help of support granted to growers for a period of three years by The Law for Distributing Free Cotton Seed to Cultivators No. 48 for 1939.[14] However, output fell off during the war years and up to 1948 because of the more attractive prices obtainable for cereals. From 1949 production began to increase substantially (in 1950 output reached 9,000 tons and the area cultivated with cotton stood at 130,000 donums),[15] due to material incentives and technical assistance for farmers, as well as to propaganda. Warriner attributes the failure of cotton production in Iraq to two reasons: there was no public authority to combat pests; and a 25% export tax on cotton levied in the interest of the local cotton industry (mainly the Iraq Spinning and Weaving Company) deterred farmers from expanding this crop because they could no longer compete with world prices, and local demand was not large enough.[16] In addition, cotton was an unpopular crop with the peasants as the labour required for its cultivation was considerable, and, unlike food crops, it was of no use to them unless it was marketed.[17]

Tobacco was cultivated in the mountainous Kurdish districts where the soil and climate were most favourable to this crop. Most of the tobacco product found its way into the local cigarette industry, and purchase of the crop became a state monopoly in 1939.

Dates ranked with barley as Iraq's most important export crop during the period 1932–50. It was estimated that Iraq was the source of 80% of the world's date production. Most of Iraq's dates were grown in the Basra region, mainly in the Shatt-al-Arab area. According to the Agricultural Census there were 18.4 million date palms, but this figure excluded all trees of non-bearing age as well as all those in private gardens.[18] Another estimate put the number of palm trees at 30 million.[19] About 350 varieties of dates were grown, but only four of these were usually exported in quantity. A British firm held a monopoly concession for the export of Basra dates. Iraq's date industry as a whole was under direct government control and was organized by the Date Board.

Fruit and vegetable production was of lesser importance. Fruit trees – mostly pomegranate, orange and apple – were cultivated mainly in the province of Sulaimaniyya. The growing of vegetables was concentrated in Baghdad and Hilla provinces, watermelons and tomatoes being the chief crops.[20]

Stock-rearing was practised mainly in north and central Iraq, where it was widespread. In the absence of complete census returns, the government could not know with certainty the actual number of domestic animals in the country. It nevertheless imposed a herd tax (*koda*) on certain animals, and the numbers of animals on which this tax was imposed provide a reasonable foundation for estimates. In FY 1938, the tax was imposed on 5,524,605 sheep, 2,223,528 goats, 82,403 camels and 59,608 buffaloes.[21]

In 1939 the *Istihlak* Tax on Livestock and Produce No. 63 for 1938 replaced the Animal Tax Law No. 15 of 1930. The number of animals on which the *istihlak* tax was imposed does not adequately reflect the number of livestock since they included only slaughtered animals or livestock sold in markets. However, an official census for livestock carried out in Iraq during FY 1951 gave the following estimates: sheep, 10 million; goats, 3 million; cattle, 1.5 million; donkeys, 1 million; buffaloes, 0.7 million; camels, 0.5 million; horses, 0.2 million.[22]

IRRIGATION AND DEVELOPMENT POLICY

In general, agricultural policy in the period under study can be divided into four headings: irrigation policy; loan policy; policy of increasing production (by means of associations, co-operatives, monopolies, farm estates and dissemination of agricultural education); and land settlement policy. This section will deal with the first three categories, which can be termed irrigation and development policy; they differed from land settlement policy in that they were more technical and less 'explosive' from a political point of view.

In January 1931 the Ministry of Irrigation and Agriculture was abolished and its duties divided between the ministries of Finance and of Economics and Communications.[23] No official reason was given for this decision; it seems that the government simply did not attach great importance to this sector. Only twenty-one years later, on the basis of a recommendation by IBRD, was a Ministry of Agriculture re-established.[24]

Despite this lack of interest in agricultural development which was the trend in Iraq of the 1930s, there were some achievements, particularly in irrigation, during that decade. In a report by the director of Operations and Intelligence of the British Air Force stationed in Iraq, it was said that 'the Government appears to take little interest in the betterment of economic conditions amongst the agricultural community', and that the continuing deterioration of this sector was leading to a 'steady drift of the agricultural community to the towns'.[25]

Between 1931 and 1939 agricultural policy was the responsibility of the directorates of Agriculture and of Irrigation, both under the auspices of the Ministry of Economics and Communications. In 1939, with the creation of a separate Ministry of Economics, the Directorate of Agriculture came under its control, while the Ministry of Communications and Works was made responsible for the Directorate of Irrigation (see Ch. 2).

Irrigation Policy

The control and utilization of Iraq's water resources were for generations – and indeed for centuries – the principal problem of the country. Unlike the Nile, the Tigris (1,850 kilometres long) and the Euphrates (2,350 kilometres long) flood their banks too late to help winter crops and too early to prepare the soil for summer crops (except for rice in the south). In other words, although Iraq is endowed with abundant water, sufficient to irrigate all the arable land, it is not available when and where it is needed. In fact, throughout the period examined in this work (and beyond it, to 1956), the danger of devastating floods was always present in the country's southern and central regions (including Baghdad); major floods occurred once every two or three years on both rivers.

After Iraq became independent, the Irrigation Directorate embarked on several projects. Foremost among them during the 1930s was the building of the Kut Barrage on the Tigris.[26] Opened in March 1939, the purpose of the barrage was to divert water to the Gharraf Canal, which was the original course of the main Tigris channel, in order to irrigate 1,456,310 donums of cultivable land, especially for winter crops in the Gharraf area.[27] However, the British noted at the time that although much stress was laid on the advantages which the scheme was to bring to the inhabitants of the Gharraf River valley,

> the benefits conferred by the barrage itself are likely to be small so long as no comprehensive irrigation schemes in the areas concerned are in existence. The only result, in fact, which the barrage seems likely to have in present circumstances is the making available of an additional amount of water for the River Gharraf itself during the flood season.[28]

Other irrigation projects included the Abu-Ghraib Canal, which was opened in 1935 to divert water from the Euphrates south of the city of Fallouja to the vicinity of Baghdad, irrigating more than 264,000 donums in the process; the Deyala Weir, constructed on the Deyala in 1939–40 (after the old weir was destroyed in 1935) to serve an area of 400,000 donums; and the Hawija Project, lying between the left bank of the Tigris and the left bank of the Lesser Zab, opened in 1940 to irrigate an area of 218,447 donums.[29]

Another important achievement during this early period (and in fact up to the end of the period under study) was the development of pump irrigation. In 1926 a law was passed to encourage use of this method by giving partial tax exemptions to all those who extended their cultivation by means of pumps,[30] and in fact there was a steady increase in the number of agricultural pumps during most of the years under study, except during FY 1941, a temporary situation due to the lack of new engines and spare parts created by war conditions.[31]

The pumps were privately owned but the installations were controlled by a licensing system. Pump irrigation (technically called lift irrigation) extended along both banks of the main rivers, throughout the delta, and occasionally in the higher reaches. It was also found on the banks of the main canals where the pumps were aligned through high ground.[32]

Pumps were used to irrigate winter crops in the Irrigation Zone. According to Sousa, the approximate area of winter crops irrigated by pumps at the end of FY 1941 was 2,621,400 donums, or half the area under cultivation for winter crops.[33] Another estimate was the one given by the Haigh report in 1949 and presented in Table 4.2, according to which the area under irrigation was estimated at 12.7 million donums, while the gross area irrigated by pumps from the Tigris, Euphrates and Deyala rivers amounted to 5.9 million donums. The Agricultural Census of 1952–3 estimated that 20% of the area utilized for agriculture was irrigated by pumps, while 49% was rain-fed and 30% was irrigated by gravity flow.[34]

Pump irrigation in Iraq benefited landowners at least as much as it benefited agriculture itself. Installation of pumps facilitated the acquisition of large tracts of land by pump owners (generally tribal sheikhs or urban merchants), for as small farmers became increasingly dependent on the pumps they correspondingly became increasingly indebted to the pump owners. 'The indebtedness very frequently led to the eventual loss of land property to the creditor.'[35]

Another major irrigation project, besides the Kut Barrage, was the Habbaniyya Barrage and flood-escape system, the main pur-

TABLE 4.2 Area Irrigated in 1949 (1,000 donums)

	Gross area	Area cultivated	
		Total	Winter crops
Euphrates			
Flow irrigation	3,109	2,666	1,160
Pump irrigation from canals	607	515	263
Pump irrigation from rivers	955	812	474
Sub total	4,671	3,993	1,897
Tigris			
Flow irrigation	2,380	2,023	760
Pump irrigation from canals	1,060	901	400
Pump irrigation from rivers	3,020	2,567	1,280
Sub total	6,460	5,491	2,440
Deyala			
Flow irrigation	1,350	1,148	572
Pump irrigation	215	183	93
Sub total	1,565	1,331	655
Total	12,696	10,815	5,002

Source: Iraq, Haigh Report, p. 90.

pose of which was to use Lake Habbaniyya, situated on the right bank of the Euphrates, for flood relief in times of dangerously high floods.[36] Work on this scheme started in 1913 but was interrupted by World War I. In 1939 work was begun again, this time to be interrupted by World War II. The decision to complete the project came after strong competition between British and European firms to win the contract, and work was finally completed in the mid-1950s.

During World War II, mainly after 1941, the study and planning of irrigation projects continued, though no major scheme was initiated. Iraq succeeded during the whole of the war in maintaining its vital irrigation services, including pump irrigation.[37]

The post-war period witnessed a strong impetus to develop agriculture in general and irrigation in particular. Iraq was then enjoying financial stability, and had accumulated large reserves of foreign currencies. In May 1945 Prime Minister Hamdi al-Pachachi informed the British ambassador in Baghdad of his government's decision 'to recruit a Commission headed by an engineer of world-wide reputation, to undertake a comprehensive study of irrigation in this country'.[38] Al-Pachachi emphasized that what Iraq desperately needed was sound internal development, and since the country's livelihood rested primarily on agriculture, this development must depend on irrigation. Such a commission was needed, he stressed, because the Irrigation Directorate could not advise on major development projects since its personnel, including the two senior British officials, were fully occupied in directing its day-to-day activities.[39] The ambassador strongly urged the Foreign Office to find a suitable person since he feared that 'if we miss this opportunity there is little doubt that the Iraq government will turn to America'. He further warned that this was 'in fact, exactly the type of capital development in which the United States would wish to participate'.[40]

In July 1946 the Iraqi government announced that an Irrigation Development Commission had been formed, to be headed by Mr F. F. Haigh of the Indian Service of Engineers, whom the Foreign Office recommended highly.[41]

The Irrigation Commission began its work towards the end of 1946, having two targets in mind: to give Iraq complete security from flood damage, and to treble the area of irrigated cultivation.

The British government was very enthusiastic about the second target, that of trebling the area of irrigated cultivation: 'The vast increase in the cultivable area of land will provide a unique opportunity for solving the stubborn problem of land settlement and registration, and for introducing a modern democratic form of land tenure in Iraq.'[42] A major reason for this enthusiasm on the part of the British, as well as of certain circles in the Iraqi government, was that an increase in cultivable land would decrease the necessity for land reform – a measure which, as we shall see, was politically volatile.

In the post-war period, agriculture continued to receive high priority in Iraq's development plans even though four different governments came to power after al-Pachachi's government formed the Irrigation Commission. (This clearly illustrates the point made in Ch. 2, that there was a certain continuity despite the frequent changes of government.) In April 1947 Prime Minister Salih Jabr reiterated what al-Pachachi had told the British ambassador two years previously: 'of the natural resources to be developed, the potential agricultural wealth of the country was first and must be first in the Government's programme. Its development would need money and expert advice, and it must go parallel with the development of irrigation.'[43]

In June 1949 Haigh's Irrigation Commission issued an extensive report on irrigation in Iraq, including quite a few recommendations concerning water utilization.[44] The commission considered Wadi Tharthar to be Iraq's most successful project for the control of Tigris flood waters.

Despite the comprehensiveness of the Haigh report, another survey was made in 1952 by an American engineering firm. Its conclusions – the KTAM report referred to earlier – are outside the scope of this work, but may be said to be very similar to those reached by Haigh's team.[45]

Irrigation policy in Iraq during the period under study was dominated by an engineering approach. Ever since William Willocks presented his report on irrigation in 1911,[46] Iraq's conception of agricultural development was limited to water-control and increasing the area under cultivation, rather than augmenting the productivity of the land already in use. The Willocks report, in fact, provided the framework for all the surveys made afterwards; even cost estimates for proposed irrigation schemes were of the same order as his 1911 figures. Of the projects he recommended only two were carried out: the Hindiyya Barrage, completed under his supervision in 1913; and the Kut Barrage, completed in 1939. But the other two big flood-control schemes, Lake Habbaniyya and Wadi Tharthar, were also a follow-up of the Willocks report.

This emphasis on water-control was, in our opinion, misplaced. It is true that by the mid-1950s Iraq had succeeded both in overcoming the continual danger to its agriculture presented by flooding and in increasing its cultivable land, but the major problem was in fact augmenting the productivity of the land already in use. As will be seen below, the government was not prepared to take action towards solving the complicated problem of land settlement; it thus sufficed itself with the construction of dams and controlling canals because such schemes required money and technology only and did not antagonize the politically strong landowners.

The British (and in the 1950s the Americans too) encouraged Iraq to embark on big projects (which, of course, meant attractive contracts for their firms), but the country's real interests were accurately perceived by a British expert who visited Iraq in 1948: 'I think it is a great pity that more attention is not being paid to the reclamation and de-salting of existing lands. This might give us more wheat in a very much shorter time than the big schemes.'[47]

Nor did the irrigation projects, important as they were, benefit all of Iraq equally. Mosul's British political adviser noted in 1942 that 'in spite of the many irrigation schemes completed in Iraq not one has yet been carried out in the mountain areas'.[48]

In a pamphlet he wrote in 1945 on the history and development of irrigation in Iraq, Ahmed Sousa, a senior official in the Irrigation Directorate, demonstrates awareness of the criticism directed against irrigation policy in Iraq, but his replies to the criticism are unconvincing. He is not convincing, for example, in refuting the charge that, in the absence of a definite development programme, most irrigation schemes were prompted by political or personal motives, and that the distribution of the agricultural areas made available by irrigation was dictated by the government's political inclinations rather than the public interest.[49] Sousa, in explaining the situation, emphasizes two 'facts': that the technical staff of the Irrigation Service was drastically reduced after 1930, and that irrigation did not receive a high proportion of the budget.[50] While the former argument might be true, the latter surely is not. Table 2.4 shows that irrigation projects received, together with army buildings and equipment, the highest share of Iraq's investment – 25% – during the period 1932–50.

Loan Policy

One of the chief impediments to economic development in Iraq (as in most underdeveloped countries) was the lack of modern credit institutions. As explained before, the few banks operating in Iraq during the period under study were foreign, and primarily concerned with commercial transactions. Credit, therefore, could be obtained only from money-lenders, and at very high rates of interest. The peasant, as we shall see, was perpetually in debt because of exorbitant interest rates.[51]

Thus, in 1936 the government stepped in and established the Agricultural and Industrial Bank. The bank's initial capital, advanced by the government, was ID 150,000.[52] The foreign banks in Iraq were approached to subscribe a further sum of ID 100,000 in return for government bonds at an annual interest of 4% and repayable in twenty-five years, but they did not react favourably to this suggestion because 'they have no desire to lock up considerable sums of money for such a long period at a relatively low rate of interest'.[53] (This is another example of the point made in Ch. 3, concerning the foreign banks being uninterested in developing the money market in Iraq.)

A year later the bank's capital was increased to ID 500,000,[54] but by 1950 the government had advanced only ID 460,000. (We shall return later to the question of the bank's capital.)

The division of the Agricultural and Industrial Bank into two separate banks in 1940 (a decision implemented only in 1946 because of the war) did not change its activities. In fact, most of the services undertaken by the bank had been provided before 1936 by the Ministry of Finance, which had a 'liberal attitude towards farmers and industrialists', but 'money loaned by the Government has seldom been repaid in full'.[55]

The bank's most important function was, obviously, providing loans, but its performance in this field was quite modest (Table 4.3). The bank attributed its shortcomings to lack of capital, and repeatedly emphasized this problem in its reports: 'The capital of the Bank, amounting to half a million Dinars and from which only 460 thousand Dinars were withdrawn until this year [1948], is not sufficient in any respect to help the farmers in their agricultural work in a country like Iraq where agriculture is considered the axis of the economy.'[56]

When the government did not come to the bank's assistance, it

TABLE 4.3 Government Loans to Agriculture, 1936-1950

	No. of loans	Amount (ID)
1936	228	40,024
1937	568	84,083
1938	648	88,756
1939	425	59,668
1940	526	73,141
1941	310	40,850
1942	100	31,450
1943	141	23,308
1944	527	97,131
1945	734	166,538
1946	718	247,797
1947	1,970	499,210
1948	463	121,247
1949	-	-
1950	526	144,621
Total	7,884	1,717,824

Sources: For 1936-46, various editions of the <u>Annual Report of the Work of the Agricultural and Industrial Bank</u>, as follows: for 1936-41, <u>Sixth Annual Report</u> (Baghdad, 1942), p. 28; for 1942-4, <u>Ninth Annual Report</u> (Baghdad, 1945), p. 15; for 1946-7, <u>Eleventh Annual Report</u> (Baghdad, 1948), p. 15. For 1947-50, <u>Fifteenth Annual Report of the Work of the Agricultural Bank for the Year 1950-1</u> (Baghdad, 1952), p. 21. (All sources cited are in Arabic.)

Note: Until 1947, loans were granted by the Agricultural and Industrial Bank, thereafter by the Agricultural Bank. Figures for 1936-47 were calculated by subtracting the number and sum of industrial loans from the total provided by the bank.

was decided in November 1948 to stop making loans, and in fact no further loans were granted until June 1950.[57] The bank had to turn to sources other than the Ministry of Finance in order to continue its work, since the total sum of loans granted by the end of FY 1949 was ID 780,000 (the total sum appearing in Table 4.3 does not take repaid loans into account), which was ID 320,000 more than its paid-up capital.[58] To this end the bank received, in early 1950, a grant of ID 100,000 from the Date Association (to help date cultivators in Basra), and a loan of a further ID 100,000 from the National Bank.[59] Subsequently, on the basis of a recommendation by the IBRD mission,[60] the government decided to raise the bank's capital to ID 2 million, but by the end of FY 1951, only ID 100,000 had been added.[61]

The bank's financial difficulties did not stem solely from the government's unwillingness to increase its captial; its lending policy contributed to this problem as well. In its report, the IBRD called for 'a careful review of the Bank's lending policies to make sure they are sound', since 'there has been a tendency for its loans to become frozen'.[62] For example, in FY 1949 only ID 108,333 of the total amount of ID 279,975 in loans falling due was actually received. (Some maturities were postponed, but for other loans not even an arrangement for repayment was made.) The IBRD report implied the reason for this situation: 'The Bank must be quite free of any political pressures and capable of granting and collecting loans without fear or favour.'[63]

In its loan policy, the bank confined itself mainly to the granting of medium-size loans (ID 100–500, the average amount of all loans being ID 250). The maximum credit supplied was ID 1,500. (In 1947 it was decided to raise this limit to ID 3,000, but the bank was able to give only two loans of this magnitude before returning to the ID 1,500 limit, which remained in force until the early 1950s.)[64] On the other hand, small loans (not exceeding ID 100), which were usually given to small farmers, constituted only a minor proportion of the total; during most financial years they ranged between 12% and 20%,[65] and occasionally (e.g. in 1942) amounted to no more than 5%.[66] These small loans were important in that they helped small farmers reduce their level of indebtedness, as well as to purchase simple machinery or animals to increase agricultural production.

The bank's greatest failure was in its inability to reach the great majority of farmers, who badly needed credit. But this failure was not accidental; rather it was the planned policy of the bank. The conditions required for medium- and large-size loans were such that the fellah was unable to fulfill them. According to the bank's regulations collateral against a loan could consist of immovable property, whether land or building (a share of less than 25% in a property was not acceptable); agricultural implements and machinery (75% of their value might be advanced); and non-perishable agricultural crops, provided they were stored in the bank's silos (50% of the estimated value of such crops might be advanced). In addition to these securities, loans could also be made against government guarantee, and against the assets and the unlimited responsibility of the co-operative societies.[67]

This meant, in effect, that the bank's lending policy was directed at big landowners only. In justification of this policy, the bank argued that since the fellah usually turned to the landlord for credit, a loan to a big landowner was in fact help, albeit indirect, to the fellah.[68] But this argument was based on a false assumption, namely, that advances made by landlords to fellaheen were free of interest. The 1933 Law Governing the Rights and Duties of Cultivators, which will be discussed in the next section, stipulated that an advance to a fellah was 'an agricultural debt'. Moreover, the 'advance' was generally in kind – seed, draft animals, machinery, and the like – and had to be repaid in the form of a larger share of the crop, thus concealing a heavy interest charge.

Besides the discriminatory lending policy, the fact that the bank had but a few branches, all of which were located in large cities, further hindered small farmers from obtaining loans.

The IBRD report called for 'a more careful scrutiny of loan applications to make sure that they are intended for productive purposes'.[69] Responding to this recommendation, the bank decided in 1951 to alter its loan policy and concentrate on lending seeds, agricultural machines, and so on – rather than money, which was often spent on purposes totally different from those for which it had been intended.[70] This policy change was important because there was no follow-up procedure, and thus no way of knowing to what uses loans were put. It is worth noting that the bank's reports indicate that the highest proportion of agricultural loans issued during the period 1936–50 went to persons living in Baghdad province (about 24%), 12% to Kirkuk province, and 10% to Basra province – all provinces where agriculture was not the dominant sector.

Besides its main activity of providing loans, the Agricultural and Industrial Bank also subscribed to the capital of some concerns (e.g. a 30% share in the Iraq Cement Company), formed other concerns with the participation of the public, and undertook still other projects entirely on its own (such as a cotton gin in 1939).[71] Most of the projects in which the bank was engaged ended in financial loss. It attributed the failure of one such project, the building of a fishing trawler meant to operate in the Persian Gulf, to 'a variety of reasons, the most important of which was that there has been no comprehensive study of the project, the lack of technical facilities, etc.'.[72] It is most likely that, as with its loans, the bank undertook these projects under political pressure or as a favour to a certain firm or businessman.

The Agricultural Bank, therefore, did not play the important role expected of it in developing agriculture, mainly because this sector of Iraq's economy was dominated by a group of big landowners interested only in their own welfare. When Iversen visited Iraq in late 1952 and early 1953, he summed up the Bank's role by saying: 'So far, however, the accomplishments of the bank have not been very great. One reason for that has been lack of resources, but it also appears to be due in part to a certain lack of initiative and sufficiently broadminded social understanding on the part of the management.'[73]

Policy of Increasing Production

In addition to the irrigation and loan policies discussed above, the managers of Iraq's economy adopted various other measures designed to develop the agricultural sector:

Associations

In January 1937 it was decided to establish an Agricultural Association which would hold annual conferences to study Iraq's agricultural conditions and to acquaint farmers with the modern, scientific methods used by more developed countries.[74] The decision was never implemented, however, and these objectives were passed on to the Agricultural Chambers created in 1938.

An Agricultural Chamber was defined by the law which established it as 'an institution set up for protecting and improving matters of agriculture', to be composed of cultivators and 'whoever wished to join with the consent of the Chamber'.[75] Its primary functions, set forth in another law, were diffusing technical knowledge among farmers and encouraging agricultural production.[76] Because of their structure, these chambers never became a lobby, and continued throughout the period under examination to be limited to technical issues.

Co-operatives

A 'Co-operative Law' was passed in Iraq in 1944, but it made little headway for the first few years. According to a report by Mr Surridge, adviser on co-operation to the Colonial Office, there were only eight co-operative associations in Iraq, all of them in Baghdad, when he visited the country in late 1946. Almost all the co-operatives were consumer associations.[77]

Upon receiving Surridge's report, the Foreign Office began to consider the possibility of the British government providing support and encouragement to the co-operative movement in Iraq (and throughout the Middle East) in order to improve living standards.[78] One of the methods mooted for accomplishing this was intensive public propaganda directed at both the government and the farmers.[79] But the British representative in Baghdad vetoed this suggestion: 'it is I fear certain that publicity in favour of the co-operative movement would be unwelcome to the land-owning classes and therefore to some extent to the Government'.[80] The IBRD report mentioned 'one really worthwhile co-operative', referring to the producers' co-operative in the Dujaila project (see below) which was formed in 1947. In 1951 it owned ten tractors with tillers, two trucks, a small flour mill and a club house.[81]

One of the major difficulties hindering the development of the co-operative movement was the farmers' unwillingness to participate as long as the 'Law Governing the Rights and Duties of Cultivators' remained unamended (see below). This unwillingness, together with the landowners' opposition, led to the movement's stagnation throughout the 1930s and 1940s. (It was only after the 1958 revolution, in fact, that co-operatives began to play a role in Iraq's agricultural development.)

Monopolies

In 1938 Iraq suffered a collapse of agricultural commodity values. Many cultivators then compounded their losses by holding on to their crops in the hope that prices would rise again, a hope which proved unfounded as the market weakened further.[82] Even when commodity prices did not actually fall, they were nevertheless drastically reduced by fierce competition between traders and shippers. The government began contemplating active intervention in the economy, and in 1939, aided by suggestions from British firms, it embarked on a policy of monopolization.

A Date Association was formed that year and given comprehensive powers. In addition to fixing prices, acting as buyer, packer and exporter if necessary, undertaking propaganda on behalf of the date industry, and making advances to date-growers, the association was also authorized to barter dates, to exercise closer control over shipments of dates, and to establish agencies abroad as well as co-operative associations of growers in Iraq itself.[83] Article 13 was the most important clause in the law. It authorized the association to enter into contracts with an exporter or exporters (subject to approval of the Council of Ministers) whereby the contracting party undertook to buy from the association, for export, specified quantities of dates at fixed prices over a given period.[84]

By the time the law was promulgated, all the arrangements for such a monopoly agreement had been worked out with a British company. A few days after the law's publication, it was announced that Messrs Andrew Weir and Co. had signed an agreement with the Date Association.[85] This agreement stipulated that the British company was committed to buy at certain prices specific quantities of three kinds of dates during the 1939, 1940 and 1941 seasons; and to buy the same quantities at a price of 10% more during the 1942 and 1943 seasons. The association for its part undertook not to grant, during the duration of the agreement, any other export licences for the three kinds of dates that the company was buying, except with the company's written approval.[86]

According to Jamil, both the association and the government intended this agreement to be temporary, until better solutions could be found for date exports. It was, however, extended several times (with some modifications due to war conditions), remaining in force until the end of the 1949 season. After reviewing its impact on each of the ten date seasons it covered, Jamil concludes that the agreement was 'a losing proposition' for Iraq.[87]

The grain monopoly produced better results. A law establishing a Grain Regulating Board, published a few months after the creation of the Date Association, gave the same monopolistic powers.[88] (Unlike the date monopoly, however, the grain monopoly was created primarily as a result of conditions arising out of the war.)

An agreement was reached in December 1939 for the purchase of 150,000 tons of barley, again by Andrew Weir and Co.; unlike the date agreement, however, it was limited to six months.[89] This agreement was advantageous to Iraq because it freed the government from having to deal with the shortage of shipping space for export which resulted from the outbreak of war. The Grain Board wanted to renew the agreement in 1940, but as Andrew Weir insisted that prices remain unchanged, no accord was reached.[90] The issue nevertheless reappeared in 1946 when, as a result of decrease in consumption and scarcity of shipping space, a new deal was signed granting Andrew Weir a monopoly for nine months in return for the purchase of 200,000 tons of barley.[91]

Another monopoly begun in 1939 was tobacco. The idea had originated in 1935 when a committee recommended the establishment of a tobacco monopoly which could raise prices and so induce growers to produce tobacco of better quality.[92] The monopoly finally established at the end of 1939 had three objectives: to improve tobacco quality; to assure farmers stable and remunerative prices; and to raise government revenues (this last objective was not explicit and depended on the other two).[93]

In reviewing the results of this monopoly, the IBRD mission concluded that the first objective had not been realized, and that the quality of tobacco had even deteriorated. The second objective was partially realized because farmers' incomes increased during the war period and remained fairly stable in the post-war period.[94] The third objective was clearly achieved: as Table 3.3 indicates, revenues from the tobacco monopoly increased from ID 186,497 in FY 1941, to ID 3,489,650 in 1946, and then decreased to ID 424,293 in 1949. In fact, revenue had become the primary objective of the monopoly. The IBRD report recommended that the monopoly be retained but emphasized the need for an agency which would limit production, since the tobacco being grown was not of sufficient quality to be marketable abroad.[95]

Of the three monopolies discussed here, the grain monopoly must be considered more successful than the other two, in that it at least achieved its primary targets. (The impact on exports will be discussed in Ch. 5.)

The Iraqi government also took various other measures intended to increase agricultural production, such as paying more attention to developing forestry and diffusing agricultural education. These steps gained momentum after the end of World War II, when British experts were engaged to improve production in different branches of agriculture. In 1948 the government began contemplating the possibility of establishing an agricultural college, but this plan was temporarily dropped because a visiting British expert recommended that the funds necessary for such a college (about ID 1 million) could be put to better use by training agricultural officers of the foreman grade, creating co-operatives and launching land settlement schemes.[96] Even with the best of intentions, however, most of the measures failed because of lack of co-ordination between government departments. For instance, when, after much difficulty, a plant pathologist and a botanist – both British – were recruited, it was reported that they 'are being misused, owing to lack of adequate laboratory facilities, and as a result both officers are becoming very discontented'.[97]

While Iraq's irrigation and development policies did score a number of achievements during the 1930s and 1940s (particularly in the field of irrigation), there is no doubt that they were disproportionately influenced by the political motives of the various governments. For every measure the Government contemplated adopting – whether to develop irrigation, to establish co-operatives, monopolies or associations, or to extend agricultural loans or technical assistance – it had to take account of the power of the big landowners. This will become even more evident in our examination of land settlement policy.

LAND SETTLEMENT POLICY

In this section, we shall briefly trace the development of Iraq's complicated land problem and the increased powers of the sheikhs during the mandate period. We shall then examine the land system itself, land settlement laws, the agricultural taxation system, relations between the sheikhs on the one hand and the Iraqi government and the British on the other, the position of the fellah, the situation in the southern province of 'Amara causing the peasants to flee to the cities, and finally, government attempts at land reform.

During their military occupation and subsequent mandate in Iraq, the British sought to create groups of supporters for their policies there. One such group was the sheikhs, whose declining authority (a process which had begun several decades before the occupation) the British bolstered. The process of tribal disintegration was reversed, and that of growing village independence from surrounding tribes was nearly halted. This was done by a number of means. First, the tribal chief was made responsible for administering the law among his tribesmen. Second, the tribal leaders' status was enhanced by their 'election' to Parliament. Third, the land tenure policy, the tax structure and the system of subsidies and cash presents all contributed to a reinforcement of the sheikhs' power.[98]

While the British were engaged in reviving the sheikhs' power, the Iraqi government occasionally attempted to interfere and revoke the sheikhs' newly granted privileges, but it soon realized that only through some form of alliance with the tribal leaders would it be able to retain power itself. 'By the middle 1920's an informal alliance had grown up between the Iraq Government and the larger landowners, whereby in return for their support, the landowners would be left as far as possible to their own devices.'[99]

Thus, by the time Iraq gained its independence in October 1932, the basic 'rules of the game' between the British, the Iraqi government and the tribal leaders were, more or less, defined. We shall now examine the basis for this relationship, whether it was strengthened or weakened during the 1930s and 1940s, and how it influenced agricultural policy in particular and economic policy in general.

The Land System

The obscure and confused condition of all forms of land rights in Iraq hindered the country's agricultural development.[100] Dowson, in his 1931 report, remarked that the tenure of some four-fifths of Iraq's cultivated land was not governed by law, and not regulated in any methodical way at all.[101]

Both Land Settlement Law No. 50 of 1932 and Land Settlement Law No. 29 of 1938 recognized the following categories of land tenure:[102]

1. *Mulk:* land held in full private ownership.
2. *Matruka:* State land specifically reserved by law for public purposes.
3. *Waqf:* land over which some rights were dedicated to a pious purpose. The law distinguished two types:
   (a) *Waqf sahih* (True *waqf*): land which was administered for the benefit of religious institutions by the Awqaf administration, or for the benefit of private persons by *mutawallis* appointed by religious courts.
   (b) *Waqf ghair sahih* (Untrue *waqf*): land from which the taxes or revenue had in the past been assigned to religious institutions by the Turkish government.
4. *Miri:* land divisible into three types:
   (a) *Miri tapu:* land where the right of ultimate ownership was retained by the state, but a usufruct right was acquired by the holder if ten years of productive use was proved. The holder could sell, mortgage, or bequeath the land but it reverted to the state if not used for at least three years.
   (b) *Miri lazma:* land held under the same conditions as *miri tapu*, but with the stipulation that the government might veto the transfer of such land if it tended to disturb the peace, a precaution designed to prevent, where necessary,

the transfer of tribal lands to people outside the tribe. *Lazma* grants were issued upon proof that the holder had made productive use of the land within the preceding fifteen years. Another difference from the *miri tapu* was that *miri lazma* reverted to the state only if not used for at least four years.

(c) *Miri sirf:* land where the state retained legal ownership and possession. This type of land could be exploited directly or indirectly at the state's discretion.

It should be noted that, although the law recognized *tapu* and *lazma* as *miri* or state lands, they were in fact hardly distinguishable from full private ownership. The stipulation that the land would revert to the state if not used for at least three years (in the case of the *tapu*) or four years (in the case of *lazma*) was rarely activated. Prior to 1939, holders of these two categories of land were generally required to pay the state for rent and water rights (payment was lower for *tapu* than for *lazma*), but in that year these assessments were abolished in return for amortization of their capitalized value over a period of ten years.[103] (A 1941 amendment reduced the debt by 20% if paid before the passage of ten years.) The large profits realized by farmers as a result of the inflated agricultural prices during World War II enabled many grantees to take advantage of these new, favourable conditions.[104]

The cadastral survey carried out by the Land Settlement Committees indicates that about 62% of the total area classified at the end of 1950 was *miri sirf*, and only 0.3% was in private ownership (*mulk*).[105]

Another characteristic of Iraq's land system was the extreme polarization of property distribution, a factor which combined with the complex system of land tenure to hinder agricultural development.

Complete data on the distribution of landholdings during the period under examination are not available. The Agricultural Census of 1952–3 provides a classification of numbers of agricultural holdings according to size-group. For the purpose of the census, a holding was defined as a farm or an agricultural estate worked or organized as a single unit. However, some individuals farmed more than one holding as defined above (sometimes in different provinces), while other holdings were jointly held by two or more persons. Therefore, the census figures cannot be used to show distribution of ownership. But, as with most of the other statistics in this work, they do serve to indicate the general trend. However, it should also be remembered that they relate to a total area of only

25.5 million donums, or about 28% of the area of Iraq's fourteen provinces; and a further drawback is that they show only the number of holdings, but not the area, in each size-group. Nevertheless, the census estimates clearly indicate that there were some very large holdings: 104 with an area of 20,000 donums or more.[106]

The Agricultural Census also shows the difference in agrarian structure between the north and the south of Iraq: the average holding was larger in the southern provinces (except for Basra, where dates were cultivated on small holdings) than in the northern provinces (except for Kirkuk).[107]

The figures which emerged from the cadastral survey carried out by the Land Settlement Committees and presented in Table 4.4 are more reliable, and show the same tendency towards polarization. As shown in Table 4.5 this survey covered an area of about 51 million donums, which constituted 54% of the area of the fourteen provinces. Table 4.4 indicates that holdings of over 1,000 donums comprised 67.1% of the total area covered by the survey, while holdings of more than 10,000 donums accounted for 24.3%.

Both the Agricultural Census and the cadastral survey underestimate the prominence of large holdings, for obvious reasons. No mention is made in the Agricultural Census of holdings exceeding 100,000 donums, while the cadastral survey claims there was only one such holding (in Kut). However, the IBRD mission reported that there were actually several holdings of well over 300,000 donums.[108] Khayyat, basing himself on data supplied by the Directorate of Land Settlement and covering privately owned land in six provinces (Baghdad, Kut, Hilla, Delaim, Kirkuk and Arbil) representing an area of 14.3 million donums, argues that there were thirteen properties of between 50,000 and 100,000 donums, and twenty-one properties of between 100,000 and 200,000 donums.[109] According to Batatu, there were eight holdings of more than 100,000 donums (two of which were over 200,000 donums); his figures also indicate that about 63% of the total agricultural area was in holdings exceeding 1,000 donums.[110]

The data presented thus far raise some questions: how was this polarization created, and were there any attempts at land reform during the period 1932–50?

Settlement of Title to the Land

In determining distribution of ownership, the settlement of title (or land settlement) constituted a decisive factor. When the new State of Iraq came into existence, the government was theoretically the

TABLE 4.4 **Distribution of Private Land Holdings (Mulk, Tapu and Lazma) according to the Cadastral Survey, by Province, 1950**

	Percentage of total area covered by Survey	Percentage of area covered by Cadastral Survey in holdings of:					
		1-100 donums	101-500 donums	501-1,000 donums	1,000-10,000 donums	10,001-100,000 donums	100,001-200,000 donums
'Amara	37.7	2.9	2.7	5.0	13.6	75.8	-
Arbil	31.7	19.9	12.7	4.7	57.4	5.3	-
Baghdad	68.7	13.8	17.1	10.7	37.5	20.9	-
Basra	20.6	25.5	16.5	6.8	43.9	7.3	-
Delaim	46.6	24.0	36.3	8.2	19.0	12.5	-
Deyala	37.9	4.1	9.8	11.3	41.3	13.5	-
Diwaniyya	26.2	16.4	19.0	9.9	34.1	20.6	-
Hilla	94.7	18.4	13.7	9.4	41.0	17.5	-
Karbela	42.5	15.7	7.6	1.6	43.8	31.3	-
Kirkuk	44.4	32.4	13.9	5.0	29.8	18.9	-
Kut	100.0	1.8	5.4	4.4	35.7	45.7	7.0
Mosul	64.2	17.1	4.1	2.8	48.8	27.2	-
Sulaimaniyya	14.3	24.7	18.1	8.9	42.4	5.9	-
Total	50.0	15.7	11.0	6.2	42.8	23.2	1.1

Source: IBRD, Economic Development of Iraq, p. 142.

Note: The Cadastral Survey did not cover Muntafiq province.

TABLE 4.5 Area of Land Settled by the Cadastral Survey 1933-50, by Type of Tenure (donums)

	Mulk	Matruka	Waqf	Miri granted in tapu	Lazma	Miri sirf	Total
1933	13,497	8,703	1,635	143,397	275,020	84,359	526,611
1934	4,236	16,916	-	316,400	374,390	334,502	1,046,444
1935	22,108	24,547	68,188	246,514	605,132	1,139,931	2,106,420
1936	10,424	7,655	43,866	112,626	290,373	437,905	902,849
1937	2,161	7,606	25,160	271,748	117,056	302,668	726,399
1938	520	22,414	17,772	290,408	556,406	1,064,678	1,952,198
1939	4,954	20,481	26,010	354,000	719,698	1,040,914	2,166,057
1940	11,579	61,937	9,622	405,665	579,410	1,183,141	2,251,354
1941	14,635	89,132	22,996	394,357	436,693	1,057,223	2,015,036
1942	18,342	113,009	90,637	484,030	585,369	2,115,684	3,407,071
1943	6,120	192,518	18,686	614,483	353,280	3,422,365	4,607,452
1944	8,223	148,709	14,104	409,535	439,420	3,049,647	4,069,638
1945	1,577	103,972	16,712	309,516	382,527	923,091	1,737,395
1946	6,622	174,830	39,855	1,059,573	401,663	1,442,041	3,124,584
1947	4,897	176,754	30,403	930,955	344,263	2,898,550	4,385,822
1948	5,998	117,060	67,323	687,735	354,087	7,086,542	8,318,745
1949	20,054	143,495	21,010	897,545	554,352	1,146,992	2,783,448
1950	4,481	353,049	76,951	889,427	424,333	3,064,934	4,813,175
Total	160,428	1,782,787	590,930	8,817,914	7,793,472	31,795,167	50,940,698

Source: Statistical Abstract 1951, p. 133.

largest landowner. However, it had no effective rights over the land, except the uncertain power to tax.

The mandatory government had not attempted to solve the problem of land settlement, except for some spasmodic and ineffectual efforts to settle the Muntafiq claims which had their roots in the tribal rivalry in this province.[111] In 1929, Sir Ernest Dowson was asked by the Iraqi government to examine the question of land settlement and make recommendations for its reform. He concluded that the problem consisted of 'the need to establish security and clarity of tenure everywhere by a general definition and settlement on a clear basis of both statutory and equitable rights to land'.[112] Two of his major recommendations were that no attempt should be made to introduce a general settlement of title in freehold ownership, but that land grants should be made, after survey, in ten-year tenancies; and that settlement of rival claims should be made on the principle of beneficial use.[113]

A few months after he published his report, Dowson sent a confidential memorandum to the High Commissioner in Baghdad, Sir Francis Humphrys, on this subject, criticizing the policy of the former High Commissioner, Sir Henry Dobbs. (Dowson had not wanted to publish this criticism in his official report.)[114] In a 1926 memorandum, Dobbs had proposed methods of reinforcing the sheikhs' position: 'Where possible the position of the existing tribal chiefs should be recognised by giving them perhaps a somewhat larger holding than other persons and possibly in some districts by imposing on them the task of collecting Government revenue, taking a percentage for the expenses of collection.'[115] Dowson strongly objected to Dobbs's approach, commenting: 'I do not myself think either simplification, or public peace or economic advance are to be realised by a deliberate policy of establishing a series of large holders as intermediaries in dealing with the mass of small holders.'[116]

Though aware of the kinds of political considerations Dobbs had thought would strengthen the British position in Iraq (such as the reinforcement of tribalism and the establishment of local magnates), Dowson insisted that Dobbs's approach was wrong if the problem was to be dealt with as one involving only land tenure.[117] It was ultimately Dobbs's approach, however, and not Dowson's which was to prevail, because the problem was clearly not an academic one of land tenure alone but rather a matter involving complex political interests.

Dowson's published report resulted in two important laws: Land Settlement Law No. 50 of 1932 and Lazma Law No. 51 of 1932. The latter created a new type of land tenure, *lazma,*[118] while the former authorized the Land Settlement Committees appointed to administer the law to grant *lazma* to people who could demonstrate that they had made productive use of land within the previous fifteen years. What happened in practice, however, was quite different from the kind of land reform the law set out to achieve:

In practice, it had been possible to obtain title on the presentation of proof that a crop was produced on the land in one year, and the land settlement committees have occasionally accepted even more tenuous proof of cultivation. In this way many sheikhs and other influential persons have managed to obtain title to large tracts of land without any payment whatsoever.[119]

Thus, in accordance with Land Settlement Law No. 50 of 1932 and Land Settlement Law No. 29 of 1938,[120] which was amended by Law No. 44 of 1939,[121] the government began distributing lands. This process continued until 1952, when the law was again amended. The pages of the *Iraq Government Gazette* of the 1930s and 1940s provide a good indication of the speed with which land was distributed and of the size of grants. During the period 1933–52, 317 regulations granting *lazma* lands were published.[122] For instance, in December 1938 Mohammad Habib, a prominent sheikh from the Rabi'a tribe and a supporter of the British, was granted *lazma* land amounting to 75,291 donums.[123] The process of assigning tribal land to large landowners accelerated greatly after 1940, with the enactment of the Law for the Sale of Miri Sirf Land.[124]

One reason for granting vast areas of land to tribal leaders was the government's increasing need for cash to finance economic projects and expand the armed forces. This was, however, but a secondary reason, since the fees received in return for the lease were quite low.[125] The main reasons were, as explained above, the policy of consolidating the sheikhs' power, the unwritten alliance between the sheikhs and the politicians, and the fact that tribal leaders were entering into partnership with politicians and urban merchants to develop their lands.

Thus the very laws which resulted from Dowson's report and were supposed to end the confused conditions of legal rights to the land became a tool in the hands of the sheikhs and politicians, enabling them to increase their power by acquiring vast holdings. Ibrahim al-Kabir, director-general of the Ministry of Finance, summed up the consequence of these laws in his memoirs: 'The result, in practice, of the land tenure bill was that large plots of land were distributed to Ministers, deputies, directors general and other people who were able to acquire them free of charge at the end of a period of three years.'[126]

Another result of Dowson's report, besides these laws, was the establishment of Settlement Committees whose primary task was to conduct a cadastral survey to define the various categories of land and their ownership; to confirm the rights appurtenant to land, such as water and drainage rights; and to delimit boundaries and define areas of land.[127] However, after eighteen years the cadastral survey – the cornerstone of the land settlement efforts – had covered only 54% of the area of Iraq's fourteen provinces and 29% of its total area. As Table 4.5 shows, some 51 million donums were surveyed between 1933 and the end of 1950; most of these lands (62%) was of the *miri sirf* type, while *miri* granted in *tapu* constituted about 17% of total settled land, and *lazma* 16%.

Four Committees of Settlement were established in Baghdad and Kut immediately after promulgation of the 1932 Land Settlement Law. In 1950 there were fourteen committees (with forty-four branches) distributed throughout the country (except in Muntafiq, where settlement of title never got underway, and in Kut, where settlement was already completed).[128] These committees did not, however, tackle the purely tribal areas:[129]

> In the areas where the tribal system still functions as a reality no land settlement has really been undertaken at all, i.e. in 'Amara (mainly rice fields), in Diwaniya where the risks are too great, and in Muntafig [*sic*], where there is an endless struggle between the Sadan [*sic*] family who claim to be the principal landowners, and the occupying peasants, which has from time to time led to outbreaks of violence. Here Government has failed to intervene.[130]

In consequence, the coverage of the cadastral survey in the different provinces was by no means uniform (Table 4.4). Thus, by the end of 1950, out of the 51 million donums surveyed by the Land Settlement Committees about 3 million donums (6%) were in 'Amara and 1.5 million donums (3%) in Diwaniyya; no land at all was settled in Muntafiq.[131] Among the reasons for this modest achievement were the fact that the settlement commissioners (mainly British) were influenced by political and personal considerations, and the corruption which spread among the committees.[132] In 1934 it was stated that one of the main difficulties facing land settlement was the insufficient numbers of competent Iraqi assistant settlement officers and British officers.[133] True as this might have been, the major factor remained government policy, which was to solidify tribal structure. Leading British advisers defended the Land Settlement Law of 1932 and argued that it was beneficial to the agricultural community as a whole: 'by the application of the law, even in its present form, large numbers of small cultivators have been given a security of tenure which they have never enjoyed before.'[134]

The only real, if ineffective, attempt to change this policy occurred in 1936. The government which came to power after Bakr Sidqi's *coup d'état* that year harshly criticized the policy of granting large blocks of land to individual owners. The MESC report on land tenure argued that this criticism was made 'probably in order to score off the British officials who had been largely responsible for the settlement policy'. Nevertheless, although British officials claimed 'that the Iraq Government itself connived at this procedure by allowing powerful owners to jump claims to land before settlement', the report admitted that the criticism was made on a sound principle.[135] However, some writers continued to argue that British influence on land tenure policy 'was only advisory',[136] or that criticism of committees 'has been commonly exaggerated' since its members 'created no rights, they recorded what rights they found to exist'.[137]

Agricultural Taxation

The system of agricultural taxes in Iraq was another important factor, besides the granting of *lazma* lands, in enhancing the big landowners' position.

Collection of land tax in Iraq was never efficient under Ottoman rule, and when the British occupied the country they faced total chaos in this area. Indeed, until 1927 tribal leaders enjoyed immunity from property tax.[138]

The impact of the Great Depression of 1929 continued to be felt in Iraq throughout 1930 and 1931. Revenues from land fell sharply because grain prices were so low.[139] The government therefore began to look for means of increasing its income from the agricultural sector. This came in the form of the *istihlak* (consumption) tax, which replaced the land tax. The new tax was based on the gross produce of land, but was levied only upon the produce which reached market. It was collected in special centres where agricultural products, livestock and fish were sold for consumption, processing or export. The duty on all types of land produce subject to the tax was fixed at 10%.[140] (In 1948 this was raised to 12%, and in 1950 lowered slightly to 11.5%.)

In 1933 the legislation was completely rewritten. The new *istihlak* tax law, while introducing no substantive changes, added definition as well as many details regarding collection and administration.[141] There were several later amendments to the 1933 law (the first in 1936) but, again, nothing substantial.[142]

Before examining the implications of this law, let us fill out the picture on agricultural taxation. The Law for the Collection of Land Rent was adopted together with the first *istihlak* law. It repealed all existing forms of land taxation, and imposed a water tax on all lands (*miri* and *mulk*) and a land rent levy on most *miri* lands.[143]

The Land Rent Law was completely revised in 1936 by the Land Tax Law. Intended to supplement the *istihlak* tax, the new levy affected government-owned and government-irrigated lands.[144] It was based upon gross produce, and was collected in cash on all cultivated lands not specifically exempted, at the following rates:[145]

(a)	*On alienated lands:*	
	Regular free-flow land	10%
	Irregular free-flow land	5%
(b)	*On miri lands:*	
	Regular free-flow land	15%
	Irregular free-flow land	10%
	Rain land	5%
	Lift land	2%
	High-lift land	1%
(c)	*Produce of tobacco, fresh and dried vegetables and fruits*	2.5%

But the land tax brought little revenue to the government, and so was replaced in 1939 by new legislation allowing land rents (*a*) and (*b*) to be abolished through the payment, in ten annual instalments, of a sum equivalent to twelve average payments.[146] Discounts for early payment, plus inflation, made this burden a light one for the rich landowners, while the poorer tenants of *miri sirf* land continued to pay the tax.[147] Land rent (*c*) remained in force as before.

As agricultural revenue was exempt from income tax, in accordance with Law No. 36 of 1939, the *istihlak* law remained the major agricultural tax throughout the period under study.

Because of the arbitrary nature of certain articles of the *istihlak* law (e.g. empowering local chambers of commerce to fix price scales, and limiting the sale and storage of agricultural produce to certain licensed premises), tax abuses and evasions proliferated.[148] (The latter were estimated at 10–30% of gross produce during the 1930s.)[149] Furthermore, the *istihlak* tax was a regressive one since it imposed the same rate on the produce of both wealthy and poor farmers. Being a levy on transaction, the tax discouraged the farmer from bringing his produce to market. Another disadvantage of the law was that it reduced the surveying of lands by the Land Settlement Committees to an issue of secondary importance for the government, as there were no longer any financial incentives to hasten the classification of land for taxation purposes.[150] But the main disadvantage was that it created a situation in which landowners were taxed lightly while the real burden was passed on to the urban consumer, who had to pay higher prices for agricultural produce.

In the discussion on government receipts we saw that agricultural taxes contributed only a modest share (14–21%) of total ordinary receipts, even though the majority of Iraq's population earned its living from agriculture. In no year during the period 1932–50 did taxes on land and land produce exceed revenues from customs and excises (Table 3.3). Of course, an increase in agricultural taxation would have meant violating the unwritten alliance between politicians and tribal leaders, and this the government was not ready to do. The 1934 annual report of the British Embassy in Baghdad made it clear that the government's policy was opposed to increasing agricultural taxes so as to make them provide a greater share of government income.[151]

The 1948 increase in the rate of the *istihlak* tax was not an adequate measure to increase revenues from agriculture. Its effect was rather to augment the already high price of food, for the producers immediately passed on the cost of the increased taxation to the consumer.[152]

Some governments, however, did want to reform land policy. The government headed by Hikmat Sulayman, which came to power in October 1936 after Bakr Sidqi's *coup d'état*, was not satisfied with the land revenue system. (The same government tried, in vain, to halt the granting of *lazma* lands.) Sulayman believed in the urgency of changing agricultural taxation (he pointed out that the system dated back to Midhat Pasha, who governed Iraq between 1869 and 1872),[153] but his motives were not purely economic: it was his intention to weaken the tribal leaders politically. Confronted by fierce opposition from the sheikhs and their allies, who threatened an armed uprising if government land policy were changed, four ministers in Sulayman's government resigned in protest against the prime minister's attitude. Sulayman's position was undermined, and his government fell in August 1937.[154]

The sheikhs were adamant in their opposition to changes in the tax system, whatever the country's socioeconomic conditions. When Iraq was facing acute inflation during World War II, the Inflation Committee recommended taxing the farmers, who were accumulating high profits. Commenting on this recommendation, the British

Embassy in Baghdad said: 'It is anticipated, however, that there will be strong opposition to any increase in indirect taxes on farmers and even stronger opposition to a direct tax, such as Income-Tax. It has to be borne in mind that the agricultural community has a large majority in Parliament.'[155] The Embassy proved correct in its judgement. But the question that must be asked is: how did the sheikhs acquire such power in Parliament, especially since Parliament was more or less controlled by the government? The answer lies in the triangular relationship between the British, the Iraqi government and the sheikhs, in which the election of sheikhs to Parliament was but one component.

THE BRITISH, THE IRAQI GOVERNMENT AND THE SHEIKHS

As explained in the beginning of this part, the British revived the power of the sheikhs during the mandate period and Iraqi politicians found it impossible to rule without the sheikhs' support. After 1932 the independent government was eager to eliminate the tribes' military power but was not prepared to wage a public battle against them. As a memorandum written by King Faisal on Iraq's problems and future and sent to his closest aides in March 1933 said:

> The solution of the land problem will bind the population to the land, and this has important implications for the sheikhs and their influence. There is no need to elaborate its advantages and it should be implemented as fast as possible. The sheikhs and aghas should not feel that the Government's intention is to wipe them out; rather as far as circumstances permit, the Government should reassure them about their livelihood and well-being.[156]

However, Faisal's death in September of that year and the accession of Ghazi, who had no popular base and was preoccupied with motor racing and broadcasting from the private radio station at his palace rather than with his country's burning issues,[157] created a vacuum the sheikhs knew how to exploit. But it should be emphasized here that the worst legislation from the fellah's point of view (as will be seen below) was promulgated before Faisal's death, which clearly indicates that Faisal, though anxious to reduce the sheikhs' power, never envisaged actually destroying it. This political imbalance continued after the *coup d'état* of 1936 and beyond, the sheikhs overcoming the short-lived efforts by Hikmat Sulayman's government to introduce land reforms.

During this period, election to Parliament was another means, besides *lazma* grants and taxation, by which the sheikhs enhanced their position. As Edmonds put it in 1937: 'For many years the "election" has been "appointment" without disguise ... If the Government does not influence the elections somebody lower down in the official hierarchy will.'[158] Edmonds called for a policy which would be a 'little more elastic' with regard to 'appointment' because elections were becoming 'a serious cause of embarrassment particularly on the Euphrates'.[159] The reasons for this embarrassment were: the *liwas* of Muntafiq and Diwaniyya had more deputies than the numbers to which they were entitled under the Electoral Law of 1924; in Diwaniyya nearly all the seats were given to tribesmen, without any representation for townsmen; and the large number of seats available in this area resulted in several being allotted to members of one tribe, thus creating jealousy among tribes from other areas.[160]

The period following the British reoccupation of Iraq in 1941 witnessed an intensive strengthening of the tribal leaders' position. When the Rashid 'Ali uprising occurred, a British cabinet committee decided 'to enlist friendship of tribes viz a viz [*sic*] Rashid Ali Regime',[161] and when the sheikhs of 'Amara and Kut did not support the 1941 movement, the British decided to reward them.[162] From 1943 onwards, the proportion of sheikhs and agas in Parliament increased substantially.[163] The sheikhs' role in the executive branch of government also grew: their share of ministerial appointments rose from nil in the period 1932–41, to 3.4% in 1941–6, and to 6% in 1947–58.[164]

Thus, granted vast areas of land, elected to Parliament and lightly taxed, this small segment of the population controlled considerable wealth and power. A British commercial secretary of the time has given us a lucid description of how a typical tribal leader, Sheikh Ajil al-Yawar of the northern Shammar tribe, conducted his affairs:

> Foreseeing the end of nomadic days he asserted his ownership of those villages which fringed the northern desert. He levied until very recently a head tax on the thousands of sheep passing through his area to Syria. He received large sums for the preservation of tranquillity in the period when the Iraq Petroleum Company were constructing their pipe line. He now supplies workers and guards to the British Oil Development Company and on the wages of each the Shaikh [*sic*] levies ten per cent; he has recently come to an agreement with the Iraq Railways to supply labour on a large scale for railroad construction in the Mosul region. Again he will collect his ten per cent ...[165]

One might imagine that with such increases in the sheikhs' wealth and power there would be a concommitant improvement in the fellah's situation, but this was not the case.

The Fellah

Ironically, the fellah's situation deteriorated after Iraq's independence, with the enactment of the Law Governing the Rights and Duties of Cultivators No. 28 of 1933[166] (in effect, the rights of the farm-owner and the duties of the fellaheen). The farm-owner became the agricultural authority who gave the orders for sowing, irrigating and harvesting (Article 3), and the fellah was obliged to carry out these orders or face severe penalties (Article 18). All advances and supplies to the fellah by the farm-owner were regarded as an 'agricultural debt' (Article 10); if the fellah delayed payment, he faced the penalties stated in Article 18. The fellah's agricultural debt was a 'preferential' one over other debts (Article 12), and an indebted fellah might have his plough and plough animals confiscated unless he continued to work on the same estate (Article 13). A fellah who did not pay his debts at his former place of employment could not be employed elsewhere (Article 15). The law empowered the farm-owner to dismiss or evict his *sirkal* (overseer of fellaheen or farm manager) or fellah if it was proved that they might be negligent. And since virtually every disaster affecting the harvest was attributed to the fellah, the fate of the *sirkal* and the fellah came to rest totally in the landowner's hands.[167]

The law stated the fellah's rights as well, but only in vague terms; as the retired inspector-general of agriculture, Mr Webster, pointed out, 'one is obliged to regard the fellah's rights as theoretical only'. Highly critical of the law, Mr Webster summed it up by saying: 'the fellah under the provisions of the present law, is doomed to perpetual indebtedness ... he is, in reality, reduced to the status of a slave'.[168]

Webster anticipated troubles among the fellaheen when the law was applied, but Sir Kinahan Cornwallis (then adviser to the Ministry of the Interior) thought it unlikely to provoke serious unrest, especially as 'the Law appears incapable of universal application throughout Iraq'.[169] Indeed, it was fortunate for the fellah that it was never the custom in Iraq to enforce laws wholeheartedly, but there is no doubt that his situation continued to deteriorate throughout the period under study.

The miserable conditions of the fellah's life were clearly reflected in the low share he received of the land's produce, which generally varied from one-third to one-half.[170] In the spring of 1933 Bonné noted this distribution of crop yields in central Iraq: the government received 10% of the total harvest, the landowner claimed as his first share 7.5%, the head of the fellaheen group (*sirkal rais*) received 2.5%, and the remaining 80% was divided into a further 40% for the landowner and 40% for the fellah. Very often, however, the fellah had to repay the credit with which he had bought the seed, at a high rate of interest, and was thus in fact left with much less than 40%.[171] But conditions varied greatly from one region to another. In 'Amara province during the 1940s, the rice peasant received half the produce if he provided the seed, and only one-third if the sheikh supplied the seed.[172] Warriner estimated that the southern landowner received between three-fifths and two-thirds of the crop (depending on whether he supplied the seed) if the land was flow-irrigated, and five-sevenths if it was pump-irrigated. In northern Iraq, she estimated the landowner's maximum share on pump-irrigated land as half the crop, and from one-eighth to one-quarter in dry-farming areas.[173] Thus, living in extreme poverty and having a serf-like relationship with the sheikh, the fellah had no way of improving his situation except by leaving the land and migrating to the cities.

Data on rural-to-urban migration in Iraq do not exist. The only available estimate is the one provided by the 1957 census: 378,996 inhabitants living in Baghdad (i.e. about 29% of its total population) were born outside the province of Baghdad, and 18% of Basra's population came from outside that province.[174] Batatu puts the number of persons migrating to Baghdad province during the years 1947–57 at 205,765.[175] While these statistics may not be accurate, they do give an indication of the seriousness of the problem.

On the whole, migration to cities originated in those provinces where the concentration of sheikhly power was extreme. The way in which land titles were settled in the south and the substantial capital expenditure needed there for irrigation served to swell the power of the landlord class. Thus, the largest volume of internal migration came from the southern *liwas*, with the central ones in second place.[176] Employment opportunites were expanding rapidly in the cities, and the fellaheen hoped that there they would find an end to their misery; but in fact once arrived, they lived in *sarifas* (reed-mat huts) in unbearable sanitary conditions, which the government took no measures to ameliorate.[177]

In order to better understand the motivation for this flight to the cities, it may be appropriate to take a close look at the southern provinces so typical of Iraqi feudalism at the time, where most of the internal migration originated.

'Amara and Kut Provinces

The most striking feature of land distribution in 'Amara, the extensive province in the Tigris marshes (where diseases like bilharzia and trachoma were rife), was its concentration of large holdings. According to the Agricultural Census, 'large holdings of 20,000 mesharas or more were found in each of the administrative sub-divisions of the *liwa* and among the 29 holdings in this size group, seven holdings were over 50,000 mesharas'.[178] Three sheikhs and the sons of four others held 1,824,841 donums, or about 53% of the total area of the holdings covered by the census. Ten other sheikhs held an additional 689,561 donums (about 19%).[179] The 483 holdings surveyed by the Agricultural Census had an average size of 6,884 donums (a stark contrast with the averages of Baghdad and Basra *liwas*, which were 407 and 25 donums respectively).[180]

Another characteristic of the agrarian situation in 'Amara was the very high percentage of rented land, amounting to over 97%, whereas only 30% of the holdings in all fourteen provinces covered by the census was rented land. Another particularity of 'Amara was that 44% of the total land in its holdings was lying fallow and about 26% was uncultivable (both proportions were high in comparison with most other provinces).[181]

This concentration of land (and thus of wealth) in the hands of a few sheikhs led to a deterioration of economic conditions in the province, which in turn led to a high migration of fellaheen to the cities. Already in 1932 it was reported that:

> The uncertainty of the leading shaikhs [*sic*] of the Bani Lam [one of the four tribes holding most of the property in 'Amara] regarding government policy, their inherent dislike of innovations and a steadily accumulating burden of debt [on the fellah], have led to large areas of agricultural land, normally leased to sub-tenants, being allowed to lie fallow; this coupled with poverty and lack of grazing, has induced a considerable proportion of the agrarian and tribal population to seek temporary residence on the Persian side of the frontier, or migrate to the cities in the hope of finding permanent employment there.[182]

Because of its political alliance with the sheikhs, the government took no tangible measure to alleviate the sufferings of the fellaheen.[183] 'Amara was notorious as a *liwa* where officials were corrupted by sheikhs forcing money on them lest they otherwise be tempted to reduce the sheikhs' land holdings.[184]

The migration from 'Amara to Baghdad and Basra had an important impact on those two provinces, where many aspects of life in the big cities, especially in Baghdad, were affected by the migrants (known as *shargawiyya*).[185]

Landholdings in Kut were nearly as concentrated as in 'Amara but the available documentation relating to agrarian life in that province is much skimpier. According to the Agricultural Census, eighteen holdings (out of 1,531) exceeded 10,000 donums and eleven holdings exceeded 20,000 donums, while the average holding in the province was 1,087 donums.[186] Many of the lands were held by absentee landlords in Baghdad who had strong connections with politicians or were themselves politicians. As Batatu points out, landholding in Kut symbolized the partnership between the sheikhs and the Baghdad absentee landlords upon which the monarchical regime largely rested.[187]

Land Reform: The Dujaila Project

Against this rather grim picture of the agrarian situation in Iraq in the 1930s and 1940s, two questions arise: was the government aware of the seriousness of the problem, and what attempts did it make at land reform?

The answer to the first question must be positive. First and foremost, awareness of the problem was reflected in the promises of vast reforms included in almost every government plan, though these promises never quite left the paper on which they were printed. A particularly convincing illustration of this awareness was the lengthy document drawn up in 1944 by the regent, 'Abd al-Ilah (who, by virtue of his political longevity, in contrast with the frequently changing governments, was the dominant figure in Iraq from 1939 until 1958). Setting out the lines on which he wished the government to work, 'Abd al-Ilah made the following proposal regarding the agrarian situation:

> The stopping of the policy of distributing land to influential persons on various pretexts and instead its distribution to the real cultivators and farmers themselves in reasonable lots. Provided that no persons shall be permitted to hide under the name of a farmer or planter and that no large estates shall be given to persons under assumed names.[188]

This document, unlike those formulated by prime ministers and senior officials, produced a tangible result: in 1945 the government decided to launch the Dujaila Project for Land Settlement. It should be emphasized that this was the only land reform project worth mentioning during the period under study.

Prime Minister Hamdi al-Pachachi defined the Dujaila land

settlement scheme as 'an extensive project aiming at the creation of a high class of prosperous cultivators who will maintain modern standards of cultivation, dwelling and social life'.[189] Its basic feature was that a tenant might, upon occupancy, receive a hundred donums of state land rent-free in exchange for ten years of continuous cultivation. After ten years the land was registered in his name, but he could not sell it for another ten years.[190]

When the Miri Sirf Land Development Law for 1945 (more commonly known as the Dujaila land settlement law) was introduced, it met with strong opposition from the sheikhs; moreover, the government had great difficulty in inducing the fellaheen to accept land grants.[191] Between 1946 and 1950, 1,058 farmers were settled in Dujaila on hundred-donum plots. The IBRD mission which visited the project was impressed by its results and described it as 'conspicuously successful'.[192] At the same time, the mission was also aware of the scheme's defects: increased salination of land because of failure to provide drainage facilities; small-scale 'landlordism' as some of the farmers brought in others to do a large part of the work on a share-cropping basis; and lack of improvement in farming methods. Nevertheless, the fellaheen's economic position was enhanced by the mere fact that they did not have to share their output with a landlord.[193]

The 1945 law was later expanded and supplemented by the 'Law for the Development of *Miri Sirf* Lands of 1951'[194] but until the 1958 revolution, legislation on land tenancy was kept within such bounds as would not be actively resisted by landowners. The result was that no real agrarian reform took place during the period 1932–50.

Although more and more virgin land was brought under the plough due to the improved irrigation and high level of investment in the agricultural sector during the 1930s and 1940s, wasteful methods of cultivation resulted in the steady deterioration of soil in the flow-irrigated plains. The IBRD mission's enquiries in 1951 indicated that as much as 20–30% of Iraq's cultivated land had been abandoned over the preceding few decades because of salt accumulation, while on a large part of the remaining land yields had declined by 20–50%, or even more.[195] Furthermore, although the area of production of most crops increased during 1932–50 (see Table 4.1) and the production of certain crops, such as barley, increased, it should be made very clear that the benefits of these accomplishments were enjoyed mainly by the landowners.

Thus, it can be said that while Iraq's agricultural policy in the period 1932–50 registered some impressive achievements, mainly in the field of irrigation, it failed, largely because of political factors, to change the country's basic agrarian structure or to improve the fellaheen's situation.

NOTES

1. Dowson, *Inquiry into Land Tenure*, p. 11.
2. Ibid.
3. As mentioned in the Introduction, Iraq's total area is 177 million donums. 94 million donums comprising the fourteen provinces, and the remaining 83 million donums consisting of the three deserts. Donum will be the area unit used in this chapter. A donum (or meshara) equals 0.62 acres, and 400 donums equal 1 square kilometre.
4. Iraq, *Report on the Agricultural and Livestock Census of Iraq, 1952–3* (Baghdad, 1954), pp. 16–17.
5. IBRD, *Economic Development of Iraq*, p. 137.
6. Doreen Warriner, *Land Reform and Development in the Middle East* (London, 1957), p. 116. Warriner quotes the KTAM report's estimate of about 8 million donums. Knappen–Tippetts–Abbett–McCarthy Engineers, *Report on the Development of the Tigris and Euphrates River Systems* (New York and Baghdad, 1954, mimeo; known as the KTAM Report).
7. *Agricultural Census*, p. 18.
8. Doris Philips, 'Rural-to-Urban Migration in Iraq', *Economic Development and Cultural Change* vii (1959), pp. 407–8.
9. A. P. G. Poyck, *Farm Studies in Iraq* (Wageningen, 1962), p. 7.
10. United Nations, *Review of Economic Conditions in the Middle East 1951–52* (New York, 1953), pp. 16–18.
11. IBRD, *Economic Development of Iraq*, p. 237.
12. *Agricultural Census*, p. 19.
13. *Statistical Abstract 1950*, p. 121. See also Dabbagh, *Études statistiques*, p. 284.
14. *Statistical Abstract 1950*, p. 130.
15. Ibid.
16. Warriner, *Land Reform*, pp. 118–19. The 25% tax was abolished in 1956.
17. Board of Trade, *Economic and Commercial Conditions*, p. 19.
18. *Agricultural Census*, p. 19.
19. *The Middle East 1950*, Europa Publications Limited (2nd edn., London, 1950), p. 169.
20. For details, see *Agricultural Census*, pp. 19–20.
21. *Statistical Abstract 1939*, p. 93.
22. *Statistical Abstract 1951*, p. 181.
23. Brown (American Legation, Baghdad) to Dept. of State, 18 Aug. 1931. ACR, Reel 5.
24. IBRD, *Economic Development of Iraq*, pp. 272–4.
25. Director of Operations and Intelligence (Air Ministry) to FO, 'Review of Events in Iraq for the Year 1934', 7 Feb. 1935. FO 371/18949, E 898/464/93.
26. Kathleen M. Langley, *The Industrialization of Iraq* (Cambridge, Mass., 1961), p. 119.
27. Ahmed Sousa, *Irrigation in Iraq* (Baghdad, 1945), p. 162.
28. Houstoun-Boswall to FO, 6 Apr. 1939. FO 371/23217, E 2647/2647/93.
29. For more details on these projects, see Sousa, op. cit., pp. 42, 162, 351–4; Abdul Wahab al-Dahiri, *The Introduction of Technology into Traditional Societies and Economies (Using Iraq as a Case Study)* (Baghdad, 1969), pp. 116–18.
30. United Kingdom, *Progress of Iraq*, p. 198.
31. *Statistical Abstract 1944 & 1945*, p. 104.
32. Iraq, Directorate General of Irrigation, *Report on the Control of the Rivers in Iraq and the Utilisation of their Waters* (Baghdad, 1951), pp. 2–3. (Hereafter: the Haigh report.)
33. Ahmed Sousa, *Iraq Irrigation Handbook*. Part I: The Euphrates (Baghdad, 1944), p. 4.
34. *Agricultural Census*, p. 18.
35. Gabriel Baer, 'The Agrarian Problem in Iraq', *Middle Eastern Affairs* iii, no. 12 (December 1952), p. 382.

36. For a detailed description of the technical aspects of this project, see Sousa, *Iraq Irrigation Handbook*, pp. 44–51.
37. Longrigg, *Iraq: 1900 to 1950*, p. 323.
38. Stonehewer-Bird to FO, 3 May 1945. FO 371/45324, E 3116/624/93.
39. Ibid.
40. Ibid. This is one of many examples showing how Anglo-American competition in the Middle East in the post-war period affected the countries of the region.
41. FO to Professor Ashley (Oxford University), 3 July 1946. FO 371/52415, E 5905/493/93.
42. Memorandum by FO on 'Development of Irrigation in Iraq', 20 Mar. 1947. FO 371/61509, E 1883/183/65.
43. Record of a meeting held at the British embassy in Baghdad on 22 April 1947 to discuss Iraq's economic development. Participants: Iraq's prime minister, the British ambassador, Iraq's minister of communications and works, and a representative of BMEO. FO 371/61621, E 3374/68/93.
44. The Haigh Report has been summarized and analysed in several works; see, for example: IBRD, *Economic Development of Iraq*, pp. 193–203; Qubain, *Reconstruction of Iraq*, pp.59–60; Lord Salter, *The Development of Iraq* (Baghdad, 1955), pp. 170–3.
45. For details about the KTAM report (for full references, see fn. 6), see: Salter, op. cit., pp. 173–7; Qubain, op. cit. 60–78.
46. William Willocks, *The Irrigation of Mesopotamia* (London, 1911).
47. Report of Crawford (BMEO) to FO on his visit to Iraq, 19 May 1948. FO 371/68409, B, E 6898/966/65.
48. Kinch to Cornwallis, 19 June 1942. Kinch's private papers and correspondence with Cornwallis (Middle East Centre, Oxford University).
49. Sousa, 'Irrigation in Iraq' (Pamphlet) (Baghdad, 1945), p. 44.
50. Ibid.
51. An Iraqi writer quotes this story to illustrate the peasant's endless debts: 'A farmer borrowed the price of three chickens which he served to a visiting guest. Interest compounded at such a rate that the farmer was forced to sell two cows to liquidate his debt.' See Ja'far Khayyat, *Al-Qarya al-'Iraqiyya* (The Iraqi village).
52. 'Fundamental Statute of the Agricultural and Industrial Bank of Iraq, Regulation No. 23 of 1936'. A copy appears in FO 371/20012, E 6285/1182/93.
53. Kerr to FO, 14 Dec. 1935. FO 371/18941, E 7552/115/93.
54. 'Law No. 27 of 1937 Amending Law No. 57 of 1935 for the Creation of an Agricultural and Industrial Bank'. A copy appears in FO 371/20803, E 2694/ 2694/93.
55. Knabenshue to Dept. of State, 30 Mar. 1936. ACR, Reel 6.
56. Agricultural Bank, *The Twelfth Annual Report on the Work of the Agricultural Bank for the Year 1947/1948* (in Arabic) (Baghdad, 1949), p. 3.
57. Agricultural Bank, *Annual Report for 1950/51* (in Arabic), p. 17.
58. Agricultural Bank, *Annual Report for 1949/50* (in Arabic), p. 3.
59. Agricultural Bank, *Annual Report for 1950/51* (in Arabic), p. 8.
60. IBRD, *Economic Development of Iraq*, p. 30.
61. Agricultural Bank, *Annual Report for 1950/51* (in Arabic), p. 8.
62. IBRD, *Economic Development of Iraq*, p. 259.
63. Ibid., p. 260.
64. Agricultural Bank, *Annual Report for 1947/48* (in Arabic), pp. 3–4.
65. From the bank's annual reports.
66. Agricultural and Industrial Bank, *Annual Report for 1942/43* (in Arabic), p. 18.
67. Articles 12–14 of Regulation No. 23 of 1936.
68. Agricultural Bank, *Annual Report for 1946/47* (in Arabic), p. 4.
69. IBRD, *Economic Development of Iraq*, p. 260.
70. Agricultural Bank, *Annual Report for 1950/51* (in Arabic), p. 9.
71. Agricultural Bank, *Annual Report for 1942/43* (in Arabic), pp. 7–8.
72. Agricultural Bank, *Annual Report for 1951/52* (in Arabic), p. 10.
73. Iversen *Monetary Policy in Iraq*, p. 31.
74. 'Current Events for the period 1–15 Jan. 1937', ACR, Reel 3.
75. 'Law for the Chambers of Agriculture No. 30 of 1938', *Iraq Government Gazette*, no. 8 (25 Feb. 1940), pp.99–100.

76. 'Regulations for the Chambers of Agriculture, no. 84 of 1939', *Iraq Government Gazette*, no. 41 (13 Oct. 1940), pp.549–52.
77. Embassy to FO, 28 Aug. 1947. FO 371/61652, E 8341/6285/65/G.
78. This was partly due to the fact that a Labour government had come into office, and its foreign minister (Bevin) favoured the encouragement of co-operatives and trade unions in the Middle East.
79. FO to Embassies in Middle East, 16 July 1947. FO 371/61652, E 6282/6282/65/G.
80. Embassy to FO, 28 Aug. 1947. FO 371/61652, E 8341/6285/65/G.
81. IBRD, *Economic Development of Iraq*, p.261.
82. 'Annual Report, Economic (A), for 1938'. FO 371/23203, E 3556/78/93.
83. 'Date Association Ordinance – No. 6 of 1939', *Iraq Government Gazette*, no. 20 (14 May 1939), pp.193–7.
84. Ibid.
85. Houstoun-Boswall to FO, 29 Apr. 1939. FO 371/23215, E 3329/1322/93.
86. Muzaffar Husein Jamil, *Siyasat al-Iraq al-Tijariyya* (Iraq's trade policy) (Cairo, 1949), pp.551–2.
87. Ibid., pp.552–60. The question of date export will be dealt with again in Ch. 5.
88. 'Grain Trade Regulating Board Law No. 32 of 1939', *Iraq Government Gazette*, no. 40 (1 Oct. 1939), pp.506–8.
89. Newton to FO, 10 Jan. 1940. FO 371/24556, E 242/203/93.
90. Jamil, *Siyasat al-Iraq al-Tijariyya*, p.572.
91. Ibid.
92. Knabenshue to Dept. of State, 20 Feb. 1935. ACR, Reel 10.
93. 'Tobacco Monopoly and Improvement Law no. 35 of 1939', *Iraq Government Gazette*, no. 2 (14 Jan. 1940), pp.17–24.
94. IBRD, *Economic Development of Iraq*, p.26.
95. Ibid.
96. Notes on a visit by Mr V.K. Maitland, forestry adviser to BMEO, 18 Nov. 1948. FO 371/68383, E 15073/60/65.
97. Ibid.
98. Batatu, *The Old Social Classes*, pp.94–9.
99. Sluglett, *Britain in Iraq*, p.232.
100. The roots of these conditions lay in Midhat Pasha's application in 1869 of the Ottoman Land Code to Iraq. See Albertine Juwaideh, 'Midhat Pasha and the Land System of Lower Iraq', in *St Antony's Papers* no. 16, 1963, pp.106–26; see also Sluglett, ibid., pp.231–8.
101. Dowson, *Inquiry into Land Tenure*, p.5.
102. Article 5 of both Land Settlement Law No. 50 of 1932, *Iraq Government Gazette* no. 23 (5 June 1932), pp.416–23, and Land Settlement Law No. 29 of 1938, *Iraq Government Gazette* no. 21 (22 May 1938), pp.317–26.
103. 'Law for Extinguishing Land Tax No. 20 of 1939', *Iraq Government Gazette*, no. 46 (12 Nov. 1939), pp.613–16.
104. Batatu, *The Old Social Classes*, p.109.
105. See Table 4.5. Figures published by the Agricultural Census are confusing, which is the reason they are not used here. It gives estimates for *tapu* and *lazma*, but lumps the remaining types together as 'other tenures and rented lands' without distinguishing among them. See *Agricultural Census*, p.17.
106. Ibid., pp.16–17.
107. Ibid., p.16.
108. IBRD, *Economic Development of Iraq*, p.141.
109. Khayyat, *Al-Qarya al-'Iraqiyya*, p.84.
110. Batatu, *The Old Social Classes*, p.54. Batatu gives the names of seven of these owners, as well as their tribal affiliations and the province in which their land was located (ibid., 48). He also gives the names and the 'strata' of 49 families who in 1958 owned more than 30,000 donums and in effect formed the nucleus of Iraqi landocracy. These families owned between them about 5.5 million donums (ibid., pp.58–62).
111. Warriner, *Land Reform*, pp.138–9.
112. Dowson, *Inquiry into Land Tenure*, p.75.

113. Ibid., pp.76–7.
114. Dowson to Humphrys, 15 Jan. 1932. FO 371/16049, E 3588/3588/93.
115. Quoted in Dowson's memorandum, ibid. A copy of Dobbs's memorandum appears in CO 730/94/15/36.
116. Dowson to Humphrys, op. cit.
117. Ibid.
118. 'Lazma Law No. 51 of 1932', *Iraq Government Gazette* no. 23 (5 June 1932), pp.423–4.
119. IBRD, *Economic Development of Iraq*, p.13.
120. Article 11(*a*) of both laws.
121. 'Law No. 44 of 1939, Supplemental to Land Settlement Law No. 29 of 1938', *Iraq Government Gazette* no. 41 (8 Oct. 1939), p.533.
122. For a list of the 317 regulations, see Mahmud Nadim Isma'il, *Al-Fihrist al-'Am lil-Qwanin wa-al-Anzima wa-al-Byanat wa-al-Ta'limat 1917–1961* (The general index for the laws, regulations, announcements and instructions, 1917–1961) (Baghdad, 1961), pp.266–77.
123. *Iraq Government Gazette* no. 52 (28 Dec. 1938), p.547.
124. 'Law for the Sale of Miri Lands No. 11 of 1940', *Iraq Government Gazette* no. 19 (12 May 1940), pp.227–9.
125. For the range of fees, see Article 34 of the 1932 Land Settlement Law and Article 36 of the 1938 Land Settlement Law.
126. Ibrahim al-Kabir Memoirs, iii, pp.82–3.
127. Article 3 of both Land Settlement Law No. 50 of 1932 and Law No. 29 of 1938.
128. *Statistical Abstract 1950*, p.109.
129. For the percentage of total area covered by the cadastral survey in each province, see Table 4.4.
130. MESC, 'Memorandum on Land Tenure in the Fertile Crescent, 1943–44'. Private papers, Middle East Centre, Oxford University. For useful background on the Sa'dun and other important tribes in Iraq, Batatu's *The Old Social Classes* is an excellent source. See also Saleh Haider, 'Land Problems of Iraq' (London Univ. Ph.D. thesis 1942), pp.69–120.
131. IBRD, *Economic Development of Iraq*, p.179.
132. Doreen Warriner, *Land and Poverty in the Middle East* (London, 1948), p.112.
133. Embassy to FO, 'Annual Report 1934'. FO 371/18951, E 940/940/93.
134. Memorandum by Edmonds to ambassador, 9 Dec. 1936. FO 624/7/623.
135. MESC, 'Memorandum on Land Tenure in the Fertile Crescent, 1943–44'. MESC private papers.
136. Warriner, *Land and Poverty*, p.117.
137. Longrigg, *Iraq: 1900 to 1950*, p.261.
138. For the development of agricultural taxation until 1931, see Guzine A.K. Rasheed, 'Development of Agricultural Land Taxation in Modern Iraq', *Bulletin of the School of Oriental and African Studies*, xxv, part 2 (1962), pp.262–5. For the summing up of the land tax situation as it existed in 1931, see *Progress in Iraq 1920–1931*, pp.112–13.
139. Sluglett, *Britain in Iraq*, p.195.
140. 'Law for the Collection of Duty (Rusoom al-Istihlak) on Land Produce No. 83 of 1931', *Iraq Government Gazette* no. 50 (6 Dec. 1931), pp.813–18.
141. 'The Istihlak Tax Law No. 59 of 1933', *Iraq Government Gazette* no. 35 (27 Aug. 1933), pp.385–90.
142. See for example the first amendment of 1936 (Law No. 49 of 1936) in Law No. 52 of 1939 in *Iraq Government Gazette* no. 45 (5 Nov. 1939), pp.592–4.
143. 'Law for the Collection of Land Rent No. 85 of 1931', *Iraq Government Gazette* no. 47 (15 Nov. 1931), pp.781–4.
144. 'Land Tax Law No. 73 of 1936', *Iraq Government Gazette* no. 30 (26 July 1936), pp.445–53.
145. Ibid., Article 7, p.446.
146. 'Law for Extinguishing Land Tax No. 20 of 1939'.
147. IBRD, *Economic Development of Iraq*, p.96.
148. See for example comments on the law by Pedler (Colonial Office), 25 Jan. 1932. CO 730/175/96432.

149. Haider, 'Land Problems of Iraq', p.615.
150. Rasheed, 'Agricultural Land Taxation', p.266.
151. Humphrys to FO, 'Annual Report on Iraq for 1934', 31 Jan. 1935. FO 371/18951, E 940/940/93.
152. Richmond to FO, 28 July 1948. FO 371/68464, E 10278/112/93.
153. Conversation between Sulayman and Ambassador Archibald Kerr, 2 Dec. 1936. FO 624/7/606.
154. See Khadduri, *Independent Iraq*, pp.113–16.
155. Comments on the report of the Iraq Inflation Committee by the British Embassy in Baghdad. FO 371/34982, E 991/9/93.
156. Faisal's memorandum appears in al-Hasani, *Tarikh al-Wizarat al-Iraqiyya*, iii, p.291.
157. Ambassador Kerr's private papers contain many anecdotes about Ghazi's personal and public life. FO 800/298.
158. Edmonds to Kerr, 24 Apr. 1937, 'Elections in Iraq'. Edmonds private papers.
159. Ibid.
160. Ibid.
161. Second Meeting of Middle East (Official) Committee, 5 May 1941.
162. Batatu, *The Old Social Classes*, p.116.
163. Ibid., p.103.
164. Ibid., p.178.
165. Report by J.P. Summerscale, commercial secretary at British Embassy, of a tour he made in northern and western Iraq, 31 May 1937. BT 60 53/1. Summerscale noted that Sheikh al-Yawar had secured for the Shammar at least the maintenance of their admittedly low standard of living, whereas many other tribes under less intelligent leadership had sunk into conditions of starvation and pauperism.
166. 'Law Governing the Rights and Duties of Cultivators No. 28 of 1933', *Iraq Government Gazette* no. 31 (30 July 1933), pp.315–23.
167. See for example a note on the law by Mr Webster, former inspector-general of agriculture, Nov. 1933, enclosed in despatch from Humphrys to FO, 22 Dec. 1933. FO 624/1/428/7.
168. Ibid.
169. Humphrys to FO, 22 Dec. 1933. FO 624/1/428/7.
170. Haider, 'Land Problems of Iraq', p.654.
171. Alfred Bonné, *State and Economics in the Middle East* (2nd edn., London, 1955), pp.131–2.
172. Batatu, *The Old Social Classes*, p.142. For more details about sharecropping see ibid., pp.142–3.
173. Warriner, *Land Reform*, pp.137–9.
174. Iraq, *The Statistical Compilation for the Census of 1957* (Baghdad, 1961), pp.169–71, 113–15.
175. Batatu, *The Old Social Classes*, p.133.
176. Philips, 'Rural-to-Urban Migration', p.420.
177. For more details, see Batatu, op. cit., pp.134–5.
178. *Agricultural Census*, p.35.
179. Batatu, op. cit., pp.130–1.
180. *Agricultural Census*, p.35.
181. Ibid., pp.17, 36.
182. Extract from Intelligence Summary (Air Force) No. 12, 15 June 1932. FO 371/16049, E 3627/93.
183. See, for example, FO 838/2 and FO 838/3.
184. British Consulate ('Amara) to British Embassy (Baghdad), 'Report for the Month of April 1947', 17 May 1947. FO 838/5.
185. The impact of the migrants lies outside the scope of this book. For more details, see Batatu, op. cit., pp.134–7; see also Philips, op. cit.
186. *Agricultural Census*, p.66.
187. John Batatu, 'The Sheikh and the Peasant in Iraq 1917–1958' (Harvard Univ. Ph.D. thesis 1960), p.150 (microfilm). The thesis constitutes, with minor alterations, the first part of his book *The Old Social Classes*.

188. Cornwallis to FO, 'Regent's proposals for improvement in administration in Iraq', 14 Mar. 1944. FO 371/40041, E 1903/37/93.
189. Henderson to Dept. of State, 7 Sept. 1944. ACR, Reel 15.
190. Norman Burns, 'The Dujaylah Land Settlement', *Middle East Journal*, v, no. 3 (Summer 1951), p.363. The article contains a detailed description of the project and its administration.
191. Qubain, *The Reconstruction of Iraq*, p.96.
192. IBRD, *Economic Development of Iraq*, p.271.
193. Ibid., p.16.
194. For details about the 1951 law, see: Warren E. Adams, 'The Pre-Revolutionary Decade of Land Reform in Iraq', *Economic Development and Cultural Change*, vi, no. 3 (April 1963), p.269.
195. IBRD, *Economic Development of Iraq*, p.17.

5

FOREIGN TRADE

Commerce was second only to agriculture in terms of the number of people it occupied in Iraq during the period 1932–50. Foreign trade played an important role in the country's development, while government policy towards the commercial sector had an impact throughout the economy, and especially on agriculture and industry.

In the first part of this chapter, Iraq's foreign trade will be examined by analysing the structure and trends of its components: imports, exports, and transit trade. Various aspects of Iraq's commercial policy will then be discussed: customs and tariffs, controls and restrictions, and trade agreements. In the third part of the chapter, the effect of Iraq's relationship with the sterling area on its trade policy will be assessed. The fourth part will deal with foreign competition for Iraq's markets, taking the British–Japanese competition of the 1930s as a case study.

STRUCTURE AND TRENDS OF TRADE

For convenience of analysis, the period under study will be divided here into three subperiods: 1932–8, 1939–45, and 1946–50. Furthermore, it should be noted that despite some deficiencies in the foreign trade statistics, such as in the balance of payments and imports evaluation, they are considered among the best statistics the government possessed during the 1930s and 1940s.[1]

Table 5.1 presents a summary of Iraq's foreign trade (excluding oil) during the period 1930–50. A few notes are in order with regard to this table. First, unlike other economic statistics, those pertaining to foreign trade were compiled according to calendar years. Second, imports were not based at c.i.f. until 1946, and are therefore defective for evaluating balance of payments. Goods imported by the British forces in Iraq or by their official institutions, imports by oil companies, and materials imported by the Ministry of Defence or for military purposes were all excluded from the import figures.

TABLE 5.1 Iraq's Foreign Trade, Excluding Oil, 1930-1950 (Iraqi dinars)

	Imports	Exports	Re-exports[a]	Deficit[b]	Transit trade
1930	5,734,984	2,893,455	...	2,841,529	2,756,518
1931	4,752,305	2,638,107	...	2,114,198	2,236,535
1932	5,733,427	2,357,473	...	3,375,954	2,067,686
1933	6,102,726	2,218,878	...	3,883,848	2,652,583
1934	6,088,193	3,165,407	...	2,922,786	3,174,308
1935	6,803,723	2,856,675	...	3,947,084	2,298,044
1936	7,177,110	3,483,649	...	3,693,461	1,641,274
1937	9,565,970	5,568,734	...	3,997,236	2,101,974
1938	9,361,004	3,472,369	216,466	5,672,169	3,526,930
1939	8,156,179	3,524,727	234,674	4,396,778	1,822,466
1940	8,692,900	3,902,504	195,601	4,594,795	3,110,600
1941	6,849,784	3,905,716	275,854	2,668,214	7,375,253
1942	12,183,682	4,479,871	223,688	7,480,123	9,183,706
1943	15,639,785	9,147,153[c]	332,842	6,159,790	10,267,478
1944	14,325,277	9,170,519[c]	317,890	4,836,868	13,597,841
1945	18,859,634	9,817,868	230,605	8,811,161	9,868,879
1946	28,039,962[d]	12,722,456	432,973	14,884,533	5,601,284
1947	39,946,140	13,800,538	904,591	25,241,011	3,342,039
1948	45,523,279	7,584,480	1,078,509	36,860,290	3,864,640
1949	40,501,372	11,207,588	1,219,869	28,073,915	2,714,172
1950	37,594,927	20,051,341	1,552,045	15,991,541	4,281,497

Source: Statistical Abstract 1950, p. 177.

[a] Until 1938, included in Exports.

[b] Deficit = Imports - Exports in the years 1930-7, and Imports - (Exports + Re-exports) in the years 1938-50.

[c] Includes exports to the British Army amounting to ID 4,014,999 in 1943, and ID 2,544,313 in 1944.

[d] From 1946 onwards, the c.i.f. value was adopted for imports.

Third, exports were quoted f.o.b., but as Murray notes, in many cases they were not genuine f.o.b. because they were underestimated.[2] Exports by oil companies were not included, and from 1939 re-exports of foreign products were also excluded. Fourth, 'transit' included all goods passing through Iraqi territory without being consumed in local markets.[3]

Balance of Trade

The most striking feature of Iraq's balance of trade, as shown in Table 5.1, was its chronic deficit, a deficit which reached a climax of some ID 37 million in 1948, the year of the financial crisis already discussed. Even when oil exports were included, the balance of trade still showed a deficit in many years. (In 1948, for instance, it was ID 25.5 million.) In order to understand the reasons for this continuous deficit, one has to look at the structure of Iraq's imports and exports. However, it is worthwhile to briefly examine the subperiods first.

As a result of the 1929 world depression, the value of Iraq's agricultural products fell in international markets, seriously affecting the country's purchasing power. To make matters worse, climatic conditions were adverse for agriculture during the years 1931 and 1932, and export of produce substantially decreased in consequence.[4]

After 1933 trade revived; the value of imports increased steadily (except for two small reductions in 1934 and 1939), and though there were further fluctuations in the value of exports, they too increased. The peak in Iraq's trade came in 1937 and was attributable both to a world-wide trade revival and to good harvest conditions in Iraq itself.

World War II greatly affected Iraq's foreign trade. Imports reached their lowest level in 1941, though there was no radical change in exports. On the other hand, the increasing world need for Iraq's agricultural products and the relatively large expenditures of the Allied forces in the country boosted the economy. Between 1941 and 1945, serving British war purposes was a top priority, and the managers of Iraq's economy were justifiably occupied with supply and inflation problems rather than with the balance of trade.

The post-war period witnessed a market increase in imports due to the strong impetus for development and the accumulation of large reserves of foreign currencies. (The first factor was dealt with in Ch. 2; the second will be discussed below in the section on the sterling area.) Exports also generally increased, but not to the same extent; their decrease in 1948, as well as the record deficit, were largely due to bad harvest conditions. With the improvement of agricultural conditions and the huge increase in oil revenues, Iraq enjoyed a considerable surplus in its balance of trade from 1951 onwards.

Iraq's different governments were disturbed by the continuous deficit in the balance of trade during the period under study. However, their perception was limited to the difference between total imports and total exports, without paying much attention to the relative proportion of capital goods and consumer goods.[5] But the persistence in the commercial account of an adverse trade balance without ill effects indicates that some kind of equilibrium of total payments was being achieved each year, in which the excess value of imports over exports was counter-balanced by tourist and other foreign expenditures in Iraq, by the government's receipt of oil royalties, and so forth. In order to have a complete picture of the balance of trade, therefore, one has to take account of these 'invisible earnings'. This can be done by examining the balance of payments.

Balance of Payments

Unfortunately, data about Iraq's balance of payments show many discrepancies and must be treated with serious caution. One major drawback is that no calculation of payments was made at all between 1939 and 1945. Another is the fact that only from 1946 were imports calculated at c.i.f. value. There were also many inconsistencies in the treatment of the activities of the oil companies and Currency Board accounts.[6] The Iraqi government itself did not place excessive reliance upon the annual statements (mainly of the 1930s) which it forwarded to the League of Nations and later to the International Monetary Fund.[7] But despite these limitations, the balance of payments can nevertheless help us visualize Iraq's trade. Hence Tables 5.2 and 5.3.

Again, the period divides into three subperiods. Table 5.2 deals with 1932–3 to 1938–9, and Table 5.3 with 1946 to 1950. (As mentioned above, there are no data for the war years.) The differences between the system of calculation in the 1930s and that of the post-war period stem from the fact that the former was based on financial years while the latter was based on calendar years. Furthermore, many changes were introduced in the evaluation of the balance of payments during the years 1946–50 as a result of Murray's report and of recommendations by the International Monetary Fund.

It will be noted that a perfect balance is obtained in neither table. From the information available, it is not possible to state whether this is due to the inadequacy of the data relative to the credit or the debit items of the account. The League of Nations pointed out, however, that while the figures for goods, services and gold were sufficiently accurate, the record of capital movements was not.[8]

Although no data are available for the war years, it is clear that they were characterized by a significant improvement in Iraq's balance of payments – thanks to the very considerable military expenditures by the Allied forces in Iraq, particularly in 1943, the high increase in world demand for Iraqi exports in the second half of the war, and the revival of transit trade, which reached a peak in 1944 (see Table 5.1; more details about transit trade will be given below).

Calculation of the balance of payments was resumed in late 1946, but data for this year appearing in Table 5.3 are not reliable since

TABLE 5.2 Balance of Payments, 1932/33 - 1938/39 (ID thousand)

	Inward or credit movements (exports)							Outward or debit movements (imports)						
	1932/3	1933/4	1934/5	1935/6	1936/7	1937/8	1938/9	1932/3	1933/4	1934/5	1935/6	1936/7	1937/8	1938/9
A. GOODS, SERVICES AND GOLD														
I. Merchandise	2,122	2,472	3,558	3,082	4,389	5,077	3,837	6,263	6,117	6,130	7,132	7,278	9,738	9,073
II. Interest and dividends	120	136	137	132	123	120	101	495	411	384	416	415	641	471
III. Other services														
1. Port and transport fees	503	609	547	460	488	602	476	-	-	-	-	-	-	-
2. Commissions and brokerage	200	174	228	304	340	488	641	-	-	-	-	-	-	-
3. Emigrants' remittances	35	36	37	38	37	34	34	79	94	74	80	98	81	80
4. Pension contributions to foreign officials	-	-	-	-	-	-	-	93	87	71	90	33	42	38
5. Tourists' expenditure	283	178	206	224	185	324	852	228	240	236	263	257	130	435
6. Disbursement by British forces in Iraq	612	582	656	684	631	575	610	-	-	-	-	-	-	-
7. Government receipts from abroad														
a. Oil royalties	655	536	989	889	900	1,026	1,968	-	-	-	-	-	-	-
b. contribution by Currency Board	-	-	15	40	81	110	60	-	-	-	-	-	-	-
8. Other items[a]	179	116	129	128	124	133	155	117	153	152	162	184	195	193
IV. Gold	810	707	460	221	151	84	163	2	16	43	40	51	32	47
Total	5,519	5,546	6,962	6,202	7,449	8,573	8,897	7,277	7,118	7,090	8,183	8,316	10,859	10,337

Surplus (+) or deficit (-) on account of:														
a. Goods and services	-2,366	-2,263	-545	-2,162	-967	-2,338	-1,556							
b. Gold	+808	+691	+417	+181	+100	+52	+116							
c. Goods, services and gold	-1,758	-1,572	-128	-1,981	-867	-2,286	-1,440							
B. CAPITAL ITEMS														
I. <u>Long-term operations</u>														
1. Amortization of government foreign debts	-	-	-	-	-	1,000		252	179	18	18	18	18	76
2. Direct long-term capital investments														
a. Value of fixed capital imported	1,199	1,061	377	258	609	430	1,007	-	-	-	-	400		
b. Local expenditure of investors	332	718	517	409	467	489	525					-		
II. <u>Known short-term operations</u>	...	115	50	609	1,174	545	236	468	454	1,456	185	1,188	76	235
Total	1,531	1,894	944	1,276	2,250	2,464	1,768	720	633	1,474	203	1,606	94	311
Net inward (+) or outward (-) movement of capital	+811	+1,261	-530	+1,073	+644	+2,370	+1,457							
Net errors and omissions	-947	-311	-658	-908	-223	+84	+17							

Sources: For 1932/3-1936/7: League of Nations, <u>Balance of Payments 1937</u> (Geneva, 1938), pp. 123-5. For 1937/8-1938/9: Baghdad Chamber of Commerce, <u>Report for the Years 1938 and 1939</u>, pp. 164-9.

[a] Other items include, <u>inter alia</u>, post and telegraph, expenditure of students and missions, diplomatic expenditure.

EP1—G*

TABLE 5.3 Balance of Payments, 1946-1950 (ID million)

	1946		1947		1948		1949		1950	
	Credit	Debit	Credit	Debit	Credit	Debit	Credit	Debit	Credit	Debit
A. Current Transactions										
1. Merchandise	26.17	27.59	31.37	40.08	21.54	46.43	28.92	41.26	55.62	38.33
2. Non-monetary gold movement (net)	-	1.59	-	0.44	0.01	-	-	-	-	-
3. Foreign travel	5.00	3.54	3.00	3.00	2.76	2.60	3.14	2.44	2.95	3.52
4. Transportation	3.13	0.12	1.09	0.39	1.33	0.13	1.44	0.15	1.57	0.33
5. Insurance	-	-	-	-	0.05	0.15	0.06	0.14	0.02	0.12
6. Investment income	1.49	7.85	1.39	7.14	1.03	2.61	0.79	6.36	1.08	22.60
7. Government, not included elsewhere (mainly military)	3.50	1.86	3.09	3.19	2.25	1.85	1.74	0.86	1.75	0.68
8. Miscellaneous	0.24	0.26	0.23	0.77	0.58	0.86	0.22	0.18	2.26	0.88
Total goods and services	37.53	42.81	40.17	55.01	29.55	54.63	36.31	51.39	65.25	66.46
Net goods and services		5.28		14.84		25.08		15.08		1.21
9. Donations (private and official)	0.30	0.53	0.30	1.09	0.31	0.79	0.32	0.21	0.31	0.23
Net donations		0.23		0.79		0.48	0.11		0.08	
10. Total (1 through 9)		5.51		15.63		25.56		14.97		1.13

B. Movement of Capital										
11. Private, excluding banking institutions (net)	0.15	2.42	5.04	-	11.53	-	9.61	-	10.72	-
12. Official and banking institutions										
a. Long-term liabilities	0.15	0.37		0.14		0.02		0.02	2.55	0.02
b. Short-term liabilities			0.16			0.31		0.58	0.05	
c. Long-term assets			-	-	7.67		0.65		1.31	0.51
d. Short-term assets	-2.82	-0.06	8.39		5.49		2.97	1.88		9.04
Total movement of capital (11 plus 12)	-2.52	2.73	13.59	0.14	24.69	0.33	13.23	2.48	14.63	9.75
13. Net movement of capital		-5.25	13.45		24.36		10.75		5.06	
Net errors and omissions (13 minus 10)		0.26	2.18		1.20		4.22			3.93

Sources: For 1946: International Monetary Fund, Balance of Payments Yearbook 1948 (Washington, 1950), p. 245. For 1947-50: International Monetary Fund, Balance of Payments Yearbook 1947-1953 (Washington, 1954), Iraq - p. 1.

they were not adjusted to the new system of calculation which began in 1947. Oil exports are included within merchandise credit, and imports by oil companies are included within merchandise debit. (Unlike in Table 5.1, imports here are c.i.f.) In the balance of capital movement most of the direct foreign investment, which constituted the major share of private capital (section 11 of Table 5.3), was made by the oil companies.

Table 5.2 and Table 5.3 both clearly indicate that Iraq's deficit in current transactions was covered by capital import. During most of the period 1932–50, the oil companies brought considerable amounts of foreign capital into Iraq for investment in their plants. However, despite the large amount of capital inflow by oil companies, the Iraqi government in certain years (mainly 1948) faced a deficit which necessitated drawing upon its sterling balances.

It should be re-emphasized, however, that most of the data presented are not accurate, and serve solely as indications. (Note the large margin of errors and omissions.)

Imports

Practically all manufactured goods used in Iraq were imported as Iraqi industry was unable to meet local demand. Table 5.4 shows the value of the ten major imports (others included timber, cement, chemical products, soap, matches, glass and rubber). The table indicates that there was a steady increase in imports (both consumer and capital goods) during the period 1932–8, reaching a peak in 1937.[9] According to a memorandum by the Iraqi government, imports expanded by over 50% in the ten years preceding World War II, the greatest expansion taking place in capital goods, which were required for canal and pump irrigation, railway construction, buildings, and municipal water and electricity supply schemes.[10]

During the first half of the war, there was only a slight reduction in imports of essential goods like tea and sugar. From the end of 1941 until 1945, however, substantial reductions occurred in nearly all types of imports, due to MESC's policy of limiting imports, and the reduced supply sources of manufactured goods. The main contraction was in the import of capital goods and transport equipment. (One should be cautious when comparing the value of imports during this period with that in the pre-war years, however, because of the significant price increase.)

The post-war period witnessed an excessive demand for imports. This was due to the market's deprivation of many goods (mainly capital), the rise in the public's purchasing power, the accumulation of large reserves of foreign currencies, and the abolition of import

TABLE 5.4 Value of Iraq's Principal Imports, 1932-1950 (ID thousand)

Year	Cotton piece goods	Iron, cast iron and steel	Boilers, machinery appliances	Sugar	Artificial silk piece goods	Tea	Automobiles and parts thereof	Clothing	Electrical machinery and apparatus	Woollen piece goods
1932	1,557[a]	837	248	397	- [b]	125	298	137	-	- [b]
1933	903	862	181	399	225	170	384	99	68	117
1934	910	503	433	381	275	243	378	260	94	211
1935	950	516	408	368	319	237	291	301	142	198
1936	805	827	490	374	352	295	271	287	198	210
1937	1,069	1,240	613	440	529	351	469	374	190	289
1938	833	1,058	996	505	420	347	398	349	242	240
1939	1,050	755	557	554	378	332	320	312	232	142
1940	855	651	272	753	532	423	201	290	226	116
1941	664	390	304	862	344	381	178	331	159	107
1942	3,413	310	131	432	277	1,057	278	308	171	149
1943	2,780	211	123	541	213	1,549	161	704	207	191
1944	3,446	286	321	1,034	119	285	294	487	102	66
1945	4,922	892	436	1,189	401	473	287	586	163	175
1946	4,281	2,565	1,744	1,797	566	412	638	1,082	643	602
1947	6,474	4,790	2,896	1,691	1,213	2,267	1,734	1,298	1,158	810
1948	7,296	4,997	4,110	3,661	374	2,123	2,176	755	1,890	1,287
1949	5,514	4,879	4,527	2,227	706	2,837	2,311	598	1,960	1,111
1950	5,054	3,707	3,650	4,763	1,350	2,881	1,761	1,152	1,835	824

Sources: For 1932-4: *Statistical Abstract 1927/28-1937/38*, p. 126; Jamil, *Siyasat al-Iraq al-Tijariyya*, p. 74. For 1935-40: Iraq, Department of Customs and Excise, *Foreign Trade Statistics 1936* (Baghdad, 1937), pp. 27-8; *Foreign Trade Statistics 1938* (Baghdad, 1941), pp. 102-17; *Foreign Trade Statistics 1939 and 1940* (Baghdad, 1942), pp. 72-86. For 1941-5: *Statistical Abstract 1944 and 1945*, pp. 154-5. For 1946-50: *Statistical Abstract 1950*, pp. 189-90.

[a] Includes artificial silk and woollen piece goods.

[b] Included with cotton piece goods.

restrictions. After 1948, however, imports decreased since some of the above-mentioned factors no longer existed, because Iraq's industrial output began to increase and was able to meet more of the local requirements, and because of the reinstatement of import licences and the imposition of new tariffs on imports, mainly consumer goods.[11]

During the years 1946–50, import prices and quantities fluctuated widely. The changes in unit values were probably the result of variations in the quality of the goods imported.[12] The rise in import prices can be attributed to developments in the world market. Thus, the increase in imports, in spite of higher prices, can be explained by the fact that there was a general expansion of economic activity in Iraq, initiated and financed chiefly by the increase in oil production.

Apart from prices, internal conditions and world supply, two other important factors affected the volume of imports: the tariffs and customs policy, and Iraq's membership in the sterling area. These factors will be discussed later in this chapter.

Exports

Except for oil, Iraq's exports consisted almost entirely of agricultural products, the most important of which were cereals (mostly barley) and dates. (In addition to the eight goods presented in Table 5.5, exports also included ghee, fish, intestines, liquorice root, etc.) The return on oil exported was paid directly to the government in the form of royalties. Income from other exports depended mainly on two factors: world prices and local weather conditions. As Table 5.5 shows, when these factors were favourable, as in 1936 and 1937, exports of most goods increased considerably. A third important factor causing fluctuations in exports was the subsistence nature of much of Iraq's agriculture: 'Although he [the peasant] makes a point of always having very adequate stocks on hand, he produces mainly for local consumption and exports of supluses are largely accidental.'[13]

In the first two years of the war, Iraq's export trade remained fairly normal, but during 1941 and 1942 harvests immensely curtailed grain exports. The figures for exports revenue presented in Table 5.5 may perhaps be misleading, in that the enhanced value of exports was due not to an increase in quantity but rather to sharp price rises. For instance, the value of grain exports in 1943 was more than ID 5 million, compared with ID 2 million in 1937, but in quantity the 1943 grain exports were only 41% of those of 1937. In fact, the quantity of exported grain returned to its 1937 level (439,000 tons) only in 1950.[14] Thus, although by the end of the war

TABLE 5.5 Value of Iraq's Principal Exports, 1932-1950 (ID thousand)

	Grain, pulses and flour	Dates	Hides and skins	Animals (live)	Cotton (raw)	Wool (raw)	Seeds	Ceramic products
1932	486	879	86	49	3	91	...	...
1933	508	835	148	74	7	132	16	...
1934	977	926	107	190	27	234	25	...
1935	472	976	128	259	36	261	12	...
1936	1,171	864	194	177	63	467	21	...
1937	2,102	974	381	300	207	1,010	55	...
1938	1,158	887	185	185	218	438	83	...
1939	1,015	963	155	247	122	631	47	...
1940	1,049	1,045	109	309	177	815	68	...
1941	438	1,018	192	394	404	965	47	1
1942	927	1,298	334	412	82	743	21	105
1943	5,381	1,922	400	86	410	383	10	194
1944	4,705	2,442	285	266	147	632	13	191
1945	4,626	2,969	767	488	25	352	4	133
1946	5,692	4,425	371	540	39	1,004	1	184
1947	6,862	4,702	155	635	363	372	128	103
1948	422	4,742	284	151	79	1,027	21	98
1949	6,053	3,174	240	360	65	534	4	134
1950	11,715	4,293	251	491	1,091	1,372	111	150

Sources: For 1932-4: Statistical Abstract 1927/28 - 1937/38, pp. 127-8. For 1935-40: Foreign Trade Statistics 1936, pp. 39-44; Foreign Trade Statistics 1938, pp. 118-25. Foreign Trade Statistics 1939 and 1940, pp. 87-92. For 1941-5: Statistical Abstract 1944 and 1945, p. 175. For 1946-50: Statistical Abstract 1950, p. 213.

exports (in value units) were triple those of the pre-war years, the actual quantities of most goods exported were much smaller.

The years 1946 and 1947 showed an increase in exports in both value and quantity, followed by a sharp decline in 1948. Improved weather conditions, a new agreement for date exports in 1950 (at higher prices) and the devaluation of the Iraqi dinar in September 1949 all led to a rise of exports to unprecedented levels in 1950.[15]

From the above discussion it can be seen that a notable characteristic of Iraq's foreign trade was wide fluctuation in both the volumes and prices of exported goods. (On the whole, fluctuations in imports were less violent than in exports.) Fluctuating exports were not only Iraq's problem, however: throughout the world the market price of barley, for example, had an average fluctuation of 13.3% during the period 1920–39, and 30% during 1940–5. It is possible, though, that this fluctuation was even stronger in Iraq because of the low quality of its barley.[16]

These facts demonstrate Iraq's vulnerability in the realm of foreign trade: while almost completely dependent on foreign markets for manufactures and major foodstuffs, it was at the same time unable to exercise any significant pressure to affect the prices of its own exports because of their very nature (with the probable exception of dates). Thus, the terms of trade developed to Iraq's detriment during most of the period under study. Iversen's research clearly indicates this deterioration during the post-war period.[17] For example, the price of the dates Iraq exported decreased by 4% between 1946 and 1950, while the price of the iron and steel Iraq imported rose by 53% during the same years.[18]

The Direction of Trade

To round out the picture of Iraq's imports and exports, it may be appropriate to examine their geographical distribution (Tables 5.6 and 5.7).

One striking feature is the concentration of foreign trade on about ten countries. Another is Britain's prominence as both importer and exporter to Iraq during most of the period under study.

As Table 5.6 indicates, the years 1932–8 witnessed the rise of Japan as Iraq's second biggest trade partner after Britain, and also an increase in the importance of imports from the United States. At the same time, Iraq continued to export most of its products to Britain. It also increased its exports to Japan and Palestine; however, as Table 5.7 shows, this increase came at the expense of exports to Iran and India.

TABLE 5.6 Imports by Principal Country of Origin, 1932-1950 (per cent)

	UK	Japan	India	USA	Germany	Italy	Iran	Syria
1932	34.9	6.8	12.4	5.2	3.8	3.7	7.2	2.5
1933	33.6	11.7	8.9	7.2	2.6	3.0	7.3	2.4
1934	25.1	20.9	6.6	6.4	5.2	2.1	8.5	2.3
1935	28.6	20.0	6.6	6.3	5.2	1.8	9.1	1.8
1936	31.7	18.8	6.8	6.4	6.5	0.6	5.7	1.6
'1937	29.5	18.3	6.9	7.6	6.6	2.7	4.0	1.7
1938	30.1	14.8	6.5	9.1	7.4	4.1	4.2	1.8
1939	23.5	18.7	7.2	7.2	6.4	3.8	5.0	1.9
1940	21.4	20.3	11.9	11.9	0.3	1.7	4.6	2.4
1941	20.0	15.6	19.4	14.3	0.1	0.3	6.4	2.1
1942	12.0	4.3	51.5	11.5	0.0	0.1	7.8	1.4
1943	10.9	0.0	55.9	6.2	0.0	0.4	6.5	7.0
1944	11.2	0.0	29.6	11.8	0.0	0.0	9.6	16.3
1945	17.5	0.0	18.0	19.0	0.0	0.0	16.4	7.9
1946	44.1	0.0	14.6	7.9	0.1	1.4	8.3	6.1
1947	43.9	0.0	12.8	8.3	0.1	6.1	4.2	5.5
1948	43.5	0.1	8.6	7.9	0.6	6.9	4.4	8.7
1949	43.3	0.5	5.3	11.4	0.7	7.6	3.2	5.2
1950	48.9	2.2	8.3	8.2	0.3	6.3	3.5	2.7

Sources: For 1932-7, Statistical Abstract 1927/28-1937/38, p. 128. For 1938-40, Foreign Trade Statistics 1939 and 1940, p. 9. For 1941-2, Foreign Trade Statistics 1942, p. 9. For 1943-5, Foreign Trade Statistics 1945, p. 9. For 1946-50, Statistical Abstract 1950, p. 183.

During the war, and especially its latter half, India came to dominate Iraq's imports, while the US position continued to improve. These developments were due to the breakdown of Iraq's trade relations with the Axis countries (before the war Germany and Italy had supplied about 8–10% of Iraq's needs), and Britain's inability to export manufactured goods. On the other hand, Iraq's exports to the United States, Palestine and Iran increased drastically during the war, while in 1943 and 1944 British and Allied forces stationed in Iraq took 44% and 28% respectively of its total exports.

The post-war period saw Britain re-emerge as the most important source of imports. Trade relations with the Axis countries were resumed as well, Italy becoming an important partner from 1947 onwards. On the exports side, India emerged as the predominant

TABLE 5.7 **Exports by Principal Countries of Destination, 1932-1950 (per cent)**

Year	UK	India	USA	Iran	Syria	France	Germany	Japan	Palestine and Trans-Jordan
1932	37.4	11.6	9.8	6.3	5.6	3.0	1.5	0.1	...
1933	31.3	10.2	12.6	7.3	9.1	2.4	3.5	0.1	5.2
1934	30.0	9.1	9.6	7.9	6.7	3.3	4.5	0.1	5.5
1935	18.5	11.6	18.6	8.3	7.8	3.0	1.9	0.1	9.0
1936	30.5	8.9	20.0	3.7	4.0	3.0	2.8	4.0	6.5
1937	27.8	6.4	20.6	1.6	3.9	4.0	3.4	8.6	6.7
1938	25.1	8.4	16.0	1.7	6.6	3.7	4.7	10.2	4.9
1939	25.7	11.8	20.9	3.6	2.8	3.8	3.5	4.8	8.1
1940	27.3	8.9	27.4	0.3	2.6	4.2	0.0	6.5	11.5
1941	14.9	7.6	26.5	0.2	10.8	0.0	0.0	0.0	11.5
1942	8.1	4.9	18.4	7.2	28.8	0.0	0.0	0.0	15.9
1943	47.8[a]	2.1	1.6	17.0	11.6	0.0	0.0	0.0	6.1
1944	38.1[b]	5.2	7.2	13.0	7.1	0.0	0.0	0.0	17.7
1945	10.9	5.3	9.8	4.3	12.2	0.1	0.0	0.0	15.0
1946	9.9	20.2	9.2	2.3	5.7	3.2	0.0	0.0	2.5
1947	15.3	25.4	4.6	2.1	1.8	5.6	0.3	0.0	5.1
1948	17.1	20.0	13.6	3.5	4.8	4.0	5.9	0.0	5.6
1949	15.7	20.9	4.1	3.6	5.3	0.4	0.5	13.0	1.7
1950	16.1	8.6	3.1	5.7	2.7	0.8	2.6	8.8	1.4

Sources: For 1932-7: Statistical Abstract 1927/28 - 1936/37, p. 10. For 1938-40: Foreign Trade Statistics 1939 and 1940, pp. 11-12. For 1941-2: Foreign Trade Statistics 1941 and 1942, p. 11. For 1943-5: Foreign Trade Statistics 1945, p. 11. For 1946-50: Statistical Abstract 1950, p. 183.

Note: Until 1938, data include re-exports as well.

[a] Including British Army (43.9%).

[b] Including British Army (27.7%).

market for Iraqi goods throughout most of 1946–50, while Britain's share also increased.

Many factors affected Iraq's trade relations: the most-favoured-nation declaration of 1932, Iraq's entry (formally at least) into World War II, its membership in the sterling area, its customs and tariffs policy, and finally, trade agreements. All these factors will be examined below. But first let us complete the general discussion by looking briefly at transit and local trade.

Transit Trade

Iraq's transit trade, particularly in the 1930s, consisted of goods consigned to and from Iran. It was dependent upon developments in Iran itself rather than conditions in Iraq. Goods in transit were not liable to Iraqi customs duty but were charged with transit dues. The principal commodities in transit to Iran were textiles, sugar, tea and manufactured goods, while goods from Iran consisted mainly of carpets and agricultural products.[19]

As a result of Iran's policy of restricting foreign imports and diverting them from Iraqi routes, transit trade declined in the 1930s in comparison with the 1920s. (As Table 5.1 shows, the average annual value of transit trade in the years 1932–8 was about ID 2.5 million.)

Transit trade began flourishing again after 1941 due to the deterioration in sea transportation in the Mediterranean and the emergence of India as the main supplier to Iraq and other Middle East countries.[20] A major element in this increase in transit trade, which reached its peak in 1944 (about ID 13.5 million), was the export of Turkish tobacco to the United States, and of American goods to Turkey. After the war, transit trade declined once more, since most trade was again channelled through the Mediterranean; it reached its lowest level in 1949 (ID 2.7 million).

Local Trade

Local trade did not play a significant role in Iraq's development. The centrality of Baghdad in the country's commerce was noted by the British commercial secretary:

> The result of my visits to other towns [in Iraq] has been to confirm the frequently repeated statement that the only important commercial centre in Iraq is Baghdad. Basra has to a small extent some separate commercial life, and also its date industry, which is independent of the capital, but the main flow of both imports and exports, the allocation of important tenders and the banking activity of the country are almost entirely regulated in Baghdad.[21]

The British Embassy was already well aware of this situation. In 1935, for example, the ambassador recommended closing the British vice-consulate at Kirkuk because

> No importers or exporters are established in the town. Local trade is in the hands of retailers who indent [*sic*] on Baghdad for their requirements. No selling agents for the British firms have been or are likely to be appointed ... The most important local product, Kurdish cigarette tobacco, has at present no sale outside Iraq.[22]

Against this background, we can now proceed to the factors which affected the structure and trends of Iraq's foreign trade policy.

COMMERCIAL POLICY

During most of the 1930s, the Ministry of Finance was responsible for shaping and implementing commercial policy. With the creation of the Ministry of Economics in 1939, most of the responsibilities with regard to trade were transferred to it, although the Ministry of Finance continued to deal with customs and excise. The Ministry of Supply also played a role in commercial policy: in conjunction with the other two ministries it conducted the controls and restriction policy. (The structure of these ministries is presented in Ch. 2.)

There were also other organizations which dealt with foreign trade. Foremost among them was the Baghdad Chamber of Commerce, created in 1926. Its budget rose from ID 1,058 in FY 1933, to ID 1,744 in 1939, ID 8,500 in 1945 and ID 18,766 in 1950. Its membership increased as well: from 355 in 1933, to 498 in 1939, and 2,456 in 1948.[23] The Basra Chamber of Commerce, created in 1928, had some 2,000 members by 1950, while the Mosul Chamber of Commerce (founded in 1947) had approximately half that number.[24]

The important question regarding these bodies of merchants from the perspective of this book is whether, as a group, they created leverage on the government and were thus able to influence commercial policy in their favour. From the evidence available, it seems that these chambers did not constitute a lobby in the real sense. First, from a legal point of view, they were not independent but rather under the supervision of the Ministry of Economics. Second, the middle and upper strata of the mercantile class during the period under study consisted mainly of British firms or non-Moslem Iraqis (Jews); the Moslems among them were 'involved more often than not in a web of interests with foreign capital'.[25] From the reports of the Baghdad Chamber of Commerce it can be seen that among the twenty-five 'first-class merchants' (defined as those whose 'financial consideration' ranged between ID 22,500 and a maximum of ID 75,000) there were twelve Britons and ten Jews. Furthermore, 215 (more than 43%) of the membership in 1939 were Jews.[26] Most of the merchants were therefore isolated from Iraq's political life: according to Batatu, out of a total of 575 ministerial appointments in the period 1921–58, only 95 (16.5%) went to members of mercantile families, of whom 84 were Moslems.[27] This is not to say that successive governments of Iraq were totally uninfluenced by the merchants, but one can argue that their relationship was far weaker with the mercantile class than with the landlords.

One final point related to the mechanism of commercial policy should be discussed before examining the various aspects of the policy itself, namely the *organization* of foreign trade. The main feature of the market organization of Iraq's export trade was its tendency to be concentrated in the hands of a few companies, mainly foreign. (For instance, Andrew Weir and Co. held the monopoly for date and grain exports during most of the period under examination.) The import trade, on the other hand, was characterized by a fairly large number of merchants dealing with consumer goods (tea, sugar, textiles, etc.), while there were only a small number of importers of capital goods (machinery and metals), due to the limited size of the market and the need for large capital for such imports.[28]

Customs and Tariffs

Modern commercial policy in Iraq seems to have passed through two stages. In the first stage, from 1861 to around 1927, the dominant objective was the procurement of funds for the augmentation of government revenue, with almost total disregard for other objectives of commercial policy.[29] The second stage, known as the 'development' phase, began in 1926–7, when commercial policy began to be seen as a tool not only for increasing revenue but also for attaining such other objectives as the protection of local agriculture and industry or the exemption from duties of 'necessary' goods, while 'luxury' or 'ostentatious' imports were discouraged.

Between 1927 and 1932 a number of laws were promulgated which exempted certain categories of 'necessary' goods from customs duties: agricultural equipment like irrigation pumps, seeds and fertilizers; industrial materials and machines; and imports for public utilities like electricity, transport and communications.[30] But this did not mean that the government stopped seeing the augmentation of receipts from customs and excises as an important aim; such receipts were in fact its principal source of revenue throughout the period 1932–50, comprising 52% of total ordinary receipts in 1932, and 47% in 1949 (see Table 3.3). Indeed, the only change after 1927 was that other, additional aims were taken into consideration as well.

The first legislation which encompassed all the above-mentioned targets was Law No. 11 of 1933. It reinforced the tendency towards protection, and clearly distinguished among imported goods according to criteria of 'necessity' and stage of manufacture.[31] While exempting 137 commodities from all import duty, the law imposed specific duties wherever possible on other commodities, for the legislators thought this kind of duty would prevent disagreements between merchants and customs officials. Among the imports so taxed were sugar, tea, coffee, sulphur, cement, tobacco, liquor, textile and woollen goods, soap and leather. (As noted in Ch. 3, the specific duty was a major defect of the tariffs system.) *Ad valorem* duties were imposed on a relatively small number of imports, but they constituted the main source of income from exports since they were applied to dates and gold.[32] There was also, according to a 1939 law, a mixed duty: in cases where both specific and *ad valorem* duties were relevant, that which resulted in the higher revenue was applied. (This was chiefly intended to hinder imports from Japan.)[33]

Jamil has calculated the rate of import duty imposed by the 1933 law on 'necessary' consumer goods at about 27–28%, and that on 'ostentatious' imports at about 37%.[34] According to his calculations, the average duty on non-manufactured commodities was 19%; on finished manufactured goods, 27%; and on semi-finished, about 22%.[35]

As shown in the previous chapter, the exemption of imported machinery from import duty had a major effect on agricultural production, in that it permitted a steady increase in the number of imported pumps for irrigation. The impact of the industrial protection policy, begun in 1929 with the law for the encouragement of industrial concerns, and established in the 1933 law, will be discussed in Chapter 6.

Law No. 11 of 1933 and its amendments had two major defects. One was that revenue collection remained a top priority. This was clearly expressed in the relatively high duties still imposed on two basic consumer goods, tea and sugar. Here one must agree with Nasrawi's argument that 'the increase in import duties was commensurate neither with the increase in imports nor with the growth of national income'.[36] The second defect was that duties on 'ostentatious' goods were not sufficiently high, except on liquor.[37]

The outbreak of World War II created a new situation for the managers of Iraq's economy: scarcity in most commodities, and inflated prices. Their customs and tariffs policy could not by itself deal with the turbulent conditions; there was a pressing need for a policy of control and restriction.

Controls and Restrictions

Regulations to control and restrict imports and exports were not a new phenomenon in Iraq's commercial policy. However, apart from restrictions stemming from sanitary, social and security reasons,[38] all efforts to limit imports during the 1930s centred mainly around the problem of the increased influx of Japanese goods.

It was only with the drastic changes in world trade conditions after 1939 that Iraq had to embark on a full-scale policy of controls and restrictions. The usual problems of balance of trade and balance of payments were reduced to secondary importance in the light of critical shortages of foodstuffs and other imported goods. In fact, commercial policy during World War II lost its real meaning and became a supply policy, the main target of which was to tackle the acute shortages, mainly of food. This was done, by licensing all imports and exports, controlling the price and distribution of essential goods, and rationing.

Towards the end of 1944, the prospect that the war would soon be over and that both supply and shipping would therefore become easier made it possible for the government to begin a policy of decontrol.[39] This process gained momentum throughout 1945, and by June 1946 it was reported that 'most commodities formerly controlled by the respective Directorates of the Ministry of Supply have now been released from control and sales restrictions'.[40]

Import licensing, however, continued to operate after 1946, control being limited to two main categories: goods from countries outside the sterling area (exceptions were made for certain capital goods, such as chemical products, metals, rubber, seeds, etc.), and all goods labelled as 'extreme luxuries' (e.g. ornaments and jewellery, silverware, artificial flowers, cigars, etc.).[41] An even more liberal policy was adopted from August 1947, when licences were required only for imports from hard currency areas.

The year 1948 was a turning point in Iraq's commercial policy: as already discussed, the country experienced a bad harvest, it participated in the war in Palestine, its oil revenue diminished due to delay in production by the oil companies and closure of the Haifa pipeline, and its foreign exchange reserves were being depleted. It also witnessed the beginning of reduced commercial activity on the part of Iraqi Jews, who had played a crucial role in the country's economic life. In order to counter-balance the serious situation which resulted from these events, Iraq imposed an embargo on grain exports in September of that year, as well as an import licensing system to cover imports not only from the hard currency area but from sterling area countries as well. Under the new system, all imported goods were placed on one of several lists. These included an 'unlimited' list (tea, sugar, cotton textiles, medical equipment); a 'limited' list for semi-luxuries (electrical appliances, automobiles, confectionery); and a 'prohibited' list to protect all goods produced in Iraq from foreign competition.[42] (This policy remained in effect until August 1952, when a more liberal import and export policy was adopted).[43]

The import licensing system was only minimally co-ordinated with the tariff system. During these years tariff was again seen as primarily a means of raising revenue. Apart from being a complex operation, the control system created a prosperous black market and a flourishing wave of smuggling, as well as many other distortions paid for, as is usual in such cases, by the man in the street.

Trade Agreements

Trade agreements are another tool, besides tariffs and controls, used by governments in their commercial policy in order to advance their countries' trade. The basis for Iraq's trade relations during the period under study was a declaration issued in May 1932 with the termination of the mandatory regime, containing Iraq's guarantees to the Council of the League of Nations. Article 11 of the declaration stipulated that, 'subject to reciprocity, Iraq undertakes to grant to Members of the League most-favoured-nation treatment for a period of ten years from the date of its admission to membership to the League of Nations'.[44] At the same time, the government reserved the right to ask any member-nation taking measures liable to affect Iraq's chief exports to open negotiations immediately to restore the balance.

At first sight, the most-favoured-nation reciprocity arrangement appeared a fair deal, but this was not in fact the case. The problem was that while other countries might not take specific measures against Iraq itself, they might well do so against items which Iraq was exporting – and the declaration did not state how Iraq could prove lack of reciprocity in such cases. Even before the declaration was made public, the British were aware of this loophole; the Foreign

Office wrote that although the declaration seemed to give Iraq adequate protection,

> in practice, this protection may amount to very little, as Iraq might easily find herself obliged to extend her minimum tariff to the majority of imports from some country which, owing to the nature of its tariff system, imposed prohibitive tariffs against goods which happened to be the main products of Iraq. For example, the principal export from Iraq is dates, which are seriously affected by high import duties in several countries.[45]

The Eastern Department of the Foreign Office recommended that the period of Iraq's obligations to other countries should not exceed two or at most five years, since a longer period would be a 'derogation of Iraq's sovereignty', and its exports would be seriously harmed.[46] Nevertheless, the declaration as published stipulated ten years. The only apparent explanation for this is that Iraq was so eager to end the mandate that it was prepared to sign nearly anything, without adequate consideration of its consequences.

The 1932 declaration diminished the need for reaching bilateral agreements. Still, the government signed a number of trade agreements, mainly during the 1930s, in an effort to improve trade balance and promote exports, especially dates. All the accords provided most-favoured-nation treatment in addition to certain other privileges for both sides. The seven agreements signed during the 1930s were: with Turkey in 1932 (came into force in 1934); with Sweden and Germany in 1935; with Palestine in 1936; with Egypt and the United States in 1938; and with Brazil in 1939.[47] The accord with Palestine, a special customs agreement, was the most beneficial for Iraq: Iraqi rice and dates were subject to reduced duties when entering Palestine, while barley and ghee were totally exempted.[48]

The world war prevented Iraq from developing its trade relations. The treaty with Germany was cancelled in 1939 (sanctions against Italy had been taken in 1935 because of its attack on Abyssinia), and Japanese imports were curtailed in 1941.

Throughout the war and its immediate aftermath, the dominant factor in Iraq's foreign trade was the link with the sterling area. (The most-favoured-nation declaration expired in 1942.) Restoration of relations with the Axis countries and the signing of two new trade agreements (with Turkey and Yemen) in 1946 did not alter this situation.

Trade agreements, therefore, did not play an important role in Iraq's commercial policy. Jamil goes so far as to argue that none of the agreements produced practical results, and that some were even to the detriment of Iraq's interests.[49] But it is undoubtedly an exaggeration to blame the agreements for the reduction in Iraq's exports. Najjar, for instance, shows that Iraq's imports from and exports to Turkey decreased substantially after their 1946 agreement,[50] but he disregards the fact that 1947 and especially 1948 were bad years in general for Iraq's trade.

Promotion of Exports

Up to now we have dealt mainly with the import side of Iraq's commercial policy. We have noted that on a few occasions (during World War II and the financial crisis of 1948) the export of certain goods was prohibited, but little mention has been made thus far of the encouragement of exports, which for Iraq consisted principally of dates and grains. (Oil will be dealt with separately in the next chapter.)

Being the largest exporter of dates in the world, Iraq naturally saw one of the main aims of its export policy as the reduction of duties on dates in countries which imported large quantities of that product, such as the United Kingdom and India. The question of lowering or abolishing duties on dates in Britain or India was interrelated in the 1930s with the continual increase of Japanese exports to Iraq then taking place at the expense of British and Indian goods. In August 1934, India raised the duty on Iraqi dates to 30% *ad valorem*, and the American attaché who reported the new measure was sure this was but India's first move to recapture its lost trade.[51]

From the beginning of his tenure of office in March 1935, Prime Minister Yasin al-Hashimi appealed to the British ambassador in Baghdad to secure the removal or reduction of the customs in the United Kingdom and India on Iraqi dates. Britain was prepared to abolish the duties but 'they are unable to do so without securing some compensating advantages for U.K. trade'. What the British wanted in return from Iraq was that it take steps to restore the UK's share of the Iraqi cotton trade, and change its tariff system with regard to motor cars and woollen goods.[52]

The first condition was fulfilled in 1936, and will be discussed below. But the Iraqis were aware that the second condition, directed against the increased sales of American cars in Iraq, would further widen the trade gap between Iraq and the United States in the former's favour. (In 1935 Iraq's exports to the US totalled ID 530,000, while US exports to Iraq stood at ID 429,000.) This, the Iraqis feared, would lead the Americans to retaliate by raising their duties on dates, and thus cancel the advantage secured by the remission of the date duty in Britain.[53]

The negotiations for an Anglo-Iraqi special customs agreement represent an example of how the Board of Trade's influence dominated British economic policy in the Middle East. The Foreign Office was of the opinion that 'the campaign to get British cars artificially in the Iraqi market will not succeed in the end', arguing that American cars were cheaper and had better service and spare parts available in Iraq.[54] The Foreign Office also frequently complained during the negotiations that the Board of Trade 'does not give sufficient consideration to local aspects of changing duties'.[55] At one point, when the negotiations were progressing, the Board of Trade produced a new demand: that Iraqi contracts for building two steel bridges over the Tigris be awarded to a British firm (which, by the way, had made a bid higher than that of any non-British company).[56]

At the end of October 1936, al-Hashimi's government was replaced by Hikmat Sulayman's and no further progress was made in the negotiations. Indeed, Iraq had by then lost interest in the matter, and in January 1937 it began contemplating the creation of a date monopoly.[57] The collapse of agricultural commodity values in 1938 created the final impetus for the policy of monopolization implemented in 1939. It should be emphasized that, quite apart from the problem of high duties, the conditions prevailing in the date trade were not encouraging in general. The competition presented by French dates was constantly increasing, especially in view of their important advantage in being so much closer to European markets. Furthermore, the competition among the many small producers of dates, and among those acting as intermediaries between producers and big export companies, tended invariably to lower date prices.[58]

In Chapter 4 we saw that the date-marketing agreements with Andrew Weir were 'a losing proposition' for Iraq in general and the date producers in particular. The impact of the monopoly on the date industry can best be gauged by examining the quantities of dates exported. (As inflation was high during the war, value of exports is not an accurate indicator.)

From Table 5.8 it can be seen that the quantity of dates exported decreased after the signing of the monopoly agreement, reaching its lowest level in 1943. Indeed, as Jamil points out, it is very difficult to understand why the Date Association decided to renew the agreement with Andrew Weir at all after the 1943 season. Equally difficult to understand is the fact that at one point the association even began to support the view of the British company *vis à vis* that of the producers, claiming that because of shipping problems,

TABLE 5.8 Date Exports, 1937-1950 (thousand tons)

Year	Quantity
1937	191.0
1938	185.6
1939	148.3
1940	132.3
1941	143.4
1942	105.6
1943	72.3
1944	107.0
1945	153.4
1946	208.1
1947	226.3
1948	214.4
1949	140.9
1950	212.0

Sources: For 1937–8, *Foreign Trade Statistics 1938*, pp.118–25. For 1930–40, *Foreign Trade Statistics 1939 and 1940*, pp.87–92. For 1941–5, *Statistical Abstract 1944 and 1945*, p.175. For 1946–50, *Statistical Abstract 1950*, p.213.

limited European markets and import controls in most of the world, date prices could not be raised, and the best way to export this commodity was therefore by a monopoly organization.[59] The most likely explanation for this stand is that British influence in Iraq seems to have reached its peak in the years 1943–4, and dates were considered important nutrition for the Allied armies. As was inevitable in the circumstances, however, the Iraqi producers reacted to the monopoly by selling more and more of their crop on the black market or simply cutting production, thus seriously harming date exports.

The grain monopoly, on the other hand, was more successful than the date monopoly, though it had less impact on trade (undoubtedly because Iraq was not a major grain exporter, and could not begin to compete with countries like Australia and the US). The creation of the grain monopoly was motivated by the outbreak of World War II, and it proved its worth by overcoming the shortage of shipping space resulting from the hostilities.

IRAQ'S RELATIONSHIP WITH THE STERLING AREA

As mentioned earlier, Iraq's membership in the sterling area was one of the most important factors affecting its foreign trade during the 1940s (and beyond). In this section we shall briefly review the background for the creation of the sterling bloc, then examine Iraq's various laws for exchange control and the negotiations between the British and Iraqi governments for the allocation of hard currencies, and finally appraise how Iraq's membership of the sterling area affected its economic development in general and foreign trade in particular.

Prior to 1939 the sterling area was an unofficial arrangement between countries which had close political and economic ties with Britain, for the purpose of facilitating their financial and trade transactions through London.[60] Iraq, as we have seen, continued to maintain the dinar's parity with the pound sterling after 1932, and to keep its foreign exchange reserves in London.

In August 1939, when the British pound was devalued, most of the non-British members – the Scandinavian and Baltic countries and Portugal – withdrew from the bloc. This left as members the British Commonwealth of Nations (except Canada and Newfoundland); the British colonies, protectorates, and mandated territories; Egypt and the Sudan; and Iraq. (The French territories, including Syria and Lebanon, were unofficial members from September 1941 to February 1944.)[61]

A month later, rigid exchange controls were introduced throughout the sterling area. Iraq alone did not adopt the new regulations, apparently because it had stocked excess goods and was able to continue importing from Japan.[62] In practice, Iraq's decision proved not very effective. The Treasury in London did not permit Iraq to use its exchange reserves as it wished; in October 1939, for instance, it rejected Iraq's demand to convert to dollars £200,000 credited to its account in several London banks in order to purchase aeroplanes from the US.[63] Furthermore, British banks in Baghdad turned down all applications by merchants for dollar exchange.

Nevertheless, there were cases in which the dollar proceeds from the sale of Iraqi products to the US were utilized to purchase American goods, much to the chagrin of the British authorities, who were unable to intervene.[64] The Treasury complained of the steady demand for dollars uncompensated for by dollar exchange. It was therefore decided in London that Iraq must institute some form of exchange control if it wanted to remain a member of the sterling bloc.[65]

In the first months of 1941, Iraqi merchants faced shortages of dollar exchange to finance their American imports.[66] By that time the British cabinet had decided not to supply Iraq with dollars unless it severed diplomatic relations with Italy.[67]

When the Rashid 'Ali uprising in May 1941 led to hostilities between Iraq and Britain, Iraq was expelled from the sterling area.[68] All Iraq's transactions with member countries had thenceforth to be referred to the Bank of England, which meant that Iraqi accounts in British banks 'have been effectively immobilised'.[69] After re-occupying Iraq in late May and installing a pro-British regime, Britain was prepared to readmit Iraq to the sterling area provided it established suitable machinery for administering exchange control decrees and imposing restrictions on imports and exports.[70]

Both conditions were fulfilled: in November 1941 the exchange control law was put into effect, followed in March 1942 by a law regulating economic life.[71] In addition to its measures for controlling foreign exchange, securities and gold, the exchange control law (amended three times) sought to discriminate in favour of imports from sterling area countries, thus reflecting the principles guiding British exchange control.[72] An exchange control committee was formed to administer the law (see Ch. 2) with which the British were quite satisfied: 'The [Iraqi] Ministry of Finance co-operated whole-heartedly in expediting the drafting and approval of the law and notifications. The Minister secured the passage of the law through Parliament with scarcely any comment. (In his own words "at least 80% of the members had no idea of its implications".)'[73]

Although dollar exchange restrictions affected certain sectors (for example, oil companies could not buy equipment at the end of 1941 because of a lack of dollars),[74] there were no radical changes in the structure of Iraq's foreign trade to the detriment of non-sterling countries. In fact, imports from the US actually increased throughout the war (except in 1943). This was due not to any ineffectiveness of the system but rather to the current reality: Britain was fighting an onerous war and could not supply Iraq with what it needed. As Table 5.6 indicates, India became Iraq's most important supplier of consumer goods during these years, while the US became the most important source of capital goods.[75]

The real impact of the sterling area on Iraq's trade began after World War II ended. By then Iraq's sterling balances with the British Treasury had reached a relatively high level: £70 million.[76] This of course was but a tiny proportion of Britain's total sterling liabilities at the end of 1945: £3,718 million (as compared with £517 million in 1939 and £1,272 million in 1941).[77] But for a small country like Iraq which was just beginning to develop and needed to import large quantities of capital and consumer goods – from whatever source – this amount was very important. Thus the period 1945–50 witnessed a long and tough struggle on Iraq's part to release more and more of these balances.

Conscious of the strong pressure on the managers of Iraq's economy to increase imports, and of the grave political consequences such pressure might lead to, the British decided towards the end of the war to release some of Iraq's sterling balances.[78] Thus, in May 1945 an agreement was signed between Britain and Iraq according to which Britain would provide Iraq with scarce currencies amounting to £3,501,624 during the calendar year 1945. This agreement established the basic principles which would guide Iraqi-British relations over the next few years with regard to hard currency allocations:

(a) The British Government will do its utmost to provide Iraq with its essential requirements from the United Kingdom.
(b) The British Government will not ask the Iraq Government to place any special limit on its foreign exchange requirements for imports of goods from countries outside the sterling area, other than the scarce currency countries, on the understanding that Iraq limit itself to imports of real need. [It should be noted that the scarce currency countries included almost all the important sources of Iraq's imports: the U.S., Canada, Switzerland, Sweden and Portugal.]
(c) The Iraq Government will retain its exchange control and strengthen its import control to ensure that scarce currencies are utilised for the purchase of essential goods only.
(d) The special Iraq dollar pool, whereby U.S. dollars acquired by Iraq were earmarked for special use, will no longer apply. All foreign exchange (including dollars) acquired by Iraq will be handed over to the general pool held by the British Government.[79]

Without any alteration in principle, the 1945 agreement was extended three times; in January 1946, £1,138,927 was provided for the first three months of 1946;[80] in April 1946, £3,176,841 was provided for the next twelve months;[81] and finally, in February 1947, £1,307,000 was allocated for the period between April and mid-July 1947.[82] This brought the total provision of scarce currencies between the beginning of 1945 and 15 July 1947 to £9,124,392.

Before proceeding to development subsequent to July 1947, let us look at the respective aims of Iraqi and British policy with regard to the sterling bloc from 1945 to mid-1947, the factors affecting them, and their impact on Iraq's foreign trade.

Throughout these thirty months, the Iraqis were continually pressing for an increase of provision of scarce currencies for imports and invisible expenditure (mainly currency for students); more freedom to spend within the allocation; and relaxation of import controls.[83] The British, satisfied with Iraq's collaboration in handling exchange control,[84] were reluctant to antagonize the managers of the Iraqi economy and were therefore responsive to some of Iraq's demands. For example, in August 1946, Britain agreed to allocate £50,000 for Iraqi students studying in non-sterling countries.[85] The plan was to let the Iraqis handle the entire operation without the Embassy having to be involved, officially, in managing the sterling balances. This was not only because the British realized that the Iraqis would resent too much involvement: their main concern was that the Americans would protest.[86]

The 'American factor' in British sterling policy towards Iraq was an important consideration (becoming, as we shall see below, even more significant after 1947). From 1945 onwards, the American minister in Baghdad continually urged his government to adopt a more active political–economic policy towards the area. There were also frequent rumours that the Americans were encouraging the merchants and the government of Iraq to demand more dollars for American imports.[87]

On the whole, the British understood that the association of countries like Iraq with the sterling area was an important tool in advancing British interests. Moreover, the sterling balances indeed worked in Britain's favour in its competition with the US in the Middle East.[88] As the conference of British diplomatic representatives in the Middle East summed up the situation:

> The fact that most of the Middle East economies have at their disposal large balances in sterling (and are, at the same time, short of dollars) in itself gives British trade an initial advantage. If schemes of development are proposed and adopted, there should, therefore, be golden opportunities for the British exporter in the Middle East.[89]

Among the factors complicating relations between Iraq and Britain was the behaviour of some Iraqi leaders in squandering their country's resources. Thus, in May 1945 it was decided to provide $100,000 for the regent's visit to the US and Canada but 'for very good reasons it was decided not to mention this generous allocation specifically in any published document'.[90] However, after the regent arrived in the US he demanded an additional $200,000 'for personal expenses'. This of course caused embarrassment in both British and Iraqi circles in Baghdad. It turned out that the regent, besides his heavy expenditure on jewellery, fur coats and other luxuries in New York, intended to buy American machinery for a textile factory which he wanted to help launch with none other than Iraq's strongman, Nuri as-Said, and Daoud al-Haidari, the Iraqi ambassador in London.[91]

Despite the second allocation, the regent nevertheless ran out of funds and borrowed $100,000 from an American millionaire, which the Iraqi government later had to repay. This extravagance was (justifiably) all the more inflammatory to British and Iraqi officials in view of the fact that the living and travelling expenses of the regent's party were covered by the US government.[92] In July 1945, therefore, it was decided by British and Iraqi officials to secretly deduct $100,000 from the allocation made in the 1945 agreement for the general import programme.[93]

Let us now return to 1947 itself, which may be considered a turning point in this aspect of the relationship between Iraq and Britain. The prelude to the change which occurred was the signing of the Anglo-American Financial Agreement in July 1946, in which Britain agreed to make currently acquired sterling freely convertible into dollars within one year. Britain further agreed to negotiate with the countries of the sterling area and other holders of sterling balances about the release of their balances in London. As a result of this commitment, Britain reached a six-month agreement with Egypt at the end of June 1947 on the release of some of its balances, and according to which Egypt withdrew from the sterling area and was consequently no longer obliged to deposit its hard currency earnings in London.[94]

A few weeks later Britain reached a similar agreement with Iraq, though more generous and flexible than the one with Egypt. Not least among the reasons for the superior terms of the Iraqi agreement was the fact that the Iraqi negotiating team strove to achieve its aims with great skill and persistence. Acknowledging that Britain had faced a difficult period both during and after the war, the Iraqi negotiators nevertheless insisted that Iraq bore no responsibility for the situation, and should not be required to pay for it. Ibrahim al-Kabir, then director of the Ministry of Finance, who played an important role in these negotiations, emphasized that 'the state of Iraq today was impressive in its poverty' and the country 'had waited 25 years for reconstruction and she could not wait any longer'.[95] He called upon Britain to be generous, as this would help create stability in Iraq; he also noted that 'the sterling balance, though small for Britain, was large and important for Iraq'.[96] Dr Saleh Haidar, also of the Ministry of Finance, presented Iraq's needs for the next five years, underlining the urgency for development projects in every sector.[97]

On the sterling question, as in other matters concerning British policy in the Middle East, there were sometimes conflicts between the British Foreign Office and the British Treasury. The latter viewed Iraq's membership in the sterling bloc from an entirely financial angle, and thought its withdrawal after 1946 would not be unwelcome. On the other hand, the Foreign Office wanted to maintain close links with Iraq in all spheres, the financial being but one. In his memoirs, Ibrahim al-Kabir relates that during the negotiations Sir Wilfrid Eady of the Treasury abruptly raised the question of Iraq's continued participation in the sterling area.

> I suspected a trap and I immediately told him that Iraq did not wish to leave the sterling bloc without giving six months notice of the withdrawal. 'No, we cannot accept this condition,' he said. I saw that my suspicion was confirmed and I said without hesitation 'We remain without çonditions'. He appeared to be dismayed at the failure of his bullying tactic and did not conceal it in the private conversation held later in the day ...[98]

After Egypt's decision to withdraw from the bloc, the Iraqi government sent a telegram to its negotiating team in London instructing them to conclude a temporary, six-month agreement on the Egyptian pattern, and inform the British that Iraq had decided to leave the sterling area. Al-Kabir immediately returned to Iraq and discovered that the decision was in fact 'due to personal motives and rivalries between ministers'. Addressing the cabinet, he stressed the harmful effects such a decision would have on the Iraqi economy just when the world economy was in turmoil. In the event, the cabinet decided to remain in the bloc, since this was 'the only policy which Iraq could follow as long as she did not enjoy full benefit of her oil and many other national resources'.[99]

Besides the persuasive arguments brought to bear, there were additional factors influencing the British to be more lenient towards Iraq. One of these was London's awareness that everything should be done to enhance Britain's relationship with Iraq in view of the latter's increasing strategic and economic importance. The British, like the Americans, were convinced that extensive development projects were the answer to communism in the Middle East, and that more allocations should therefore be given for capital imports. Furthermore, American–British competition in the area during these years also had its effect: the British could no longer arrest the increase in American influence, and therefore felt it 'essential that we should never lay ourselves open to the accusation of blocking American expansion'.[100] (It should be remembered that in 1946 and 1947 Britain desperately needed America's economic help, and thus did not want to antagonize it in areas like the Middle East.)

A third factor was the Palestine question, which was a source of tension in London's relationship with Baghdad. The British reasoned that if they could not satisfy Iraq on the Palestine issue, it would be unwise to disappoint it on the sterling question as well.

All these factors combined together to produce a five-year financial agreement governing Britain's release of Iraqi sterling balances, signed in London on 13 August 1947.[101] The main provisions, which were effective retroactively to 15 July, were:

1. A release of £15 million during the five years between July 1947 and July 1952, with a maximum of £4 million during each of the first two years.
2. A special release of £5 million to facilitate the change in conditions from those prevailing before 15 July.
3. A working balance of £2 million to meet any temporary shortage in foreign currency for overseas payments.
4. The release of the equivalent of any unspent balance remaining on 15 July of the scarce currencies allocated to Iraq under the agreement of 1945.
5. Other releases included the value of all credits opened and confirmed but outstanding on 15 July, the value of outstanding orders placed by the Iraqi government with the Crown Agents, the oustanding amount of the Port of Basra debt, and the outstanding amount of the advances made to the Iraq Government by oil companies working in Iraq (this last figure came to some £4.2 million).

All the releases listed above were to be freely convertible for payments in any currency area.

Unfortunately for Iraq, this agreement did not last long. On 20 August the chancellor of the Exchequer announced that, owing to the rapid rate at which American credit was being expanded, the British government found it necessary to suspend the free convertibility of the releases made to Iraq and other countries of the sterling area.[102]

Although quite disappointed, Iraq decided that in light of the emergency Britain was facing it was prepared to co-operate, 'both as an ally and a friend and as a member of the sterling area in order to ease the situation with maximum speed'.[103] Banks in Iraq were instructed to suspend all transactions involving new dollar liabilities. However, in spite of this ban on dollar dealings, the volume of documentary credits opened for business over the following two months was approximately equal to that registered during July. A very large proportion was for cotton piece-goods from the US.[104] (It seems that merchants knew how to exploit loopholes in the regulations.)

In October 1947 negotiations began between Britain and Iraq to reach a new agreement. Both sides played the same cards as in their negotiations a few months earlier. Britain's secretary of state emphasized, in his meeting with the Iraqi regent in London, that 'the two countries sink or swim together, and it is in Iraq's own interests to moderate her demands and requirements'.[105] On the other hand, Iraq's prime minister, Salih Jabr, reiterated his country's immediate need for development projects, and asked the British to help him in this sphere because he was constantly being attacked by the opposition for his co-operation with Britain on the sterling area question.[106]

According to the agreement signed on 17 November, Britain undertook to ensure that sterling standing to Iraq's credit would be made available to meet any deficit in Iraq's balance of payments with the scarce currency countries. For its part, Iraq promised that between October 1947 and 30 June 1948 it would enter into no commitments in excess of £986,000 with the Belgian monetary area, or of £4,327,000 with the rest of the scarce currency countries.[107] As a result of the Belgian government's protests against Belgium being singled out in the agreement, the British agreed that Iraq could spend more in Belgian francs, provided its purchases in other hard currencies were correspondingly reduced.[108]

In April of 1948, the year of Iraq's major financial crisis, its minister of finance informed the British ambassador in Baghdad that Iraq had exhausted its scarce currency allocation made under the agreement (which was due to expire at the end of June), and desperately needed an additional allocation to buy foodstuffs.[109] Indeed, Iraq's sterling balances had plummeted in comparison with the post-war years (£70 million in 1945, £67 million in 1946, £59 million in 1947, and £45 million in 1948).[110] In June 1948 the agreement was extended for one year, enabling Iraq to receive £750,000 for its commitments to Sweden, and £5,500,000 to other scarce currency countries. No substantial change was introduced except that the German mark was added to the list of scarce currencies.[111] In July, the agreement was re-extended for three months: Iraq was allocated £1,375,000 for all scarce currency countries, and an additional £187,000 for Sweden.[112] This was followed by a temporary agreement reached in November 1949, in which Iraq was allocated $1 million a month while continuing to deposit its hard currency earnings in the sterling area pool.[113] Finally, a more liberal agreement was concluded in August 1950:

Belgium, Japan and West Germany were no longer considered to be within the hard currency area, and Iraq was allocated some £7.1 million for the year between October 1949 and September 1950.[114]

Before attempting to appraise the sterling area as a system affecting Iraq's trade and economic development, a few words should be added as an epilogue to the above discussion. Between 1950 and 1958, a number of agreements more generous towards Iraq were reached, made possible both because Iraq's balances were growing at a faster rate due to oil revenues and because Britain's own economic position was also improving. After its 1958 revolution, however, Iraq decided to formally sever its ties with the sterling area, which it did at the end of June 1959.

Iraq's relationship with the sterling area was interconnected with other issues, such as control over money supply (the Currency Board being in London), the non-existence of a national bank until 1949, the role of commercial banks in Iraq's finances, and Iraq's close political and economic ties with Britain. The impact of Iraq's membership in the sterling area on its foreign trade and economic development has already been extensively treated by other writers, though their conclusions have differed greatly. However, since none of them had access to the British government documents opened to the public only recently, it might be worthwhile to add a few points to their arguments, and to clarify a few others.

Foremost among the defenders of Iraq's membership in the sterling area was the Danish economist Carl Iversen.[115] Some of the advantages he notes are indeed valid. The dinar's link with the pound sterling created stability and inspired confidence, both internally and externally. It dissipated the misgivings felt by the mercantile community, who had opposed the change from the Indian rupees and the dropping of the dinar's parity with gold. But other advantages claimed by Iversen are less convincing. It is quite exaggerated, for example, to argue that Iraq enjoyed free access to London capital and money markets in raising loans. From the British documents cited in the discussion of foreign loans in Chapter 3, it can be seen how Iraq was manipulated and even forced to make political and economic concessions for every loan it received.

F. Shehab, on the other hand, belittles the advantages of the sterling area and tries to refute every point put by Iversen.[116] In so doing he underestimates the importance of political considerations and argues, rather theoretically, that although there would have been many dangers had Iraq left the bloc, such dangers are experienced by any country wishing to pursue an independent monetary course. While there is truth in this argument, it fails to take the complexities of the situation into account. Iraq's economic decision-makers tried to derive whatever benefits they could from the sterling relationship because it was an indispensable part of a large framework of co-operation with Britain. To argue that this large framework worked to Iraq's detriment is another question entirely. It should also be noted that there are no indications that Egypt's position improved drastically after it left the sterling area in 1947. Another important point is that we are dealing with a period when Iraq was not receiving high revenues from oil; it would seem that Shehab did not pay sufficient attention to these twenty years, and rather based his conclusions on the period 1950–8.

That is not to say that the sterling area worked to Iraq's benefit; however, it is doubtful whether, under the political and economic conditions of the 1930s and 1940s, not only in Iraq but in the world-wide constellation of large and powerful countries *vis à vis* small and weak ones (mainly colonies and ex-colonies), there was a better alternative.

One cannot deny, however, that the system of the sterling area prevented Iraq from having an independent monetary policy. The best example of this was the 1949 devaluation of the pound sterling: Britain announced on 18 September 1949 that the pound would be devalued from $4.03 to $2.08, and two days later Iraq followed suit. As a result, Iraq's sterling balances were depreciated in terms of American dollars by about 30.5%.[117] Similarly, there is no doubt that between 1945 and 1950 Iraqi imports from the scarce currency area were largely determined by the amounts of currencies made available to Iraq under its various agreements with Britain. This meant limitations on Iraq's imports of essential goods, mainly from the US (between 1946 and 1950 Britain once again became Iraq's main supplier: 44.7% of Iraqi imports originated in the UK, as opposed to only 8.7% in the US – see Table 5.6), and this was indeed an impediment to Iraq's development.

In retrospect, then, it can be said that membership in the sterling area presented Iraq with more disadvantages than advantages, but it is highly doubtful whether, in the given economic and political situation, Iraq could have left the bloc and succeeded in launching an independent monetary policy.

TRADE COMPETITION IN IRAQ

British Commercial Interests in Iraq

Apart from oil interests and trying to obtain as many contracts as possible for British firms, Britain's commercial policy in Iraq aspired to retain for the UK the position of dominant supplier of Iraq's needs. We shall now briefly consider Britain's predominance in Iraqi trade, and then examine in detail Britain's reaction to competition for that trade.

Britain's predominance in Iraq's trade pre-dated 1932. Prior to World War I, the UK's share of Iraq's total imports averaged between 45% and 50%, while India's share constituted an additional 25%. This trend continued throughout the 1920s, although there was a falling-off as compared with the pre-war years: an average of 35% of Iraq's total imports.[118]

The 1930 Treaty of Alliance between Iraq and Britain, which paved the way for Iraq's independence, guaranteed the special position enjoyed by the British in Iraq. As the British ambassador pointed out, 'There is no reason to apprehend that British trade will diminish to any marked extent, as long as the privileged position in Iraq, secured to Great Britain by the Treaty of Alliance, is maintained.'[119] And when in 1934 Britain's position in Iraq was questioned in some London circles,[120] he defended British policy by pointing out the economic advantages it brought:

> The foreign commercial interests in Iraq are, owing to the existence of the British connexion, predominantly British. With the exception of a foreign department store or two, and one American date-growing and exporting firm, there are no foreign business houses of any importance other than British. The greater part of the country's foreign trade is carried in British ships. The foreign capital sunk in the country is almost exclusively British ... All important insurance business is in the hands of British firms.[121]

In order to secure and consolidate these advantages, the British varied their methods, sometimes exercising political or economic pressure (the latter kind was manifested in granting loans, lowering duties on Iraqi exports, etc.), sometimes simply by using the extensive influence wielded by the British advisers working for the Iraqi government.

One of the major threats to British commercial interests in Iraq was foreign competition. A striking example of how Britain reacted to such competition and how the resulting rivalry affected Iraq's foreign trade is the thrust for Iraqi markets made by Japan in the 1930s.

British–Japanese Competition for Iraq's Markets

British–Japanese competition during the 1930s was not restricted to Iraq. The political and economic background to this competition, which penetrated many parts of the world, is outside the scope of this work.[122] However a few points should be noted, since most aspects of the two countries' competition in Iraq were dictated by events occurring far away from it.

The devaluation of the Japanese yen in December 1931 had remarkable effects on Japan's export trade. The combination of low wages, good workmanship and favourable exchange rate meant that Japan could offer goods at prices with which no other country could compete.[123] At the same time, the Great Depression of 1929 had adversely affected the production of the Western industrial countries. From 1932 Japanese goods, mainly cotton and textiles, began appearing in markets to which Japan had not previously exported, to the alarm of the countries which had hitherto controlled those markets, like Britain.

From the British government's point of view, the fact that Japanese competition most severely affected the old and vulnerable Lancashire textile industry presented a difficult problem, as cotton interests in Lancashire were able to exercise a powerful influence over Britain's commercial policy for many years.[124] British reaction to Japanese competition was an extension of the system of Imperial Preference adopted in 1932 to protect the products of the British Empire from foreign competition.[125]

Iraq, like Egypt and Palestine, was among the countries in which a significant increase in Japanese imports took place from 1932 onwards.[126] As Table 5.9 shows, Iraq's imports of textile and textile articles from Japan increased from ID 147,000 in 1931–2 to ID 577,000 in 1933–4 and continued to rise steadily until reaching ID 1,524,000 in 1937. For most of the 1930s, Japan was the second largest exporter to Iraq after Britain.

The increase in Iraq's imports of Japanese textiles can be attributed to two reasons. The first and major one was the low price of the Japanese goods compared with the British ones. As the Board of Trade put it: 'In almost all classes of goods Japanese prices are at least one third lower than those of similar United Kingdom products. The quality of the Japanese goods may in some cases be inferior but in the market the price factor is decisive in effecting sales.'[127]

TABLE 5.9 Iraq's Imports of Textiles and Textile Articles from Japan and Britain, 1931-1951 (ID thousand)

	Japan	Britain
1931-2	147	551
1932-3	308	506
1933-4	577	374
1934-5	983	186
1935[a]	1,159	257
1936	1,181	327
1937	1,524	380
1938	1,199	341
1939	1,364	222
1940	1,373	227
1941	918	215
1942	486	361
1943	87	530
1944	12	477
1945	1	862
1946	-	2,828
1947	-	3,405
1948	26	2,929
1949	179	2,077
1950	740	2,087
1951	3,169	2,024

Sources: For 1931/3 – 1934/5: *Economic Conditions in Iraq, 1933–35*, p.21. For 1935–1951: *Summary of Foreign Trade Statistics 1927–1960*, pp.110, 112.
Note: Textile and textile articles includes cotton piece-goods, silk piece-goods, artificial silk piece-goods, woollen piece-goods and clothing.
[a]The method of compilation used by the Department of Customs and Excise was altered in 1935 from financial years to calendar years.

The price factor undoubtedly *was* decisive. As the standard of living in Iraq was very low during the 1930s, the purchasing power of most Iraqis was consequently weak. Thus, for the majority of the population, price was much more important than quality.

The second reason for the increase in Japanese imports lay in Iraq's relationship with the sterling area. While Japan abandoned the gold standard and depreciated its yen, Iraq's commitment to the sterling area meant that the exchange rate would always be in the yen's favour.[128]

The first British reaction to Japanese competition in Iraq, as elsewhere, came from the textile industry, which was most severely hurt. Messrs Herbert Whitworth Ltd. of Manchester wrote to John Rumney Remer, MP:

> Although this territory [Iraq] is not within the British Empire, you are well aware that many many millions of money and a huge toll of lives has been spent during and since the war in putting this Country on a sound footing, which recently has enabled it to take a place in the League of Nations ... We are Iraq's biggest customer for her exports. Therefore why should we allow Japanese looms to do all the supplying of hcr principal imports?[129]

However, the Colonial Office, the Board of Trade and the Foreign Office were all of the opinion, during 1933, that Iraq (and indeed other countries) should not be asked to introduce discriminatory measures against Japan.[130] At that point the British government did not want to further antagonize Japan, since there were indications that the Japanese government had reacted to the anti-Japanese boycotts in China and to India's repeated tariff increases on Japanese goods by accelerating its commercial expansion.[131] Moreover, 'there was no evidence in 1933 of a serious decline in British trade in an important industry as a result of Japanese competition'.[132] Nevertheless, the Manchester Chamber of Commerce, articulating Lancashire interests, began to single out Japanese competition as the chief source of their predicament, and hence asked the British government to see to it that Japanese goods were discriminated against. More and more questions on the subject were being asked in the House of Commons. Thus, in July 1933, Captain Fuller, MP, asked the president of the Board of Trade: 'if he is aware of the intensity of Japanese competition in Iraq, which has resulted in a great loss of orders to Manchester merchants; and if any steps can be taken to negotiate an agreement with Iraq in order to preserve our market against unfair competition there?'[133]

The British press joined the textile lobby in its campaign to persuade the government to take action. When King Faisal of Iraq visited London in 1933 to obtain a loan for his government, a British paper published in Baghdad called for measures which would protect British interests: 'While the Iraq mission is here [London] our Government must ask for and insist upon reciprocity and fair treatment. Japan must not be allowed to walk away with the fruits of all the lives, labour and money which have been devoted to the building of Iraq on a solid foundation.'[134] Replying in the Iraqi press, the Iraqi government protested that it was bound by its international obligations to follow an open-door policy, and that there was no question of discrimination or of any intention on Iraq's part to evade fulfilment of its undertakings to Great Britain. It further argued that Japanese textile factories were submitting the lowest bids for government contracts, and it was thus obliged to award them these contracts.[135]

By 1934 the Board of Trade had bowed to the pressure of the textile industry. The Foreign Office, noting this change, continually pointed out that grave consequences might ensue if the Japanese government discovered that the British were pressing Iraq and other independent countries to take discriminatory measures against Japan.[136]

The failure in March 1934 of London-based negotiations between British and Japanese cotton and rayon industrialists[137] left the Foreign Office no option but to consent to the Lancashire demands that Britain should influence such foreign countries as Iraq and Egypt to take action to restore British trade and thus reduce Japan's.[138] Britain itself took measures that year, to be followed by other countries like Egypt in 1935. (India, as mentioned earlier, increased its tariffs in 1932 and again in 1933, to 75% *ad valorem* on Japanese goods.)[139]

In Iraq, the main argument used by the British against the Japanese (the Iraqis later endorsed it) was that Iraqi exports to Japan were negligible. Dates were unknown in Japan, and an attempt to introduce them into the diet of Japanese troops in 1936 proved unsuccessful. Grains were readily available from China, Australia and India, and Japan therefore had no need to import such commodities from a more distant country such as Iraq. All in all, less than 1% of Iraq's exports prior to 1936 went to Japan.

Before taking any action, the Iraqi government held talks with the Japanese delegation attending the 1933 International Financial and Economic Conference in London, but to no avail.[140] Further rounds of equally unsuccessful discussions aimed at increasing Japanese imports from Iraq took place in 1934 and spring 1935.[141]

At the end of 1935, the Japanese government suggested the creation of a special fund to compensate Japanese importers for their loss in importing Iraqi products. In February 1936, the Japanese authorities were ready to lower tariffs on imported dates if Iraq would commit itself not to raise duties on Japanese textiles. According to Jamil, Iraq rejected both suggestions without examining them.[142]

The unsuccessful negotiations with Japan, coupled with growing pressure from Britain (as mentioned earlier, one condition for lowering tariffs on Iraqi dates imported into Britain was that Iraq reduce its imports from Japan), led Iraq to enact Regulation No. 22

of 1936, which was put into effect in May 1936. The most important clause of this law was Article 1, which provided that textiles of Japanese origin could not be cleared through customs for home consumption

unless the person desiring to clear such goods can prove to the satisfaction of the Collector of Customs and Excise, export to Japan, for home-consumption, of Iraqi produce, other than Oil and Oil Products, to the extent shown below:

(a) 15% of value of goods desired to be cleared from the date of the coming into force of this Regulation to 31 March, 1937.
(b) 25% of value of goods desired to be cleared during the year ending on 31 March, 1938.[143]

To the British it was obvious that the 'situation now created seems to afford valuable opportunity for recovery of lost markets by British and Indian exporters of piece goods'.[144]

Iraq now asked Britain to lower duties on Iraqi dates in return for its concession to British goods. The British made their compliance contingent on Iraq's altering tariffs on motorized vehicles in Britain's favour; but, as was shown earlier, the Iraqis could not do so for fear of American reaction.

In response to Iraq's customs restrictions, Japanese firms expressed their readiness to buy large quantities of salt from Iraq,[145] and the Iraqi press reported that large shipments of wheat were being sent to Japan.[146] The British ambassador in Baghdad described the situation thus:

It may presumably be taken for granted that the Japanese will do everything possible to maintain the value of their exports of piece-goods to this country, which at present amount to about £1,000,000 a year. Already they are encouraging Iraqi importers to send samples of possible Iraqi exports to Japan and are offering an additional inducement in the shape of free freight for such goods as may be carried in Japanese bottoms ... Trade in Japanese piece-goods has become so profitable to Iraqi merchants that no efforts will be spared to comply with the regulation in order to keep the Japanese trade going.[147]

The British were satisfied with Iraq's measures against Japanese imports. However, it was only with reluctance that they accepted Iraq's request that British consular officers in Japan should authenticate Japanese customs clearance certificates in respect of Iraqi goods consigned to Japan. The reason for this reluctance was that the British did not want to give the Japanese the impression that they were 'conspiring against their trade'.[148]

A few months after the new Iraqi regulations were put into effect, the British found themselves very disappointed that the system did not in any way check the flow of Japanese goods into Iraq: 'The market for the Japanese good in Iraq has shown itself much more elastic in practice than was generally supposed possible and the net benefit to United Kingdom piece-goods exporters of the present Iraqi restrictions on Japanese piece-goods imports has proved nugatory.'[149]

Import permits proving that the Iraqi merchant had exported ID 15 of goods to Japan in order to be able to import ID 100 of Japanese textiles were available on the black market; the merchants purchased them and passed the cost on to the retail buyer. But even so, the resulting increase in the price of Japanese textiles was not sufficient to enable British products to compete successfully. Ambassador Kerr predicted that

> even when the ratio of Japanese purchases to sales of cotton textiles is raised to one quarter in March 1937, there will still be no great difficulty in disposing of the requisite amount of Iraq exports to Japan without any further appreciable reaction upon the prices at which Japanese cotton piece-goods can be sold in Iraq.[150]

Kerr was right. Although the Iraqi government raised the ratio of Iraqi exports to Japanese imports to 25% from April 1937,[151] there occurred no decline in Japanese imports to Iraq. Again the merchants were able to pass on to the public the increased costs without appreciably lessening the gap between Japanese prices and those of British manufacturers.[152] In fact, as Table 5.9 indicates, the value of Japanese textiles and textile articles imported into Iraq continued to increase, while the value of British goods imported decreased.

In late 1937 the Iraqi government published Regulation No. 76 of 1937, which increased the ratio of Iraqi goods (other than oil and oil products) required to be exported from Iraq to Japan to 35% of the value of Japanese textiles imported to Iraq between 1 April 1938 and 31 March 1939.[153]

During 1938, Iraq's imports of Japanese piece-goods declined. This was only partially due to the restrictive regulations, however; an additional factor was the general deterioration that year in Iraq's foreign trade, both imports and exports (Tables 5.4 and 5.5). Furthermore, the Iraqi market was overstocked with Japanese textiles imported during 1937.[154] Meanwhile, it had begun to be increasingly difficult for Japanese importers of Iraqi produce to arrange, under the percentage system, credits satisfactory to the principal banks – all of them British – operating in Iraq.[155]

Under further regulations (Law No. 16 of 1939), the ratio of 35:100 between Iraqi exports and Japanese imports was made applicable to all Japanese goods, instead of textiles only.[156] By then, Iraq had adopted the ratio system as an integral part of its commercial policy, issuing regulations which provided that the ratio of 25:100 between exports and imports would apply to six other countries besides Japan.[157]

Iraqi exports, however, were unable to keep up with the new policy. Not only that, but in order to meet the new requirements Iraqi products were being sold to countries like Japan at prices lower than those at which they had previously been exported to other countries.[158]

As a result of this situation, Law No. 16 of 1939 was repealed, making the ratio of 35:100 between exports and imports applicable, as before, only to textile imports from Japan. Another factor impelling Iraq to moderate its policy was the outbreak of World War II, which, as we have seen, had a two-fold impact, in that it led both to an increase in the world demand for Iraqi products, and created the necessity for Iraq to increase its imports.

In spite of all these developments, Japan's trade with Iraq continued to prosper: Iraq's imports of Japanese textiles and textile articles increased from about ID 1.2 million in 1938 to ID 1.4 million in 1940 (see Table 5.9), and a Japanese Trade Bureau was established in Baghdad in July 1939 with the object of furnishing Japanese merchants with pertinent information.[159] But Iraq's exports to Japan were far from the ratio of 35:100 in 1939: total exports to Japan amounted to no more than ID 169,000, as against total imports of ID 1.5 million. Iraqi merchants were allowed to increase their purchases from Japan regardless of the difficulties that might arise in meeting their commitments to the Iraqi customs authorities in respect of the provision of certificates covering exports to Japan.[160] Consequently, a serious shortage of import certificates developed, and this in turn led to an increased premium on these certificates from about 3% to 11%, reaching 15% by the end of 1939. Textile importers made representations to the government, but it was announced that no change in the ratio policy was contemplated.[161]

During 1940 Iraq's trade with Japan was disrupted by two factors. The first was the attempt of Japanese exporters to refuse payment in sterling for both pending and future contracts. Initially the Japanese shippers tried to insist on credits being opened in US dollars, but when they realized this demand would not be met they suggested rupees as a basis of payment for Japanese goods.[162]

The second factor contributing to the disorganization of trade was the rise in the premium for export certificates covering Iraqi shipments to Japan from the already high figure of 15% to 17%.[163] In July the Department of Overseas Trade reported that it had reached 18%.[164] Meanwhile, Japanese exporters continued to refuse to accept sterling in payment for exports to Iraq. The result of these developments was, as the Department of Overseas Trade reported in August, that 'apart from transactions which have been arranged on the basis of free dollars, virtually no orders have been placed in Japan by local merchants for nearly three months'.[165]

While imports from Japan did not decrease in 1940, their upward trend was checked. Total imports of textiles increased by less than 1% (from ID 1.36 million to ID 1.37 million) but these figures should be treated cautiously since an intense inflationary process set in from early 1940 (see the textile wholesale price index in Table 3.8).

The Iraqi press, while praising trade relations with Japan, began to demand that Japan help Iraqi merchants who were experiencing difficulties in their trade affairs due to the Japanese regulations restricting import and export trade to members of the Japanese Export and Import Association.[166] Aware of this criticism, and in order to revive the flow of Japan's exports to Iraq, the large import firm of G.G. Abdeni and Co. Ltd., acting on behalf of Messrs Mitsubishi, signed a contract with Iraq's Ministry of Economics on 7 October 1940 to buy the entire Iraqi cotton crop of 1940.[167]

At a meeting held at the British Ministry of Economic Warfare at the end of 1940 to discuss Britain's trade relations with Iraq, the subject of Japanese competition was raised. Mr Marrs of the Board of Trade expressed his uneasiness over the ratio system as 'it would appear that the Japanese, by the terms of their purchase of the cotton crop, had secured what amounted to a monopoly of the piece-goods trade'.[168]

The British, alarmed by the growth of Japanese–Iraqi trade relations, and realizing that the customs restrictions they had pressed Iraq to implement since 1936 had not checked the flow of Japanese imports, decided on a new method. In a memorandum prepared by the Ministry of the Treasury, it was recommended that: 'The Iraq Government should be pressed to control the import of cotton textiles from Japan, which has been increasing, and we should ensure that no payment for imports from Japan is made in dollars.'[169] The Bank of England instructed the British banks in Iraq not to finance Japanese shipments in dollars (as Japanese exporters were demanding).[170] The banks also refused to open credits in Japan except against a deposit of 100% in cash, an act which indeed impeded business between the two countries.[171]

As world conditions continued to deteriorate, Iraq faced immense problems in securing basic commodities for its population. Thus, in December 1940 it repealed all customs restrictions *vis à vis* Japan, and instituted new regulations according to which Iraqi importers were asked to pay 15% in cash in lieu of showing evidence that goods had been exported to Japan to the value of 35% of their imports.[172]

From the British ambassador's point of view, the new customs regulations were drafted largely for the benefit of Messrs Abdeni (who bought the cotton crop of 1940). Sir Basil Newton reported a strong rumour to the effect that the prime minister, Rashid 'Ali, had personally made £50,000 on the cotton deal, and that he and other prominent Iraqis had collaborated with Messrs Abdeni in their negotiations for the cotton contract, as well as for the convenient amendments to the quota restrictions on trade with Japan.[173] Ibrahim al-Kabir confirms these allegations in his memoirs, arguing that the 'only people who took advantage of these anomalous operations were those who traded in the purchase and sale of export certificates like George Abdeni who was the friend of the Prime Minister and presumed to be the instigator of the scheme'.[174]

In 1941 the value of Japanese exports to Iraq decreased by 33% (see Table 5.9). Considering the inflationary prices at the time, the decrease was even more significant. It resulted more from world conditions and Japan's military attack on the US than from British efforts to check Japanese imports through exchange control. Yet it seems that the latter had some effect as well.

Under British pressure, Iraq decided in November 1941 to sever relations with Japan on the grounds that it had encouraged Rashid 'Ali's movement.[175] Subsequently, Japanese exports to Iraq continued to decrease rapidly; by 1944 they were totally insignificant. But, interestingly enough, even in early 1945 Japanese cotton goods were finding their way to Baghdad markets. British reports had the Russians selling Japanese goods in Persia (at a handsome profit, as part of their campaign to obtain rials to finance their various activities there), whence they were smuggled into Iraq.[176] It was also reported that a number of Kurds brought to Baghdad Japanese textiles said to have been distributed to them by Russian agents.[177]

Japanese exports to Iraq resumed in 1948. Although they did not present a threat to British exports until the end of the period under study, by 1951 the value of Japanese textiles exported to Iraq once again exceeded that of British textiles.

The British–Japanese competition for Iraqi markets discussed here is a good example of how international commercial rivalry can affect a small and relatively weak country. Theoretically, the competition should have worked to Iraq's benefit. But reality proved otherwise. British influence in Iraq was powerful at the time, with Britain holding the bargaining cards in any negotiations. Iraq was dependent on Britain in a number of respects, the most important being the fact that Britain was its sole supplier of military equipment. Even when there were opportunities to exploit the competition, Iraq's decision-makers did not manoeuvre adeptly. For instance, they gave in to British demands that Japanese goods be discriminated against, and only later, when their leverage was dissipated, did they ask Britain to lower its duties on Iraqi dates.

The ratio policy Iraq was forced to adopt *vis à vis* Japan created many distortions in Iraq's foreign trade: exports to Japan were increased only at the expense of exports to other countries, and sometimes even at lower prices. Total exports, therefore, did not increase at all. At the same time, no effective lobby formed in Iraq to fight this policy: import merchants were not affected by it, since they passed on the cost of the mandatory export certificates to the buyer, while export merchants benefited from it, for it constituted an indirect subsidy to them.

Even from Britain's point of view the ratio policy was a failure, as it made nearly no impact on the flow of Japanese goods into Iraq, or elsewhere for that matter. It was only World War II that brought Britain's commercial competition with Japan to an end.

Britain's Other Competitors in Iraq

Britain had other competitors for Iraq's markets besides Japan, but none of them constituted a real threat to British predominance in Iraq's foreign trade.

Commercial relations between Iraq and the Soviet Union prospered for a very short while in 1931 when, as a result of the Persian Trade Monopoly Law, Soviet goods were diverted to Iraq. The Iraqi Council of Ministers agreed to the establishment in Baghdad of a branch office of the Russian Eastern Company to facilitate trade between the two countries.[178] But the British High Commissioner, under instructions from London, pressed King Faisal to suspend the council's resolution.[179] After the war, the Soviet Legation in Baghdad asked Iraq to stop treating the Soviet Union as a 'closed market' for the purpose of imports and exports. In 1946 it offered to supply Iraq with white sugar at a very cheap price, but British and American influence prevented the deal from going through.[180]

Another country which competed with Britain during the 1930s was Germany. Beginning in 1934, German products (mainly cement and iron) were exported to Iraq as part of an arrangement known in Hebrew as *Ha'avara* (transfer), which had as its purpose the release of frozen credits in Germany belonging to German Jews emigrating to Palestine. Each emigrant was allowed to release 30% of his frozen assets in the form of exports. When such exports met with opposition by the British administration in Palestine, the *Ha'avara* organization began directing them to Iraq.[181]

Although a trade agreement between Iraq and Germany was reached in 1935, the strict exchange and import policy Germany had adopted the previous year prevented any significant development in bilateral trade between the two countries.[182] The British for their part did everything possible to discourage such trade relations,[183] and in 1939 the ratio policy discussed above was made applicable to Germany.

In any event, after 1938 trade with Germany began to decrease rapidly as a result of the severance of connections between German firms and their Jewish representatives in Iraq, as well as because of a partial boycott of German goods (and German ships) by Iraqi Jewish merchants.[184]

After 1945 trade relations with Germany were resumed, but they remained insignificant until 1950. Britain's only serious competitor in Iraq after the war was the US. American trade with Iraq had in fact begun to prosper during the war itself, when Britain could not supply Iraq with its needs. American competition, however, was not restricted to trade as was the Japanese; as we saw in Chapter 1, it rather endangered British interests in all sectors of Iraq's economy.

On the whole, it can be said that Iraq's foreign trade policy was more co-ordinated in the 1940s than in the 1930s. Issues influenced by the war and its aftermath, such as the sterling area problem, elicited a fair degree of consistency despite the frequent changes of government. On the other hand, external issues imposed on Iraq, such as the British–Japanese competition of the 1930s, did not contribute to the development of policy coherence. Both decades, however, were characterized by the concept that the major purpose of tariffs is to increase government revenue.

NOTES

1. Murray, *Statistical Organisation in Iraq*, p.104.
2. Ibid., p.113.
3. Iraq, Central Bureau of Statistics, *Summary of Foreign Trade Statistics, 1927–1960*, General Remarks.

4. Board of Trade, Department of Overseas Trade, *Economic Conditions in Iraq, 1933*, Report by C. Empson, Commercial Secretary to His Majesty's Embassy at Baghdad (London, 1933), p.12.
5. See Jamil's criticism of this approach, *Siyasat al-'Iraq al-Tijariyya*, pp.370–1.
6. For more details about the balance of payments and the deficiencies in its calculation, see Murray, *Statistical Organisation in Iraq*, pp.129–31; Zalzalah, *Iraq in the Sterling Area*, pp.173–5.
7. Memorandum by Iraqi government in reply to aide memoire presented by British Embassy in Baghdad, 13 Apr. 1939., FO 371/23208, E 2821/374/93.
8. League of Nations, *Balance of Payments 1937*, p.125.
9. The increase in consumer goods imports took place in spite of the increase of tariffs on them in 1933 (see the section on tariffs policy).
10. Memorandum by the Iraqi government, enclosed in a despatch from Murray (statistical adviser to Iraqi government) to BMEO, 24 Aug. 1948. FO 957/48, 108/18/18. The figures were based on Murray's work with Iraq's Statistical Bureau.
11. See A.H. al-Najjar, *Siyasat al-Tijarah al-Kharijiyya fi al-'Iraq fi fatrat ma ba'ad al-Harb al-'Alamiyya al-Thaniya* (Foreign trade policy in Iraq after World War II) (Baghdad, 1968), pp.95–7.
12. Iversen, *Monetary Policy in Iraq*, pp.75–6.
13. Board of Trade, Department of Overseas Trade, *Report on Economic Conditions in Iraq, 1933–1935*, by J.P. Summerscale, Commercial Secretary to His Majesty's Embassy at Baghdad (London, 1936), p.,17.
14. *Foreign Trade Statistics 1938*, p.118; *Statistical Abstract 1950*, p.213.
15. The 1950 date export agreement is outside the scope of this book.
16. *Instability in Export Markets of Under-Developed Countries* (New York, 1952), p.12.
17. Iversen, *Monetary Policy in Iraq*, p.77.
18. Ibid., pp.74, 76.
19. United Kingdom, *Economic and Commercial Conditions*, pp.24–5.
20. Knabenshue to Dept. of State, 'Current Events for the Period 1–15 Nov. 1941', ACR, Reel 16.
21. Report by J. Summerscale to DOT, 8 Apr. 1936. FO 371/20016, E 2442/2440/93.
22. Kerr to FO, 18 Nov. 1935. FO 369/2409, K 12790/9893/293.
23. From the reports of the Baghdad Chamber of Commerce.
24. Mohammad Salman Hasan, *Al-Tatawar al-Iqtisadi fi al-'Iraq* (Economic development of Iraq) (Beirut, 1965), pp.462–3.
25. Batatu, *The Old Social Classes*, p.282.
26. Baghdad Chamber of Commerce, *Report for the Years 1938 and 1939*.
27. Batatu, op. cit., p.312.
28. For a detailed description of the organisation of foreign trade, see Hasan, *Al-Tatawar al-Iqtisadi, fi al-'Iraq*, pp.138–54, 262–72.
29. For details about the first stage, the 'revenue' phase, see Hasan's thesis, 'Foreign Trade in the Economic Development of Modern Iraq, 1869–1939' (Oxford Univ. D.Phil. thesis 1958), pp.210–26. Most of the material in Hasan's *Al-Tatawar al-Iqtisadi* is drawn from his thesis.
30. For details about Law No. 30 of 1927 and its amendments, see Jamil, *Siyasat al-'Iraq al-Tijariyya*, pp.57–61.
31. For the full text of the Law, see *The Iraq Directory*, Commercial Section, pp.35–41.
32. Ibid., pp.42–88.
33. The 1933 law was amended in 1934 (Law No. 3), 1935 (Laws Nos. 29 and 65) and 1939 (Law No. 10). For a comprehensive treatment of the 1933 law and its amendments, see Jamil, *Siyasat al-'Iraq al-Tijariyya*, pp.169–209.
34. Ibid., pp.196–200.
35. Ibid., pp.202–7.
36. Al-Nasrawi, *Financing Economic Development*, p.138.
37. Jamil, *Siyasat al-'Iraq al-Tijariyya*, pp.249–51.
38. For a detailed list of restricted and prohibited imports, see ibid., pp.181–4.
39. Thompson to FO (Tel. 444), 16 Sept. 1944. FO 371/40058, E 5685/193/93.
40. *MEESB* (June 1946), p.6.

41. Iraq's Ministry of Supply, Notification No. 70 of 1946. Enclosed in the despatch on 'Economic Conditions in Iraq for October 1946', FO 371/52423, E 11397/652/93.
42. For more details about the lists, see IBRD, *Economic Development of Iraq*, pp.162–5.
43. For a discussion of the change in policy, see Zalzalah, 'Iraq in the Sterling Area', pp.370–4.
44. The full text appears in Davis, *Constitutions, Electoral Laws, Treaties of States*, pp.197–203.
45. Memorandum by Eastern Department, FO, for the British representative on the Council of the League of Nations, 21 Jan. 1932. FO 371/16030, E 369/9/93.
46. Ibid.
47. For details about each treaty, see Jamil, *Siyasat al-'Iraq al-Tijariyya*, pp.315–329.
48. *Board of Trade Journal* (18 Mar. 1937), p.420.
49. Jamil, op. cit., p.314.
50. Najjar, *Siyasat al-Tijarah al Kharijiyya fi al-'Iraq*, pp.479–80.
51. James Moose (American Legation, Baghdad) to Dept. of State, 'Current Events for the Period 15–31 Aug. 1934'. ACR, Reel 3.
52. FO to Ambassador Kerr, 28 Mar. 1935. FO 371/18951, E 1555/811/93.
53. Kerr to FO, 25 July 1936. FO 624/7/377.
54. Memorandum by FO, 19 Aug. 1936. FO 371/2011, E 377/30/93.
55. FO to Board of Trade, 4 Sept. 1936. FO 371/22011, E 5469/1052/93.
56. Kerr to FO, 'Annual Report on Iraq for 1936', 30 Jan. 1937. FO 371/20803, E 1055/1055/93.
57. Ambassador to FO, 'Annual Report on Iraq for 1937'. FO 371/21856, E 794/794/93.
58. For a detailed discussion of these problems, see Jamil, *Siyasat al-'Iraq al-Tijariyya*, pp.541–4.
59. Jamil, op. cit., pp.555–60.
60. For a historical background, see Raymond Mikesell, 'Sterling Area Currencies of the Middle East', *Middle East Journal*, ii (April 1948), 161–4.
61. James Ansara, 'Report on the Sterling Area System in the Middle East', June 1945. T 236/207.
62. Zalzalah, *Iraq in the Sterling Area*, p.212.
63. FO to Embassy (Baghdad), 4 Oct. 1939. FO 371/23218, E 6808/6809/93.
64. Memorandum by FO (based on information from British banking circles in Iraq), 16 May 1940. FO 371/24560, E 2031/932/93.
65. Waterfield (Treasury) to FO, 19 Aug. 1940. Ibid.
66. Knabenshue to Dept. of State, 10 Dec. 1940. ACR, Reel 18.
67. Cabinet meeting of 17 Feb. 1941. CAB 65/17, 18(41)2.
68. FO to Embassy (Angora) (Tel. 1027), 6 May 1941. FO 371/30057, R 4947/40/44. After the Rashid 'Ali uprising, the staff of the British Embassy in Baghdad were transferred temporarily to Angora.
69. *The Economist* (17 May 1941), p.662.
70. FO to Embassy (Baghdad), 13 July 1941. FO 624/22/126.
71. For details about the law regulating economic life, see p.121.
72. 'Exchange Control Law No. 71 of 1941'. A copy appears in FO 624/22/126. It underwent three amendments: (1) Law No. 33 of 1942; (2) Law No. 56 of 1943; (3) Law No. 33 of 1947. Copies appear in FO 371/61650, E 7444/453/93.
73. Cornwallis to FO (Tel. 340), 6 Dec. 1941. FO 624/22/126.
74. Memorandum by IPC, end of 1941 (no exact date). T 160, 1157/17889.
75. *Summary of Foreign Trade Statistics, 1927–1960*, p.111.
76. Basri estimated the balances at £74 million, of which £43 million were reserves held by the Iraq Currency Board in London, in a sense representing the cover for Iraq's currency. See Basri, *Mabahith fi al-Iqtisad al-'Iraqi*, p.169. Another estimate put the balance at £70 million; see: Phillip W. Bell, *The Sterling Area in the Post-War Period* (Oxford, 1965), p.95.
77. T. Balogh, 'The International Aspect', in G.D.N. Worswick and P.H. Ady (eds.), *The British Economy 1945–50* (Oxford, 1952), p.481.
78. Memorandum by Treasury, 1 Feb. 1945. T 236/1177.
79. 'Agreement between His Majesty's Government in the United Kingdom and the Iraqi

Government concerning Iraq Foreign Exchange Requirements for 1945', Baghdad 28 May 1945. Cmd 6646.
80. 'Correspondence between His Majesty's Government in the United Kingdom and the Iraqi Government concerning the Prolongation of Existing Arrangements regarding Iraqi Foreign Exchange Requirements', Baghdad 17 Jan. 1946. Cmd. 6742.
81. 'Correspondence between His Majesty's Government in the United Kingdom and the Iraqi Government concerning the Prolongation of Existing Arrangements regarding Iraqi Foreign Exchange Requirements', Baghdad 8 Apr. 1946. Cmd. 6803.
82. 'Exchange of Notes between His Majesty's Government in the United Kingdom and the Government of Iraq concerning the Prolongation of Existing Arrangements regarding Iraqi Foreign Exchange Requirements', Baghdad 10/22 Feb. 1947. Cmd. 7110.
83. Stonehewer-Bird to FO, 24 Mar. 1946. FO 371/52367, E 1085/9/93.
84. Stonehewer-Bird to FO (Tel. 76), 16 Nov. 1945. T 236/1180.
85. FO to Embassy (Tel. 48), 10 Aug. 1946. FO 371/52367, E 7664/9/93.
86. Thompson (British Embassy, Baghdad) to Pinsent (Treasury), 11 Sept. 1945. E 11/2339.
87. Cornwallis to FO, 21 Mar. 1945. FO 371/45290, E 2197/89/93.
88. Memorandum by Lingerman (First secretary to the Embassy – Commercial), 'American Trade Competition in Iraq', Oct. 1944. FO 921/263, 81/44/9.
89. Summary of the conference of British representatives in the Middle East which met in London on 5–17 Sept. 1945. BT 11/2681.
90. Stonehewer-Bird to FO, 18 June 1945. FO 371/45293, E 4686/89/G93.
91. Ibid.
92. Pinsent (Treasury) to Baxter (FO), 31 July 1945. FO 371/45293, E 5718/89/G93.
93. Embassy to FO (Tel. 540), 17 July 1945. FO 371/45293, E 5231/89/G93.
94. See Mikesell, 'Sterling Area Currencies', pp.169–70.
95. Minutes of Sterling Balance Negotiations between Iraq and the United Kingdom, 20 June 1947. T 236/1190.
96. Ibid.
97. Ibid.
98. Ibrahim al-Kabir memoirs (unpublished), iii, p.160.
99. Ibid., pp.160–1.
100. Stonehewer-Bird to Bevin, 'Memorandum on the United Kingdom–Iraq Financial and Economic Position', 3 Apr. 1947. FO 371/62420, UE 2817/176/53.
101. 'Financial Agreement between the Government of the United Kingdom and the Government of Iraq', London, 13 Aug. 1947. Cmd. 7201.
102. Embassy to FO, 'Report on Economic Conditions in Iraq for August 1947', FO 371/61661, E 8782/641/93.
103. Memorandum from Iraq's Ministry of Finance to British Embassy in Baghdad, 28 Aug. 1947. FO 371/61651, E 8291/453/93.
104. BMEO (Cairo) to FO, 4 Nov. 1947. FO 371/61513, E 10514/183/65.
105. FO notes of the secretary of state's interview with the regent of Iraq, 14 Oct. 1947. FO 371/61595, E 9553/3/93.
106. Busk to FO (Tel. 1063), 10 Nov. 1947. FO 371/61654, E 10520/453/93.
107. 'Financial Agreement between the Government of the United Kingdom and the Government of Iraq', Baghdad 17 Nov. 1947. Cmd. 7269. The term 'scarce currency countries' included, apart from the Belgian monetary area, the American account area, the Portuguese monetary area, Canada and Newfoundland, Switzerland and Liechtenstein, Argentina, Sweden and Japan.
108. Busk (Embassy, Baghdad) to FO, 20 Nov. 1947. T 236/1196.
109. Mack to FO (Tel. 402), 14 Apr. 1948. T 225/24.
110. *Statistical Abstract 1950*, p.282.
111. 'Exchange of Notes between the Governments of the United Kingdom and Iraq Prolonging the Supplementary Financial Agreement of 17 November 1947', Baghdad 27 June 1948. Cmd. 7490. For the discussions preceding the agreement, see T 236/1197, T 236/1193 and FO 371/68467.
112. Mack to FO, 5 Oct. 1949. FO 371/75167, E 12553/1117/93.
113. Embassy to FO (Tel. 994), 16 Nov. 1949. FO 371/75159, E 13835/1113/93.

114. Zalzalah, *Iraq in the Sterling Area*, pp.274–5.
115. Iversen, *Monetary Policy in Iraq*, pp.250–79.
116. F. Shehab, 'Iraq', *Bulletin of the Oxford University Institute of Statistics*, xxi, no. 4 (1959), pp.291–307.
117. Mack to FO, 'Economic Report for September 1949', 21 Oct. 1949. FO 371/75149, E 13255/1101/93.
118. Memorandum by British Embassy in Baghdad to FO on British commercial interests in Iraq, 29 May 1934. FO 371/17858, E 3526/190/93.
119. Humphrys to FO, 1 Feb. 1934. FO 371/17858, E 962/190/93.
120. See p.15.
121. Humphrys to FO, op. cit.
122. Cotton-textile competition played a crucial role in the foreign policy not only of Japan and Britain but of the United States as well. Some writers see in this competition an important factor leading to World War II. For an interesting general work on the subject, see Osamu Ishii, 'Cotton-Textile Diplomacy: Japan, Great Britain and the United States, 1930–1936' (Rutgers Univ. Ph.D. thesis 1977).
123. Ann Trotter, *Britain and East Asia 1933–1937* (London, 1975), p.27.
124. Barnard Ellinger, 'British Foreign Policy in relation to the Lancashire Cotton Industry', *International Affairs* (March–April 1937), pp.245–62.
125. H.W. Arndt, *The Economic Lessons of the Nineteen-Thirties* (London, 1944), pp.102–7.
126. Memorandum by Chaplin (FO) on Japanese trade in neutral markets, 10 Sept. 1935. FO 433/2.
127. Board of Trade, *Report on Economic Conditions in Iraq, 1933–35*, p.8.
128. Jamil, *Siyasat al-'Iraq al-Tijariyya*, pp.331–2.
129. Syres (Dominions Office) to Ronald (FO), 29 Dec. 1932. FO 371/16049, E 6912/3606/93.
130. FO to Board of Trade, 26 July 1933. FO 371/17870, E 3696/1392/93.
131. Ishii, 'Cotton-Textile Diplomacy', p.147.
132. Trotter, *Britain and East Asia*, p.28.
133. *Hansard*, Parliamentary Debates, House of Commons, 4 July 1933, cclxxx, p.156.
134. *Iraq Times*, 29 July 1933.
135. Knabenshue to Dept. of State, 2 Aug. 1933. ACR, Reel 4.
136. FO to Board of Trade, 26 July 1934. FO 371/17870, E 3696/1392/93.
137. For details of the negotiations and an explanation of their breakdown, see Trotter, *Britain and East Asia*, pp.31–3.
138. Memorandum of first meeting of cabinet committee on Japanese competition, 27 Mar. 1934. CAB 27/568. This committee was formed to consider the economic and political consequences of the breakdown of negotiations between British and Japanese cotton and rayon industrialists.
139. *The Economist* (24 Mar. 1934), p.621.
140. Jamil, *Siyasat al-'Iraq al-Tijariyya*, pp.332–4.
141. Board of Trade, *Report on Economic Conditions in Iraq, 1933–35*, p.7.
142. Jamil, op. cit., p.334.
143. *Iraq Government Gazette*, 23 May 1936. A copy appears in FO 624/377/6.
144. Kerr to FO, 25 May 1936. Ibid.
145. Knabenshue to Dept. of State, 8 June 1936. ACR, Reel 3.
146. Knabenshue to Dept. of State, 19 Aug. 1936. Ibid.
147. Kerr to FO, 11 June 1936. FO 371/20011, E 3563/1052/93.
148. Memorandum by J.G. Ward (FO), 15 July 1936. FO 371/20011, E 4778/1052/93.
149. Comments by D. Scott Fox (FO) on restrictions on Japanese goods, 16 Nov. 1936. FO 371/20012, E 7478/1052/93.
150. Kerr to FO, 16 Nov. 1936. Ibid.
151. *Board of Trade Journal* cxxxviii (5 May 1937), p.669.
152. Board of Trade, *Report on Economic and Commercial Conditions in Iraq, 1935–1937* by J.P. Summerscale (London, 1938), p.7.
153. *Board of Trade Journal* cxxxix (2 Dec. 1937), p.739.
154. The American minister at Baghdad reported that the stocks of Japanese textiles in Iraqi

markets were sufficient to meet the country's requirements for two years. See despatch of 7 May 1939, ACR, Reel 3.

155. Peterson to FO, 'Economic Report (B) on Iraq', 24 Oct. 1938. FO 371/21853, E 6515/434/93.
156. *Board of Trade Journal* cxlii (20 Apr. 1939), p.599.
157. Ibid. The six countries were Germany, Czechoslovakia, the Soviet Union, Poland, Italy and Switzerland.
158. According to Jamil, the Iraqi cotton that began to be exported to Japan was sold at a price lower than in previous years when it was exported to Liverpool. See Jamil, *Siyasat al-'Iraq al-Tijariyya*, p.342.
159. Newton to FO, 5 July 1939. FO 371/23217, E 4923/4923/93.
160. DOT to FO, 'Economic Conditions in Iraq, Apr. 1940', FO 371/24556, E 1139/203/93.
161. DOT to FO, 'Economic Conditions in Iraq, Jan. 1940', ibid.
162. DOT to FO, 'Economic Conditions in Iraq, May 1940', ibid.
163. Ibid.
164. DOT to FO, 'Economic Conditions in Iraq, July 1940', ibid.
165. DOT to FO, 'Economic Conditions in Iraq, Aug. 1940', ibid.
166. *Al-Bilad*, 14 Oct. 1940.
167. Newton to Halifax, 12 Nov. 1940. FO 371/24561, E 3057/1342/93.
168. Minutes of a meeting at the Ministry of Economic Warfare (MEW) on 18 December 1940. MEW to FO, 23 Dec. 1940. FO 371/24556, E 3075/203/93.
169. Waterfield (Treasury) to Coverley-Price (FO), 19 Aug. 1940. FO 371/24560, E 2476/932/93.
170. Newton to FO, 2 Jan. 1941. FO 371/27086, E 55/55/93.
171. Newton to FO, 12 Nov. 1940. FO 371/24561, E 3057/1242/93.
172. 'Customs Notifications No. 17 of 1940', *Iraq Government Gazette*, 15 Dec. 1940. A copy appears in FO 371/27086, E 679/55/93.
173. Newton to FO, 25 Jan. 1941. FO 371/272086, E 680/55/93.
174. Al-Kabir memoirs (unpublished), iii, p.112.
175. Cornwallis to FO, 17 Nov. 1941. FO 371/27095, E 7576/191/93.
176. Cornwallis to FO, 9 Jan. 1945. FO 371/45322, E 429/429/93.
177. Cornwallis to FO, 'Economic Conditions for Feb. 1945', FO 371/45322, E 1355/429/93.
178. Acting High Commissioner to Lord Passfield (secretary of state for the colonies), 26 June 1931. CO 730/168/88255.
179. Acting High Commissioner to Lord Passfield, 16 July 1931. Ibid.
180. BMEO, 'Activities of Major Powers in M.E. Territories', Monthly Progress Report, Mar. 1946. FO 371/52337, E 3828/341/65.
181. Kerr to FO, 'Memorandum respecting German Economic Penetration in Iraq', 23 Apr. 1936. FO 371/20010, E 2512/97393.
182. For an interesting discussion of Germany's foreign trade policy towards countries like Iraq, see Larry Neal, 'The Economics and Finance of Bilateral Clearing Agreements: Germany 1934–8', *Economic History Review* xxxii, no. 3 (August 1979), pp.391–404.
183. Even when the large German corporation I.G. Farben had developed a new serum against syphilis, a German contract with the Iraqi Health Ministry was stopped by the British Embassy. See: H.H. Kopietz, 'The Use of German and British Archives in the Study of the Middle East: The Iraqi Coup d'Etat of 1936', in Kelidar (ed.), *Integration of Modern Iraq*, p.49.
184. Houstoun-Boswall to FO, 'Annual Report, Economic (A) for 1938', 10 May 1939. FO 371/23203, E 3556/78/93.

6

INDUSTRY, OIL AND LABOUR

MANUFACTURING INDUSTRIES

Following World War I, economic policy in Iraq stressed infrastructure and agriculture. In the last years of the mandate, however, there began a movement for the development of local industries. This was essentially a 'national' movement, the object being to reduce imports of manufactured articles.[1]

The first turning point came in 1927 with Law No. 20, whose target was to increase national production by exempting from tariffs building materials and equipment for agricultural cultivation, industrial output and water supply. This was followed two years later by Law No. 14 of 1929, which became the cornerstone of government policy throughout the 1930s and 1940s.

When the mandate ended, industry in Iraq was still undeveloped, consisting mainly of cottage workshops, but nevertheless stronger than before the mandate. Industrial activities were undertaken by some Iraqi entrepreneurs from among the mercantile community, and were thus no longer restricted to foreign or government initiative. Cotton ginning, building and construction, and date and cigarette processing plants were the main manufacturing industries at this time.[2]

Main Industries

Iraq's manufacturing industries at the end of the 1940s can be divided into six general categories:[3]

Textiles

Cotton. By 1950 there were three gins operating in Baghdad on locally-produced cotton. During the 1930s most of the ginned cotton was exported, but a considerable proportion of it began to be used by the Iraq Spinning and Weaving Company when it was formed in 1947.

Wool. There were three wool mills in Baghdad, with an average yearly output of some 500,000 metres of cloth, all of which was used locally. These factories accounted for about 90% of Iraq's production of woollen textiles. In addition, hand-weaving was widespread as a cottage industry. The total number of hand looms is not known, but has been estimated at 3,000.

Rayon. One small mill in Mosul produced rayon cloth from imported yarn.

Clothing. Apart from the few knitting factories mentioned above, there was no production of clothing.

Shoes and Boots

Shoes and boots were predominantly hand-made, but there were seven factories using electrically operated machinery. Production was estimated at 40,000 pairs of shoes and boots per annum. (As imports from the Bata firm of Czechoslovakia dropped because of high tariffs, local production increased by about 20%.)

Liquor and Tobacco

Distilleries. There were a number of distilleries producing arak, the national alcoholic beverage (made from dates or grapes), and also methylated spirits for local use.

Beer. A brewery began production in August 1948, using high-quality Iraqi barley. Output was estimated at 3.75 million pints a year.

Cigarettes. There were five factories in Baghdad, all using local tobacco, with an estimated output of 1,300 million cigarettes a year. There were also various other, smaller factories, most of which were not power-operated.

Building Materials

Bricks. Brick factories ranked highest among the concerns benefiting from the 1929 Law for the Encouragement of Industry (cigarettes being second). This industry expanded considerably during World War II, due to the constant military demand for roads and railways. The expansion continued in the post-war period when, as a result of the rise in the public's purchasing power, there was an increased demand for housing. By 1948, as Table 6.1 indicates, the brick industry was the biggest employer of labour after the oil industry, and it paid the highest average daily wages. Local production was sufficient to meet domestic needs, except for certain special types of bricks.

Cement. A cement factory in Baghdad began to operate in May 1949, with an initial production of 250 tons a day.

TABLE 6.1 Employment and Average Daily Wage, by Industry, 1948

	No. of workers	Average daily wage (fils)
Food	2,435	314
Beverages and refreshments	1,155	324
Tobacco	2,492	210
Vegetable oils and soap	457	284
Printing and binding	650	231
Tanning and shoes	2,135	366
Spinning and weaving	3,562	167
Mining	872	199
Mechanics	2,735	338
Water, electricity and telephone	1,222	285
Construction materials	6,115	381
Oil	13,133	357
Tailoring	1,025	287
Carpentry	1,435	371
Miscellaneous	809	310
Total	40,232	-

Source: Industrial Bank, Second Annual Report for the Financial Year 1948/49, p. 50.

Oils and Soap

Vegetable Oils. There were five factories in Baghdad producing vegetable oils for edible purposes and for soap manufacture. Most of the raw materials were indigenous. Annual production was put at 10,000 tons.

Soap. Apart from the prevalent 'bazaar' soap-manufacturer, there were eleven factories in Baghdad with a total estimated capacity of about 15,000 tons per annum.

Other Industries

Among Iraq's other important industries were matches, printing, tanning, glassware and an ammunition factory. Some of these, such as matches, were able, more or less, to supply the country's needs.

The above outline clearly indicates how undeveloped Iraq's industry was. Probably its most important turning point was World War II. Although only a few new manufacturing concerns were established during the war, those already in existence made considerable profits. (Textile and cigarette factories reported 100% profits.)[4] This attracted widespread interest, mainly among the mercantile class. For the first time in Iraq's history, industry began to be considered as profitable as trade or landowning. This new perception, combined with the increase in the public's purchasing power and the government's growing awareness of the importance of industry (even creating a separate Industrial Bank), all gave a great impetus to industrial development, the results of which were felt during the 1950s.

The main question then is: why did no significant development take place in the industrial sector during the 1930s and 1940s? The answer can be found in government policy, the objective problems facing Iraq (and most other developing countries), and the British attitude towards industrialization in Iraq.

Government Policy towards Industrialization

Industrial policy was the responsibility of the Directorate of Industrial Research, which was part of the Ministry of Economics and Communications. In 1939, with the creation of the Ministry of Economics, the Directorate was abolished and a Department of Industry was established. Various committees also dealt with industrial policy, mainly the Industrial Development Committee, formed in 1943 to develop enterprises other than cigarette factories and distilleries. These bodies, however, made but a small contribution to industrialization; some barely functioned (nothing was ever heard from the Industrial Development Committee), while others limited themselves to the bureaucratic procedures of supervising and surveying industries.

As already stated, industry was not given high priority in Iraq's economic policy. This was clearly reflected in government expenditure for capital development works: during the period 1931–50 only 4.8% of the total expenditure was allocated to 'industry and other development schemes', which probably meant even less than that for manufacturing industries proper (see Table 2.4).

This low priority for industrialization stemmed from the government's conception that Iraq was basically an agricultural country, and development policy must therefore emphasize agriculture. The subject of agriculture versus industry has been extensively examined elsewhere, both in a general theoretical context and with specific reference to Iraq.[5] We shall therefore not dwell on the theme, but it must be considered.

The Iraqi government's policy crystallized out of the British perception, which saw in Iraq an agricultural country exporting raw materials needed for British industries. In the late 1940s and early 1950s, British and other Western organizations surveying Iraq's economy forcefully advocated the notion that Iraq should place top priority on agricultural development.[6] Only after the 1958 revolution did Iraq deviate from this strategy. (Unfortunately, however, it then went to the opposite extreme of emphasizing industry to the neglect of agriculture.)[7] The issue was, and is, not which sector to prefer, but rather how to develop both simultaneously. This was well expressed in an international symposium on industrial development:

> Industrialisation and the development of agriculture are in no way alternative goals of the development policy, but complementary and mutually supporting processes. An imbalance between the growth of agriculture and industry can have unfortunate consequences on the growth of the economy as a whole.[8]

Having placed such low priority upon industrialization and with so little direct investment in the manufacturing sector, government policy towards industrialization was limited to two areas. The first was the encouragement and protection of local industry by granting exemptions from duties and taxes while simultaneously imposing tariffs on competing imported goods. The second was extending loans to factories.

Encouragement and Protection of Local Industry

The policy of encouraging and protecting local industry, as shown earlier, was begun in 1927 and reinforced by the 1929 law, which allowed certain exemptions from income and property taxes, and from customs duties. The use of unoccupied government land was also allowed, provided that the industries established thereon fulfilled certain conditions: produced finished goods in a form different from that of the raw materials, used other than manual power, did not permit non-Iraqi labour to exceed 10% of the total (excluding the technical staff), and made an initial investment of at least 30,000 rupees (approximately ID 2,250).[9] This policy gathered momentum with the enactment of Law No. 11 of 1933, which levied tariffs on imported goods according to their 'necessity' and stage of manufacture.

This policy of protectionism was not created in a vacuum; rather, it was the result of intensive pressure by local industrialists. In 1933, for instance, the Society for the Encouragement of Local Products (established a few years earlier) published a petition signed by eighty members of local footwear industries 'complaining bitterly against foreign competition', and requesting that prohibitive customs duties be imposed on imported footwear (mainly the cheap shoes manufactured by Bata of Czechoslovakia) 'as the lives of 18,000 Iraqi families are threatened'.[10] Similarly, local industrialists (who at the time came from the mercantile class) were pressing the chamber of commerce to intercede with the Ministry of Finance to increase tariffs on competing imports.[11]

The impact of the 1929 law can be assessed from the fact that between 1932 and 1947 the number of industrial establishments benefiting from it increased from 31 to 101.

As the conditions for qualifying for inclusion under the law were relaxed (e.g. the initial investment required was reduced to about ID 1,500), it seems unlikely that any industrial enterprise of the necessary size would refrain from taking advantage of its benefits. (The law was not applicable, however, to the oil, date and wool industries, because their products left the country in a form not different from the raw material.) It should be noted that with the creation of the Industrial Bank the benefits provided by the law began to be withdrawn (unofficially), which may explain why the number of concerns benefiting from the law in 1948 declined drastically, to 17.[12]

On the whole, the impact of the encouragement policy was quite modest; the number of concerns benefiting from the law never exceeded 101. This was not due to drawbacks in the law, which offered every possible tax exemption to non-manual industries, but rather to the wider policy of preferring agriculture to industry, as well as to objective factors (to be explained later), which led to a situation in which only a small number of industries existed by the end of the 1940s.

As for the protection policy, embodied in the 1933 customs law, it benefited three industries: cigarettes, liquor and shoe manufacture. As imports of products competing with these three industries dwindled in the face of the high tariffs imposed on them, local production prospered and multiplied.[13] The impact of tariffs on other industries, however, was less significant: the tariffs were either too low to inhibit imports or, more important, Iraqi industries could not satisfy local demand. This was 'inevitable because there were only a few worthwhile industrial projects to be protected'.[14] The latter case is illustrated by the woollen textile industry, which remained unprotected during the 1930s because the government was of the view that the local industry could not satisfy local needs, and that what it did sell was at relatively high prices.[15]

Loan Policy

The Agricultural and Industrial Bank was created, as we have seen, in 1936. A comparison of the industrial loans it granted in the years 1936–46 (Table 6.2) with the agricultural loans during the same period (Table 4.3) clearly indicates that the bank was primarily an agricultural one: during these eleven years, agricultural loans totalled ID 808,425, compared with only ID 71,425 for industrial loans. Indeed, it is hard to see how the industrial loans could have been effective at all (except for such years as 1942 and 1946).

In 1940 it was decided to separate the bank's functions, but this was implemented only in 1946 due to the war. The law of 1940 creating the Industrial Bank stated that its purpose was to develop and assist Iraqi industry and to carry on banking business related to this end. The bank was permitted to establish industrial enterprises of its own, sponsor and subscribe to public and private companies,

TABLE 6.2 Government Loans to Industry, 1936-1949

	No. of loans	Amount (ID 1,000)
1936	3	0.7
1937	8	3.2
1938	14	6.9
1939	13	3.2
1940	12	5.9
1941	7	6.3
1942	3	20.2
1943	4	0.9
1944	3	1.1
1945	7	15.9
1946	7	7.4
Sub total	81	71.7
1947	54	172.1
1948	35	50.3
1949	81	132.1
Sub total	170	354.5
Total	251	426.2

Sources: See Table 4.3.

make loans to industrialists, and act as an agent for the import of machinery and raw materials.[16]

The bank's capital was ID 500,000 in 1946 (doubling by 1951), which was obviously insufficient to fulfil its aims.[17] Nevertheless, the number and amount of its loans considerably increased in comparison with the pre-1946 period; as Table 6.2 shows, its loans in 1947–8 were five times those of the preceding eleven years. Due to the bank's conservative policy, however, most of them were under ID 500 and for very short terms.[18] Such small loans could not of course help industrialists acquire new machinery.

Industries based on the processing of agricultural products received the highest proportion of loans during FY 1946–9,[19] which is not surprising since they were the best developed industries in the country at the time. Loans to factories in the Baghdad region predominated, while the southern region received more than the northern.[20]

Another important function of the bank was investment in industrial enterprises. In the period preceding 1950 it was involved in five projects: the Iraq Cement Company, the Vegetable Oil Extraction Company, the Iraq Trading and Grain Milling Company, the National Leather Industry Company, and the River Dredging and Land Reclamation Company.[21] During FY 1946–9, the bank made net profits from its industrial share holdings. Iversen, while criticizing it for not investing in less profitable enterprises and thus justifying its role as a state bank, admitted that on the whole 'the Industrial Bank has apparently in a way been very successful with these schemes'.[22]

Unlike the case of the Agricultural Bank, it was not the Industrial Bank's lending policy that made it less effective than it could have been; rather, it was the government's lack of interest in industrial development. Up to 1950 the Industrial Bank was handicapped by a shortage of capital, a situation rectified only after the creation of the Development Board.[23]

It would be too simplistic, however, to attribute the underdevelopment of Iraqi industry solely to government strategy. There were also other, genuinely objective problems hindering Iraq's industrial development.

Obstacles to Industrialization[24]

Infrastructure

Lack of infrastructure is one of the more complicated issues facing developing countries. A more convenient term than infrastructure might be 'social overhead capital', which includes: 'all public services from law and order through education and public health to transportation, communications, power and water supply, as well as such agricultural overhead capital as irrigation and drainage systems. Its hard core is probably transportation and power.'[25] Thus, lack of electricity and water facilities precluded the establishment of industries in many parts of the country. Iraq therefore had to devote about 40% of its total expenditure on capital development works in this period to 'social overhead capital' (see Table 2.4).

Manpower

After two decades of developing infrastructure, the lack of skilled and semi-skilled labour remained the most problematic factor impeding Iraq's development. The advantages of the availability of cheap labour were more than offset by the necessity of training, and by the high overhead costs connected with the building of new concerns.[26] Most industries were dependent on foreign technicians, experts and foremen, which, although inevitable in the early stages of any industrial development, had many drawbacks (higher costs, acclimatization to local conditions, etc.).

Capital

Lack of financial resources and scarcity of local capital are usually prime obstacles to industrialization in developing countries, and this was the case in Iraq during the 1930s and 1940s. (With the immense increase in oil royalties in the 1950s, capital scarcity became a secondary issue.) Undeveloped money markets and the low level of savings exacerbated this problem. But even when it was possible for certain groups (i.e. landlords and merchants) to invest, they preferred real estate, trade and agriculture to industry. Those few who were interested in industry usually had political backing, an illustrative example being the close relationship between Nuri as-Said and Nuri Fattah, which made the latter 'king of Iraq's textile industry'.[27]

The fact that Iraq lacked a viable middle class which could expand its trade activities into industrial ones added to the difficulties of raising money for industrial schemes. In any event, most industries were family ventures, raising their capital within the family circle. There were a few large industries (cement, beer, cotton spinning and weaving, artificial and natural silk textiles) which were owned by joint-stock companies, and even distributed annual profits,[28] but the number of such enterprises never exceeded ten. Unfortunately, the Industrial Bank did not fill the gap created by the lack of entrepreneurs.

Limited Market

The small Iraqi population, with its low purchasing power, afforded but narrow scope for large-scale industry, a problem further aggravated by the Iraqis' tendency to buy foreign goods in the belief that they must be better (quite a common phenomenon in developing countries). The limited market which resulted naturally deterred investors from launching industrial enterprises.[29] Many investment opportunities studied by the Industrial Bank – such as the manufacture of artificial silk, or of paper and cardboard from straw – had to be abandoned because of this factor.

The above problems were compounded by the political instability, which generally discouraged investment, and because of a general unawareness of the importance and potential of industrial development.

Finally, it seems that the oil royalties Iraq began to receive in 1934 created a general confidence that more oil would be found, thus reducing even further the incentive for government to develop manufacturing industries on a large scale.

British Attitude towards Industrialization in Iraq

Because of Britain's considerable influence in Iraq, its attitude towards the development of any sector in the economy was significant. In the particular instance of manufacturing industries, documentation on British policy is scanty. This is not surprising in view of the fact that Britain, as indicated earlier, saw Iraq as an agricultural country supplying raw materials, and because of the low priority industry occupied in Iraq's economic policy and development plans. In this context, it should also be noted that British loans to Iraq were intended not for industrial development but rather to meet specific financial crises.

The outbreak of World War II and the creation of MESC generated some interest in the industry of Iraq (and other Middle East countries). But industry was only of secondary importance to MESC, which had to tackle food shortages, inflation and problems of shipping space. No directorate for industry was created within the organization,[30] and only a few reports on the subject were prepared, mostly surveys of existing industries. (This was in sharp contrast to the ample material on not only the existing conditions in agriculture but also its future potential.)[31] The monthly *Middle East Economic and Statistical Bulletin* issued by MESC and the minister of state resident in the Middle East rarely mentioned developments in the industrial sectors of the countries it covered. In fact, a major source of friction between MESC and local leaders in the region was the former's frequently reiterated determination to prevent the establishment of industries 'likely to become uneconomical after the war'.[32] This caused the agency to be looked upon as 'another manifestation of commercial imperialism', whose target was to increase American and British industrial exports to the area at the expense of local development.[33]

The creation in 1945 of the BMEO in Cairo helped raise interest in industry, as it was felt that industrialization was necessary for any improvement in living standards, but this interest was still not up to the level of that taken in agriculture, oil, foreign trade and labour. BMEO's attitude towards industrial development in the Middle East was summed up by Sir Arnold Overton: 'We should go very slow here. With the costs of production in the Middle East as high as they are at the moment, new industries could, I think, only survive for so long as the present world shortage continues, unless the home market was protected for them by a high tariff wall.'[34]

Industrial development did not, therefore, occupy a secondary place only in Iraq's economic policy and machinery; it was also but a minor feature of Britain's Middle East economic policy and machinery.

OIL

Although a number of concessions were granted during the period 1932–50, it was the arrangements made with oil companies before Iraq joined the League of Nations which laid the corner-stone for the development of this sector of Iraq's economy. This work highlights certain facets of oil policy which have not been dealt with elsewhere, or were discussed without recourse to contemporary British or American documents. The most significant of these facets is probably the triangular relationship linking the Iraqi government, the British government and the oil companies. An examination of this relationship is, in our opinion, essential to understanding the important treaties of the 1950s which have been analysed in other works and which lie outside the scope of this book. But before undertaking such an examination, some background on the oil concessions and oil's contribution to Iraq's economy is called for.[35]

Oil Companies Operating in Iraq and their Concessions

Four companies worked in Iraq during most of the period under study, foremost among which was the Iraq Petroleum Company (IPC). The original concession, granted in 1925 to the Turkish Petroleum Company (as it was known until 1929), covered the whole of the *wilayets* of Baghdad and Mosul.[36] A seventy-five-year agreement concluded in March 1931 (the major concession setting the guidelines for all further concessions) granted IPC an area of 35,126 square miles, the main oilfield being in Kirkuk.[37] The company was to construct a pipeline with a total capacity of not less than 3 million tons per annum and pay four shillings (gold) per metric ton, with a guaranteed minimum annual payment of £400,000 (gold). IPC's shareholders were: the Anglo-Persian Oil Company (now British Petroleum), 23.75%; Royal Dutch–Shell, 23.75%; Compagnie Française des Petroles, 23.75%; Standard Oil Company of New Jersey, 11.875%; Socony, 11.875%; and Gulbenkian, 5%.[38]

From the very beginning, the British tried to gain predominance in their access to Iraqi oil concessions. Using their influence on the mandatory government, British Oil Development, Ltd. (BOD) obtained, in April 1932, a seventy-five-year concession covering an area of 41,302 square miles west of the Tigris.[39] At that time 45% of BOD's shares were British, 31% Italian, 12% German and 12% Franco-Swiss; but by 1935 the Italians were the majority shareholders, with 52%.

The British were troubled by BOD's concession being controlled by outsiders, and discussions took place between the Foreign Office, IPC and the British Embassy in Baghdad to decide upon a course of action. The British ambassador to Baghdad, Sir Francis Humphrys (who was to become chairman of IPC in 1941) thought it would be 'inadvisable to withhold support from the BOD Company on account of the present Italian influence'. He was worried that if the BOD concession were allowed to lapse 'it is unlikely to be taken up except possibly by American interests, over whom we should have no control at all'.[40] The Foreign Office, however, was more disturbed by the Italian majority and overruled Humphrys' objections. J.C. Sterndale Bennett wrote:

> It would be more satisfactory if the British group were predominant, and if we could have some assurance that in supporting the BOD Company there would be some ultimate benefit to ourselves, and that we should not be merely supporting an organisation which might become a dangerous competitor of the IPC.[41]

Thus, in 1936 IPC organized a subsidiary, Mosul Holdings, Ltd., for the purpose of acquiring shares in Mosul Oil Fields, Ltd., which had been established by the non-Italian shareholders. A year later, IPC was in effective control of Mosul Oil Fields. In 1941, BOD assigned its 1932 concession to Mosul Holdings, Ltd., renamed Mosul Petroleum Company (MPC).[42]

The third oil company operating in Iraq, Basra Petroleum Company (BPC), another subsidiary of IPC, obtained, in July 1938, a seventy-five-year concession to an area covering 87,236 square miles contiguous to Kuwait.[43] (The BPC and the MPC concessions, although worded like that of IPC, were different in that they had to give the Iraqi government 20% of the oil they produced free of charge.)

Finally, there was the Khanaqin Oil Company (KOC), which was formed in 1925 to acquire and operate the concession held by the Anglo-Persian Oil Company in the strip of land along the Iraq–Iran frontier known as the 'transferred territories'. It produced oil from the Naft Khaneh field for local consumption. Early in 1932 the Rafidain Oil Company, also a subsidiary of IPC, was organized to undertake the marketing of oil products within Iraq, drawing its supplies mainly from KOC.[44]

Thus, by the end of the 1930s IPC had a monopoly over the production of Iraq's oil. This generated fears among Iraqi politicians. Adding to their apprehension was the fact that IPC's shareholders, with the exception of Compagnie Française des Petroles and Gulbenkian, also had extensive oil interests elsewhere, which, the Iraqis believed, made IPC less motivated to increase oil production in Iraq. At the same time, the Iraqi government was aware of IPC's financial strength and its technical ability to develop Iraq's resources.[45] The Iraqi government, therefore, was faced with a difficult task in the 1930s and 1940s: protecting the national interest by breaking the IPC monopoly, while simultaneously inducing the oil companies to increase production and develop the oil fields. This task was indeed a top priority in Iraq's economic policy since, as will be seen in the next few pages, the contribution made by oil to Iraq's economy was considerable.

Importance of Oil to Iraq's Economy

The impact of the oil industry on the local economy can be examined in seven ways.

1. *Contribution to gross national product.* This was estimated to be 10% in 1948.[46] (As the oil industry continued to grow in

the 1950s so did its contribution to the economy, reaching 28% in 1958.)[47]

2. *Contribution to foreign exchange receipts.* In 1948 Iraq's foreign exchange receipts were put at $111 million: $38 million (34.2%) derived from the oil industry, $41 million from exports of goods, and $32 million from other current earnings. Again, with the growth of the oil sector its contribution reached about 59% in 1957.[48]

3. *Contribution to government budgets.* As Table 6.3 indicates, oil revenues as a percentage of total government receipts ranged from 25.2% in 1938 to 7.5% in 1948. (The decrease in 1948 was due to the closure of the Haifa pipeline as a result of

TABLE 6.3 Oil Production and Revenues, FY 1932-FY 1950

	Oil production (1,000 metric tons)	Oil revenues	
		(ID 1,000)	as % of total government revenues
	(1)	(2)	(3)
1932	122	524	12.4
1933	115	540	13.0
1934	1,030	995	19.8
1935	3,664	598	11.2
1936	4,011	600	10.0
1937	4,255	731	10.6
1938	4,298	1,977	25.2
1939	3,963	2,014	21.9
1940	2,514	1,576	16.2
1941	1,566	1,463	14.4
1942	2,595	1,463	10.6
1943	3,572	2,794	15.4
1944	4,146	2,225	11.8
1945	4,607	2,316	11.4
1946	4,680	2,327	9.3
1947	4,702	2,346	9.0
1948	3,427	2,012	7.5
1949	4,067	3,238	11.3
1950	6,479	5,286	15.8

Sources: Col.(1): for 1932-48, UN, Statistical Yearbook 1948 (New York, 1949), p. 135. For 1948-50; UN, Statistical Yearbook 1952, (New York, 1952), p. 108. Col.(2): from Table 3.3. Col.(3): Col.(2) as percentage of government revenues which appear in Table 3.3.

the Palestine war.) Although it was only during the 1950s that oil revenues became the government's major source of income (reaching 61% in 1959), oil royalties still played a crucial role in developing Iraq in the 1930s and 1940s.

4. *Contribution to capital formation.* Data are lacking but as most of the oil royalties were channelled into capital development projects (discussed in Ch. 2), there is no doubt that oil contributed to capital formation in Iraq.

5. *Employment.* In spite of oil's important share in the national product, relatively little manpower was employed by the oil companies. Between 1932 and 1945 the total average labour force employed in the oil industry was some 4,400 (the majority by IPC).[49] It was only in the post-war period that the number of employees increased significantly, reaching 14,556 in 1947.[50] The relatively low level of employment was due mainly to the nature of the oil industry: a high ratio of capital to labour.

6. *Supply of fuels and raw materials:* While oil constituted one of Iraq's most important sources of energy, local consumption of oil products was relatively small (a major reason for this being the undeveloped state of Iraq's manufacturing industries). In 1949 consumption of oil products was estimated at 9,141 million barrels.[51]

7. *Local expenditures by oil companies.* The level of local expenditures by oil companies was low as most of their investments were made outside Iraq. Hasan argues that the oil companies' expenditure on wages and local purchases never exceeded 5% of the value of oil exports,[52] but this is an underestimate. Iversen, based on more reliable estimates, shows that in certain years, 1949 for instance, local expenditures reached as much as 45% of oil exports.[53] However, it remains true that the oil companies' local expenditures were low, and their impact was to increase Iraq's propensity to import.

It is obvious from any analysis of Iraq's oil industry according to the above seven criteria that the major contribution of oil was a financial one: to government budgets, to foreign exchange receipts, and so forth. It was less significant in contributing directly to the country's development: there was a lack of 'physical linkages' between the oil sector and other sectors of the economy. The non-existence of such 'physical linkages' was the result of a situation in which the oil industry neither supplied nor demanded of the other sectors significant quantities of investment goods, and was exacerbated by the fact that very few of the profits accruing to the oil companies were reinvested in Iraq.[54] Moreover, the oil industry's contribution to the development of local skills and know-how was limited because operations were restricted to the production stage alone. (The question of building a local refinery will be discussed below.)

Nevertheless, the significance of oil to Iraq's economy during the period 1932–50[55] should in no way be underestimated. A small undeveloped country under strong foreign influence and with limited resources, Iraq was in desperate need of money to develop its economy and raise its standard of living. This has to be borne in mind when coming to analyse the triangular relationship of the Iraqi government, the British government and the oil companies.

The Relationship between the Iraqi Government and the Oil Companies

Oil policy was one aspect of Iraq's economic policy where consistency was maintained. The many governments which came to power after independence were faced with a *fait accompli* in the sphere of oil concessions, which made it easier for them to have a clearly defined set of targets in their oil policy. When new issues arose (such as the reopening of the Haifa pipeline), Iraqi politicians were able to reach consensus on how to tackle them even though they had to deal not only with the oil companies operating in Iraq but also with the British and sometimes with the US government.

One issue between the Iraqi government and the oil companies concerned the receipts due to Iraq. During the period under study, the major element of Iraq's revenues was tonnage royalty from IPC's concession, paid at the rate of four shillings (gold). The increase in oil revenues, as shown in Table 6.3, was concomitant with an increase in oil production. However, Iraq continually demanded revision of the payments formula and was unwilling to wait till the end of the twenty-year period stipulated by the 1931 convention for which a royalty of four shillings (gold) was prescribed.[56] IPC, with the support of the British government, had the upper hand in this issue, and it was only in 1950 that the rate of payments was raised to six shillings (gold) per ton.

The question of receipts was also connected with another major bone of contention between IPC and the Iraqi government: level of production. As payment was per tonnage, the Iraqis constantly demanded that the oil companies increase production so that royalty payments would increase. They accused IPC of pursuing a policy of limited production, a charge which turned out to be justified. A report by the US Federal Trade Commission declassified in 1974 makes it clear that IPC in Syria used a variety of devices to delay the laying of pipelines. As the Penroses explain: 'oil production in the Middle East proved to be so prolific that the oil companies found it desirable to hold back their development in order to prevent a very great fall in prices'.[57] IPC's answer to such charges was that it was impossible to expand oil exportation because of the capacity of the pipelines.[58]

World War II had an adverse effect on the development of Iraq's oil resources. The plan to double the pipelines to the Mediterranean was postponed, and the geological survey in Basra was halted in May 1940. Most of the companies' staff left Iraq, either for reasons of safety or to join their countries' armed forces. Italy's entry into the war in June 1940 and the closure of the Mediterranean to cargo ships further interfered with the exportation of Iraqi oil.[59] As a result of these developments, production fell from 4.3 million tons in 1938, to 2.5 million in 1940, and 1.6 million in 1941 (Table 6.3).

With the end of the war, the unsettled issues from the pre-war period reappeared. To these were added new Iraqi complaints, such as the low percentage of local personnel employed in senior positions in the oil companies and the question of Iraqi shareholding.

The oil concessions provided that, in the event of a public issue of shares, Iraqis should be given preferential opportunity of acquiring 20%. This was a measure demanded by the government for itself and/or its public. However, no public issue of shares had occurred by the end of the period under study.[60]

The subject of Iraqi and foreign labour employed by the oil companies was more sensitive for the government, as it drew much public attention. The total number of foreigners ranged from 140 (in 1941) to 814 (in 1949). Although this constituted only 4% and 6% respectively of the total number of employees,[61] what was significant to the Iraqis was that foreigners occupied all the important positions; there was much bitterness that Iraqis were not being trained to replace foreigners at technical jobs.[62] Here the companies, particularly IPC, were willing to try to meet Iraqi demands, and by the end of the 1950s a respectable cadre of skilled Iraqi labour was employed on their staffs. (The relationship between the oil companies and their employees will be discussed below.)

Another demand with roots in the 1930s that had been shelved during the war and re-emerged in the post-war period was the construction of a local refinery. In 1935 Iraq asked the British to provide an expert to advise on this. The British expert reported unfavourably, arguing that the limited size of the Iraqi market did not justify such an undertaking. But Iraq insisted that the existing arrangement, under which the Anglo-Persian Oil Company supplied oil products for northern and central Iraq from its refinery on the Alwand River (marketing them through another subsidiary, the Rafidain Oil Company) while southern Iraq was supplied by the Abadan refinery in Iran, was an infringement of Iraqi sovereignty.[63]

In early 1946 Iraq raised the issue again, and informed the British Embassy in Baghdad of its intention to build a refinery at Baiji in northern Iraq.[64] British officials at the Foreign Office and the Ministry of Fuel and Power objected to the proposal since 'it would be contrary to the interest of British oil companies'.[65]

Only a year later, Iraq's Ministry of Economics issued a public invitation for tenders for the supply and erection of the proposed oil refinery at Baiji.[66] The British were alarmed because 'the U.S.A. is being given every opportunity to compete', and immediately adopted a more pragmatic policy: 'However little this project may appeal to us, there seems no way of dissuading the Iraqi Government from putting it into effect. In these circumstances it is at least to be hoped that British tenderers will secure the contract.'[67]

Contacts between the Iraqi and American governments took place in 1948 and 1949 about building the refinery,[68] with Iraq asking the US to persuade Britain to withdraw its opposition to the project.[69] But only in 1951 did the Iraqi government actually engage an American contractor to build a small refinery, not at the site originally contemplated but at Dora in southern Baghdad.[70]

The final major issue preoccupying Iraq's oil policy was the continual demands for loans and financial aid from the oil companies. In general, whenever the Iraqi government needed money it turned to the oil companies either for a direct loan or to ask them to agree that oil royalties constitute a security for a loan raised in London money markets. The oil companies, for their part, always wanted something in return for their financial help, unless thë were strongly pressured to forgo this by the British government.

In Chapter 3 the question of raising foreign loans was examined in detail. It was shown how negotiations began at the end of 1936 and were terminated in August 1937 with great disappointment on the Iraqi side; only £1 million was raised instead of £3 million, and the loan was redeemed nine years before its original redemption date.

The second attempt to obtain financial help from the oil companies, in 1939, was successful. IPC, having obtained a concession for its subsidiary BPC in 1938 and encouraged by the British government,[71] agreed to an advance of £3 million free of interest. Being aware, however, of the critical financial situation confronting the Iraqi government,[72] IPC was able to extract something in return for its advance. The May 1939 agreement stipulated that in return for the £3 million advance made by the companies (payable in six semi-annual instalments and recoverable from future royalties), the Iraqi government would alter BOD's drilling obligations, and extend by seven years the time limit within which BOD must export oil.[73] By reducing the number of drilling rigs in operation from nine to three, BOD was saving £175,000; it was also estimated that by postponing exports for seven years, another £800,000 (gold) was being saved.[74] Thus, although their loan to the Iraqi government was interest-free, there is no doubt that IPC and BOD did not make a bad deal for themselves – not only financially, but also from a public relations point of view.

In 1943 Iraq received another advance from the oil companies, which came about in the following way. As mentioned above, the war adversely affected oil production in Iraq. In July 1941, BOD and BPC requested a moratorium as they were facing difficulties in discharging their obligations under their respective conventions, due to (*a*) their inability to obtain additional drilling equipment from either Britain or the US; (*b*) dislocation of their operations owing to loss of transport, stores and other equipment during the Rashid 'Ali uprising; and (*c*) the difficulty of maintaining adequate personnel in Iraq in war conditions.[75]

Negotiations thus began between the oil companies and the Iraqi government. In November 1941 the latter, aware that it held strong cards in these talks, unexpectedly asked for a loan of £1.5 million in return for a moratorium on drilling operations. The oil companies totally rejected the request and decided they had no alternative but to invoke *force majeure*.[76] The British government immediately came to the oil companies' aid and tried to persuade the Iraqi government to retreat from its demand of a loan, but to no avail.[77]

Negotiations continued throughout 1942, with the Iraqis insisting that the oil companies come forward 'with a suitable compensation against the loss which Iraq will sustain'.[78] Although British influence was very powerful at the time, the Iraqis strongly believed in their ability to achieve a *quid pro quo* for the moratorium; they informed the oil companies of their willingness to go for arbitration, while implicitly threatening to cancel the concessions.[79]

British officials were confident that Iraq would not cancel the concessions because the oil companies continued to pay the dead rent, but they were also conscious that Iraq's bargaining strength was 'the company's fear of arbitration and our dislike of it at any rate during the war'.[80] In spite of the fact that by 1943 the US government had stepped in and informed the Iraqi government of its support for the American companies participating in the mother company, IPC,[81] the Iraqis consistently refused to modify their requirements. As a result, the British realized that the oil companies would have to either accept arbitration or come to terms with Iraq.[82]

The oil companies chose the second alternative. An agreement was concluded on 22 March 1943 between the Iraqi government on the one hand and IPC, MPC and BPC on the other, according to which Iraq accepted a moratorium on BPC's and BOD's operations retroactively from 2 May 1941, while prolonging their concessionary periods for drilling and production until two years after the armistice with Germany, Italy or Japan, whichever came last. In return, Iraq would receive a loan of £1 million on 1 June 1943, and another of £500,000 on the first of January following signature of the armistice.[83] (See Table 3.5.)

The Relationship between the British Government and the Oil Companies

The 1943 moratorium is interesting not only as an illustration of how a consistent oil policy could prove fruitful, but also because it clearly indicates the extent of British support for the oil companies. The British government's connection with the oil companies was obvious even before the beginning of concessions in Iraq,[84] and in 1934 the British ambassador emphasized that his country's interests were 'very closely bound up with the promising oil industry in Iraq'.[85] Although IPC had American, French and Italian shareholders, it was clear to all that it was a British firm; moreover, its 1931 convention specified that IPC should remain a registered British company and that its chairman should at all times be a British subject.[86] Furthermore, all responsible IPC positions in Iraq were filled by Britons, and the machinery and material necessary to the company's operations were predominantly of British manufacture.

After Iraq became independent, the close contacts, coordination of positions and exchange of information between the British government and the oil companies continued regularly. British officials, however, continually emphasized that the companies were 'quite separate from His Majesty's Government'.[87] For instance, during the negotiations for the 1943 moratorium there were two sets of talks going on simultaneously: between oil company representatives and Iraq's Ministry of Economics, and between the British ambassador in Baghdad and the Iraqi prime minister. As a Treasury representative put it, 'These must be kept technically separate but of course we have to concert with the company.'[88] When agreement was reached, the chairman of IPC, Sir Francis Humphrys (an ex-ambassador to Iraq), formally conveyed the company's thanks to the Foreign Office for its help 'in securing the satisfactory settlement'.[89]

Nevertheless, relations were not always smooth between the British government and IPC. When a strike broke out in Kirkuk in April 1943, the British ambassador in Baghdad was furious that IPC did not report the incident or consult the Embassy. Writing to the Foreign Office, he complained that:

> This is all, in my view, very deplorable, but I would not bother to report it to you were it not that it is, I understand, quite typical of the way the oil companies here behave. Their line is that they never tell us anything until they are in really serious trouble, and then they rush round at the last minute and expect us to settle things.[90]

Later, talks were held in London between the Foreign Office and IPC in which it was decided that IPC's representatives would report adequately to the Embassy and that the Embassy, for its part, would take more initiative in contacting them.[91]

The question of granting Iraq loans and advances posed another problem in the relationship between the oil companies and the British government. The latter, alert to the danger a financial crisis in Iraq would present to British interests there, habitually turned to IPC whenever the Iraqi government was in trouble. IPC, however, was not enthusiastic about extending loans without a *quid pro quo*. During the 1948 financial crisis the British government often asked the oil companies to help Iraq, and in each instance they responded with a new set of demands. British officials frequently expressed discontent with the way oil representatives perceived the internal situation in Iraq:

> The interests of the oil companies in Iraq are so inseparably bound up with the maintenance of the social and economic stability in the country that we find it hard to understand how the IPC group can face such an imminent threat of chaos [the 1948 financial crisis] with anything but the most serious misgivings for their own future.[92]

On the whole, however, such cases of friction were unusual. There was more harmony than discord, and the oil companies, in return for British government assistance in their dealings with Iraq, were ready to help Britain achieve its political aims there. This was readily apparent when the oil companies abstained from paying royalties to the Rashid 'Ali government as a means of pressure;[93]

indeed, it was only after the re-establishment of a pro-British regime in Baghdad that IPC resumed payments.[94] (It had continued to pay the dead rent in order to maintain the company's legal status, but the Eastern Bank, a British bank which handled the Iraqi government's accounts, blocked the money.)

American Oil Interests in Iraq

The 1943 moratorium, in which the US joined hands with Britain and the oil companies in pressuring Iraq to act against its interests, was not exceptional. Another illustration of such co-operation, one which had even more important political implications, was the reopening of the Haifa refinery after the establishment of the State of Israel. As a result of the war in Palestine, the pumping of Iraqi oil to Haifa (whence it was exported mainly to Europe) was stopped. The Americans were alarmed that such stoppage might harm their Marshall plan of reconstructing Europe, but the Iraqis were reluctant to allow crude oil movements to Haifa as long as the refinery was under Israeli control.[95]

Reopening the refinery became an urgent issue for all the parties concerned. When Iraq wanted financial assistance from IPC in 1948, the reopening became 'an indispensable condition of any loan to be extended by the Iraq Petroleum Company'.[96] At the end of that year, both British and IPC officials believed there was about an even chance of solving the problem, and that the chief difficulty was 'how to deal with public opinion in Iraq and in neighbouring countries'.[97]

The issue remained high on the agenda during the 1949 negotiations in London between the Iraqi government and IPC concerning the price per ton of oil paid to Iraq, with IPC maintaining, according to the Foreign Office, that:

> under no circumstances can they agree to pay any higher rates of royalty until the Haifa pipeline is reopened. They say that they are losing a substantial volume of production, and profit to be derived therefrom, while on the other hand the costs of maintenance of the line are in no way abated.[98]

The British hinted to the Iraqis that there might be a relaxation of the arms embargo (imposed by Britain on all countries which participated in the Palestine war) if pumping were resumed.[99] At one point Iraq's prime minister was ready to agree to the refinery being reopened if it were internationalized, but this idea was totally rejected by Israel.[100] Finally, towards the end of 1949, British and American officials realized 'it was politically impossible for any

Iraqi Government to pump oil to Haifa even for export only',[101] and indeed the pipeline remained closed.

But, as discussed in Chapter 1, American interests in Iraq (and throughout the Middle East) were not always harmonious with those of the British, and oil was no exception in the rivalry between the two powers.[102] In 1931, for instance, the State Department protested to the British government against the granting of an oil concession in Iraq to IPC 'without first giving the nationals of all countries a chance to submit tenders',[103] and in subsequent years the Americans continued to insist on such equality.[104] The British, however, were not keen to allow this.

The Iraqis were aware of the ongoing competition between Britain and the US (and not only in the sphere of oil interests), and knew how to exploit it. Prime Minister Nuri as-Said would complain regularly to the Americans about IPC and British intervention in Iraqi affairs, which he said was preventing the development of economic relations between Iraq and the US.[105] He repeatedly expressed Iraq's eagerness to buy American materials, claiming this was made impossible by the sterling area restrictions, and he encouraged the US government to do 'everything possible in order to bring about an increase in the extraction of petroleum in Iraq'.[106] Whether or not Nuri was just playing the Americans off against the British, the fact is that his tactics achieved their aims.

By the end of the war, and with the weakening of Britain's position, the Americans began to put their demands quite explicitly: 'We want a cessation of British political interventionism in the process of obtaining petroleum concessions in areas directly or indirectly dependent upon British sovereignty.'[107] Furthermore, in the post-war period the Americans actually supported the Iraqis on many important issues in their negotiations with the British government and the oil companies, such as the building of a local refinery, as we have seen. And although Iraqi–American relations were hampered by the Palestine war, by the end of the period under study the US had begun to express increasing support for Iraq in its dealings with the oil companies. A memorandum by the American ambassador to Iraq stated: 'I feel strongly that the British, Dutch, United States and French interests concerned in IPC should, for the sake of the whole Western position in this area, and emphatically in their own interests, give the Iraqis a better deal in the matter of their oil.'[108] This US support undoubtedly assisted Iraq greatly in attaining higher royalties in 1950, and the 50–50 agreement of 1952.

Appraisal of Oil Policy in Iraq

Was Iraq's oil policy successful? It is indeed hard to answer with a simple yes or no. Until the end of the 1940s the Iraqis themselves were dissatisfied with the results they had achieved. They maintained that 'the benefit derived by Iraq from its oil sources is not commensurate at all with the abundancy of these sources.'[109]

Examination of the six main points of contention, discussed above, between the government of Iraq and the oil companies (royalties, level of production, shareholding, Iraqi vs foreign labour, building a local refinery and financial aid) indicates that from the Iraqi standpoint no progress at all was made in some of them (e.g. shareholding), while more tangible results were recorded in others (e.g. training of Iraqi manpower). As for the two basic matters of royalties and production, the period 1932–50 set the background for the significant achievements of raising royalties to six shillings (gold) per ton in 1950, and the 50–50 agreement of 1952 (effective from 1 January 1951). The continuous struggle and tough negotiations of the 1930s and 1940s enabled Iraq to increase production, solve its financial problems and launch extensive development programmes in the 1950s.

Could it have done better? Before answering this, a very important fact should be emphasized: oil concessions in Iraq, on the whole, were more favourable to the host country than elsewhere in the Middle East or in Venezuela.[110] In the years 1934–50, before the adoption of the 50–50 formula, Iraq received a higher royalty per ton – an average of $1.75 – than Saudi Arabia and Iran, both of which received $1.60, or Venezuela with $1.26 (in the period 1934–43).[111] This does not mean, however, that Iraq's interests were not harmed by the nature of the concessions (e.g. IPC's monopoly and the fact that the contribution of oil to Iraq's economy was primarily limited to revenue), or that Iraqi bitterness towards the oil companies had no basis. But, as in the matter of the sterling area, Iraq of the 1930s and 1940s faced a strong constellation: in this case it was the oil companies backed by the most powerful countries in the world,[112] and it is therefore highly dubious whether better results could have been achieved.

Finally, a few words should be added about the profits which accrued to the oil companies operating in Iraq. Throughout the period under study, the IPC group repeatedly declined to answer requests by the Iraqi government for detailed information on oil sales, prices and expenses, and oil company archives are still closed to the general public. Mikdashi, basing his estimates on the dividends distributed to shareholders (Compagnie Française des Petroles, Socony and Gulbenkian), leaves no doubt that IPC profited substantially from its investments in Iraq.[113]

LABOUR

The emergence of a labour movement and the state of its development are indications of a country's advance and the level of its industrialization. In this part, we shall round out the study of Iraq's industrial sector by examining the conditions of the labour force in its manufacturing and oil industries, and the impact of labour laws, trade unions, and labour policy (of both the Iraqi and the British governments) on the development of the Iraqi labour movement.

Details about the conditions of labour employed in the oil companies and manufacturing industries during the 1920s and 1930s are scanty. According to a 1931 report, there was no fixed standard of working hours per week in the oil companies; the average was fifty. However, one important fringe benefit available to workers in the oil companies, the railways and Basra Port (and not enjoyed elsewhere) was free medical treatment.[114]

The lack of laws regulating working hours and wages is attributable not only to the undeveloped state of industry and the low priority of industrialization in the government's economic policy, but also to the weakness of the labour unions. The pioneer in Iraq's trade union movement was Mohammad Salih al-Qazzaz, who applied to the Ministry of the Interior for permission to open a labour club in 1924. Though refused, he continued to hold meetings until 1929, when the government authorized the formation of a Mechanics Union under his presidency.[115] Its growth was slow and its activities limited. On 3 December 1930, the first strike in the history of Iraqi industry took place when members of the Mechanics Union employed in a railway shop in Baghdad objected to a cut in their wages unless a similar reduction was made in the wages of their foreign colleagues.[116]

A few months before formal independence, a law forbidding strikes or strike calls was enacted.[117] As a result, the Mechanics Union was banned and Qazzaz was arrested. However, he was released the same year and later succeeded in forming an engineers' society, which in 1933 became the Labour Union Society. In mid-1935 it was declared illegal, some of its members having been caught distributing pamphlets urging a general strike. From then until the end of 1944, the government refused to sanction the formation of any labour movement.[118] There were, however, a number of unofficial unions during the 1930s, of which the most important were the motor drivers, the barbers and the printers.[119]

Meanwhile, an important turning point in Iraq's labour history occurred: in 1936 a labour law was passed (at the suggestion of the International Labour Office). It defined industrial undertakings; regulated conditions and hours of work, and compensation for death, injury or disease; safeguarded workers' rights in forming associations and labour unions; forbade child labour; and stipulated provisions for setting up individual factory labour councils as well as an umbrella council composed of representatives of labour unions and government.[120] A 1937 amendment to the law limited daily working hours to eight, following a wave of strikes in the oil companies.[121] A further amendment that year stipulated that workers were entitled to one day off each week, and to annual leave and sick leave with full payment,[122] and a 1942 amendment improved compensation and vacation terms.[123]

The Labour Law does not appear to have had any significant effect on the development of trade unionism. This was because the government did not implement those clauses which gave unions legal recognition. Even at the time of the law's enactment, a British official commented: 'It is clear from the Law that the [Labour] Associations will be subject to very close official supervision, and it is unlikely that they will be allowed to attain any great political importance.'[124] However, the law did serve to increase workers' awareness of their conditions. As the 1937 Annual Report of the British Embassy reported: 'During the year labour questions have for the first time begun to assume importance in internal affairs. There were quite a number of strikes [by the workers] to improve their working conditions.'[125]

During World War II there was growing unrest among Iraqi workers. The continual price increases (see Table 6.4) and the shortage of goods brought the trade unions to the fore. But attempts to organize labour remained haphazard and limited, due to the government's opposition and to mass ignorance about trade unionism.[126] Nevertheless, towards the end of the war it was felt in Baghdad that labour problems could no longer be disregarded. A British expert, Professor Peer, was sent to Iraq by MESC to study the problems which would arise with the peace-time discharge of thousands of local workers employed by the British Army.[127] Although Peer's report mainly dealt with new outlets for employment, it induced both Iraqi and British officials to conclude that something should be done to improve labour conditions.[128] Thus, immediately after the report was presented to MESC, the Iraqi

TABLE 6.4 Average Cost of Living Index in Baghdad, 1939-1950 (base = 1939)

	Foodstuffs	Clothing	Fuel and light	Rent	Other items	General index
1939	100.0	100.0	100.0	100.0	100.0	100.0
1945	655.4	790.8	456.0	333.0	449.5	590.3
1946	628.3	768.3	425.7	333.0	422.9	566.8
1947	688.7	792.9	407.9	333.0	402.4	601.4
1948	805.8	841.1	411.0	333.0	413.0	673.1
1949	599.6	777.5	412.9	333.0	362.7	539.8
1950	548.5	646.9	413.5	298.0	332.4	490.8

Source: Statistical Abstract 1951, p. 332. (For an explanation on calculation of the index, see Statistical Abstract 1947, p. 238.)

government authorized unionization of carpenters, shoe-makers, weavers and printers; a month later it permitted the establishment of the Railway Workers' Union.[129]

Attitudes towards unions, however, did not change with their legal recognition, and government circles continued to suspect their motives.[130] The British Embassy in Baghdad reported that Colonel Smith, director-general of the Iraqi State Railways, was keeping an eye on developments in the Railway Workers' Union, and that he was 'privately encouraging members to squeeze out those who are at present organising the Union and elect instead men who are active railway workers and not merely political opportunists'.[131] The Embassy decided not to interfere with Colonel Smith's way of conducting affairs but added in its report:

> 'political opportunists' or not, leaders with some education and independence will be necessary if workers in this country are to improve upon their present miserable status. They were unlikely [to do so] ... if merely organised into 'Company Unions' which is evidently what Colonel Smith would like to see.[132]

By the end of the war, both the Iraqi and British governments had become quite worried about the extent of communist influence upon the trade union movement. The British, and later the Americans, began impressing on all 'responsible Iraqis' that the 'first line of defence against communism is an advanced social programme', since communism 'only flourished in discontented countries'.[133] British officials became interested in the Iraqi Communist party and its activities,[134] especially after the large-scale railway workers' strike of 15–30 April 1945. The workers demanded higher wages, and the British had no doubt that their strike was 'prolonged by communist agitation'.[135]

Britain, now under a Labour government, continually urged the Iraqi government to take immediate steps to regulate working conditions in order to effectively combat the spread of labour disputes, such as those plaguing the oil companies (mainly in Kirkuk) and other industries in 1946.[136] Two months after the long and serious strike in Kirkuk, BMEO's labour adviser, Mr Audsley, was sent to Iraq to report on working conditions in the oil sector. His findings showed that wages in the oil companies were somewhat higher than those in other industries (Table 6.1), but that no wage paid anywhere kept pace with the rising cost of living index.[137]

While it is true that the oil companies generally offered better wages and fringe benefits than did most other Iraqi industries,[138] two factors made them fertile ground for long strikes. First, the fact that they were controlled by foreigners, mainly British, made the workers particularly bitter. The second, less sentimental factor was the relationship between management and labour. A British Embassy official visited oil company sites and found working conditions there satisfactory, but he was appalled by the atmosphere:

> the relation between management and labour is outwardly that of 'sahibs' and 'niggers', and this aspect is accentuated by the luxury in which the management and British staff live, and their remoteness. There is no unofficial social contact between British and Iraqis; in fact, I gathered that such contact is discouraged.[139]

The local manager of IPC, Mr Skliros, also confirmed that 'there was almost completely no intercourse between the I.P.C. and the local inhabitants'.[140]

The oil companies disregarded these issues. Moreover, their habit of dismissing workers on very short notice further exacerbated relations between management and labour. British officials investigating Iraqi press charges that 'anybody who dares to disobey is discharged immediately' found them to be correct,[141] but the companies' general policy was to decline answering or commenting upon press criticisms on the grounds that any response would spark a controversy.[142]

Thus, strikes periodically broke out at the oil companies. Some were immediately attributed to 'Communist instigations',[143] while others were dealt with as 'genuine industrial disputes',[144] but as their number increased there was a growing awareness of the need for extensive study of labour problems in the country.

Audsley returned to Iraq in June 1948, and the following month presented a comprehensive report on labour there.[145] His principal conclusion was that the wage–price question lay at the crux of Iraq's labour problems. He found that wage levels were still, as in 1946, not keeping pace with the general cost of living (which, as Table 6.4 shows, increased by more than six and a half times between 1939 and 1948, while food and clothing increased eight-fold during the same period).[146] Having calculated that even the very lowest subsistence level required a minimum wage of about 350 fils per day, Audsley discovered, using a very wide sample, that the average daily wage paid to unskilled labourers was only some 230 fils. In fact, as Table 6.1 indicates, only in four industries (construction, tanning, carpentry and oil) was the average daily wage higher than 350 fils. Audsley was also struck by the completely unbalanced wage structure characterizing Iraq's various principal industrial undertakings, the outstanding difference being between the wage rates paid by IPC on the one hand and by other large concerns such as the Iraqi State Railways, Basra Port and the Royal Air Force Station at Sha'iba on the other. (Minimum wage rates in these concerns ranged from 200 to 230 fils.)

Audsley reported that during his discussions with British officials in the above concerns, he felt that 'there is a certain psychological resistance on the part of senior British executives who have been in the country a long time to a realisation of the wretchedness of the workers' living conditions and the potentially explosive nature of the labour situation'.[147] He was aware, however, that the main source of blame in the situation 'undoubtedly rests with the Iraqi landowners, grain merchants and certain politicians who connive to maintain a stranglehold on the market and to keep prices high in order to make private fortunes'.[148] Regarding trade unionism, Audsley found that the official attitude was as hostile as it had been before unions were legalized in 1944,[149] and that the great majority of workers were politically unaware. In the event, no major development occurred in this field until the 1958 revolution.

The 1940s ended with no radical changes in Iraq's labour situation, though working conditions had significantly improved in comparison with the 1920s and 1930s. Ironically, Iraq had the most progressive labour laws among Middle East countries. The problem lay in their enforcement, both by government and by employers. In June 1949, Audsley examined the compliance of four Middle East countries with the requirements of the International Labour Organization. In spite of its modern laws, Iraq was found to have a worse record than Egypt, Lebanon or Syria.[150] Audsley reported that the Iraqi laws were not implemented at all in the realms of equal pay for women, training of women, social security and settlement of labour disputes; and only poorly enforced with respect to labour inspection, employment services, child protection, freedom of association and co-operative organizations.[151] Unlike Egypt, for example, where strong political links existed between the labour movement and a powerful political party (i.e. the Wafd),[152] no major party in Iraq (except the illegal Communist party) consistently championed the cause of labour. Whenever labour problems arose, the opposition simply used them to criticize government policy, but without offering any constructive suggestion for improving working conditions.

It is evident, then, that although there were certain achievements in Iraq's manufacturing industries during the period under study, government policy towards their development did not change significantly but rather continued to perceive them as secondary in importance to other sectors of the economy. On the other hand, the government devoted considerable effort to enhancing Iraq's position *vis à vis* the oil companies, as oil royalties became more and more vital to its budgets. Labour issues were tackled only when problems erupted; generally, the far-reaching laws which were enacted to improve working conditions were inadequately enforced.

NOTES

1. United Kingdom, *Progress of Iraq*, p.215.
2. Langley, *Industrialization of Iraq*, pp.35–54.
3. Based on Board of Trade, *Economic and Commercial Conditions*, 16–17; MESC, 'A Survey of Iraq', 1943. FO 922/153/1936 (contains a list of names and location of all factories); DOT, 'Economic Survey of Iraq', 24 Apr. 1944. FO 371/40051, E 2564/78/93; 'Industries in Iraq', 1945. BT 11/2692, BT 11/2693, BT 11/2695. The results of the Industrial Census of 1954 have not been used as they do not reflect the situation of the 1930s and 1940s; between 1950 and 1954 many new industries were created and production increased, a result of the Development Board's plans. For details about the census, see Langley, op. cit., pp.89–100.
4. Langley, op. cit., p.58.
5. See, for example, A.O. Hirschman, *The Strategy of Economic Development* (New Haven, 1958); M.J. Flanders, 'Agriculture versus Industry', in 'Development Policy: The Planners' Dilemma Re-examined', *Journal of Development Studies* v (April 1969), pp.171–90; N. Kadhim, 'The Strategy of Development Planning and the Absorptive Capacity of the Economy: A Case Study of Iraq' (Colorado Univ. Ph.D. thesis, 1974).
6. Prominent examples are: IBRD, *Economic Development of Iraq*; Iversen, *Monetary Policy in Iraq*; Salter, *Development of Iraq*.
7. For a discussion of this period, see: Ferhang Jalal, *The Role of Government in the Industrialisation of Iraq 1950–1965*, (London, 1972).
8. United Nations Industrial Development Organisation, *General Issues of Industrial Policy*, UNIDO monographs based on the proceedings of the International Symposium on Industrial Development held in Athens in 1967 (New York, 1969), p.9.
9. The full text appears in: Report by His Majesty's Government in the United Kingdom

of Great Britain and Northern Ireland to the Council of the League of Nations, *Administration of Iraq for the Year 1929* (London, 1930), pp.171–3. The law was amended in 1930 (Law No. 45), 1936 (Law No. 63), and 1939 (Law No. 21). During the war the law was again amended (1941) according to the country's needs at the time, but its basic principles remained more or less unchanged.

10. Knabenshue to Dept. of State, 8 Apr. 1933. ACR, Reel 13.
11. See, for example: Baghdad Chamber of Commerce, *Annual Report 1935–36*, pp.34–40.
12. A new law for the encouragement of industry was enacted in 1950; see: Langley, *Industrialization of Iraq*, p.82.
13. For details, see: Jamil, *Siyasat al-'Iraq al-Tijariyya*, pp.235–9.
14. Ibid., p.424.
15. Hasan's thesis, 'Foreign Trade in the Economic Development of Modern Iraq', p.235.
16. 'Law for the Creation of the Industrial Bank – No. 12 of 1940', *Iraq Government Gazette* no. 30 (28 July 1940), pp.383–5.
17. Industrial Bank, *Annual Report for 1946/7 and 1947/8* (in Arabic), p.11.
18. For the procedure of applying for and receiving a loan, see Langley, *Industrialization of Iraq*, pp.144–8.
19. Industrial Bank, *Annual Report for 1946/7* (in Arabic), p.45; Industrial Bank, *Annual Report for 1948/9* (in Arabic), p.52.
20. Industrial Bank, *Annual Report for 1946/7* (in Arabic), p.41; Industrial Bank, *Annual Report for 1948/9* (in Arabic), p.54.
21. Industrial Bank, relevant *Annual Reports* (in Arabic).
22. Iversen, *Monetary Policy in Iraq*, p.33.
23. For a detailed analysis of the Industrial Bank's activities in the 1950s and 1960s, see: Jalal, *The Role of Government in the Industrialisation of Iraq*.
24. The majority of the problems discussed here apply to most other Middle East and developing countries as well. For a general work on the Middle East, see Kurt Grundwald and Joachim O. Ronall, *Industrialisation in the Middle East* (New York, 1960).
25. Hirschman, *Strategy of Economic Development*, p.83.
26. Bernard D. Weinryb, 'Industrial Development in the Middle East', *Quarterly Journal of Economics* lxi (May 1947), p.472.
27. Batatu, *The Old Social Classes*, pp.316–18. Batatu describes how this relationship deteriorated in the 1950s, but by then Nuri Fattah had established himself.
28. For more details about lack of resources and enterprise, see 'Abdul Ghani al-Dali, 'Problems of Industrial Enterprise in Iraq', *Middle East Economic Papers* (Beirut, 1954), pp.37–50.
29. For a theoretical discussion of this problem, see: R. Nurkse, 'The Size of the Market and the Inducement to Invest', in D.E. Novak and R. Lekachman (eds.), *Development and Society* (New York, 1964).
30. There was only an assistant director for industrial production. The directorates were: food, trade relations, materials, medical requirements, transport and administration. See plan of organization in Wilmington, *Middle East Supply Centre*, pp.204–5.
31. For a list of MESC reports, see ibid., pp.211–17.
32. F. Boardman, 'Civilian Requirements from War to Peace: the Middle East Supply Centre', *Department of State Bulletin* xiii (December 1945), p.995.
33. Wilmington, 'Reappraisal', p.158.
34. Memorandum by Sir Arnold Overton (BMEO), 30 Nov. 1945. FO 957/1.
35. See for example: Penroses, *Iraq*; Stephen Hemsley Longrigg, *Oil in the Middle East*, 2nd edn. (London, 1961).
36. Two important works deal with the pre-independence period: Marian Kent, *Oil and Empire* (London, 1976), which deals with British policy in Mesopotamia in the first two decades of this century; and Helmut Mejcher, *Imperial Quest for Oil: Iraq 1910–1928* (London, 1976).
37. For the full text of the 1931 concession, see: Organization of Petroleum Exporting Countries (OPEC), *Selected Documents of the International Petroleum Industry* (Vienna, 1974), pp.7–28.
38. Ibid. For comments on IPC's concession, see FO 371/15307, E 3183/5/93.

39. OPEC, *Selected Documents*, pp.29–50. For details about negotiations preceding the convention and comments on it, see CO 730/171.
40. Comments by Sir Francis Humphrys included in FO memorandum on BOD's activities in Iraq, 1934. FO 371/17871, E 5055/1752/93.
41. Minutes by Bennett (FO), ibid., E 6854/1752/93.
42. 'Oil Resources in the Middle East', report by FO research department, 1945. FO 371/45274, E 1823/1823/65.
43. For full text, see: OPEC, *Selected Documents*, pp.50–70. For comments, see Peterson to FO, 2 Feb. 1939. FO 371/23215, E 1319/1079/93.
44. Benjamin Shwadran, *The Middle East, Oil and the Great Powers 1959* (2nd e., New York, 1959), pp.250–1. See also Longrigg, *Oil in the Middle East*, pp.66–83, for a concise history of all concessions during the 1920s and 1930s.
45. For a discussion of IPC's monopoly and Iraqi fears, see: Penroses' *Iraq*, pp.138–44.
46. Charles Issawi and Mohammad Yeganeh, *The Economics of Middle Eastern Oil* (New York, 1962), p.143.
47. Ibid.
48. Ibid., p.146.
49. *Statistical Abstract 1940*, p.116.
50. *Statistical Abstract 1947*, p.115.
51. Issawi and Yeganeh, op. cit., p.155.
52. Hasan's thesis, 'The Role of Foreign Trade in the Economic Development of Iraq', in M.A. Cook (ed.), *Studies in the Economic History of the Middle East* (London, 1970), p.371.
53. Iversen, *Monetary Policy in Iraq*, pp.73, 98.
54. For a detailed study of the various aspects of the lack of physical linkages in an economy, see Sinan Ridha al-Shabibi 'Optimal Industrialisation with Uncertain Oil Revenues: Dynamic Multisector Models, 1974–1984' (Bristol Univ. Ph.D. thesis, 1974), pp.57–62.
55. For oil's impact on the economy in the 1950s and 1960s, see: al-Nasrawi, *Financing Economic Development.*
56. The application of the 'gold clause' was in itself another source of controversy with IPC (but not with MPC and BPC as their concessions precisely defined the gold conversion rate) following Britain's renunciation of the gold standard in September 1931 and the consequent depreciation of sterling. For more details about receipts, see Zuhayr Mikdashi, *A Financial Analysis of Middle Eastern Oil Concessions* (New York, 1966), pp.105–7.
57. Penroses, *Iraq*, pp.73–4.
58. For a detailed discussion of the level of production by the oil companies, see Hameed al-Qaysi's 'An Economic Appraisal of Iraq Petroleum Concessions – A Comparative Study' (Columbia Univ. Ph.D. thesis, 1961), pp.37–74.
59. Ibid., pp.42–4.
60. Longrigg, *Oil in the Middle East*, pp.189–90.
61. *Statistical Abstract 1940*, p.116; *Statistical Abstract 1951*, p.189.
62. Iraq's minister of economics to IPC, 19 Oct. 1948. FO 371/68479, E 14001/620/93.
63. Penroses, *Iraq*, p.159.
64. Embassy to FO, 1 Mar. 1946. FO 371/52424, E 709/709/93.
65. Ibid., E 1622/709/93.
66. Embassy to FO, 14 May 1947. FO 371/61866, E 4462/4462/93.
67. Baker (FO) to Elderton (Board of Trade), 2 June 1947. Ibid.
68. Embassy to FO, 25 Oct. 1948. FO 371/68479, E 14067/620/93; Embassy to FO, 13 Aug. 1949. FO 371/75179, E 10247/1533/93.
69. Embassy (Washington) to FO, Report on the meeting of Iraq's foreign minister with officials from the Dept. of State, 27 Oct. 1949. FO 371/75140, E 13178/10345/93.
70. Penroses, *Iraq*, p.160.
71. The reasons behind the British decision to encourage granting Iraq an advance from the companies, and to extend a direct loan from the British government six months later, were discussed in the section on loans in Chapter 3.
72. The British reported that the shortage of funds was so acute that the minister of finance was forced to draw on the revenues of the municipalities of Baghdad, Basra and Mosul

and was contemplating paying civil servants only 50% of their salaries in cash, with promissory notes for the remaining 50%. Newton to FO, 6 June 1939. BT 11/1053.

73. For full text, see BT 11/1053.
74. Newton to FO, op. cit.
75. Cornwallis to FO, 27 July 1941. FO 371/27096, E 4818/227/93.
76. Cornwallis to FO, 1 Nov. 1941. Ibid., E 7173/227/93.
77. Cornwallis to FO, 25 Nov. 1941. Ibid., E 7785/227/93.
78. Iraq's minister of economics to BPC, 10 May 1942. T 160/1157/17859.
79. Ibid.
80. Comments by Beckett (Treasury) on the letter from Iraq's minister of economics to BPC, 29 May 1942. Ibid.
81. Secretary of state to minister resident in Iraq, 12 Feb. 1943, *FRUS*, 1943, iv, pp.645–7. For talks with Iraq's prime minister, see ibid., pp.650–3.
82. Cornwallis to FO (Tel. 28), 9 Jan. 1943. T 160/1157/17859; FO to Embassy (Tel. 135), 17 Feb. 1943. Ibid.
83. For full text, see FO 624/31; for comments, see T 160/1157/17859.
84. See the works of Kent, Mejcher, and Sluglett.
85. Humphrys to FO, 1 Feb. 1934. FO 371/17858, E 962/190/93.
86. Article 32 of the 1931 convention, OPEC, *Selected Documents*.
87. Comments by Beckett (Treasury), 29 May 1942. T 160/1157/17859.
88. Ibid.
89. Note on a meeting at the FO with Humphrys, 30 June 1943. FO 371/34981, E 3861/2/93.
90. Mack to FO, 5 May 1948. FO 371/68479, E 6413/620/93/G.
91. FO to Mack, 1 June 1948. FO 624/130, 78/11/48.
92. BMEO (Cairo) to FO, 23 Nov. 1948. FO 624/141, vol. iv.
93. Bridgeman (Petroleum Dept.) to Crosthwaite (FO), 3 Mar. 1941. FO 371/27062, E 773/1/93.
94. FO minute by Seymour, 26 May 1941. FO 371/27096, E 2563/227/93.
95. For a description of all the positions on this issue, see: memorandum by the assistant chief of the Petroleum Division (Dept. of State), 10 Sept. 1948. *FRUS*, 1948, v, pp.42–4.
96. Memorandum by FO to the ME (Official) Committee, 24 Dec. 1948. FO 371/68467, E 15800/112/93.
97. Minute by Burrows (FO) on a meeting with Wheatley (IPC), 20 Dec. 1948. FO 371/68479, E 16187/620/93.
98. FO minute by Chadwick, 12 July 1949. FO 371/75179, E 8724/1533/93.
99. Brief for the secretary of state's conversation with the Iraqi ambassador in London, 11 July 1949. FO 371/75136, E 8573/1026/93.
100. Mack to FO, 'Report on Wheatley's Conversation with Nuri as-Said', 2 Mar. 1949. FO 371/75178, E 851/1533/93.
101. British Embassy (Washington) to FO, 27 Oct. 1949. FO 371/75140, E 13178/10345/93.
102. For general works on the subject of American interests prior to World War II, see: John DeNovo, *American Interests and Policies in the Middle East 1900–1939* (Minneapolis, 1964); Baram, *The Department of State in the Middle East*.
103. American Legation (Baghdad) to Dept. of State, 29 Dec. 1931. ACR, Reel 1.
104. See 'Right of American Interests to Equal Opportunity to Bid for Oil Concessions in Iraq'. *FRUS*, 1931, ii, pp.604–11.
105. Summary of conversation between Nuri and Henderson on 'American Interests in Iraqi Oil', 29 Feb. 1944. ACR, Reel 18.
106. Memorandum on conversation between Nuri and Dept. of State officials, 29 May 1945. *FRUS*, 1945, viii, p.490.
107. Memorandum by the acting chief of the Petroleum Division (Dept. of State), 31 May 1945. *FRUS*, 1945, viii, p.51.
108. Memorandum by Edward Crocker, 30 Jan. 1950. *FRUS*, 1950, v, p.641.
109. Iraq's Ministry of Economics to IPC, 19 Oct. 1948. FO 371/68479, E 14001/620/93.
110. Qaysi's thesis, *Iraq Petroleum Concessions*, compares the economic features of Iraqi oil concessions with those of Venezuela, Saudi Arabia and Iran by examining eight components: area of the concession; exploration and minimum production provisions; financial obligations; integration between the oil industry and the economy; con-

servation; employment and training obligations; duration of concessions; and refining obligations.

111. Ibid., pp.187–190 and Table 16.
112. The impact of this backing was mainly shown in the section on the relationship between the British government and the oil companies, and to a lesser extent in the section on American interests.
113. Mikdashi, *Financial Analysis of Oil Concessions*, pp.101–5.
114. Despatch No. 357, 10 Apr. 1931. CO 730/167/88231.
115. Memorandum by the Research Dept. (FO), 21 Mar. 1949. FO 371/75049, E 5609/10111/65. (Hereafter: Research Dept. memo 1949.)
116. Mahmud M. al-Habib, 'The Labour Movement in Iraq', *Middle Eastern Affairs*, vii, no. 4 (April 1956), p.142.
117. 'Law for the Maintenance of Public Peace at Strike, No. 70 of 1932', *Iraq Government Gazette* no. 38 (18 Sept. 1932), pp.604–5.
118. Research Dept. memo, 1949.
119. 'Labour Organisations in Iraq', Extract from Iraq Police Abstract of Intelligence No. 6, 11 Feb. 1933. FO 624/1/155.
120. Labour Law No. 72 of 1936. A copy appears in FO 624/7/407.
121. Clark to FO, 23 Mar. 1937. FO 371/20795, E 2417/14/93.
122. Scott to FO, 26 Oct. 1937. FO 371/27096, E 6573/14/93.
123. Law No. 36 of 1942. A copy appears in FO 371/31360, E 5542/17/93.
124. Bateman (British Embassy) to FO, 10 June 1936. FO 371/20013, E 2483/1419/93.
125. Annual Report 1937. FO 371/21856, E 794/794/93.
126. Research Dept. memo 1949.
127. According to his report, in March 1944 there were some 37,000 civilians working for the British Army (in October 1943, more than 38,000). The majority were unskilled labourers; the rest, artisans and clerks. The full report (July 1944) appears in LAB 12/123.
128. See comments on the report by MESC officials in FO 921/302, 117(17)44/2.
129. Thompson to FO, 18 Aug. 1944. FO 371/40098, E 5305/5305/93.
130. Henderson to Dept. of State, 15 Sept. 1944. ACR, Reel 17.
131. Thompson to FO, 15 Sept. 1944. FO 371/40098, E 6090/5305/93.
132. Ibid.
133. Thompson to Bevin, 8 Oct. 1945. FO 371/45281, E 7496/6265/65.
134. See, for example, a report by the British Defence Security Office. Ibid.
135. Research Dept. memo 1949.
136. Stonehewer-Bird to FO, 19 July 1946. FO 371/52456, E 7015/3860/93.
137. Stonehewer-Bird to FO, 25 Oct. 1946. Ibid., E 10773/3860/93.
138. E.A. Kinch, 'Social Effects of the Oil Industry in Iraq', *International Labour Review*, lxxv (Mar. 1957), pp.193–206.
139. Minute by Wells (Embassy, Baghdad), 7 Apr. 1948. FO 624/130.
140. Report by Skliros on his visit to Kirkuk, 26 Oct. 1946. FO 624/105/1239.
141. British Consulate-General (Basra) to Embassy (Baghdad), 10 Aug. 1949. FO 624/176/734.
142. Ibid.
143. Mack to FO (Tel. 478), 4 May 1948. FO 371/68479, E 5748/620/93.
144. Minute by Wells, 21 May 1948. FO 371/68479, E 3702/620/93.
145. His full report appears in FO 371/68458, E 12918/77/93.
146. The wholesale price index increased less during the period 1939–48: from 100 to 558. See Table 3.8.
147. Audsley's report, op. cit.
148. Ibid.
149. The government, through its CID (Criminal Investigations Department), kept track of the movements of all union activists and leaders. For an interesting collection of reports, see Air 23/589.
150. Audsley to Waterlow (BMEO), 17 June 1949. FO 371/75049, E 7545/10111/65.
151. Ibid.
152. See Marius Deeb, 'Labour and Politics in Egypt, 1919–1939', *International Journal of Middle East Studies*, x, no. 2 (May 1979), pp.187–203.

CONCLUSION

Economic policy in Iraq betwen 1932 and 1950 can be divided, from a historical point of view, into three subperiods, each with its distinctive problems. Throughout the period, however, Britain's influence had a decisive impact on the economic management of Iraq, with Britain's own economic problems therefore a significant factor in shaping Iraq's economic policy.

The first subperiod was from 1932 to 1939 (from independence to the outbreak of World War II), during which time Iraq was recovering from the world depression and trying to develop its resources. The two main problems it then faced were a deficit in its balance of trade and a lack of financial sources for development.

Trade policy in this period was concerned – or even obsessed – with trade deficit in its narrowest sense, that is, merely looking at the difference between the total values of imports and exports without considering whether the imports were capital or consumer commodities. This coincided with the rise of Japan as a principal supplier of Iraq's imports, mainly textiles. As Japanese goods competed with British products not only in Iraq but in many other parts of the world as well, including in Britain itself, Britain saw fit in 1932 to adopt a policy of 'Imperial Preference', which was extended to the Crown Colonies the following year.[1] Although Iraq was neither a colony nor even a mandate, at least formally, it was requested to apply high tariffs and a quota system to keep cheap Japanese textiles out. While this may have benefited the British export trade, it clearly depressed the standard of living of the Iraqi population.[2]

Iraq's second chief problem in this subperiod – a shortage of capital for development – was also seriously affected by Britain's economic policy. In the face of financial difficulties, it was only natural for the Iraqi government to turn to Britain for help. At the end of 1931, however, the British government had decided to impose a complete, though unofficial, embargo on foreign lending[3] – a policy which was to make it extremely difficult for Iraq to raise a loan abroad, and which therefore, to a certain degree, hampered the country's growth.

During the second subperiod, the war years, Iraq faced problems of inflation, supply control and a curb on imports due to the restrictions imposed on sterling area members. Until mid-1941 the country's economy was almost normal; prices rose little and currency in circulation scarcely increased. But conditions quickly deteriorated thereafter. A poor harvest, the decrease in imports (caused *inter alia* by the exchange controls imposed in consequence of Iraq's entrance into the sterling area) and heavy military expenditure by the Allied forces combined to produce conditions of menacing inflation. The situation in Britain itself strongly affected Iraqi policy: while Iraq was accumulating large sums of hard currencies, it could not spend them to import necessary commodities because Britain was facing an acute shortage of hard currencies,[4] which led the Treasury to impose severe restrictions on countries in the sterling area. The importation of manufactured articles and certain foodstuffs was limited to inadequate levels, a situation aggravated by maldistribution of supplies and by hoarding. Moreover, the war widened the gap between rich and poor by opening lucrative opportunities for merchants, landowners and army contractors.

But the war also had its benefits for Iraq: communications were developed, exports boosted, local industry stimulated, agricultural production increased, and hard currency reserves substantially enhanced.

During the third subperiod, 1945–1950, three factors played a most important role in shaping economic policy: Britain emerged not only victorious from World War II but also, relative to its previous stature, weak and poor; a powerful new element appeared in Iraq and throughout the Middle East – that is, the United States; and Iraq's development needs were even more urgent after the long years of stagnation.

Britain in these years continued to suffer from a shortage of hard currencies, and sterling area problems became increasingly complicated.[5] Iraq, on the other hand, continually pressed for an increased share of the hard currencies it had gained during the war, to finance its growing import needs. The resulting series of tough negotiations and agreements between the two countries assumed high priority for Iraq's leaders.

Unable to supply its allies' demands, Britain found it increasingly hard to dominate Iraq in the presence of growing American influence in the area, and therefore had no alternative to seeking a *modus vivendi* with the Americans, both in Iraq and in the Middle East as a whole. During this time the British also augmented their advisers in Iraq, and in a further effort to safeguard British economic interests there, tried to press the Iraqis into establishing a Central Development Board with both British and American members. Moreover, because Britain could no longer satisfy Iraq's needs by itself, international organizations like the World Bank were approached to help Iraq in its development schemes.[6]

Apart from the events marking the transitions between these subperiods, there were several other crucial turning points in the first two decades of Iraq's independence. The year 1941, for example, witnessed the Rashid 'Ali uprising, with its resulting repercussions upon Iraq's economy and entrance into the sterling area. The year 1948 was even more important in Iraq's economic history: the Palestine war and its disastrous effects on the budget, coupled with a bad harvest, caused one of Iraq's severest financial crises. That year also marked the beginning of the end of the significant commercial role that Iraq's Jewish community had assumed for centuries.[7]

There are many historians and former British officials who continue to argue that Britain's role in Iraq after its independence was minor. For example, in a letter to the writer replying to a question about the role of the advisers in Iraq, a British official who had served as consul in Baghdad and Mosul emphasized that 'none of these Advisers, except Edmonds, had any influence at all on Iraqi thinking', and that 'British Advisers working after Iraq's termination of the Mandate may well have only marginal contributions to make to your researches, since they had no creative role to play'.[8] British documents of the 1930s and 1940s, however, show that exactly the opposite was true, and that Britain's very specific aims in Iraq were consistently pursued and implemented by both its diplomatic personnel and the British advisers working with the Iraqi government. This book has shown the considerable extent and depth of British interests in Iraq, and the dominant role they played in every sector of the economy.

It should be emphasized that although Iraq constituted but a small market for British products, the British firmly believed in the wisdom of not forgoing a single contract, whatever its scale, on the theory that an aggregate of small markets adds up to a big one. Hence Britain's strenuous efforts to eliminate all competition in Iraq.

In addition to the constraint imposed by British interests, the managers of Iraq's economy also had to take into account the interests of certain local groups (landowners, merchants and elements within the state apparatus itself). This was due to the fact that the basis of power in Iraq was narrow, and without the support of these groups (a tiny minority of the population, but disproportionately wealthy and strong), governments could not rule.

This close connection between politics and economics did not benefit Iraq. Mohammad Mahdi Kubbah, who was president of Iraq's Independent Party and served as minister in a number of governments, put his finger on this problem in 1948:

> It was an unfortunate fact that, ever since the foundation of the Iraqi Government, Iraqi economy had been exploited for the benefit of a section of the Iraqi people instead of for the benefit of the people as a whole. Those who had profited were the politicians, the big merchants and the senior Government officials.[9]

Given Iraq's predominantly agrarian population and embryonic middle class, it was only the state itself which could mobilize the country's resources to change the economic climate and distribution of wealth. Only the government of Iraq could undertake the large projects vital to the country's economic growth – except for the exploitation and development of its oil industry, for which even the state, newly independent as it was, lacked the necessary expertise and finance, and which it therefore had to seek from foreign oil companies. But in exercising this role, the government had to contend with the internal and external constraints mentioned above. The result was that Iraq's economy was managed in such a way as to minimize any possibility of collision with the constraining forces. Thus, no agrarian reform was instituted, lest it infringe upon the landowners' interests. Similarly, British interests caused cheap Japanese textile imports to be discriminated against, and development scheme contracts to be awarded to British firms even when they were the highest bidders. Not surprisingly, therefore, the main areas of economic progress in Iraq during the 1930s and 1940s were those, like irrigation and infrastructure, where the government did not have to contend with the interests of either internal or external factors.

In addition to the problem of constraints, there were two other factors which played a role in shaping the management of Iraq's economy: the Iraqization process and increased US involvement in the area.

The Iraqization process, aimed at reducing foreign influence to a minimum, began even before independence and continued to gain momentum throughout the period under study. The belief, held by most Iraqis, in an independent economy was reflected in the opposition to foreign loans and to the granting of concessions to oil companies, the desire to replace foreign officials and workers by Iraqis, and the effort to create national organizations which would take over the functions of foreign firms and banks operating in the country (hence the creation of the state-controlled Rafidain Bank to replace the British Eastern Bank in managing government accounts, and the establishment of the National Bank to replace the London-based Currency Board).

The drive for Iraqization tended to unify Iraq's decision-makers, whose generally limited ability to achieve policy consistency was most often successful, as shown in this study, when the issue involved foreign interests, particularly British ones. This was clearly the case with regard to the sterling area question and negotiations with the oil companies. On other occasions, when the British connection was not so obvious, conflicting internal interests precluded a consistent policy – for example, with regard to agriculture.

The increased involvement of the United States in the Middle East, especially from the second half of World War II onwards, contributed to this process of Iraqization. The vigorous competition between Britain and the US in almost every sphere of Iraq's economy gave the Iraqis a valuable card to play in their dealings with the British. This factor, coupled with the UK's military and economic weakness after the war, induced the British to be more amenable to Iraq's demands.

Despite its many limitations and constraints, Iraq nevertheless attained some significant achievements during the period 1932–50. A number of important institutions were created which were to feature prominently in the country's development – including the National Bank, the Industrial Bank and the Mortgage Bank. There was also a growing awareness of the value of industrialization and the urgent need for agrarian reform, and there was considerable improvement in the fields of education, health, social services, labour laws, and so on. For instance, the number of students increased significantly. In 1932 the total number of children in primary schools was 43,244; by 1950 it was 169,869. The number of students in intermediate and secondary schools increased from 2,688 to 27,575 during the same period.[10] Another indication of the improved standard of living was the lowered infant mortality rate: in 1932 it was 331 per thousand babies in Baghdad and Mosul, and 591 per thousand in Basra; by the end of 1949 it had dropped to 128 per thousand in Baghdad, 80 per thousand in Mosul and 120 per thousand in Basra.[11] Moreover, achievements subsequent to the chronological framework of this work, like the 50–50 oil agreement of 1952, cannot be detached from what happened in earlier years.

While more could undoubtedly have been achieved, it should be remembered that the world-wide trend towards economic self-sufficiency and tariff barriers, particularly in the interwar period, was not to the benefit of Iraq or other developing countries. Furthermore, with the development of the international economic crisis of 1929–30, the difference in prices on world markets between the raw materials exported by developing countries and the industrial products exported by developed ones widened to the disadvantage of the former. This study has shown that even when Iraq had a defined policy (sterling area, oil) it faced a strong constellation of factors operating against it, and this problem should be taken into consideration when assessing Iraq's economic performance in the years 1932–50.

Iraq's economy in the 1930s and 1940s strongly resembled that of colonized countries. Anthony Hopkins has developed a model for West Africa in which he distinguishes between the open economy of colonized countries and the closed economy of independent ones.[12] Most of the principal characteristics of the open phase of development he describes correspond to the situation in Iraq. First, such countries export a limited range of agricultural and mineral commodities in exchange for manufactured products, mainly consumer goods. Second, one or more sectors of the economy are dominated by expatriate interests. Third, the major industrial powers are able to exert considerable influence on economic policy; their chief target is to maintain sales of their manufactured goods and to restrict the entry of goods manufactured by rival industrial powers. Fourth, the open economy's monetary system is dependent upon that of the major power, while banking arrangements are concerned mainly with financing the activities of expatriate firms; the system assists the development of trade with the major power, without involving that power in any monetary responsibilities towards the open economy.

The closed phase of development in Hopkins' model is marked by national monetary institutions, limited expatriate influence, and an economic policy more firmly controlled by indigenous authorities.

By now it will be apparent that Iraq of the 1930s and 1940s lay somewhere between the open and the closed prototypes of Hopkins' model. Formally independent, and characterized by an ongoing process of Iraqization and the creation of national institutions, Iraq cannot be said to have had a colonized economy.

On the other hand, its similarity to the open prototype is so striking that we must conclude that during the first two decades of statehood Iraq's economy more closely resembled that of a colonized country than that of an independent one.

The period under study ended in 1950 with Iraq having a per capita income of about ID 30 ($85) and a national income of ID 151 million (1949 figures).[13] Another estimate, made a year later, was very similar, showing a per capita income of ID 32 and a national income of ID 168 million in 1950.[14]

By all standards, therefore, Iraq remained a poor and undeveloped country. Although the windfall of oil revenues gave a tremendous boost to its economy during the 1950s, the basic ingredients of malaise were still there. Even after the government embarked on its impressive development schemes, it still hesitated to tackle the basic issue of wide inequality in income distribution, because of the same internal and external constraints which had impeded economic policy during the 1930s and 1940s. However, awareness of the need for fundamental reforms increased among the population. The 1958 revolution was perhaps an inevitable culmination of this process, in that it attempted to reduce the effects of both the internal and the external constraints Iraq had been labouring under since independence, the former by instituting land reform and other measures intended to curb the power of the sheikhs (and thus reduce income inequality) and the latter by eliminating the advisers, conducting tougher negotiations with the oil companies and generally following a more independent economic policy.

NOTES

1. Arndt, *The Economic Lessons of the Nineteen-Thirties*, pp.105–6.
2. Ibid., p.107.
3. Ibid., pp.110–11.
4. R.S. Sayers, *Financial Policy 1939–1945*, History of the Second World War (London, 1956), pp.273–85.
5. J.R. Sargent, 'Britain and the Sterling Area', in G.D.N. Worswick and P.H. Ady (eds.), *The British Economy 1945–1950* (Oxford, 1952), pp.531–49.
6. William Diamond, 'Activities of the International Bank in the Middle East', *Middle East Journal*, iii, Oct. 1949, pp.455–61.
7. No work has been published on the role played by Jews in modern Iraq's economic life. The community dwindled from about 150,000 in 1948 to some 30,000 in 1951, and it took many years for Iraq to replace the numerous bankers, merchants and government officials among them.

8. Letter to the writer by Sir Laurence Grafftey-Smith, 18 Apr. 1979.
9. Conversation between Ambassador Mack and Kubbah, 6 Mar. 1948. FO 624/134, 224/81/48.
10. *Statistical Abstract 1927/1928–1937/1938*, pp.54–6; *Statistical Abstract 1950*, pp.70–3.
11. *Statistical Abstract 1927/1928–1937/1938*, p.80 *Statistical Abstract 1950*, p.21. The *Statistical Abstract* emphasizes that these figures refer to births and deaths officially registered by the authorities, but that numerous cases escaped registration and therefore could not be estimated.
12. Anthony Hopkins, *An Economic History of West Africa* (London, 1973), pp.168–72.
13. United Nations, *Final Report of the United Nations Economic Survey Mission for the Middle East*, p.43.
14. K.G. Fenelon, *Iraq; National Income and Expenditure 1950–1956* (Baghdad, 1958), p.17. Haseeb's calculations of the national income are probably more accurate but they refer to the period 1953–61, and as oil revenues increased significantly between 1950 and 1953, his estimate of the national income in 1953 (ID 245.9 million at current prices) does not reflect the situation in the 1930s and 1940s. See K. Haseeb, *The National Income of Iraq 1953–1961* (London, 1964), pp.13–32.

BIBLIOGRAPHY

ARCHIVAL SOURCES

Records

British Records at the Public Record Office

Air Ministry

Air 23: Overseas Commands, 1932–49.
Air 23: Operations Record Books, Commands, 1932–49.

Board of Trade

BT 11: Commercial Department Correspondence and Papers, 1932–49.
BT 60: Department of Overseas Trade Correspondence and Papers, 1932–49.

Cabinet

CAB 21: Registered files.
CAB 23: Cabinet Minutes, 1932–9.
CAB 24: Cabinet Memoranda, 1932–9.
CAB 27: Committees General Series, 1932–9.
CAB 65: War Cabinet Minutes, 1939–45.
CAB 66: War Cabinet Memoranda, 1939–45.
CAB 78: Middle East Supplies Committee, 1941–7.
CAB 92: War Cabinet Committees on Supply, Production, Priority and Manpower, 1939–46.
CAB 95: War Cabinet Committees on the Middle East and Africa, 1939–45.
CAB 110: Joint American Secretariat (Policy matters in the field of Anglo-American supply)
CAB 128: Cabinet Minutes, 1945–9.
CAB 129: Cabinet Memoranda, 1945–9.

Colonial Office

CO 537: Colonies General Supplementary Original Correspondence, 1932–48.
CO 730: Iraq Original Correspondence (the main source for the mandate period).
CO 732: Middle East Original Correspondence (includes interdepartmental correspondence on Middle East issues), 1932–49.
CO 813: Iraq's Government Gazette, 1930–1932.

Foreign Office

FO 141: Archives of British Embassy in Cairo (includes documents on British policy in the Middle East and papers relating to British–Japanese competition in the area).
FO 371: General Correspondence, Political (Iraq, series 93, is the main source for political affairs after independence and is also very important for economic issues; Eastern, series 65, includes documents on British policy in the Middle East), 1930–49.
FO 406: Confidential Print Eastern Affairs, (documents relating to Arabia, Iraq, Palestine, Syria and the Levant), 1932–46.
FO 433: Confidential Print Economic Affairs, General (includes correspondence concerning economic and trade conferences, economic surveys and trade statistics), 1932–9.
FO 624: British Embassy and Consular Correspondence in Iraq, 1933–49.
FO 837: Ministry of Economic Warfare (papers relating to Iraq's trade relations with Britain and the Axis during World War II).
FO 838: British Consulate in 'Amara, 1941–9.
FO 921: Minister of State, Cairo, 1942–6.
FO 922: Middle East Supply Centre, 1941–5.
FO 957: British Middle East Office, Cairo, 1946–9.

Ministry of Labour

LAB 13: Overseas Department, 1932–49.

Treasury

T 160: Finance, 1932–48.
T 161: Supply and Establishment Divisions, 1931–49.
T 231: Exchange Control Division, 1939–49.
T 236: Overseas Finance Division, 1938–49.

American Records

American Consular Reports (ACR) from Baghdad, 1931–44 (sixteen reels of microfilm).
General Correspondence, 1945–9 (National Archives, Washington DC).

Private Papers

Anthony Eden (papers relating to his service as secretary of state for foreign affairs, 1936–8 and 1940–5), at the Public Record Office, FO 954.
C.J. Edmonds (papers relating to his service in Iraq, 1915–45), at the Middle East Centre, Oxford University.
Ibrahim al-Kabir (memoirs relating to his service with the Iraqi government, including his tenure as director-general of the Ministry of

Finance), at *Moreshet Yehudei Bavel* (Iraqi Jewish Heritage Foundation), Tel Aviv.

Archibald Kerr (papers relating to his service as ambassador in Iraq, 1935–7), at the Public Record Office, FO 800.

E.A. Kinch (his correspondence, when political adviser in Mosul, with Sir K. Cornwallis and others, 1941–4), at the Middle East Centre, Oxford University.

Middle East Supply Centre Papers, 1942–6, at the Middle East Centre, Oxford University.

UNPUBLISHED THESES AND ARTICLES

'Ali, 'Abdul Munim. 'A Study of the Banking System and its Role in the Economic Development of Iraq' (George Washington University Ph.D. thesis, 1958).

Batatu, John. 'The Shaikh and the Peasant in Iraq 1917–1958' (Harvard University Ph.D. thesis, 1960).

Gross, Nahum T. and Jacob Metzer. 'Public Finance in the Jewish Economy in Interwar Palestine' (Maurice Falk Institute, Discussion Paper no. 776, Jerusalem, July 1977).

Haider, Saleh. 'Land Problems of Iraq' (London University Ph.D. thesis, 1942).

Hasan, Mohammad Salman. 'Foreign Trade in the Economic Development of Modern Iraq 1869–1939' (Oxford University D.Phil thesis, 1958).

Ishii, Osamu. 'Cotton Textile Diplomacy: Japan, Great Britain and the United States, 1930–1936' (Rutgers University Ph.D. thesis, 1977).

Kadhim, M. 'The Strategy of Development Planning and the Absorptive Capacity of the Economy: A Case Study of Iraq' (Colorado University Ph.D. thesis, 1974).

Kalian, Edward 'Abdul Kareem. 'Money and Banking in Iraq, 1914–1958: A Study in Economic History' (Columbia University Ph.D. thesis, 1966.

Al-Qaysi, Hameed, 'An Economic Appraisal of Iraq Petroleum Concessions – A Comparative Study' (Columbia University Ph.D. thesis, 1961).

Al-Shabibi, Sinan Ridha. 'Optimal Industrialisation with Uncertain Oil Revenues: Dynamic Multisector Models, 1974–1984' (Bristol University Ph.D. thesis, 1974).

Zalzalah, 'Abdul Hasan. 'Iraq in the Sterling Area 1932–1954' (Indiana University Ph.D. thesis, 1957).

OFFICIAL PUBLICATIONS

Iraq

Publications of the Iraqi Government

Census of Iraq 1947 (three parts).
Census of Iraq 1957.
Foreign Trade Statistics, 1927–50.
Hisabat al-Dawla al-'Iraqiyya (Accounts of the State of Iraq), 1930–50.
Iraq Directory, 1936.
Iraq Government Gazette, 1930–50.
Project Funds Agreement between the Government of Iraq and the National Bank and the International Bank for Reconstruction and Development (Washington, 1950).
Report on the Agricultural and Livestock Census of Iraq 1952–3 (Baghdad, 1954). ['Agricultural Census'.]
Report on the Control of the Rivers of Iraq and the Utilization of their Waters (Baghdad, 1951). ['Haigh Report'.]
Statistical Abstract, 1927/1928–1958.

Semi-Official Publications

Agricultural and Industrial Bank, 1936–46.
Agricultural Bank, 1946/7–1950/1.
Baghdad Chamber of Commerce, 1935/6–1950/1.
Industrial Bank, 1949/50–1950/1.
Iqari Bank, 1949/50–1950/1.
National Bank of Iraq, 1949/50–1950/1.
Rafidain Bank, 1941–50.

Britain

Publications of the British Government

Command Papers

Treaty of Alliance between the United Kingdom and Iraq, with an Exchange of Notes, Baghdad 30 June 1930. (Together with Notes Exchanged Embodying a Separate Financial Agreement, London 19 August 1930.) Cmd. 3797.
Agreement between His Majesty in respect of the United Kingdom and His Majesty the King of Iraq regarding the railway system of Iraq, with exchange of notes, Baghdad 31 March 1936. Cmd. 5282.
Agreement between His Majesty's Government in the United Kingdom and the Iraqi Government concerning Iraq foreign exchange requirements for 1945, Baghdad 28 May 1945. Cmd. 6646.

Correspondence between His Majesty's Government in the United Kingdom and the Iraqi Government concerning the prolongation of existing arrangements regarding Iraqi foreign exchange requirements, Baghdad 17 January 1946. Cmd. 6742.

Correspondence between His Majesty's Government in the United Kingdom and the Iraqi Government concerning the prolongation of existing arrangements regarding Iraqi foreign exchange requirements, Baghdad 8 April 1946. Cmd. 6803.

Exchange of notes between His Majesty's Government in the United Kingdom and the Government of Iraq respecting the status of the Iraqi diplomatic mission in London and the precedence of His Majesty's Ambassador at Baghdad, London 2 August 1946. Cmd. 6918.

Exchange of notes between His Majesty's Government in the United Kingdom and the Government of Iraq concerning the prolongation of existing arrangements regarding Iraqi foreign exchange requirements, Baghdad 10/22 February 1947. Cmd. 7110.

Financial Agreement between the Government of the United Kingdom and the Government of Iraq, London 13 August 1947. Cmd. 7201.

Financial Agreement between the Government of the United Kingdom and the Government of Iraq, Baghdad 17 November 1947. Cmd. 7269.

Treaty of Alliance between His Majesty in respect of the United Kingdom of Great Britain and Northern Ireland and His Majesty the King of Iraq, with Annex and Exchange of Letters, Portsmouth 15 January 1948. Cmd. 7309.

Exchange of notes between the Governments of the United Kingdom and Iraq prolonging the Supplementary Financial Agreement of 17 November 1947, Baghdad 27 June 1948. Cmd. 7490.

Hansard, Parliamentary Debates, House of Commons

Reports on the administration of Iraq

Annual Reports by His Majesty's Government to the Council of the League of Nations:

Administration of Iraq for the year 1929 (London, 1930).

Administration of Iraq for the year 1930 (London, 1931).

Progress of Iraq during the period 1920–1931 (London, 1931).

Administration of Iraq for the year 1931 (London, 1932).

Administration of Iraq for the period January to October 1932 (London, 1933).

Semi-official Publications

Reports by Board of Trade, Department of Overseas Trade

Economic Conditions in Iraq, 1933, by C. Empson (London, 1933).

Report on Economic Conditions in Iraq, 1933–1935, by J.P. Summerscale (London, 1936).

Report on Economic and Commercial Conditions in Iraq, 1935–1937, by J.P. Summerscale (London, 1938).
Iraq, Review of Commercial Conditions (London, 1945).
Economic and Commercial Conditions in Iraq, 1949, by F.H. Gamble (London, 1950).
Middle East Supply Centre, *Middle East Economic and Statistical Bulletin*, 1943–5 [*MEESB*].
Naval Intelligence Division, *Iraq and the Persian Gulf*, Geographical Handbook Series (1944).
Sayers, R.S. *Financial Policy 1939–1945, History of World War II* (London, 1956)

United States

Department of State, *Foreign Relations of the United States* (*FRUS*), 1930–50.

Germany

Documents on German Foreign Policy 1918–1945, Series D (1937–45).

PRESS

Al-'Alam al-'Arabi (Baghdad).
Al-Bilad (Baghdad).
Board of Trade Journal (London).
The Economist (London).
Financial Times (London).
The Iraq Times (Baghdad).
The Middle East 1950, Europa Publications (London).
The Times (London).
Al-Zaman (Baghdad).

BOOKS AND ARTICLES

'Abd al-Baqi, Ahmad. *Mizaniyyat al-Dawla al-Iraqiyya Tahdiruha wa-Tahliluha* (The Iraq State Budget: Its Preparation and Analysis) (Baghdad, 1947).
Adams, Doris Goodrich. *Iraq's People and Resources* (Los Angeles, 1958).
Adams, Warren E. 'The Pre-Revolutionary Decade of Land Reform in Iraq', *Economic Development and Cultural Change* xi, no. 3 (April 1963), pp.267–88.
Arndt, H.W. *The Economic Lessons of the Nineteen-Thirties* (London, 1944; reprinted Cass, 1963).
Baer, Gabriel. 'The Agrarian Problem in Iraq', *Middle Eastern Affairs* iii, no. 12 (December 1952), pp.381–91.
——. 'Ha-Mashber ha-Kaspi be-Iraq' (The financial crisis in Iraq), *Ha-Mizrah he-Hadash* i, no. 1 (January 1950), pp.122–7.

Balogh, T. 'The International Aspect', in G.D.N. Worswick and P.H. Ady (eds.), *The British Economy 1945–1950* (Oxford, 1952), pp.476–510.

Baram, Phillip J. *The Department of State in the Middle East 1919–1945* (Philadelphia, 1978).

Basri, Meer. *Mabahith fi al-Iqtisad al-'Iraqi* (Studies in Iraq's Economy) (Baghdad, 1948).

Batatu, Hanna, *The Old Social Classes and the Revolutionary Movements of Iraq* (Princeton, 1978).

Bell, Phillip W. *The Sterling Area in the Postwar Period* (Oxford, 1956).

Boardman, F. 'Civilian Requirements from War to Peace: The Middle East Supply Center', *Department of State Bulletin* xiii (December 1945), pp.994–9.

Bonné, Alfred. *State and Economics in the Middle East*, (2nd edn. London, 1955).

Burns, Norman. 'The Dujaylah Land Settlement', *Middle East Journal* v, no. 3 (Summer 1951), pp.362–6.

Cohen, Stuart A. *British Policy in Mesopotamia 1903–1914* (London, 1976).

Constantine, Stephen. *The Making of British Colonial Development 1914–1940* (Frank Cass, London, 1984).

Al-Dabbagh, Hashim, *Études statistiques sur le développement économique d l'Irak* (Baghdad, 1960).

Al-Dahiri, 'Abdul al-Wahab. *The Introduction of Technology into Traditional Societies and Economies (Using Iraq as a Case Study)* (Baghdad, 1969).

Al-Dali, 'Abdul Ghani. 'Problems of Industrial Enterprise in Iraq', *Middle East Economic Papers* (Beirut, 1954), pp.37–50.

Davis, Helen Miller. *Constitutions, Electoral Laws, Treaties of States in the Near and Middle East* (2nd edn., Durham, 1953).

Deeb, Marius, 'Labour and Politics in Egypt, 1919–1939', *International Journal of Middle East Studies* x, no. 2 (May 1979), pp.187–203.

Denovo, John A. *American Interests and Policies in the Middle East 1900–1939* (Minneapolis, 1964).

——. 'The Culbertson Economic Mission and Anglo-American Tensions in the Middle East, 1944–1945', *Journal of American History* lxiii (1977), pp.913–36.

Diamond, William. 'Activities of the International Bank in the Middle East', *Middle East Journal* iii, no. 4 (October 1949), pp.455–61.

Dowson, Ernest, *An Inquiry into Land Tenure and Related Questions* (Letchworth, 1931).

Ellinger, Bernard. 'British Foreign Policy in Relation to the Lancashire Cotton Industry', *International Affairs* (March–April 1937), pp.245–62.

Fevelon, K.G. *Iraq; National Income and Expenditure 1950–1956* (Baghdad, 1958).

Flanders, M.J. 'Agriculture versus Industry in Development Policy: The

Planners' Dilemma Re-examined', *Journal of Development Studies* v, no. 3 (April 1969), pp. 171–90.
Food and Agriculture Organization (FAO), Mediterranean Development Project, *Iraq*, Country Report (Rome, 1959).
Grundwald, Kurt and Ronall O. Joachim. *Industrialization in the Middle East* (New York, 1960).
Habermann, John Stanley. 'The Iraq Development Board: Administration and Program', *Middle East Journal* ix, no. 2 (Spring 1955), pp. 179–86.
Al-Habib, Mahmud M. 'The Labor Movement in Iraq', *Middle Eastern Affairs* vii, no. 4 (April 1956), pp. 137–43.
El-Haj, Ribhi Abu. 'Capital Formation in Iraq, 1922–1957', *Economic Development and Cultural Change* ix, no.4 (July 1961), pp. 604–17.
Harris, George, *Iraq* (New Haven, 1958).
Hasan, Mohammad Salman. 'Growth and Structure of Iraq's Population 1867–1947', *Bulletin of the Oxford University Institute of Statistics* xx, no. 4 (1958), pp. 339–52.
——. 'The Role of Foreign Trade in the Economic Development of Iraq, 1864–1964: A Study in the Growth of a Dependent Economy' in M.A. Cook (ed.), *Studies in the Economic History of the Middle East* (London, 1970), pp. 346–72.
——. *Al-Tatawar al-Iqtisadi fi al-'Iraq* (Economic Development of Iraq) (Beirut, 1965).
Al-Hasani, 'Abdul Razzaq. *Tarikh al-Wizarat al-'Iraqiyya* (History of the Iraqi Ministries), eight vols. (Sidon, 1953, vols. VII and VIII in 1955).
Haseeb, K. *The National Income of Iraq 1953–1961* (London, 1964).
Himadeh, Sa'id. *Al-Nizam al-Iqtisadi fi al-'Iraq* (The economic structure in Iraq) (Beirut, 1938).
Hirschman, A.O. *The Strategy of Economic Development* (New Haven, 1958).
Hopkins, Anthony. *An Economic History of West Africa* (London, 1973).
Hunter, Guy. 'Economic Problems: The Middle East Supply Centre' in George Kirk (ed.), *The Middle East in the War* (London, 1952), pp. 169–93.
International Bank for Reconstruction and Development. *The Economic Development of Iraq* (Baltimore, 1952).
International Monetary Fund, *Balance of Payments Yearbook.*
Ireland, P.W. *Iraq: A Study in Political Development* (London, 1937).
Isma'il, Mahmud Nadim. *Al-Fihrist al-'Am lil Qawanin wa-al-Anzima wa-al-Bayanat wa-al-Ta'limat 1917–1961* (The general index for the laws, regulations, announcements and instructions, 1917–1961) (Baghdad, 1961).
Issawi, Charles and Mohammad Yeganeh. *The Economics of Middle Eastern Oil* (New York, 1962).
Iversen, Carl. *Monetary Policy in Iraq* (Copenhagen, 1954).
Jalal, Ferhang. *The Role of Government in the Industrialisation of Iraq 1950–1965* (London, 1972).

Jamil, Muzaffar Husein. *Siyasat al-'Iraq al-Tijariyya* (Iraq's trade policy) (Cairo, 1949).

Jawad, Hashim. *The Social Structure of Iraq* (Baghdad, 1945).

Jwaideh, Albertine. 'Midhat Pasha and the Land System of Lower Iraq', *St Antony's Papers* no. 16 (1963), pp. 106–36.

Kelidar, Abbas (ed.). *The Integration of Modern Iraq* (London, 1979).

Kent, Marion. *Oil and Empire* (London, 1976).

Khadduri, Majid. *Independent Iraq 1932–1958* (2nd edn., London, 1960).

Khayyat, Ja'far. *Al-Qarya al-'Iraqiyya* (The Iraqi village) (Beirut, 1950).

Kinch, E.A. 'Social Effects of the Oil Industry in Iraq', *International Labour Review* lxxv (March 1957), pp. 193–206.

Kirk, George. *The Middle East 1945–1950* (London, 1954).

Kubbah, Mahmud Mahdi. *Mudhakkarati fi Samim al-Ahdath 1918–1958* (My memoirs in the Core of Events 1918–1958) (Beirut, 1965).

Langley, Kathleen M. *The Industrialization of Iraq* (Cambridge, Mass., 1961).

League of Nations, *Balance of Payments.*

——. *Statistical Yearbook.*

Lloyd, E.M.H. *Food and Inflation in the Middle East 1940–1945* (Stanford, 1956).

Longrigg, Stephen Hemsley. *Iraq: 1900 to 1950* (London, 1953).

——. *Oil in the Middle East* (2nd edn., London, 1961).

Louis, Wm. Roger. *The British Empire in the Middle East 1945–1951* (Oxford, 1985).

Main, Ernest, *Iraq from Mandate to Independence* (London, 1935).

Mejcher, Helmut. *Imperial Quest for Oil: Iraq 1910–1928* (London, 1976).

Mikdashi, Zuhayr. *A Financial Analysis of Middle Eastern Oil Concessions 1901–1965* (New York, 1966).

Mikesell, Raymond. 'Sterling Area Currencies of the Middle East', *Middle East Journal* ii, no. 2 (April 1948), pp. 160–74.

Murray, John. *A Report on Statistical Organisation in the Government of the Kingdom of Iraq* (Baghdad, 1948).

Al-Najjar, A.H. *Siyasat al-Tijarah al-Kharijiyya fi al-'Iraq fi fatrat ma ba'd al-Harb al-'Alamiyya al-Thaniya* (Foreign trade policy in Iraq after World War II) (Baghdad, 1968).

Al-Nasrawi, Abbas. *Financing Economic Development in Iraq* (New York, 1967).

Neal, Larry. 'The Economics and Finance of Bilateral Clearing Agreements: Germany 1934–1938', *Economic History Review* xxxii, no. 3 (August 1979), pp. 391–404.

Nurkse, R. 'The Size of the Market and the Inducement to Invest' in D.E. Novak and R. Lekachman (eds.), *Development and Society* (New York, 1964).

Organization of Petroleum Exporting Countries (OPEC). *Selected Documents of the International Petroleum Industry* (Vienna, 1974).

Penrose, Edith and E.F. *Iraq: International Relations and National Development* (London, 1978).

Philips, Doris. 'Rural-to-Urban Migration in Iraq', *Economic Development and Cultural Change* vii, no. 4 (July 1959), pp.405–21.
Poyck, A.P.G. *Farm Studies in Iraq* (Wageningen, 1962).
Prest, A.R. *War Economies of Primary Producing Countries* (Cambridge, 1948).
Qubain, Fahim I. *The Reconstruction of Iraq: 1950–1957* (New York, 1958).
Rasheed, Guzine A.K. 'Development of Agricultural Land Taxation in Modern Iraq', *Bulletin of the School of Oriental and African Studies* xxv, part 2 (1962), pp.262–74.
Salter, Lord. *The Development of Iraq* (Baghdad, 1955).
Sargent, J.R. 'Britain and the Sterling Area' in G.D.N. Worswick and P.H. Ady (eds.), *The British Economy 1945–1950* (Oxford, 1952), pp.531–49.
Shehab, F. 'Iraq', *Bulletin of the Oxford University Institute of Statistics* xxi, no. 4 (1959), pp.291–307.,
Shwadran, Benjamin. *The Middle East, Oil and Great Powers 1959*, (2nd edn. New York, 1959).
Sluglett, Peter, *Britain in Iraq 1914–1932* (London, 1976).
Sousa, Ahmed. *Iraq Irrigation Handbook, part I: The Euphrates* (Baghdad, 1944).
——. *Irrigation in Iraq* (Baghdad, 1945).
——. 'Irrigation in Iraq' (pamphlet) (Baghdad, 1945).
Trotter, Ann. *Britain and East Asia 1933–1937* (London, 1975).
United Nations. Department of Economic Affairs, Public Finance Information Papers, *Iraq* (New York, 1951).
——. *Final Report of the United Nations Economic Survey Mission for the Middle East*, part I (New York, 1949).
——. *General Issues of Industrial Policy, Proceedings of the International Symposium on Industrial Development held in Athens in 1967* (New York, 1969).
——. *Instability in Export Markets of Under-Developed Countries* (New York, 1952).
——. *Review of Economic Conditions in the Middle East 1951–1952* (New York, 1953).
——. *Statistical Yearbook.*
Warner, Geoffrey. *Iraq and Syria 1941* (London, 1974).
Warriner, Doreen. *Land and Poverty in the Middle East* (London, 1948).
——. *Land Reform and Development in the Middle East* (London, 1957).
Weinryb, Bernard D. 'Industrial Development of the Middle East', *Quarterly Journal of Economics* lxi (May 1947), pp.471–99.
Willocks, William. *The Irrigation of Mesopotamia* (London, 1911).
Wilmington, Martin W. *The Middle East Supply Centre* (London, 1972).
——. 'The Middle East Supply Centre: A Reappraisal', *Middle East Journal* xi, no. 2 (Spring 1952), pp.144–66.
Wilson, Arnold T. *Loyalties: Mesopotamia 1914–1917* (London, 1930).
Young, Edward Hilton. *Reports on Economic Conditions and Policy and Loan Policy* (Baghdad, 1930).

INDEX

For Product Safety Concerns and Information please contact our EU
representative GPSR@taylorandfrancis.com
Taylor & Francis Verlag GmbH, Kaufingerstraße 24, 80331 München, Germany

www.ingramcontent.com/pod-product-compliance
Ingram Content Group UK Ltd.
Pitfield, Milton Keynes, MK11 3LW, UK
UKHW020017200926
475702UK00014B/1938

* 9 7 8 0 7 1 4 6 3 3 0 5 3 *